The W
Book One

Other books by Laura Knight-Jadczyk

*The Secret History of the World
and How to Get Out Alive*

9/11: The Ultimate Truth

*The High Strangeness of Dimensions, Densities,
and the Process of Alien Abduction*

The Horns of Moses
(Coming Soon)

Laura Knight-Jadczyk

THE
WAVE
BOOK ONE

Riding the Wave

Red Pill Press
2007

Copyright © 1994-2007 Laura Knight-Jadczyk
http://www.cassiopaea.org/
ISBN-13: 978-1-897244-26-5

All Rights Reserved. No part of this publication may be reproduced, stored in a retrieval system, or transmitted in any form or by any means, electronic, mechanical, or otherwise, other than for "fair use", without the written consent of the author.

Printed and bound in Canada by Red Pill Press, 10020-100 Ave., Grande Prairie, Alberta, T8V 0V3.

Some material in this book appeared in a slightly different form in the books *The Secret History of the World, Amazing Grace,* and *The High Strangeness of Dimensions, Densities and the Process of Alien Abduction.*

TABLE OF CONTENTS

Foreword Speculations on Time Travel and Superluminal Communication
by a Theoretical Physicist/Mathematician ... 7

Author's Letter to the Reader ... 19

Note to the Reader on the Subject of Aliens and UFOs ... 36

Autobiographical Background of the Author
Necessary to the Context of The Wave ... 79

Chapter 1 Riding the Wave ... 208

Chapter 2 Multi-Dimensional Soul Essences ... 229

Chapter 3 Dorothy and The Frog Prince Meet Flight 19 in Oz or,
"I don't think we're in Kansas anymore!" ... 249

Chapter 4 The Cassiopaeans Get Taken Out of the Closet
and Go for a "Test Drive" ... 292

Chapter 5 Perpendicular Realities, Tesseracts, and Other Odd Phenomena... ... 324

Chapter 6 Animal Psychology or That which was A, will be A. That which
was not-A, will be not-A. Everything was and will be either A or not-A. ... 356

Chapter 7 Balloons, Anti-balloons and Fireworks Or Laura Falls Into the Pit
and Ark Comes to the Rescue ... 390

Afterword ... 407

Bibliography ... 409

FOREWORD

SPECULATIONS ON TIME TRAVEL AND SUPERLUMINAL COMMUNICATION BY A THEORETICAL PHYSICIST/MATHEMATICIAN

The term "Cassiopaeans" appears in many places in this book. The name Cassiopaea was given by a source identifying itself by saying "we are you in the future" which Laura Knight-Jadczyk contacted via an experiment in superluminal communication in 1994.

"We are you in the future"

This is what "they" declare: that "they" – The Cassiopaeans – 6th density Unified Thought Form Beings – are Us in the future. What a bizarre concept. Or is it?

Is that possible? Can such a statement find a place in accepted theories? Or it is in an evident contradiction with everything that we – that is, physicists – know about Nature and its laws?

Putting aside for the moment the issue of whether existence in a pure state of consciousness is possible, is traveling in time possible, even if only in theory? Is sending and receiving information from the future or sending information into the past allowed by our present theories of relativity and quantum mechanics? If information can be sent, does this also imply that physical matter can be "sent", via some sort of TransDimensional Remolecularization? And if so what are the laws, what are the restrictions? What are the means?

Well, frankly speaking, we do not know, but we may have a clue. Kurt Gödel, after he became famous for his work on foundations of mathematics, went on to study the Einstein general theory of relativity and made an important contribution to physics: he discovered a class of otherwise reasonable cosmological solutions of Einstein equations – except for one point: they contained causal loops!

At first these causal loops were dismissed by relativists as being "too crazy". The arguments against these model universes even became rather personal, commenting upon the state of mind of the inventor! (A not terribly unusual phenomenon in the heated debates within so-called "ivory towers" of academia.)

A "Causal Loop" means the same thing as "Time Loop". It can be described as going into the future and ending up where you started at the original time and place. It is called "Causal" because, in Einstein's Theory of Relativity, Time is a relative concept and different observers can experience Time differently, so the term "causal" is used to avoid using the term "time."

But, little by little, it was realized that causal – or Time – loops *can* appear in other solutions of Einstein equations as well – usually they correspond to some kind of "rotation" of the universe.

Causal loops make time travel not only possible, but probable. But then, causal loops lead to unacceptable logical paradoxes, and physics does not like such paradoxes at all – they are a serious problem!

But, the subject of communicating with the past or receiving information from the future *is* being discussed in physics even in terms of the flat, not-curved-at-all space-time of Lorentz and Minkowski. Hypothetical faster-than-light particles – tachyons – can serve as the communication means. They make an "anti-telephone" – a telephone into the past – possible.

But do tachyons exist? Or *can* they exist?

Well, that is still a question that has not been answered definitively for some.

And, the truth is that paradoxes must never be ignored. They always indicate that some important lesson is to be learned; that some essential improvement or change is necessary. The same holds true for the paradoxes involved in the idea of receiving information from the future. We cannot simply go back into Saturday and tell ourselves the winning lottery numbers of Sunday. If this were possible, then it should also be possible for some future, future self to tell a future self *not* to tell! Thus we have a paradox: we, in the future, have intervened into the past making our communication from the future impossible!

A paradox: if we communicated, we have not communicated, and if we do not communicate, then we have communicated! Impossible in a linear, non-branching universe!

Is there a possible escape from the paradox, an escape that leaves a door open, even if only a little – for our anti-telephone?

Indeed, there is, and not just one, but several ways out.

First of all – the evident paradox disappears if we admit the possibility that the communication channels are inherently noisy; that is a normal situation when we deal with quantum phenomena. So, if the communication into the past is a quantum effect – we are saved from evident paradoxes. Quantum Theory can be useful!

Sending a signal into the past, we are never 100% sure if the message will be delivered without distortion. And conversely, receiving info from the future we are never 100% sure if this comes from an authentic broadcast or is a spontaneous and random creation of the receiving end. If this is the case, and if certain quantitative information – that is, theoretic relations between receiving and transmitting ends – are secured to hold, then there are no more paradoxes even with reasonably efficient information channels.

In other words: there *can* be broadcasts from the future to the past, but *there will be few "receivers"*, and of those few, *even fewer that are properly tuned*. And even those that are properly tuned may be subject to "static". Even if there is no static, those receivers that can receive pure information will experience the static of "non-belief" and distortion after the fact from society.

There is also another aspect of such an information transfer which is that the probabilities involved are connected with a *choice event*; with the choosing of one among many possible futures.

It may happen that branching of the universe corresponds to each such event. Branching of the universe into an infinite tree of decisions has been discussed within quantum measurement theory – it even has the name of "Many Worlds interpretation of quantum theory".

Two of the well-known physicists who consider the many worlds interpretation more than just an exercise in theorizing are John Archibald Wheeler and David Deutsch.

The Many Worlds Interpretation has one serious weakness: it has no built in algorithm for providing the timing of the branchings. Thus it is a certain framework rather than a complete theory.

There is, however, a theory that fills in this gap in the Many Worlds Interpretation – and this theory I know quite well, and in fact I know it better than most others for the simple reason that I developed it in collaboration with Philippe Blanchard (University of

Bielefeld) in 1988 as an integral part of the Quantum Future Project. It is called Event Enhanced Quantum Theory (EEQT for short notation). (A complete list of references and much more info on this subject can be found on my "Quantum Future" project page[1] on the World Wide Web).

The fact that our generally accepted theories of the present do not prevent us from thinking that time travel is, perhaps, possible, does not necessarily imply that we know how to build the time machine!

On the other hand, it is perhaps possible that the time machine already exists and is in use, even if we do not understand the principle of its work, because it goes much too far beyond our present theoretical and conceptual framework. It is also possible that some of the machines we think are serving a totally different purpose do, in fact, act as time machines. Many things are possible…

Now, back to superluminal communication, or "channeling" in general and the Cassiopaeans in particular: the fact that sending information into the past is possible does not necessarily imply that any information that pretends to be sent from the future is such indeed! But, if we generally accept that extraterrestrial life is possible, and we use all of our knowledge and resources to search for life beyond our Earth, then we also need to include the understanding that receiving information from the future is equally possible. With this perspective, science should search for any traces of such information.

What kind of information channels are to be monitored in search of such broadcasts? What kind of antenna arrays do we need? How must we direct them into a particular "future time"? Say, into the year 3000? Or 30,000? Or 300,001?

My answer is: nothing like that is necessary. All that we need we already have, namely *our minds*.

And indeed, assuming that the knowledge and technology of the future is (or *can be*) much more advanced than ours, then it is only natural that any broadcast from the future *will be addressed directly into the mind*.

Even today there are techniques of acting directly on our minds. They are not always used for our benefit; nevertheless they do exist. But if communications from the future are possible, why don't we

---

[1] http://quantumfuture.net/quantum_future/

receive these broadcasts on a daily basis? If our minds can serve as receivers, then why aren't we all aware of the transmissions?

I think that the answer has to do with multiple realities and branching universes, and perhaps any civilization which would receive messages from the future on a daily basis has ceased to exist because communication through time is a very dangerous game. You produce paradoxes, and these paradoxes remove the paradoxical universes from the repository of possible universes; if you create a universe with paradoxes, it destroys itself either completely or partially. Perhaps just intelligence is removed from this universe because it is intelligence that creates paradox. Perhaps we are very fortunate that even if we can receive *some* of these messages from the future, we still continue to exist.

Suppose our civilization were to advance to the point where everyone can communicate with themselves in the past; they have a computer with a special program and peripheral device that does this. It becomes the latest fad: everyone is communicating with themselves in the past to warn of dangers or upcoming calamities or bad choices, or to give lottery numbers or winning horses. But, what is seen as a "good event" or "benefit" for one, could be seen to be a "bad choice" or "calamity" to someone else!

So, the next step would be that "hackers" would begin to break into the systems and send false communications into the past to deliberately create bad choices and calamities for some in order to produce benefits for themselves or others.

Then, the first individual would see that false information has been sent and would go into their system and go back even earlier to warn themselves that false information was going to be sent back by an "imposter" and how to tell that it was false.

Then the hacker would see this, and go back in time to an even earlier moment and give false information that someone was going to send false information (that was really true) that false information (that was really false) was going to be sent, thereby confusing the issue.

This process could go on endlessly with constant and repeated communications into the past, one contradicting the other, one signal canceling out the other, with the result that it would be exactly the same as if there were *no* communication into the past!

There is also the very interesting possibility that the above scenario *is* exactly what is taking place in our world today.

It is also possible that, whenever a civilization comes to the point that it can manipulate the past and thereby change the present, it would most probably destroy itself, and probably its "branch" of the universe, unless there comes a cataclysmic event before this happens which would act as a kind of "control system" or way of reducing the technological possibilities to zero again, thus obviating the potentials of universal chaos. In this way, cataclysmic events could be a sort of preventive or pre-emptive strike against such manipulations, and may, in fact, be the result of engineered actions of benevolent selves in the future who see the dangers of communicating with ourselves in the past!

So, the probability is this: if there *is* communication from the future, it *may*, in fact, be constantly received by each and every one of us as an ongoing barrage of lies mixed with truth. Thus, the problem becomes more than just "tuning" to a narrow band signal, because clearly the hackers can imitate the signal and have become *very* clever in delivering their lies disguised as "warm and fuzzy" truths; the problem becomes an altogether different proposition of believing nothing and *acting* as though *everything* is misleading, gathering data from all quarters, and then making the most *informed* choice possible with full realization that it may be in error!

Using our computer analogy: we can't prevent hackers from hacking, but, what we can do is make every effort to prevent them from hacking into *our* systems by erecting barriers of knowledge and awareness. Hackers are always looking for an "easy hack", (except for those few who really *like* a challenge), and will back away as you make your system more and more secure.

How do you make your computer (or yourself) immune to hackers?

It is never 100% secure, but if all preventative measures are taken, and we constantly observe for the signs of hackers – system disruption, loss of "memory", or energy, damaged files, things that don't "fit", that are "out of context" – we can reduce the possibility of hacking. But, we can only do this if we are *aware* of hackers; if we *know* that they will attempt to break into our system in the guise of a "normal" file, or even an operating system or program that promises to "organize" our data for greater efficiency and ease of function or "user friendliness", while at the same time, acting as a massive drain on our energy and resources – RAM and hard drive.

As a humorous side note: we could think of Windows Operating system as the "ultimate hacker from the future" who, disguised as a sheep, is a wolf devouring our hard disk and RAM, and sending our files to God only knows where every time we connect via the internet!

And of course, there are viruses. Whenever we insert a floppy disk or CD into our computer, we risk infection by viruses which can slowly or rapidly, distort or destroy *all* the information on our computer, prevent *any* peripheral functions, and even "wipe" the hard disk of all files to replace them with endless replications of the viral nonsense. The human analogy to this is the many religions and "belief" systems that have been "programmed" into our cultures, and our very lives, via endless "Prophet/God" programs, replacing, bit by bit, our own thinking with the "dogma and doctrines of the faith".

Enough of the computer analogies. I think that the reader can imagine any number of variations on the theme and come to an understanding of how vulnerable we are to "disinformation" in the guise of truth from either the future, the past, or the present.

Among the many critics of "channeling", in general, and my wife's work in particular, which is quite different both in theoretical approach and content, there are those who say "Channeled Information is crap. It is 100% disinformation."

I can't take such claims seriously.

Why?

I am a scientist. I look at things in a somewhat different way than other people. I am more critical. I am even more critical than most of my colleagues. So, when I see a statements like these, or even "channeling is a satellite transmission", I get very suspicious.

Why so?

I immediately see that anyone who says things like this is speaking nonsense – in *these* sentences. And when I see someone speaking nonsense in couple of sentences, and when this somebody is so affirmative – *then* I can't take this person seriously in all the rest.

What are the facts? What are the possibilities?

Certainly there is a possibility that some (most?) of the channeling *today* comes via satellites or other means of programming. That *is* not only possible but probable.

The next question we should ask is: *Why*?

The evident answer is: to twist, to disinform, via New Age-type naive people. Based on an assessment of the facts of technology and the morality (or lack of) amongst the Elite rulers of our world, it is highly probable that if there was information that would tend to free humanity from their controls, they would co-opt it immediately exactly as I have described above in my computer analogies.

Can the Cassiopaean channeling be disinformation or come as a result of such technology and/or programming?

This would not be so easy. We are not naïve, we are critical of our work. We think, we analyze, we test and do research.

Could *some* of our "communications" have been influenced this way?

Yes. There is such a possibility.

Can *all*, or even 95% be received this way?

No. Because there are too many instances in which the Cassiopaeans were answering questions to which normal "satellite type" of intelligence, without being able to instantly read the minds of everyone on this planet, could not have had access.

Therefore, I think the statement that *all* channeling is crap and disinformation, and that 95% is via satellites shows that the individuals who make such claims are:

a) Unable to think logically,

b) Not interested in discovering the truth.

This is the main difference between their approach and ours. While we are ready to question everything, and *always* look for new facts, other individuals declare, "*We know the Truth*". Here it is! And then we find one or another easily detectable nonsense statement that is claimed to be absolute, and this discredits everything else they say.

The Devil is always in the details.

Whenever someone claims: "All white is black" – I get suspicious. And I am turned off to everything else they say. Not because "white being black" is impossible, we know there *are* paradoxes, but *because* the person uses this three letter word: "all".

As for parallel realities, yes, probably this is part of the clue. As for satellites trying, once in a while, their dirty tricks – yes, this is possible. And we *are* taking it into account. But *always* we are trying to apply our logical thinking, our "judgment". But we know that this 3rd density reality check is *never sufficient* when dealing with possible hyperdimensional realities. But it is *always necessary*. Which means, in practical terms:

1) Always use it to the max.

2) Never think you can rely completely on it alone!

What I want to state clearly is this: this channeling, the Cassiopaean channeling, *is* different than other channeling. It was different from the very beginning, it continues to be so, and it will continue to be different. We may give it a name: Critical Channeling. It is such by intent, not by chance. It is channeling in which, by intent, the messenger is as important as the message itself. They are inseparably entangled in a quantum way; an interfering quantum amplitude. They form a oneness, a whole. To separate the message from the messenger would be, in this Cassiopaean quantum experiment, like closing one hole in a double slit experiment. You close one hole, and the whole pattern is different, not just a part of it. As I have written above:

There *can* be broadcasts from the future to the past, but *there will be few "receivers"*, and of those few, *even fewer that are properly tuned*. And even those that are properly tuned may be subject to "static". Even if there is no static, those receivers that can receive pure information will experience the static of "non-belief" and distortion after the fact from society.

It is in this context – that my wife is one of those few receivers who has worked very hard to properly "tune" to transmissions from the future – that I call the Cassiopaean Communication "Critical Channeling".

What is this "Critical Channeling"? In what way is it different than other channeling?

It would take a lot of space and time to describe it in details. One day we will do it. But for now, let me just make this observation: the Cassiopaean channeling has characteristics of a scientific experiment. Think of scientists in their lab, working on the great laws of the universe. They perform an important series of experiments. They are trained professionals, they know their stuff, they know their laboratory equipment and its quirks. But they are human beings. Once in a while someone will make some dirty joke, once in a while they will have to discard a series of data because mice have messed up their equipment during the night. Now, think, what advantage it would be if they would write in their paper the dirty joke, include the mice data, the ink blobs, etc., etc.

That is not the way of science. And the Cassiopaean experiment will proceed as a scientific one. With scientific standards in mind. The Cassiopaean channeling is Critical Channeling. It is in this respect that it is *different* from other channeling. And it will stay so.

The difference is in the approach. We are searching for the truth. Others who make unilateral statements that all channeling is crap are sure that they know it and would like to impose it on other people, or manipulate other people into believing what they say. And naturally, when such individuals state such things, they claim that it comes from God or some equally authoritarian source, but when someone else dares to have a different way of finding the truth, it is necessarily "100% disinformation" and "crap".

We try to share our thoughts, and when necessary, we are ready to learn and *change*. And that is what is most important. This attitude of being open.

What if such claims are right, that all channeling is crap and disinformation? Even if I consider it as highly improbable, can it be true?

Of course, being a scientist, and using my brain in order to judge, I had to consider also this possibility, however improbable it may look to me. And I concluded that such a claim cannot be true. Here is my reasoning: it goes via "*reductio ad absurdum*" – which is often used in logic and in mathematical proofs. You assume something to be true, and then by a chain of logical deductions you come to the conclusion that your assumption cannot be true. Somewhat tricky – but useful.

Applying this method to the claim that "all channeling is 100% disinformation because it is coming via satellite", let us suppose it is true. In order to be true it must include the capability of reading and controlling *everybody's* mind at *all* times.

But if that is the case, then why would the persons making such claims be exempt from this control?

Therefore, by logic, anyone who makes such a statement is also being influenced by programming and by satellites (if everybody is, then so is he). If so, then what such a person writes is skewed. And, because such debunkers are often so loud, and so sure, about this subject for no valid reason, it is a logical conclusion that what they are saying is *not* true, that the claim that all channeling is crap is, itself, disinformation.

So we see that starting from the assumption that such a claim is right (satellites affect everybody), we come to the conclusion that the claim is wrong (because it is simply repeating the satellite disinformation). So, here we have *reductio ad absurdum.*

But we can go even further. Can we find a reason why debunkers would state such evident nonsense with such certainty?

Well, here we can have a hypothesis too. If, as we know by the above analysis, *not all* channeling is from satellites, that *some* channeling can provide us with real information from "benevolent higher beings", from "us in the future", or from "Mind-God and Oversoul", call it as you will, then it is only natural that there will be forces trying to discredit *this* channeling. So, we have solved one problem here. If a critic calls all channelers disinformation agents, and if he is right, or even partly right, then we have reasons to suppose that such an individual is an agent of those forces.

There is one more exercise in logical reasoning and critical thinking that comes to mind. Most critics are not clear about what channeling is, so let me take the particular example of using the Ouija board, as my wife, Laura, does. Why does she use the Ouija board?

Laura went to great lengths to research the subject of channeling before she ever began her experiments. Based on facts and data, it was clear that using a "peripheral device" in a full state of consciousness was the optimum method to screen out noise. In particular, such a method makes it far more difficult for satellites, or other programming signals coming from human and hybrid technology, when and if they come, to affect the message. At least two persons are needed, full consciousness, critical thinking, often coffee, fresh minds, loud discussion of the data as it comes, and the board. Thinking in terms of possible quantum physics involved in mind-matter interactions, it is clear to me that the methods she uses are more likely to be robust and shielded against deliberate bombarding from outside by mind controlling signals, whether technological or "psychic". On the other hand, talking directly to "Mind-God" as so many other channels do is far more susceptible to interference. For example, a weak outside EM signal can be talking directly to a tiny implant in our teeth, and we will take it for our Oversoul...

So, by logical thinking and by critical analysis we come to a working hypothesis. But, please, do not jump to the conclusion that we have solved all the problems. Important problems are still out there and need to be addressed. The above analysis does not confirm anything 100%. It gives indications. To answer the question as to whether or not the Cassiopaean Communications is exactly what it says it is – transmissions from Us in the Future – a full analysis, that takes into account not one but many aspects, is necessary. Completely different methods must be used. If A is an opponent of B, and if we find that A is wrong, that does not mean that B is right! To see whether B is right or not – is a different problem.

Let me just note that we have discussed these issues on many occasions on our website[2], with other groups or individuals and quite often, those who started as skeptics have later admitted openly that these Cassiopaeans have an amazing record.

Arkadiusz Jadczyk, Ph.D.

---

[2] http://www.cassiopaea.org

AUTHOR'S LETTER TO THE READER

This book has been a long time coming. Since the first of the series of articles appeared on the internet in late March or early April of 2000, I have been deluged by requests from readers to bring the material out in a regular book. And, since I began to publish *The Wave*, there has been an unbelievable series of attacks on us personally, our children, our friends, associates and even our internet discussion group members. I had no idea that just sharing my experiences and research was going to create such an earthquake.

On the website, *The Wave* series stands alone with introductions and biographical material hyperlinked to other pages on the site. Bringing *The Wave* out as a book requires a certain "beginning" so that the reader who is not familiar with the website will not be lost and wonder just what the heck is going on. With that in mind, I have included material that will "set the stage," so to say, for the New Reader. Those of you who are familiar with our publications might want to read this already familiar material anyway because, here and there, I have added further details in response to additional reader requests.

One of the things I want to add at the beginning here is that I never, ever, intended for my life to become "public property" as a consequence of my work and my writing. Those of you who have read my partial autobiography, *Amazing Grace*, know that the likelihood of me ever being a "public person" was so remote, considering my "niche" in this world, that even if, like many others, I occasionally dreamed of doing something "worthwhile" for humanity, it never was more than exactly that: an occasional dream that my practical nature scanned cursorily and relegated to the "nonsense" file. That is, until I encountered Tom French, a journalist with the St. Petersburg (Florida) Times. He described that meeting in the article he subsequently wrote about me as follows:

> I met Laura for the first time on the afternoon of Saturday, Feb. 25, 1995, at the east branch of the Clearwater Library. She and I were there for the meeting of a local chapter of the Mutual UFO Network, better known as MUFON, an organization that investigates reports of UFOs and alien abductions. I had not been aware that there was any such chapter in Tampa Bay, much less that it had enough

members for them to congregate en masse at the public library. I wanted to know more, so I went.

This was in the early stages of the current national obsession with all things UFO-related. The X-Files was only in its second season, the so-called alien autopsy video was not yet airing on the Fox network, and the only person I knew personally who had seen a UFO – or at least, who had admitted such a thing to me – was my former hairdresser.

Still, the congregants at the library were excited that Saturday. They knew that a ground swell of interest in other worlds and other intelligences was gaining momentum around the country; they sensed that they were in the first wave of a profound shift in the public's willingness to consider the possibility that alien visitations might just be a verifiable fact of life on this planet. After years of being derided, these people were finally getting some attention and respect.

To say that Laura made an impression that day is an understatement. When it was her turn to speak, she instantly seized control of the room. She had so much presence, she was almost radioactive. And hers was no ordinary presence. She was not about to be mistaken for a movie star; she was overweight and slightly mussed, and her clothes were almost defiantly unfashionable. She wore leggings that, as I recall, were a little too tight and a tunic adorned with amber beads and painted gold spirals. I took one look at her and said to myself, "I bet she has a bust of Elvis in her living room."

Somehow, though, Laura used all these qualities to her advantage. She was too much, and knew it, and did not care; if anything, she reveled in her over-the-topness, which gave her tremendous freedom and power. Her eyes flashed; her hair flowed freely; her slightly crooked smile ignited the atmosphere around her.

In a short talk, apparently delivered without any notes, Laura gave an overview of her life, telling a little about her childhood, her work as an exorcist, her hypnosis session with the woman with the missing time, the night she and the kids saw the two ships above their swimming pool. She also spoke about some recent experiences with a spirit board, which as I understood it was similar to a Ouija board but more elaborate. Using this spirit board, she said, she and F*** and some other friends had begun communicating with what she called "sixth-density beings" from the stars that make up the Cassiopeia constellation.

Laura's story was easily the wildest I heard that day. It didn't matter. She was smart, charming, completely real. She joked about herself, her kids, her husband, her family's decidedly off-beat riff on middle-class life. She even joked about these sixth-density beings, whatever they were. "The boys from Brazil," she called them, and the way she said it made me laugh, even though I had no clue what she was talking about. She was giving a performance, and I was not the only one in the audience who enjoyed it.

Cherie Diez, a Times photographer with whom I'd worked for many years, had come with me to the MUFON meeting. The two of us were searching for someone unusual to follow for the newspaper. After seeing and listening to Laura that day, Cherie and I believed that we had found a subject who exceeded our every expectation.

In between our work on other projects for the paper, we were drawn again and again to Laura's house in New Port Richey, hanging out for hours at a time with her and her family and friends. What we saw, every time we visited, was a woman leading a life on her own terms, defining herself every day.

Laura's life was crammed with seemingly incongruous elements. She was a walking smorgasbord of the paranormal, yes. But she was also a mother of five, making dinner and doing the laundry while she pursued aliens and demonic spirits. She was a glorious amalgamation, a mixture of Bette Midler, Father Damien, Donna Reed and Agent Scully.

Laura defied all categories. She did not, would not fit into any box, including one that I had tried to stick her into that first day at the MUFON meeting. When I toured her home, I found no bust of Elvis in the living room. But on her mantel, above the fireplace, there was an eerie, almost ghostly ceramic pitcher bearing the likeness of Edward VIII. Laura's grandparents had bought it in 1937, just after Edward gave up the English throne to marry Wallis Simpson. So much for my stereotyping.

Laura's house was one huge encyclopedia of her life, overflowing with things that testified to the breadth of her curiosity and interests. On the walls hung Victorian prints from her grandparents, a painting of Jesus, a map of the world, pieces of her children's artwork, oversized reproductions of tarot cards, Star Trek posters the kids had put up...

Though some of her children occasionally were enrolled in the public schools for a semester or two, Laura still home-schooled them for the most part. She seemed to be doing a good job. Jason and his siblings – he was the middle child, and the only boy – were smart and well educated. They were constantly drawing, reading, playing the piano, inventing their own secret codes, working out math problems for fun; whenever I asked them anything about history or science or literature, they usually showed themselves to be far ahead of most other children their age.

In some ways, their lives were strange. Like their mother, at least a couple of the children claimed to have paranormal abilities; several years before the movie Sixth Sense came out, Jason told me, without a trace of a smile on his face, that he could see the spirits of dead people, walking around him on the street.

Yet for all these oddities, Jason and his siblings were still just kids. They complained about taking out the trash. They argued about who would get to sit in the front seat of the family van. They could watch TV for hours on end, sprawled across the furniture in front of the set like lazy jungle cats.

Aletheia and Anna, the two oldest girls – they were 16 and 13 when I met them – were embarrassed by their mother. This was not surprising. Virtually every teenage girl is appalled by her mom at one time or another. But in their case, Aletheia and Anna were appalled because their mother gathered with friends on Saturday nights, channeling communications from sixth-density beings. "Mom," Aletheia would say, "can't you play bingo? Would you please sell Tupperware, for God's sake?"

As Cherie and I went on interviewing Laura, asking her to fill in the blanks from over the years, the children listened, adding their own details and impressions of what they had seen themselves. In many ways, they were Laura's witnesses. They had been on hand for much of what she described to us, and they corroborated her stories...

Laura was constantly reading another handful of books on Atlantis, and cataloging her dreams, and contemplating the nature of evil, and drawing up astrological charts, and writing massive treatises on vampires and aliens, and driving away to UFO conventions, and firing off e-mails about the latest alien sighting in Brazil...

Sometimes she seemed tired and distracted; occasionally she would call me sounding a little down. But that was all. Most of the time, she seemed too busy to be depressed. She moved in a constant whirlwind, driving the kids around, throwing another load of laundry into the dryer, reading up on crop circles, typing transcripts of the channeling sessions...

She was always blasting one kind of music or another on the stereo. She swooned to Beethoven, Brahms, countless operas and choral pieces, not to mention Pink Floyd; predictably, one of her favorites was Dark Side of the Moon. She loved to go to movies, to escape on excursions with F*** and other friends, to brush her daughters' hair and laugh at Jason's imitations of Data, the android from Star Trek: The Next Generation. And she never lost her sense of humor.

Once, we stopped at a diner for breakfast. The waitress, taking Laura's order, asked if she wanted home fries or grits. "Who's cooking the grits?" said Laura. The waitress stopped writing and looked up from her pad. "My brother," she said, smiling uncertainly. "Was he born in Florida?" Laura asked. "No." "Then I'll take the home fries."

Laura was always hard to keep up with. Cherie and I followed along as best we could. We sat in on one of Laura's spirit detachments; we attended several of the channeling sessions she and F*** were leading. In addition, we spoke with many of the people around Laura...

From the start, we recognized the possibility that Laura could have lied to us about the exorcisms and many other things as well. She could have made up her memories of the reptilian face[3] at the window, the dreams, the breaking glass. If she had wanted to do so – and it would have required the cooperation of not only her children, but many other people as well – she could have been staging an almost impossibly elaborate hoax on us for several years. Neither Cherie nor I saw anything to indicate such a hoax.

After spending several years in her company, we never found any evidence to suggest that Laura was some con artist, faking her studies of the paranormal to gain money or attract publicity. Everything about her suggested someone who was trying her best to give a full and accurate account of her life. When I asked difficult questions, she did not hedge. On her own, she shared with me sensitive moments from her past, moments where she had made a mistake or done something she regretted, such as a suicide attempt in her early 20s when she was distraught over the breakup of a relationship and the death of her grandfather. It was not easy for her to talk about these things, but she did.

In addition, the overwhelming volume of her activities – not just the channeling sessions themselves, but thousands of pages of notes, essays and papers – testified to the genuine depth of Laura's interest. She was clearly devoted to these questions long before we entered her life; she talked about the exorcisms and the channeling that first day at the MUFON meeting before she knew we were in the audience. Once we sought her out, Laura repeatedly expressed ambivalence about her story appearing in the newspaper.

At times, when she worried about how readers might react to her story, she even asked us to reconsider writing about her at all.

Money never appeared to be the driving force behind Laura's activities. She lived modestly, driving a used van and raising her kids in a house that was in constant need of repair.

Laura showed scant interest in making money from her paranormal activities. She charged minimal fees for her sessions, but they never amounted to much. Several years ago, when she made some transcripts of her channeling sessions for us, we paid her $100; since then, she has given us hundreds of more pages of these transcripts and has refused to accept a penny more for her trouble.

---

[3] Actually, Tom was mistaken to call this a "reptilian face" because that is not how I described it. The only thing I could say about it was that it seemed to be made up in "black-face" make-up, with white around the eyes.

If she was out to make a buck, she was terrible at it...

Other possibilities occurred to me. I wondered if maybe Laura had imagined the face at the window and all the other strange episodes as a way of injecting drama into her life. Was it possible that she was bored, or lonely, or simply so desperate to find something to occupy her mind that she had created this huge fantasy? What if all of it – the exorcisms, the spirit detachments, the channeling with the Cs – was just some massive, unruly play that her subconscious was constantly staging to keep things interesting?

Then, of course, there was the simplest explanation. What if Laura was a victim of some psychosis? This was a possibility Laura repeatedly raised herself. "Sometimes I think I'm losing my mind," she said to me. "Is this what being mad is like? Because, you know, some really crazy people can really seem sane." Every time she brought up this possibility, Laura dismissed it. She said that she had occasionally been to counselors and psychologists, as many of us have. But to her knowledge, she told me, she has never been diagnosed with any mental illness.

Early on, I considered asking Laura to be evaluated by a psychiatrist, at the newspaper's expense. What if a doctor could put a name on whatever was happening with her? What if he or she told us that Laura was manic-depressive, delusional, even schizophrenic?

Ultimately, though, I never asked Laura to put herself under the microscope. It didn't feel right. The more time I spent with her, the less I wanted to try to force her into another box. Whatever was happening with her, there was something remarkable about the way it was playing itself out. She was raising her children, enjoying her friendships with F**** and others, reading and learning all the time, exploring the reaches of her imagination. The woman was leading a life. It wasn't a perfect life, not even close. But it was hers, and it was extraordinary, and I was not about to interfere...

Things were happening in front of me that I could not explain. Laura did things, little things, that I could not figure out. Like the letters that came off the board when she was channeling. Sometimes she recited them so fast, they came out in a single flowing stream. How did she do that? If she was just making up the answers, or her subconscious was making them up, how did she compose them so quickly, without hesitation or interruption? These were not just "yes" or "no" answers. Sometimes the answers were long and complicated. Some of them sounded like things Laura would say; I could imagine her thinking them up, and then breaking them down and calling them out in the individual letters. But other times, the answers didn't sound like Laura at all. They sounded like they came from someone else, someone who knew things it seemed unlikely Laura would know. Either way, I could not understand how she sometimes managed to call out the letters so fast. I would listen to the letters pouring out, and I would try to hear the words hidden inside them, and my brain could not keep up. The letters melted together into one long non-stop blur. Maybe it proved nothing. Maybe all these things showed was that Laura was smarter and quicker than anybody I'd ever come across...

After all this time, I cannot begin to tell you what is truly happening with Laura. I do know that she remains as intriguing as ever. From the moment I met her, she has made me consider possibilities that would not have occurred to me otherwise. She has forced me to see and think in new ways. This is Laura's true gift. The only special ability of hers to which I can swear.

When I share Laura's story with people, they ask me what it means. I tell them I do not know. I cannot prove that sixth-density beings, hailing from a constellation in the sky, actually hooked her up with a second husband who was perfectly suited for her but who lived across the ocean. All I know is, Laura is real, and Ark is real, and against all the odds, they found each other and are now married. Isn't that enough?

I find it amazing that Laura has spent so much of her life pursuing aliens and dark entities, when in the end she caught hold of something far more elusive.

We talk about love all the time, but how do we know it's real? We can't see it, can't nail it down, cannot begin to prove exactly what it is. Love is an idea, an invisible notion without form or substance, that we accept on faith. And yet we spend our lives chasing it. We crave it, long for it, cry ourselves to sleep over it. We do these things, because we feel what love means inside us, and that is all we need to know that it is real.

When I go to see Laura and Ark these days, I think about these things. I see them together, and it reminds me that the invisible is sometimes within reach...

In recent months, Laura and Ark have devoted a great deal of time to a sprawling Web site that discusses their lives, their theories, the channeling with the Cs. Those who read through its contents will see that my descriptions of the channeling have only skimmed the surface of that subject.

Laura's curiosity remains as epic as ever. Not long ago, I noticed two piles of books – her current reading material – stacked precariously beside her chair in the living room. The titles included The Atlas of Early Man, The Myth of the Eternal Return, Mysteries of the Alphabet, The Etruscans and Subquantum Kinetics. Not all of her selections were so intellectual. Wedged in the middle of the books was a copy of Woman's World magazine, which she was scanning for new diets. Her desire to unlock the mysteries of the cosmos burns just as fiercely as when I first met her.

Recently I asked what her goals were for the years ahead. She gave me her list. "A," she told me, "change the universe. B, transcend space and time, which includes time travel into the future and into the past. Or, C, transition into another density and effect all of the above."

In the meantime, Laura and Ark have each other. The two of them talk for hours on end. They almost never go out, except when she wants to venture to Sam's Club to hunt for bargains. "We don't go anywhere," she says happily. "We don't do anything." There is a different feeling now to Laura's life. It feels less scattered than before, less uncertain, immeasurably more calm. Inside the house, there is a palpable, tangible sense of contentment.

Recently I asked her what she has learned. Not so much about aliens or UFOs, but about her heart. Laura paused and thought for a moment. "In my mind," she said, "life is an ongoing miracle. It really is a miracle. And the one thing I have learned just in the past few years is that if you don't see something miraculous in your life, if it seems dark or sad or it seems like a burden, the most miraculous thing you have is your ability to choose to be that miracle. I mean, to be it. I think once people choose to be a miracle, the universe reflects that back to them."

Some people would call this luck. Laura would not.[4]

Even though, as Tom described it above, I was very hesitant to even allow him to tell my story, I finally made the decision – after many meetings and discussions with him – to agree to do it. The expected Central Florida audience wasn't that large and I figured I could handle any problems that might issue from such exposure. Certainly, if that had been all that ever happened, it would have been a "flash in the pan," and then fade out to obscurity.

Except for the website.

Except for *The Wave*.

As Tom pointed out, in the months immediately prior to the publication of his lengthy article, written after five years of my association with him, Ark and I had devoted a lot of time to the

---

[4] Thomas French, "The Exorcist in Love: A tale of possibilities", *St. Petersburg Times* (St. Petersburg, Fla., February 13, 2000).

website. The main reason we had launched the website was exactly due to the events Tom described in his article: we had been working with a process that most definitely seemed to work in life changing ways. No, it wasn't easy and it consisted in divesting oneself of illusions, a painful process under the best of circumstances. But do, please note, that last exchange Tom reported. I do, indeed, consider life to be a miracle and that we all have the ability to BE a miracle, but as Ark is fond of saying: the devil is in the details. So, the website was launched to describe all the details that could, step by step, help those others like us who had spent their lives as we had: in illusion that time and again led to disappointment and suffering. We had learned that the key was to move from illusion and lies into truth. But that wasn't a simple process because the layers of lies and illusions in which we live are like an onion, you peel and peel and peel, and when you get to the center, what is there? As I told Tom, you then find that you have to BE your own miracle, be your own light in the darkness.

Tom was our witness. As he wrote, "There is a different feeling now to Laura's life. It feels less scattered than before, less uncertain, immeasurably more calm. Inside the house, there is a palpable, tangible sense of contentment." And this motivated me to try to share what we had learned, what we had experienced via the Cassiopaean Experiment.

From my point of view, I simply had a website – like millions of other ordinary people – where I shared my hobby – the thing that interested and excited me – with others who might have similar hobbies. Sure, my hobby – my quest, if you like – was searching for the truth, the bottom line of our existence, but I theorized that there certainly might be others with similar interests. Naively, I thought that "war stories" could be shared the way cat fanciers share the photos of their favorite felines or the way those who are interested in cuisine share recipes. After all, a cat fancier or a chef is never attacked for preferring one breed of cat or one type of cookware over another; they are not accused of all sorts of vile intentions of forcing everyone else to prefer that type of cat or cookware. Nor do cat fanciers and chefs find themselves in the position of having their privacy invaded, their character impugned, their lives destroyed by libel and slander, or physical threats of bodily harm made against them and their family. On March 2nd, I wrote about my website to an internet friend as follows:

> I put up the *Jesus* transcripts on the site yesterday... there has been an overwhelming interest in the *Jews* page for some time now, ever

since it was discovered by some Jewish folks who then linked it to some sort of discussion page.

You might also want to look at santilli.htm to see the note that Ark added yesterday... when we found it, we cracked up! Yesterday was an "odd" day, too!

I have also been trying to keep up with my gardening... am getting close to the end of the "spring preparations" phase, but feel time running out on me in that respect. Wanted to do far more than I am going to be able to do based on present progress. I guess that gardening is just in the blood – long line of farmers... But, the kids, who regularly made fun of my obsession, now say that we have the best yard on the street! (SOMEbody's got to!)

As you can see, my life was still fairly normal at that point. I had not yet begun *The Wave*. At that point, I was just collecting excerpts from the Cassiopaean Transcripts together into "subject" groupings, going through them to remove personal information to protect my privacy and the privacy of the few people who had attended our sessions, and putting them up as web pages.

I barely knew how to do web pages, and I was learning as I went, having a lot of fun. Those readers who remember my early efforts will recall the tacky backgrounds, graphics and "theme music" I was adding to every page. It was only after readers began to write to me and complain that it took so long to load the pages with all the graphics and music, and that they had a hard time printing the material that I began to strip the pages of all the "bells and whistles" to the current, plain look of the website. During this period of time, we were paying substantial money to send our son to the commercial art school he wanted to attend. Now, he does the graphics and design of the website and all I do anymore is write. Of course, the attackers accuse us of having a "slick website" and suggest that there must be illegally gotten money behind it, or at least money from nefarious sources.

Speaking of writing, I had done a lot of it over the years, beginning with my book length project entitled *The Noah Syndrome*. I learned to type doing that one. But I wasn't really a "writer" at that point. I was stilted and formal and the fact is, I still often regress to that style. But in a very real sense, I learned to write by writing for the website. I won't say that I have any definite "stylistic grace" or that I can even claim to be a "writer," but I sure have produced more material than I ever imagined I would. That fact, too, comes under attack. I'm damned if I do, and damned if I don't. If I say nothing, if I just publish the transcripts without commentary on the background of the sessions, I am accused of "hiding" important information because I am egotistical and want to be the only one who has the answers. If, on the other hand, I try to answer every request for information about my experiences – never mind that I couch my answer in terms that it is only my experiences, or my opinion, and that I am open to new data, that I am still a work in progress – then I am "egotistically writing about myself." Go figure!

The fact is that my current way of "writing," if we can call it that, only developed out of the many, many requests from readers for more information. Every "subject page" I put up on the website with no commentary except for a few brief sentences to connect excerpts separated by time, brought forth inquiries and correspondence from readers or other "researchers" in particular subjects. On the same day that I wrote the email I quoted above, about my gardening and "normal life," I wrote the following to another correspondent who had read the Cassiopaean material on the Twin Sun subject:

>On 2 Mar 2000, at 19:56, Barry Warmkessel wrote:

>I have read your twin sun website and find that data in it is very similar >to my own. We have defined a dark star in our solar system which we >have dubbed Vulcan. We have an IRAS object for it (like an infrared >photograph), orbit elements (period, inclination, etc.) mass and magnitude. >You can find it at: http://www.barry.warmkessel.com/

Hi,

We had a look.

Trust me, it is NO great satisfaction to have the C's material validated! Particularly in this sense. But, as they say: knowledge protects... even if you don't WANT to know something!

As you may know, my husband is a mathematical/physicist and we did have a look at Mueller's book after receiving this info, but couldn't get a straight answer out of any of the folks we wrote to in inquiring about some astronomical insights on any of this. So, we have been in a sort of vacuum with it. Ark *did* do some calculations with various periods, but came up with nothing satisfactory because, other than what we were given, we really had no data.

Some folks think it is "not nice" when the C's give part of an answer and then leave us hanging, but then, when the "rest of the answer" comes from a third party with no "agenda," it does tend to make it more of a "learning experience" and makes it "stick." So, maybe they ARE wiser than we are.

Anyway, what we would like to know is: with your astronomical insight (we are complete amateurs in this realm) do you have a visualization... sort of a "picture" of the orbits with numbers and so forth? Can such a thing be modeled?

Did you have a look at what the C's said about the mass of the "dark companion" relative to Sol? How does this calculate?

If it is okay, I would like to put a link to your page from my index page.

Yes, we have some "weird" stuff... but, we DO try to keep an analytic attitude toward all of it.

Mr. Warmkessel kindly wrote back:

I do not know of your group at all, but I suspect you get your information via channeling with a board or something like that. This is OK by me. Whatever works. Channeling is not 100% accurate, but good channelers can get error rates as low as only 10% to 15%.

To which I responded:

Yup. And that's why we call it an "experiment." We work at it, making adjustments in all sorts of ways... and it is a group effort, and *not* a single individual. And, another thing, no one of us ever has a clue what is "coming through," because it simply by-passes our conscious minds. We have to have the words read back to us as we proceed. Tedious, yes, but much better for corruption control, as I call it.

And so, things were still rather quiet through most of March. Much of my correspondence consisted of exchanges with various family members and genealogy club members with whom I was discussing my genealogy project which had obsessed me for the past several years. I actually spent more time working on that than I did working on the website.

But there were also many questions from readers who wrote to me about the odd references the Cassiopaeans repeatedly made to *The Wave*. This subject appeared in so many contexts that it was difficult to separate it out into a "subject file" for the website. But, since so many people wanted me to deal with that subject next, I decided I would give it a try. After I had pulled out all the sections of the transcripts that mentioned it and pasted them into a document chronologically, I realized that I would have to write just a bit more than a few connecting sentences to make it "flow." And by this time, I most definitely wanted it to flow better; otherwise, I knew I would get another deluge of questions to answer! The body of material along with my estimated commentary was supposed to be only about 100 pages. I divided it up into chapters, thinking that nine was a good number, and had it all set up and ready to write the connecting text. I planned to do one page per day, and be done in less than two weeks. It was going to be simple and then I could get back to my genealogy and my gardening and my reading.

As I mentioned at the beginning here, the first two parts went up in late March or early April. I didn't even record the day. I put the two pages up simultaneously because they "went together," and were going to be the "introduction" to the Cassiopaean material.

The first email in my archives that refers to *The Wave* series is dated April 5th. That is probably the actual day the pages were uploaded to the site. Part 3 was uploaded on the 8th. I have a record of that since all those who wrote to me about the first two parts asked to be notified as soon as a new chapter was published. Immediately, the emails began to arrive. The first one is as follows, including my reply:

>On 8 Apr 2000, at 18:30, M*** B*** wrote:

>Just a quick note of encouragement: your Wave series is >absolutely wonderful – great info and funny. You're a treasure.

Hi,

Thanks! All encouragement appreciated as SOME letters are not so encouraging!

Thankfully, though, that kind are in the minority.

Only 6 more sections to go on the Wave series, and we have some additional info that will be appended to the Flight 19 business in the next couple of days.

Thanks for writing.

Laura

Notice how confident I was that I only had six more sections to go, and then I would be done with it. Also note my reference to the fact that some people were writing "not so encouraging" letters." Here is another of the beginning avalanche of letters:

>On 10 Apr 2000, at 11:47 G*** R***wrote:

>I am wondering what Ark has to say about this wave. The subject >of waves in physics is a very important one!

Well, remember, I am only on part 3 of 9 sections... Ark's questions and the answers to them will be coming up soon. This subject has been quite a topic over the past few years to say the least!

Laura

Again and again I was saying: oh, it's only going to be 9 parts, it will be a breeze, I'll be done in a few days and we can all get back to normal. As the letters continued to come in, I began to realize that I was going to have to do a more comprehensive coverage. Things that I didn't think were too important, and almost left out because they were so strange, were producing amazing resonance with other people!

Meanwhile, on April 20th, we received an email from a movie producer who wanted to "buy the rights" to my life story.

On 19 Apr 2000, at 12:00, Joseph Nasser wrote:

> We are a television movie production company interested in your compelling life story. We are very sensitive to the importance of your privacy and will change names and places of occurrence if you desire. In addition, the amount of time you put into the movie is entirely your decision. Some people choose to be very involved, but most choose only a brief interview with a writer. We are prepared to offer you full financial compensation for the rights to your life story.
>
> I have enclosed a list of our movie credits which will show you that we are an active, legitimate company. As you will notice, one of the projects we recently put into development is Project:Stargate which concerns the US Governments attempts to use psychics for espionage purposes. We are very sympathetic to stories involving the paranormal. I hope to speak with you soon.
>
> If you or not interested in the possibility of a movie I fully understand and wish you all the best. Thank you for your time and consideration.

Part of what I wrote back to him is as follows:

> As you may have also guessed, when I made the decision to allow Tom French "inside" my life for five years, the choice naturally entailed a certain level of loss of privacy. It was a choice that I did not make lightly, and my chief concern was that the events of my own life could be beneficial to others. That idea is still central to all that we do, though somewhat tempered by recent experiences to allow for the possibility of having everything twisted and distorted and misunderstood. I was braced for negative reactions and was quite surprised that there were almost none. Rather, there was an overwhelming outpouring of correspondence from people with similar experiences, or those looking for help.
>
> At present, it is curious to me that someone wishes to purchase the rights to my life story. Does this mean that I can't write about it myself? And tell ALL the details... all that was omitted by Tom, all that I have, thus far, even omitted from the "personal version" on

my website? For the most part, these omissions have been for my own safety.

Does purchasing the rights to my story mean that it will sit on a shelf as an "option" that is never acted on?

The answer was, basically, yes to all questions. I would be selling the rights to my own life story and would be prevented from writing it myself in any context. What is more, the "option" could sit forever on a shelf and never reach the light of day. Further details revealed that I would have almost no input into the "spin" of the story itself. I said "no thanks."

Indeed, as Tom French noted, I was terrible at making money!

What struck me as odd about the whole thing was that this offer came exactly at the point that I had made the decision that there was going to be no way I could write about *The Wave* the way I had originally planned it. Based on the number and types of questions that the first three chapters were eliciting from readers, I knew that I was going to have to write about the background of the material, the experiences that led from one question to another; why I had asked this question and not that question of the Cassiopaeans, and so on. In short, to write *The Wave*, I would have to write about my life.

Just to give you some idea of what I was dealing with: I wrote almost 4,000 emails in 2000, and I did not respond to every single email I received. That is an average of about 11 emails a day. Very often, they were to individuals who were seekers and had questions requiring rather long and detailed answers. In 2001, I wrote 11,226 emails.

On April 26, I asked my small circle of internet friends – consisting of about a dozen people – if they would be up to chatting with new people. I was so deluged with emails that I found myself spending all my time writing personal answers to them, and then writing the same answers over again to others. It seemed far more efficient to turn some of these questions over to the several people with whom I had been corresponding for some time so that they could attempt to discuss things together, or I could simply write one answer to a question and send it to all of them at once. They all agreed that it was a fine idea, and so our first "discussion group" was born – due to the publication of *The Wave*.

At about the same time, Parts 5 and 6 of *The Wave* were published. The whole project was taking a *lot* longer than I had anticipated and I was dancing as fast as I could just to keep up with the "waves" I seemed to be making. On April 29th, I posted the following to this newly formed discussion group:

> I finished Wave 7 yesterday and will be doing keywords and getting it loaded on the site within the next two hours. It deals with some of the things we have been talking about in the past couple of days... and still more to come. Working on Wave 8, but took some time out to set in some marigolds that would have been too big to move next week...

As you can see, I still had illusions of being able to garden! I guess that I didn't realize that I had more or less begun to garden in a different way. By May, the discussion group had grown so large that we decided to move it to an "e-group" discussion forum for ease of management.

And so it went. I will not continue in this line because I have described the further events that occurred behind the scenes of writing *The Wave* in what is now known as *The Adventures with Cassiopaea* series. Yes, that will be published in book form soon, also. For now, we are just happy to have finally been able to get this first volume of *The Wave* completed!

Let us move on now to the necessary background material for any new readers. Those of you who are old friends I hope will forgive me for considering it necessary to add this to *The Wave* when you are so familiar with the text itself as it stands on the website.

November 7, 2004

NOTE TO THE READER ON THE SUBJECT OF ALIENS AND UFOS

Almost thirty years ago, I received my first formal training in hypnosis. Over the years, I not only sought out additional training, I employed this skill on behalf of many troubled individuals. Until 1994, I had never encountered what is popularly known as an "abductee" – that is, an individual claiming to have been abducted by alleged aliens. I have to admit that when I did, it presented certain problems both in terms of having a well-established technique to deal with it, as well as my own categories of what is or is not possible.

I often tell people in a sort of joking way: of all the people who *never* wanted to know anything about aliens and UFOs, I deserve a place at the head of the line. Very few people really understand how deeply serious this remark is. When I opened the door to consider the possibility – quite remote as I thought – of the *possibility* of "other worldly" visitors, life as I knew it ended. That was eleven years ago. But then, a completely new life was born from the ashes. The road from there to here has been difficult, to understate the matter, and complicated by all the High Strangeness that seems to surround the subject. This introduction is from my book on the subject of so-called alien abductions, entitled *The High Strangeness of Dimensions, Densities and the Process of Alien Abduction*.

The term "high strangeness" is attributed to Dr. J. Allen Hynek who addressed the United Nations on the subject of UFOs on November 27, 1978 in the following way:

> Mr. Chairman, there exists today a world-wide phenomenon... indeed if it were not world-wide I should not be addressing you and these representatives from many parts of the world. There exists a global phenomenon the scope and extent of which is not generally recognized. It is a phenomenon so *strange and foreign to our daily terrestrial mode of thought* that it is frequently met by ridicule and derision by persons and organizations unacquainted with the facts...
>
> I refer, of course, to the phenomenon of UFOs... Unidentified Flying Objects... which I should like to define here simply as "any aerial or surface sighting, or instrumental recording (e.g., radar, photography, etc.) which remains unexplained by conventional methods even after competent examination by qualified persons."

You will note, Mr. Chairman, that this definition says nothing about little green men from outer space, or manifestations from spiritual realms, or various psychic manifestations. It simply states an operational definition. A cardinal mistake, and a source of great confusion, has been the almost universal substitution of an interpretation of the UFO phenomenon for the phenomenon itself.

This is akin to having ascribed the Aurora Borealis to angelic communication before we understood the physics of the solar wind.

Nonetheless, in the popular mind the UFO phenomenon is associated with the concept of extra-terrestrial intelligence and this might yet prove to be correct *in some context...*

We have on record many tens of thousands of UFO reports... they include extremely intriguing and provocative accounts of strange events experienced by highly reputable persons... events which challenge our present conception of the world about us and which may indeed signal a need for a change in some of these concepts...

Mr. Chairman, any phenomenon which touches the lives of so many people, and which engenders puzzlement and even fear among them, is therefore not only of potential scientific interest and significance but also of sociological and political significance, especially since it carries with it many *implications of the existence of intelligences other than our own...*

Speaking then for myself as an astronomer, and I believe for many of my colleagues as well, there is no longer any question in my mind of the importance of this subject...

Mr. Chairman, I have not always held the opinion that UFOs were worthy of serious scientific study. I began my work as Scientific Consultant to the U.S. Air Force as an open skeptic, in the firm belief that we were dealing with a mental aberration and a public nuisance. Only in the face of stubborn facts and data similar to those studied by the French commission... have I been forced to change my opinion...

The UFO phenomenon, as studied by my colleagues and myself, bespeaks the action of some form of intelligence... but whence this intelligence springs, whether it is truly extra-terrestrial, or bespeaks a higher reality not yet recognized by science, or even if it be in some way or another a strange psychic manifestation of our own intelligence, is much the question. We seek your help, Mr. Chairman, in assisting scientists, and particularly those already associated with the many formal and informal investigative organizations around the world, by providing a clearing house procedure whereby the work already going on globally can be brought together in a serious, concentrated approach to this most outstanding challenge to current science.

I would like to draw your attention to particular remarks made by Dr. Hynek in the passage quoted above:

> [A] global phenomenon ... *so strange and foreign to our daily terrestrial mode of thought*... it carries with it many implications of the existence of intelligences other than our own... [It] bespeaks the action of some form of intelligence... but whence this intelligence springs, whether it is truly extra-terrestrial, or bespeaks a higher reality not yet recognized by science, or even if it be in some way or another a strange psychic manifestation of our own intelligence, is much the question...

These remarks address the "High Strangeness" factor. "High Strangeness" describes those UFO cases that are not only peculiar but that can often be utterly absurd. In some cases, there are events before, during, and after the "sighting proper" imbued with elements of time and space distortion, bizarre synchronicities, strange states of consciousness, beings that act absurd, strange 'creatures' associated with the sighting, but not necessarily part of the sighting, anomalous phone calls, electronic glitches, paranormal events including poltergeist type activity, and what are popularly known as MIBs – Men in Black.

French scientist, Jacques Vallee, and Eric Davis write in a paper about High Strangeness:

> A primary objection to the reality of Unidentified Aerial Phenomena events among scientists is that witnesses consistently report objects whose seemingly absurd behavior "cannot possibly" be related to actual phenomena, even under extreme conditions... Skeptics insist that superior beings, celestial ambassadors or intelligent extraterrestrial (ETI) visitors simply would not perpetrate such antics as are reported in the literature.

In one case, a farmer in Minnesota, Mr. Simonton, claimed that a craft hovered in his barnyard and strange swarthy oriental looking men offered him a jug which he filled with water and then gave him pancakes. Dr. Hynek had the little cakes analyzed and found they lacked any salt content. Vallee noted that saltless cakes are often a feature of fairy myths.

Another case was that of a Belgian farmer who saw a UFO land in his field. He approached the craft and a small "alien" came up to him and asked him for the time! The farmer replied with the requested information. The alien told him he was wrong and pointed a wand at him which paralyzed him until the alien had departed in his craft.

When the authorities investigated the case, they found a circle of destroyed flora on the landing site, and it was reported that even the soil was damaged from something like extreme heat exposure.

When you read enough raw data from the many thousands of cases, you get the deep impression that the witnesses are telling the truth about what they have experienced. Why would a couple of farmers make up such ridiculous, nonsensical stories? Testimony was obtained to show their mental stability and competence. They never made any money from their stories, and they certainly weren't after fame. In fact, they suffered more from telling their stories than if they had just kept quiet.

Such cases are not isolated. There are many with such bizarre elements. Something is certainly happening to these people, and it is something that has both physical and psychological components. Nevertheless, this High Strangeness factor is a problem because it's all too easy to dismiss or ignore such "reports" because of these ridiculous claims. One has to wonder if this "High Strangeness" isn't deliberate – and for that very reason. This brings us to consider the signal to noise factor.

Dr. Hynek wrote in a paper presented at the AIAA 13th Aerospace Sciences Meeting Pasadena, Calif., January 20-22, 1975, entitled "The Emerging Picture of the UFO Problem":

> But one element that is common to all scientific endeavor is the problem of signal-to-noise ratio; in the UFO phenomenon this problem is a major one. The UFO problem is, initially, a signal-to-noise problem. *The noise is, and has been, so great that the existence of a signal has been seriously questioned.* Isaac Asimov, whom no one could accuse of lacking in imagination, writes:

> "Eyewitness reports of actual space ships and actual extraterrestrials are, in themselves, totally unreliable. There have been numerous eyewitness reports of almost everything that most rational people do not care to accept – of ghosts, angels, levitation, zombies, werewolves, and so on... The trouble is, that whatever the UFO phenomenon is, it comes and goes unexpectedly. There is no way of examining it systematically. It appears suddenly and accidentally, is partially seen, and then is more or less inaccurately reported. We remain dependent on occasional anecdotal accounts". (*From the December 14, 1974 issue of TV Guide, a media magazine with a very great circulation and hence powerful in forming public opinion.*)

Here we see a very important part of the UFO problem, that of the presentation of data to men of science, and to men, like Asimov and others who excel in writing about science.

Scientific efforts can be seriously hampered if the popular image of a subject is grossly misleading. Funds can be curtailed and good men of science who wish to give time to the subject are apt to face misrepresentation whenever their work receives any public attention. Ball lightning is just as much an unknown as the UFO phenomenon, yet scientists can openly discuss these "balls of light" but are likely to be censured if they talk about similar unidentified lights which last much longer, are brighter, and move over greater distances, but are labeled UFOs. Proper presentation of the UFO phenomenon to the media may not seem an integral part of the UFO problem, per se, but its effects loom large.

The signal-to-noise aspect of the UFO problem is aggravated to a high degree because the signal is a totally unexpected signal, and represents an entirely new set of empirical observations which do not fit into any existing framework in any of the accepted scientific disciplines. One may even contemplate that the signal itself signals the birth of a new scientific discipline.

I return to the out-of-hand dismissal of the UFO phenomenon by persons like Isaac Asimov, in part, because of the poor presentation of the data to such persons. This is an important facet of the UFO problem itself and must be taken into account if we are to make any progress with the study of the signal.

An analogy may be useful here: In the isolation of radium, Mme. Curie was obliged to work through tons of pitchblende to obtain a minuscule amount of radium. Yet there was no question of the signal in the "pitchblende noise". The radioactivity of the pitchblende was unquestioned. Let us suppose that instead there had been a rumor – an old wives' tale, or an alchemist's story – that there existed a miraculous unknown element which could be used in the transmutation of elements, and which had miraculous healing powers and other exotic properties. Would any scientist, on the basis of such an alchemist's tale, have done what Mme. Curie did to lift the signal out of the noise of tons of pitchblende? Hardly. Mme. Curie *knew* that there was a signal – it wasn't a rumor. And although the labor was immense, there was a definite, scientifically accepted methodology for separating the signal from the noise.

Now, in the UFO problem we did not know at the start that there was a signal – there were merely tales, unacceptable to scientists as a body. Only those of us, through a long exposure to the subject, or motivated by a haunting curiosity to work in the field and to get our hands dirty with the raw data, came to know there was a signal.

We *know* that we cannot find a trivial solution to the problem, i.e., a common sense solution that the phenomenon is either entirely a matter of misidentification, hallucinations, and hoaxes, or a known phenomenon of nature, e.g., of a meteorological nature. We know that there exists a subset of UFO reports of high strangeness and high witness credibility for which no one – and I emphasize – *no one*, has been able to ascribe a viable explanation. But the Isaac Asimovs and the trained scientists, as well as large segments of the public, do not know this. And we cannot expect them to know this unless we present data to them properly and thus provide motivation to study the subject. We who have worked in the UFO field are somewhat in the position of Einstein who wrote to Arnold Sommerfeld in response to Sommerfeld's skepticism of the General Theory of Relativity:

"You will accept the General Theory of Relativity when you have studied it. Therefore I will not utter a word in its defense."

Emotional defense of the UFO phenomenon is pointless; the facts, properly presented, must speak for themselves.

With the noise level so high, and with the popular interpretation of UFOs as visitors from outer space rather than simply what their initials stand for, Unidentified Flying Objects – an unidentified phenomenon whose origin we do not know – it is very difficult for one to be motivated to study the subject.

The noise in the UFO problem is two-fold. There is the obvious noise, and also the more "sophisticated" noise, which might even be part of the signal. The obvious noise is akin to that well known to any scientist. An astronomer recognizes the noise of errors of observation, of instrumental errors, or that introduced by atmospheric distortion, by photon statistics, etc.

In our problem the noise is likewise comprised of errors of observation (though to a much greater degree), but also to wishful thinking, deliberate substitution of interpretation of an event for the event itself, as, "I saw a space ship last night" for "I saw a light in the sky last night", and the totally extraneous noise of the unbalanced imaginations of the pseudo-religious fanatics who propagate unfounded stories and who uncritically accept anything and everything that appeals to their warped imaginations...

The question of whether the UFO phenomenon is a manifestation of some type of intelligence, whether extraterrestrial, "meta-terrestrial", or indeed some aspect of our own, is a critical one.

Certainly, in those close encounter cases in which creatures or occupants, ostensibly the pilots of the craft, are reported, intelligent behavior of some sort seems obvious. Even if the occupants are robots, a more distant intelligence is implied. The almost universally reported response to detection by these occupants is an important part of the picture; upon detection the creatures are reported to disappear quickly and take off. Except in certain cases, there appears to be no desire for any involvement with the human race...

Given the elements of the present picture of the UFO phenomenon, it is clear that any viable hypothesis that meets these picture elements satisfactorily will be, according to present views, "far out".

There have been other times in the history of science when striking departures from classical concepts were necessary. Since new hypotheses must in some way use present knowledge as a springboard, it is a sobering thought to contemplate that the gap between the springboard of the known and a viable UFO hypothesis might even be so great as to prevent the formulation of an acceptable hypothesis at present.

Thus, for example, only a century ago, an inconsequential period of time in total history, the best scientific minds could not have envisioned the nuclear processes which we now feel certain take place in the deep interiors of stars. The question of energy production on the sun capable of maintaining the sun's prodigious outflow of energy for hundreds of millions of years – a time period demanded by the fossil history millions of years – was simply not answerable by any hypothesis conceivable to the scientists of a century ago.

It is indeed sobering, yet challenging, to consider that the entire UFO phenomenon may be only the tip of the proverbial iceberg in a signaling an entirely new domain of the knowledge of nature as yet totally unexplored, as unexplored and as unimagined as nuclear processes would have been a century ago.

Dr. Hynek is often referred to as the father of rigorous scientific UFO investigation. He was a scientific consultant for the Air Force's UFO investigation, Project Bluebook which later research shows to have been intended to debunk the subject. But after studying so many credible cases, Dr. Hynek was to go on to found the Center For UFO Studies (CUFOS). He also invented the classification for UFO sightings, terming the phrase 'Close Encounter.' He is the author of the landmark UFO book, *The UFO Experience: A Scientific Study*. Dr. Hynek served as director of CUFOS until his passing in 1986.

Regarding Hynek's idea that we may be dealing with "an entirely new domain of the knowledge of nature", his friend and associate, Jacques Vallee has interesting comments to make:

[C]urrent hypotheses are not strange enough to explain the facts of the phenomenon, and the debate suffers from a lack of scientific information. Indeed, from the viewpoint of modern physics, our Cosmic Neighborhood could encompass other (parallel) universes, extra spatial dimensions and other time-like dimensions beyond the common 4-dimensional spacetime we recognize, and such aspects could lead to rational explanations for apparently "incomprehensible" behaviors on the part of entities emerging into our perceived continuum.

As it attempts to reconcile theory with observed properties of elementary particles and with discoveries at the frontiers of cosmology, modern physics suggests that mankind has not yet discovered all of the universe's facets, and we must propose new theories and experiments in order to explore these undiscovered facets. *This is why continuing study of reported anomalous events is important: It may provide us with an existence theorem for new models of physical reality.*

Much of the recent progress in cosmological concepts is directly applicable to the problem: Traversable wormholes (3-dimensional hypersurface tunnels) have now been derived from Einstein's General Theory of Relativity (Morris and Thorne, 1988; Visser, 1995). In particular, it has been shown that Einstein's General Theory of Relativity does not in any way constrain spacetime topology, which allows for wormholes to provide traversable connections between regions within two separate universes or between remote regions and/or times within the same universe.

Mathematically it can also be shown that higher-dimensional wormholes can provide hypersurface connections between multidimensional spaces (Rucker, 1984; Kaku, 1995).

Recent quantum gravity programs have explored this property in superstring theory, along with proposals to theoretically and experimentally examine macroscopic-scale extra-dimensional spaces (Schwarzschild, 2000).

Thus it is now widely acknowledged that the nature of our universe is far more complex than observations based on anthropocentric self-selection portend...

No experiment can distinguish between phenomena manifested by visiting interstellar (arbitrarily advanced) ETI (extra-terrestrial intelligence) and intelligent entities that may exist near Earth within a parallel universe or in different dimensions, or who are (terrestrial) time travelers...

If we must formulate a view of the problem in a single statement at this point, that statement will be:

Everything works as if UAPs (Unidentified Aerial Phenomenon) were the products of a technology that integrates physical and psychic phenomena and primarily affects cultural variables in our society through manipulation of physiological and psychological parameters in the witnesses.[5]

As I have written in my books and publications on our website, www.cassiopaea.org, and elsewhere, I have *never* seen an alien[6] that I know of. I have no conscious awareness or memory of any such thing as a "typical abduction" or an encounter with an alien in any semblance of a conscious state of mind. Indeed, I am going to talk about certain "encounters" that are "highly suggestive", but there is a certain ambiguity about them that relates directly to this issue of "state of mind", and this ambiguity leaves the event always in question as far as I am concerned. I certainly have as good an imagination as the average person if I need it to solve a problem, but after raising five children, there is little "imaginative flying" going on in my head and a lot of being practical and finding out what is really going on.

In my book, *Amazing Grace*, I chronicled a number of my own experiences of surpassing strangeness, though I never thought of these events in terms of "aliens". Until I was 41 years old, I never saw anything that I might have thought – by any stretch of the imagination – could be a UFO, and when, at that late date, I finally did see something of such extraordinary configuration and behavior, I immediately tried to find a "plausible excuse" for it so I could "go back to sleep". But, as Hynek said, there are certainly things for which we cannot find a common sense solution. It is at such a point, when all avenues of identification and explanation have been exhausted, that the individual who is "motivated by a haunting curiosity" goes to work in the field, gets their hands dirty in the raw data, and realizes that there is, most certainly, a signal even if it is a signal that suggests an intelligence so strange and foreign to our daily terrestrial mode of thought that we are stunned by the implication. That implication can be shattering to our sense of safety: that the UFO phenomenon may be signaling *"an entirely new domain of the*

---

[5] Jacques F. Vallee and Eric W. Davis, "Incommensurability, Orthodoxy and the Physics of High Strangeness: A 6-layer Model for Anomalous Phenomena", *National Institute for Discovery Science*, Las Vegas.

[6] Including the "face at the window" that Tom French describes as a "reptilian alien." I never described it as such. Indeed, at the present time, I consider it a possibility, but as I said above: I have never seen an alien that I *know* of as an alien with any certainty.

knowledge of nature as yet totally unexplored, as unexplored and as unimagined as nuclear processes would have been a century ago". It was partly as a consequence of this event that I began the experiment that resulted in the Cassiopaean Transmissions. After a certain amount of research, after facing the High Strangeness factor repeatedly, I understood clearly something that Jacques Vallee proposes in his paper cited above:

> The cognitive mismatch or Incommensurability Problem between human and ET cultures will guarantee that the latter will develop communication techniques *other than radio*. ET cultures may be sending radio and optical signals to Earth now but they may also be sending signals in a variety of other forms such as holographic images, psychic or other consciousness-related signals, modulated neutrinos, gamma ray bursters, wormhole-modulated starlight caustics, signals generated by gravitational lensing techniques, modulated X-rays, quantum teleported signals, or some quantum field theoretic effect...

Vallee has touched upon the very issues that my husband, Arkadiusz Jadczyk, has discussed in the Foreword to this book. Most of this material included in the Foreword was published by him long before Vallee wrote the above paper, though it seems likely that Vallee was moving in this direction for quite some time as evidenced in his book *Forbidden Science*. In the Epilogue, Vallee talks a little bit about physics, parallel realities, hyperspace:

> Cosmology now recognizes the possibility, indeed the inevitability, of multiple universes with more than four dimensions. Communication and travel within our universe are no longer thought to be absolutely constrained by the speed of light and a constant arrow of time. Even travel into the past may be considered without necessarily creating insurmountable paradoxes. This is a tremendously exciting development. It opens up vast new realms for theoretical and experimental endeavor...
>
> If we look at the world from an informational point of view, and if we consider the many complex ways in which time and space may be structured, the old idea of space travel and interplanetary craft to which most technologists are still clinging appears not only obsolete, but ludicrous. Indeed, modern physics has already bypassed it, offering a very different interpretation of what [an] "extraterrestrial" system might look like...
>
> For some time various knowledgeable friends have urged me to take my research behind the scenes again. I intend to follow their advice. I cannot justify remaining associated with the field of ufology as it presents itself to the public today. Furthermore, I suspect that the

phenomenon displays a very different structure once you leave behind the parochial disputes that disfigure the debate, confusing the researchable issues that interest me. The truly important scientific questions are elsewhere.

While it is true that Dr. Hynek, Dr. Vallee, and my husband, Dr. Jadczyk, were working for years in the direction of these ideas, what is amazing is that the Cassiopaean Communications – myself in the future – also discussed the same things in considerable detail with me, an amateur whose driving interest was in finding out why the world was the way it was and humanity's role within it. Certainly, this is often the same drive that operates in scientists – those scientists who actually do "good science" with an open mind – but it necessarily has different results from the efforts of the layperson in most cases. In my own case, however, the results have been quite similar: scientific theories and mind-expanding concepts regarding an "entirely new domain of the knowledge of nature". This was the gift of the Cassiopaeans.

At the same time, there is much in the Cassiopaean Material that is strikingly similar to philosophical concepts native to certain esoteric teachings, most particularly Sufi and ideas brought forward by Georges Gurdjieff and Boris Mouravieff. Both of the latter claim to be presenting something called "Esoteric Christianity". What I have discovered in my own research is that this "Esoteric Christianity" is quite similar to Archaic Siberian Shamanism, the degraded remnant of what must have been the "religion" of the Northern Peoples – the Megalith builders – in prehistoric times. I have traced these developments and laid out all the clues in my book *The Secret History of the World*.

How we view our world and our place in it is entirely dependent on what we know about what went before. What became overwhelmingly apparent as I continued in my research was that the true history of man has been so distorted by "official culture" as to make it almost impossible for the average person to really understand why the world is as it is, and what possible role humanity may play in the grander scheme of things.

Tracking the processes of history certainly gave me an uneasy feeling that there was some sort of "pattern" to it which certainly could not be a conspiracy in human terms. Until I opened my mind to the possibility of "alien interactions with humanity", and began to consider the many implications of such ideas – most particularly time loops and alternate universes – nothing about the history of mankind made any sense at all.

Most assuredly, historians of ancient times face two constant problems: the scarcity of evidence, and how to fit the evidence that *is* known into the larger context of other evidence, not to mention the context of the time to which it belongs. Very often historians have to use what could be described as a more or less "legal method" for deciding which bit of evidence has more or less weight than another. For example, most of what we know about ancient times comes to us in polemics written by adversaries of a particular group or idea. These polemics survived because they were "favored" by the elite rulers or conquerors, and the "inside knowledge" of the group in question is lost because they may have been destroyed along with their material. In this respect, it is much easier to "refute than confirm". A difference of emphasis can be as telling as a new discovery.

Fortunately, ancient history is not "static" in the sense that we can say we know all there is to know now simply because the subject is about the "past". For example, the understanding of ancient history of our own fathers and grandfathers was, of necessity, more limited than our own due to the fact that much material has been discovered and come to light in the past two or three generations through archaeology and other historical sciences.

But more important to this process is the consideration of manipulation of facts. If you are judging history by a kind of legal method, it becomes crucial to know who is or is not likely to be telling the truth. Often, the only way to determine that is to evaluate what Georges Dumézil referred to as the "line of force". When we have taken a particular text apart and have ascertained, as much as possible, the approximate legitimacy of each element, there still remains another question that actually constitutes the essence of the matter: What are the main trends of the whole? What are the lines of force running through the *ideological field* in which the details are placed? This is often where religion enters the picture, acting as the lens through which we view our past and the scale by which we judge the merits of testimony.

Regarding religion, and most particularly the religions that hold sway over our world such as Christianity born of Judaism, we simply cannot overstress the importance of deep and serious study. We cannot ignore the question of whether or not Christianity and Judaism and Islam are "true", and if they are *not*, then why have they spread and persisted? And if they are not true, we need to evaluate a proper response to them.

As many regular readers of our website know, almost from day one of the publication of the Cassiopaean material, we have been accused of being a "cult". I've had a lot of trouble dealing with that accusation because every "claim" that we are a "cult" has been a lie, and all of the accusations have been made by individuals who clearly *are* members of *real cults* – scary ones, too.

The Oxford English dictionary entry for 'cult' states: 1. a system of religious worship, esp. as expressed in *ritual*. 2. A devotion or homage to a person or thing. 2b. A popular fashion esp. followed by a specific section of society 3. denoting a person or thing popularized in this way.

It is clear that the above description could easily apply to any of the organized religions prevalent today. Christianity, Judaism, Islam, Buddhism (and others) are replete and indeed founded on ritual and "devotion to a person or thing". However, they are not generally referred to as "cults".

The term cult, in its modern and widely understood form, is reserved for any group formed under a *hierarchical structure*, where some form of *coercion or manipulation* of the group members exists. Generally there is also some *focus of worship*, be it the group leader(s) or some other outside personage or thing such as Jesus, Jehovah/Yahweh, Allah or the Tooth Fairy.

The issue of *justification for worship or allegiance* – that is, *the coercion and manipulation* – is usually tied to the perceived or stated benefits or potential benefits to be derived from belief, worship or allegiance. In other words, promises are made of heavenly rewards that can never be demonstrated or proven (no one has ever come back to tell us that heaven exists, nor is there any proof), promises of survival of the end of the world – to be the "Chosen People" who rule – or wine bearing *houris* who minister to the martyr in paradise – are all included in the *promises of the main cults* that dominate our world: Judaism, Christianity and Islam.

We, on the other hand, take the approach of a sort of scientific mysticism – where mystical claims are submitted to rational analysis and testing, and the required scientific proofs are modified to allow for the *nature of evidence from theorized realms outside our own* where ordinary scientific proofs might not apply.

And yet, again and again, we have had to address this issue of being labeled a "cult" because the accusations and mud keep flying.

In the beginning, it was very hard for me to understand why – after all, I was just a mother of five kids with a hobby publishing the results of my studies on the Internet, and one would think that doing that was allowed in a democratic society – but it became obvious that there are some fairly powerful groups on the planet who must be scared to death of this ordinary housewife as is evident from the extraordinary amount of effort put into trying to shut me up!

So far, when we have tracked the origins and connections of our accusers, we generally end up at powerful Christian or Jewish organizations with covert government or military ties that have a vested interest in maintaining their cultic controls over peoples' minds. At this point, the Islamic groups haven't gone after us, but that's only because we have been pointing out that the Moslems are on the short end of the stick in this go-round.

The fact is, as far as I am concerned, Islam – as a monotheistic religion that promotes an "object of worship" – is no better than Christianity or Judaism – all three of them are, historically speaking, vile, bloody, violent cults. What is going on in the Middle East today – this conflict that threatens to blow up the whole planet (and if you don't know that this is the case, you have not been paying attention!), is just more of the same old cult nonsense that has been playing out for the past two millennia.

Faith that can "move mountains" is promoted by cults – also known as the standard Monotheistic religions – as the necessary thing that the "faithful" must cultivate in order to receive the benefits that are promised by the hierarchy.

The example of Abraham's willingness to sacrifice his son, Isaac, has been trotted out for ages as the supreme example of how one is to approach the "god". One must be willing to give the god anything and everything! This "Faith" is an essential part of the "covenant" with the god – a sort of "act of trade", so to say.

The story about the almost sacrifice of Abraham in the Bible is actually nearly identical to the Vedic story of Manu. These acts of sacrifice were based on what was called *sraddha* which is related to the words *fides, credo, faith, believe* and so on.

The word *sraddha* was, according to religious historians Dumézil and Levi, too hastily understood as "faith" in the Christian sense. Correctly understood, it means something like the trust a workman has in his tools to "shape or create" reality and techniques of sacrifice were, in the way of tools, similar to acts of magic!

Such "faith" is, therefore, part of a "covenant" wherein the sacrificer knows how to perform a prescribed sacrifice correctly, and who also knows that if he performs the sacrifice correctly, it *must* produce its effect.

In short, it is an act that is designed to gain control over the forces of life that reside in the god with whom one has made the covenant.

Such gods as make covenants are not "literary ornaments" or abstractions. They are active partners with intelligence, strength, passion, and a tendency to *get out of control if the sacrifices are not performed correctly*. In this sense, the sacrifice – the "faith" – is simply black magic.

In another sense, the ascetic or "self-sacrificer", is a person who is *striving for release from the bondage and order of nature* by the act of attempting to mortify the self, the flesh; testing and increasing the will for the purpose of winning tyrannical powers while still in the world. But again, we see that through this self-sacrifice, he or she seeks *mastery of the gods*. It is, in short, manipulation and coercion at its most subtle to promote "faith" as the bringer of salvation.

What seems to be so is that it is generally individuals who have been "disenfranchised" or who feel helpless and at the mercy of the forces of life – whether they manifest through other people or random events – who are those most likely to seek such faith, such a covenant with a god. They feel acutely their own inability to have an effect in the world, and they turn their creativity inward to create and maintain their subjective "faith" in opposition to objective reality.

What is crucial to understand is that Fundamentalists of all kinds are basically "giving their will" away in exchange for promised benefits. This free will is their own power of creativity – their own possibility for growth and development that can only commutate and expand in the process of uncertainty, taking risks, and making free and willing exchanges with others that do *not* include dominance and manipulation.

The "absolute certainty" of the Fundamentalist locks them into Entropy, and their creative energy goes to feed a vast system of illusion. These systems are the creation and maintenance of the Idols they worship. Like the paranoid schizophrenic, they devise baroque and ingenious systems of perception and define them as "given by god". They then spend an enormous amount of energy editing out all impressions that are contrary to their system of illusion.

Another aspect of the Man who must be Right that manifests in religious beliefs is that Fundamentalists look down on others who do not share their faith. It is, at root, an "us vs. them" system that focuses its ironclad preconceptions so rigidly on "future benefits", that its adherents simply lose sight of the here and now.

Fundamentalists are more interested in dogma than in actual deeds in the moment. It is extremely important to get others to believe in their illusion in order to confirm its "rightness", even if they claim, on the surface, that "everyone has the right to their own opinion". The fact is, they cannot tolerate anyone else's opinion if it is different from their own because it threatens their "rightness".

This rightness *must* be maintained at all costs because, deep inside, the Right Man (or woman) is usually struggling with horror at their own helplessness. Their rightness is a dam that holds back their worst fears: that they are lost and alone and that there really is no god, because how could there be a god who loves them if they have to suffer so much? Their inability to feel truly loved and accepted deep within is, in effect, like being stranded in a nightmare from which they cannot wake up.

Faith. This is the thing that a "charismatic leader" utilizes to induce his followers to engage in violence against other human beings.

This "faith" can be induced by manipulations and promises of heavenly or other rewards, this "rightness" of one's views, of one's god, and what the god is supposedly "revealing" to the leader, and this can then be used to manipulate other people to do one's bidding.

And so it seems that the requirement of "faith" and "worship" of an object of cultic value such as Jehovah, Yahweh, Jesus or Allah is the means by which human beings can be induced to commit atrocities upon other human beings.

We see that the image of Abraham, who was willing to sacrifice his own son, is not so compelling a picture after all. It merely symbolizes a sort of mindless belief in the orders of someone or something "out there" that certainly may not have the best interests of humanity at heart.

We can perceive, in the willingness of Abraham to sacrifice his son, the Right Man terror of Cain who killed his brother because his sacrifice was not accepted. A god who picks and chooses what sacrifice is "good enough" – setting brother against brother – is certainly a "jealous god", and such a god is a psychopath.

The main template of Christianity – received directly from Judaism – is that of *sin*. The history of *sin* from that point to now, is a story of its triumph.

Awareness of the nature of *sin* led to a growth industry in agencies and techniques for dealing with it. These agencies became centers of economic and military power, as they are today.

Christianity – promoting the ideals of Judaism under a thin veneer of the "New Covenant" – changed the ways in which men and women interacted with one another. It changed the attitude to life's one certainty: death. It changed the degree of freedom with which people could acceptably choose what to think and believe.

Pagans had been intolerant of the Jews and Christians whose religions tolerated no gods but their own. The rising domination of Christianity created a much sharper conflict between religions, and religious intolerance became the norm, not the exception.

Christianity also brought the open coercion of religious belief. You could even say that, by the modern definition of a cult as a group that uses manipulation and mind control to induce worship, Christianity is the Mother of all Cults – in service to the misogynistic, fascist ideals of Judaism!

The rising Christian hierarchy of the Dark Ages was quick to mobilize military forces against believers in other gods and most especially, against other Christians who promoted less fascist systems of belief. This probably included the original Christians and the original teachings.

The change of the Western world from Pagan to Christian effectively changed how people viewed themselves and their interactions with their reality. And we live today with the fruits of those changes: War Without End.

Which brings us back to the Control System of our reality:

> [A] global phenomenon ... *so strange and foreign to our daily terrestrial mode of thought*... it carries with it many implications of the existence of intelligences other than our own ... [It] bespeaks the action of some form of intelligence... but whence this intelligence springs, whether it is truly extra-terrestrial, or bespeaks a higher reality not yet recognized by science, or even if it be in some way or another a strange psychic manifestation of our own intelligence, is much the question...

> It is indeed sobering, yet challenging, to consider that the entire UFO phenomenon may be only the tip of the proverbial iceberg in a signaling *an entirely new domain of the knowledge of nature as yet totally unexplored*, as unexplored and as unimagined as nuclear processes would have been a century ago.

It is this *"entirely new domain of the knowledge of nature"* that has been the concern of the Cassiopaean Transmissions from the very beginning. It is the nature of this domain that is the subject of their communications regarding aliens, alien abductions, hyperdimensional realities, and related subject matter. This is the central core of the book you now hold in your hand.

***

As I have written, I've spent much of my life trying to find reasonable explanations for complex and mysterious events, struggling to fit the anomalous experiences of my own as well as other people, into acceptable categories, trying to find prosaic explanations. The ironic consequence of this was that I was often compelled to shove logical observations under the rug of the mundane world, and in that sense, you could say that my imagination certainly was exercised! Because of these experiences and the fact that they did not "fit" into the "reality construct" of our society, I realized that part of our world is marginalized to an extreme degree, and this was troubling to me. I struggled mightily to bridge the gap between High Strangeness and the reality that our culture accepts as valid and real, establishing reasonable categories into which I could pigeonhole anomalies so as to not deny the evidence, while still giving credibility to the social and cultural norms of what is or is not possible.

When a person knows that there are "strange things out there" on the one hand, and, on the other, that these strange things are regularly ridiculed and debunked, it becomes necessary to do something! The result is usually that a long list of terrestrial experiences are effectively fenced off from scrutiny for the simple reason that they may be considered abnormal or even sinful. That's not a healthy way to live.

Like many, many people, I never asked for strange things to happen in my life. I most definitely fought a losing battle to pretend they weren't happening or that there was a "normal explanation" for them. I often wondered how many other people in the world had suffered because their deep realities had been ridiculed? At the most extreme end are people considered insane because their perceptions are different. But there are also vast numbers of people who have had many odd experiences who are afraid to speak of them, who hold them close inside, wondering daily if they're losing their minds, or perhaps even whether they are being subjected to some sort of demonic torment.

Charles Fort, decrying the state of anomalies investigation, wrote in his book *LO!*:

> Our data have been bullied by two tyrannies. On one side, the spiritualists have arbitrarily taken over strange occurrences, as manifestations of the departed. On the other side, conventional science has pronounced against everything that does not harmonize with its systematization's. The scientist goes investigating, about as, to match ribbons, a woman goes shopping. The spiritualist stuffs the maws of his emotions. One is too dainty, and the other is gross. Perhaps, between these two, we shall some day be considered models of well-bred behavior.

Let me try to explain: there is a little known fact about hypnosis that is illustrated by the following story:

A subject was told under hypnosis that when he was awakened he would be unable to see a third man in the room who, it was suggested to him, would have become invisible. All the "proper" suggestions to make this "true" were given, such as "you will *not* see so-and-so" etc... When the subject was awakened, lo and behold! the suggestions did *not* work.

Why? Because they went against his belief system. He did *not* believe that a person could become invisible.

So, another trial was made. The subject was hypnotized again and was told that the third man was *leaving the room,* that he had been called away on urgent business, and the scene of him getting on his coat and hat was described. The door was opened and shut to provide "sound effects", and then the subject was brought out of the trance.

Guess what happened?

He was *unable to see* the Third Man.

Why? Because his perceptions were modified according to his beliefs. Certain "censors" in his brain were activated in a manner that was acceptable to his *ego survival instincts.*

The ways and means that we ensure survival of the ego is established pretty early in life by our parental and societal programming. This conditioning determines what *is* or is *not* possible; what we are "allowed" to believe in order to be accepted. We learn this first by learning what pleases our parents and then later we modify our belief based on what pleases our society – our peers – to believe.

To return to our story, the Third Man went about the room picking things up and setting them down and doing all sorts of things to test the subject's awareness of his presence, and the subject became utterly hysterical at this "anomalous" activity! He could see objects moving through the air, doors opening and closing, but he could *not* see the *source* because he did not believe that there was another man in the room.

So, what are the implications of this factor of human consciousness? (By the way, this is also the reason why most therapy to stop bad habits does not work – they attempt to operate against a "belief system" that is imprinted in the subconscious that this or that habit is essential to survival.)

One of the first things we might observe is that everyone has a different set of beliefs based upon their social and familial conditioning, and that these beliefs determine how much of the *objective* reality anyone is able to access.

In the above story, the *objective* reality *is what it is*, whether it is truly objective, or only a consensus reality. In this story, there is clearly a big part of that reality that is inaccessible to the subject due to a *perception censor* that was activated by the suggestions of the hypnotist. That is to say, the subject had a strong belief, based upon his *choice* as to who or what to believe. In this case, he had chosen to believe the hypnotist and not what he might be able to observe if he dispensed with the perception censor put in place by the hypnotist who activated his "belief center" – even if that activation was fraudulent.

And so it is with nearly all human beings: we believe the hypnotist – the "official culture" – and we are able, with preternatural cunning, to deny what is often right in front of our faces. What is most disturbing in the case of the hypnosis subject described above is that he is entirely at the mercy of the "Invisible Man" because he chooses not to see him. Is it possible that – in a similar way – we are under the control of a "hypnotist" who does not have our best interests at heart?

Let's face it: we are all taught to avoid uncomfortable realities. Human beings – faced with unpleasant truths about themselves or their reality – react like alcoholics who refuse to admit their condition, or the cuckolded husband who is the "last to know", or the wife who does not notice that her husband is abusing her daughter.

In *States of Denial: Knowing about Atrocities and Suffering*, Stanley Cohen discusses the subject of denial which may shed some light on the context in which we find the "alien phenomenon" situated.

Denial is a complex "unconscious defense mechanism for coping with guilt, anxiety and other disturbing emotions aroused by reality". Denial can be both deliberate and intentional, as well as completely subconscious. An individual who is deliberately and intentionally denying something is acting from an individual level of lying, concealment and deception. I don't think that we are dealing with this in the present case. What we are dealing with is denial that is subconscious and therefore organized and "institutional". This implies propaganda, misinformation, whitewash, manipulation, spin, disinformation, etc.

Believing anything that comes down the pike is not the opposite of denial. "Acknowledgement" of the probability of a high level of Truth about a given matter is what should happen when people are actively aroused by *certain* information. This information can be 1) factual or forensic truth; that is to say, legal or scientific information which is factual, accurate and objective; it is obtained by impartial procedures; 2) personal and narrative truth including "witness testimonies".

I should add here that skepticism and solipsistic arguments – including epistemological relativism – about the existence of objective truth, are generally a social construction and might be considered in the terms of the hypnotized man who has been programmed to think that there "is no truth".

Denial occurs for a variety of reasons. There are truths that are "clearly known", but for many reasons – personal or political, justifiable or unjustifiable – are concealed, or it is agreed that they will not be acknowledged "out loud". There are "unpleasant truths" and there are truths that make us tired because if we acknowledge them – if we do more than give them a tacit nod – we may find it necessary to make changes in our lives.

Cohen points out that "All counter-claims about the denied reality are themselves only maneuvers in endless truth-games. And *truth, as we know, is inseparable from power*". Denial of truth is, effectively, *giving away your power.*

There are different kinds of denial. First, there is literal denial which is the type that fits the dictionary definition, the assertion that something did not happen or does not exist. This most often occurs in very painful situations where there are conflicts of love: the wife would say that the husband could not have molested his daughter, therefore the child must be making it up. This also seems to apply to denial of the state of our manipulated reality. Our love for our parents, our need for their approval, is often transferred to our peers, our employers, and the State. To think about stepping outside of the belief system that makes us "belong" is just too frightening. It assaults our deepest sense of security.

The second kind of denial is "interpretative". In this kind of denial, the raw facts that something actually happened are not really denied – they are just "interpreted". If a person is reasonably intelligent, and is faced with evidence of phenomena that do not fit into the belief system of one's family, culture, or peer group, there is nothing to do but to interpret – to rationalize it away. "Swamp gas" and the Planet Venus given as an explanation for UFOs are good examples. Another is Bill Clinton's "But I didn't *inhale*" interpretation of his marijuana use. And then, there was the famous "I didn't have sex with Monica" interpretation.

I have to admit that this latter type of denial was the one that gave me the most "comfort". I couldn't deny many strange things, so I worked very hard to create acceptable categories for them. Sure, my categories were wider and more liberal than those of ordinary people who were not involved in the kind of work and research that engaged my thinking, but they were restricted categories nevertheless. I drew a line against "aliens and UFOs" and that line was, for many years, uncrossable.

The third kind of denial is termed by Cohen as implicatory denial where there is no attempt to deny either the facts or their conventional interpretation; what is ultimately denied are the psychological, political and moral implications that follow from deep acknowledgement. For example, the idea that America is being run by a madman with designs on the entire planet is recognized as a fact, but it is not seen as psychologically disturbing or as carrying any moral imperative to act.

Cohen discusses five different contexts of psychological denial: 1) perception without awareness, 2) perceptual defense 3) selective attention, 4) cognitive errors and 5) inferential failures. His conclusion is that "the scientific discourse misses the fact that the ability to deny is an amazing human phenomenon ... a product of sheer complexity of our emotional, linguistic, moral and intellectual lives".

As my husband, Ark,[7] has written, science seems to be controlled by money. Scientists, for the most part, *have* to work on those things that get funding. There is nothing terribly unusual about that since it is a general rule for everyone. If you don't get money for your work, you starve, and then you don't do any work at all. Yes, that's somewhat simplistic, but still relevant to the subject here.

A few years back, our research group assembled a Timeline[8] of secret and not-so-secret scientific projects – and those involved in them. The result was a compelling view of the fact that science has most definitely been used in a very detrimental way in our world. However, when such ideas – backed by the kind of extensive data we assembled – are brought to public attention, they are generally dismissed as "conspiracy theory" and are thus deemed unworthy of attention.

So please, bear with me a moment here and let's apply a little logic to the problem.

The first thing we want to think about is the fact that the word "conspiracy" evokes such a strong reaction in all of us: nobody wants to be branded as a "conspiracy thinker"; it just isn't "acceptable"; it's "un-scientific" or it's evidence of mental instability. Right? That's what you are thinking, isn't it?

In fact, I bet that the very reading of the word even produces certain physiological reactions: a slight acceleration of the heartbeat, and perhaps a quick glance around to make sure that no one was watching while you simply read the words "conspiracy theory" silently.

Have you ever asked yourself *why* the word evokes such an instantaneous emotional reaction? Have you ever wondered why it stimulates such strong "recoil"? After all, it is only a word. It only describes the idea of people in "high places" thinking about things and doing things that manipulate other people to produce benefits for themselves. Certainly, everyone "knows" that this happens all the time. No one would even raise an eyebrow if you said: "Well, everybody knows that politicians are corrupt and just playing politics

---

[7] Arkadiusz Jadczyk, internationally known mathematical/theoretical physicist, expert in hyperdimensional physics.

[8] http://www.cassiopaea.org/cass/timeline.htm

to get rich". But if you really stop to consider the ultimate implications of such a statement, you would have to admit that this could be a real problem about which you might wish to do something. But then, of course, what could you do? We see here what Cohen has called "implicatory denial" where there is no attempt to deny either the facts or their conventional interpretation; what is ultimately denied are the psychological, political and moral implications that follow from *deep acknowledgement*. We can casually admit things in states of implicatory denial, which then leads us directly into "interpretative denial" where the raw facts that something may actually be happening – such as a conspiracy – are not really denied – they are just "interpreted" or rationalized away. We are then more easily able to slip into literal denial, that there is no "conspiracy", and then the painful truth of our true condition is ameliorated and we can return to our sitcoms, ballgames and weekend barbeques.

Historian Richard M. Dolan studied at Alfred University and Oxford University before completing his graduate work in history at the University of Rochester, where he was a finalist for a Rhodes scholarship. Dolan studied U.S. Cold War strategy, Soviet history and culture, and international diplomacy. As an expert, his opinion of "conspiracy theory" is that *from a historical point of view, the only reality is that of conspiracy*. Secrecy, wealth and independence add up to power. Deception is the key element of warfare, (the tool of power elites), and when winning is all that matters, the conventional morality held by ordinary people becomes an impediment. Secrecy stems from a pervasive and fundamental element of life in our world, that those who are at the top of the heap will always take whatever steps are necessary to maintain the status quo.

And maintaining the "status quo" in science *has* to be one of the main objectives of the Power Elite. And how do they do that?

By "official culture".

Official culture, understood this way, from the perspective of elite groups wishing to maintain the status quo of their power, means only one thing: COINTELPRO. Here I do not mean the specific FBI program that was created to counter the anti-war movement of the 60s and 70s, but the concept of the program, and the likelihood that this has been the mode of controlling human beings for possibly millennia. Certainly, Machiavelli outlined the principles a very long time ago and little has changed since.

The fact is, I like to call it "Cosmic COINTELPRO" to suggest that it is almost a mechanical system that operates based on the *psychological nature of human beings*, most of whom *like* to live in denial. After all, "if ignorance is bliss, 'tis folly to be wise". This is most especially true when we consider the survival instinct of the ego. If the official culture says that there is no Third Man in the room, and if it works through the inculcated belief systems, there is little possibility that the "subject" will be able to see the source of the phenomena in our world. It will always be an "invisible Third Man."

Using the model of the 70s COINTELPRO as a guide to what may be going on in our world, let us consider the fact that the FBI has been shown to have concentrated on *creating bogus organizations and promoting bogus ideas as a form of control.*

"There exists in our world today a powerful and dangerous secret cult." So wrote Victor Marchetti, a former high-ranking CIA official, in his book *The CIA and the Cult of Intelligence*. This is the first book the U.S. Government ever went to court to censor before publication. In this book, Marchetti tells us that there *is* a "Cabal" that rules the world and that its holy men are the clandestine professionals of the Central Intelligence Agency.

In our opinion, the CIA is but one "arm" of the cult, just as Benedictines were but one order of the Catholic Church. To borrow from, and paraphrasing, Marchetti:

This cult is patronized and protected by the highest level government officials in the world. It's membership is composed of those in the power centers of government, industry, commerce, finance, and labor. *It manipulates individuals in areas of important public influence – including the academic world and the mass media.* The Secret Cult is a global fraternity of a political aristocracy whose purpose is to further the political policies of persons or agencies unknown. It acts covertly and illegally.

The most effective weapons of COINTELPRO are ridicule and debunking. Notice that Marchetti points out that this is done via manipulation of individuals in areas of important public influence – including the *academic world* and the *mass media*.

Bottom line is: if you have bought into the emotionally manipulated consensus of "official culture" that there are no conspiracies, that there is no "Third Man", it is very likely that you are being manipulated by fear of ridicule. You are in denial. You have been hypnotized by the suggestions of the holy men of the Secret Cult. And you have chosen to believe them over your own possible observations and senses.

Why is it so that the very individuals who should be diligently studying the UFO/alien phenomenon do not?

Why is it so that scientists – most particularly physicists and mathematicians of a good and honest disposition – seem to be the ones who most actively resist the very idea that their profession *may* have been taken over and "vectored" by conspirators who do not have humanity's best interests at heart?

Why do scientists – those to whom the power elite *must* look for solutions to their "power problems" – think for one instant that their profession is exempt from conspiratorial manipulation and management?

That just isn't logical, is it?

In the physical sciences, very often machines and instruments are utilized to "take measurements". In order to achieve accuracy with even the most precisely tooled device, certain tests are undertaken to establish the "reading error" of the gadget. What we would like to suggest is that the "official culture" that establishes what may or may not be taken "seriously" is a planned and deliberate "reading error" built into the "machine" of science – our very thinking – the suggestions of the "hypnotist".

Without a historical context of science, there is little possibility that a sincere scientist – who is generally not much interested in history, based on my own experience – will ever be able to establish the "reading error" of his machine – his thinking.

There are only so many hours in the day, only so many days in the year, and only so many years in the life of a scientist. The amount of study that is necessary to discover the threads of "conspiracy", where they lead and what they lead to or away from, is actually overwhelming. I know: I've spent about 30 years doing it. What's more, I began my research from a skeptical point of view that "conspiracy" was paranoid thinking, and I was determined to find the way to demonstrate that there was *no* conspiracy. I wanted to create categories where anomalies could be discussed rationally within the accepted bounds of our social and cultural constructs. Unfortunately, not only did my plan fail – my hypothesis was utterly demolished by the hard facts.

One thing I did learn was that finding those "hard facts" was very difficult and time-consuming. And that is deliberate. After all, how good a conspiracy is it if it is so easily discovered? It is clear that in such a *high stakes arena as the Global Control agenda* now being overtly pursued by the Bush Reich – after years and years of the "secret science" – whatever conspiracies exist, will be managed with all the resources and power of those elitists who wish to retain control. That is a formidable obstacle.

I would also like to mention the fact that, even though I am the one who has collected and sorted data, my husband, a mathematical-theoretical physicist, *has* assisted me in analyzing it. At first he did it to humor me. And then, as he applied his knowledge of mathematics to the various problems I brought to him, he began to realize that science *can* be applied to these problems, and once that is done, it strips away the denial mechanism, and one is left with the inescapable conclusion that nothing is as it seems and never has been. We live in an ocean of lies, disinformation, manipulation, propaganda, and smokescreens.

Too bad more competent scientists do not bring their skills to the solving of these problems. But that is precisely what the "Secret Cult" does *not* want to happen. And that is precisely *why* the most subtle and far-reaching of the "COINTELPRO" operations have been run *on scientists themselves*.

Physics and mathematics are the *numero uno* professions that have been used – historically speaking – to support the power elite. They are the ones that give the elite their "tools of power", their bombs and mind control technology. It is logically evident that the governing elite have a vested interest in making sure that the money goes only to projects that 1) will augment their control; in which case such projects will be buried and no one will know about them; or 2) projects that do not threaten their control, in which case we may assume that they are funding research in the public domain that leads *away* from the "important" issues.

In short, if it's popular, gets funded, is allowed out in the open, you can almost guarantee that it is smart but useless.

You can take that to the bank.

Here is where we come back to the context. If we take it as an operating hypothesis that there does exist a powerful elite whose interests are served by science, and who have a vested interest in public science never approaching the "secret science", we have adjusted our "machine tolerances" and can look at the problem in a different way.

But then we face the problem of "what is good science?"

A general definition would be that good science is that which contributes to the increase of knowledge within the scientific community overall, providing better methods of solving problems.

By this definition, there is a *lot* of "respectable science" that is not "good science". Also, by this definition, there is a lot of "good science" that is not "respectable". In fact, based on our short review of "conspiracy", we might even think that most "respectable science" is deliberately vectored toward being very "smart but useless". Then we might suspect that the very best of the "good science" is deliberately ridiculed, attacked, or otherwise suppressed at a very early stage.

This, of course, brings us to the question: who, or what is behind it?

Actually, this would be a question that might be best answered by scientific analysis. When one is considering such things as COINTELPRO, the confusing elements of double and triple reverse psychology might be sorted out by those who are trained to use mathematically logical constructs. However, they are the very ones who are most turned off by the very idea.

We suggest that is deliberate.

Why? Perhaps we can find an answer in something discussed by UFO researcher and writer, Don Ecker, in his article, "The Human Mutilation Factor":

> In the last forty years of UFO research, one of the most baffling questions that have plagued researchers has been "Is the UFO Phenomenon dangerous to humanity?"
>
> Over the years, there have been numerous cases where the phenomenon has figured into human deaths, but as a rule, most cases have been officially ruled accidental. When speaking of cases where death has resulted, usually most assume cases where military pilots have died as a result of "chasing" the phenomenon. One of the most famous of these military chases that is discussed whenever the subject of death and UFOs is raised, is the famous "Mantell Case". This case is so well known that I will not discuss it here, but there are many others. In one of the less well known cases, during the mid 1950's, a military jet interceptor was observed on radar being "absorbed" into a UFO over the Great Lakes. No trace of pilot or aircraft was ever found. In another case reported in the excellent work "Clear Intent" was the case of the "Cuban MIG Incident". In this case a Cuban MIG was locking on his weapons radar when the aircraft exploded in mid-air. The wing man was certain that the UFO had fired some type of weapon, but other than the jet

exploding, no other smoke, flame or other obvious weapon firing was observed.

The matter of either overt or covert hostility on the part of UFOs has always been treated warily by serious researchers. On the one hand, if the enigma is hostile, then several questions must be faced. What if anything should the powers in authority tell the public? Is the government capable of handling a threat of this type? Is the public ready to face an issue as potentially terrifying as a "possible threat from somewhere else?" Other than incidents involving military involvement, have there been cases where civilians have been injured or killed during some type of UFO encounter? Is it possible that the reported cases of UFOs and their occupants abducting unwilling humans for some type of medical or genetic experimentation could be true? Now, if any of this is factual, then what ramifications do the Human Race face in light of the above?

According to Mr. Phil Imbrogno, during the research that led to the writing of *Night Siege: The Hudson Valley UFO Sightings* by Dr. J. Allen Hynek, Philip Imbrogno, and Bob Pratt, Imbrogno has stated that on several occasions, Hynek specified that he wanted no mention of the dozens of human abductions that they had already uncovered at that time, to be mentioned in the book. Hynek was afraid of the adverse publicity if word of this aspect leaked out to the public. After Hynek's death, Imbrogno stated publicly on Compuserve and other public forums, facts of abductions, animal mutilations, and EVEN several cases of mysterious deaths of humans, that he indicated COULD possibly be linked to the UFO Phenomenon.

While researching several stories for UFO Magazine, I interviewed a number of prominent UFOlogists, over the last several months, and in each case, the question of human deaths, in connection with animal mutilations, invariably was raised. Most readers of this text will be familiar with Mr. John Keel, who many regard as the last of the Great UFOlogists. From the earliest days of modern UFOlogy, Keel has been a force to reckon with. The author of numerous books that address various aspects of UFOlogy, and magazine articles too numerous to mention, Keel has a unique slant on the subject that most will never experience. According to Keel, *the phenomenon has always had an unexplained hostility towards humans*, that have led to untold numbers of deaths. While Keel will be the first to explain that he rejects the ET hypothesis, he does not doubt the phenomenon a bit. In what many UFOlogists consider as one of Keel's best works *The Mothman Prophecies* [footnote: E. P. Dutton & Co., Inc. 1975], Keel related report after report of animal mutilations involving cattle, dogs, horses and sheep, and also related what were called "vampire killings" of four humans in Yugoslavia, were the victims were "mutilated and drained of blood".

After having spoken to John Ford, the Chairman of the Long Island UFO Network, for a news story for UFO Magazine, I became even more convinced that the aspect of potential UFO hostility should be investigated. Ford relayed a numbing number of animal mutilations, human disappearances, human abductions, covert Federal involvement in areas that suffered high numbers of animal mutilations, and even armed military helicopters that chased UFOs over civilian communities. Ford, who is an officer of the Federal Court system, did investigations into the disappearances of mostly young adults over a year period, in areas of high UFO overflights, and after having several personal friends who were police officers of the local municipalities look into the situation, came to the conclusion that the facts were being suppressed. The reason given was that there was "no need to panic the public". Although no ironclad proof can be made for direct UFO intervention, the circumstances are extremely suspect.

After growing up in an age where the entire human race can be decimated by nuclear, biological and chemical weapons, the human race somehow manages to keep slogging on. I have seen more people "panicked" over a shortage of gasoline than imminent nuclear holocaust, yet somehow when the subject of UFOs crop up, the government doesn't want to panic anyone. It really makes me wonder what they know, that I should. I really don't think that they are going to talk to anyone soon...

In the new issue of *UFO Magazine*, I have written an update on the investigation of what appear to be more mutilations involving humans.

During the November 1989 Omega conference hosted by John White, Whitley Strieber castigated UFO Magazine for running my story on human mutilations in Vol. 4 Number 3. In that news story, I related the results of an investigation I was conducting on what appeared to be a series of human deaths that greatly resembled animal mutilations. Also, I included a report from Wm. "Bill" Knell of the Long Island Skywatch organization.

Knell had been conducting research into an inordinate number of missing children in the area of Westchester County. According to Strieber, he had received "hundreds" of phone calls from concerned citizens about the story. (That in itself is suspect, as anyone knows who has ever tried to call Strieber. Strieber has an answering service or secretary that screens each call, takes a message and then Whitley decides on whom he will speak with.) Anyway, I digress. Knell has many police contacts, and after checking with them, there were no contacts from Whitley. (One could surmise that what really had Whit in a snit was the way the print media had lambasted his flick, *Communion*, and his recent books, such as *Majestic*. He had just called all journalists "prostitutes".)

According to Knell and officers from the New York State Police, and the Connecticut State Police, the reported figures were in no way accurate, but the weirdest happening was when Knell received an inquiry from an Asst. Medical Examiner from Westchester County. The Asst. ME wanted to know everything Knell could relate on humans that had been mutilated. When Knell pursued this, it turned out that 3 morgues (2 in New York, 1 in Connecticut) had been "hit" in the middle of the night. Newly arrived human cadavers had been mutilated by removal of face, genitals, eyes, parts from the stomach, rectum, thyroids, etc. The morgues were immediately investigated by the police, but nothing could be placed on the employees. There were reduced staff at that time of night, and the events occurred in different areas. High Strangeness indeed. According to the Asst. ME, the incidents were immediately concealed from the media and public. More than likely the reasons were that there was no explanation, nor were the incidents going to be solved in the near future. As an aside, there were also quite a few animal mutilations that were occurring in New York and Connecticut, and once again no solutions were forthcoming for these events.

The Satanic explanation was examined, and according to the reporting witness, did not hold water.

Charles Fort, mentioned above, was an obsessive collector of anomalous events. Fort traveled to the major metropolitan libraries of his day where he would read through the various scientific journals of the day, looking for "damned data".

"Damned data" includes strange phenomena and experiences which included reports of falls of strange things from the sky, strange things seen in the heavens, and strange disappearances. Fort was not just critical of the efforts of science to explain our reality, he was downright contemptuous of it. He would gleefully and fiendishly mock astronomers, meteorologists, and other scientists and their efforts to either deny or explain away anomalous occurrences. He derided their pompous attempts to deny what they could neither understand nor explain. His notes were published as *The Book of the Damned*. Fort once remarked that the only conclusions he could draw from all his research, was that Earth was "owned" by some beings who we could neither see nor comprehend. He said:

I think we're property.

***

Now we want to look at one of the most troubling aspects of the UFO/alien problem that we have only touched on briefly: what does it mean for religion?

My answer is that it is not only science that is being vectored by COINTELPRO, but our general cultural experience which has been molded for millennia by religion. Nowadays, in the presence of widespread sharing of information relating to anomalous appearances of what are now being called UFOs and "aliens", we find that another form of disinformation has led to the identification of Jesus with the "interstellar astronaut" theory. Yes, Jesus is an "alien".

Dr. Vyatcheslav Saitsev of the University of Minsk claimed that Jesus came from outer space. His idea was that Jesus was a representative of a higher civilization, and that this is the explanation of his supernatural powers. He noted, *"In other words, God's descent to Earth is really a cosmic event."*

He may not be so crazy. Considering the work of COINTELPRO to conceal, distract, disinform, the question is: which God?

At the present time there is a veritable frenzy of publishing books purporting to reveal the "Greatest Secrets" of all time. All of them seem to have a similar, general trend, which is to support a certain "derivation" of the mysteries in terms of Egyptian secrets, technology, and religion. This trend is the subject of the book by Lynn Picknett and Clive Prince, *The Stargate Conspiracy*, which is a useful overview for the novice in terms of achieving a basic understanding of the fact that there is, indeed, something very mysterious going on all over the planet in terms of shaping the thinking of humanity via books, movies, and cultural themes.

Picknett and Prince suggest that the central theme of the conspiracy is the "manipulation of beliefs about the origins and history of human civilization, in particular of beliefs about the existence of an advanced civilization in the ancient past and its influence on the earliest known historical civilizations, primarily that of Egypt". What Picknett and Prince fail to note is that the beliefs about the origins and history of human civilization have been manipulated for millennia to keep humanity in the dark. Anyone who doubts that this is often done quite consciously and deliberately ought to have a look at a few remarks of Cornelius Tacitus about the Roman Raj in Britain:

> The following winter was spent on schemes of the most salutary kind. To induce a people, hitherto scattered, uncivilized and therefore prone to fight, to grow pleasurably inured to peace and ease, Agricola gave private encouragement and official assistance to the building of temples, public squares and private mansions. He praised the keen and scolded the slack, and competition to gain honor from him was as effective as compulsion. Furthermore, he trained the sons of the chiefs in the liberal arts and expressed a preference for British natural ability over the trained skill of the Gauls. The result was that in place of distaste for the Latin language came a passion to command it. In the same way, our national dress came into favor and the toga was everywhere to be seen. And so the Britons were gradually led on to the amenities that make vice agreeable – arcades, baths and sumptuous banquets. They spoke of such novelties as 'civilization', when really they were only a feature of enslavement.

If anyone cares to suggest that this sort of manipulation has not continued down to the present day, I suggest an in-depth examination of some of these periods of history wherein great "advances" manifested, including the personal writings of the individuals involved. It is quite a revelation to discover that a great "idea" has been imposed upon us simply because the alternative view, which had more supporting evidence, was not useful to the control agenda of the authorities.

What is taking place at our present moment in history via what can only be called religious revivalism, including its manifestation as the so-called New Age Movement with its subset of specialization in UFOs and aliens, is what is known in popular intelligence parlance as "damage control", a vast COINTELPRO operation against the revelation of Truth in its proper context. In place after place, in all fields of scientific study, discoveries are being made that contradict what we have been taught to believe about our world, our history, religions and origins. The only way the Secret Cult that controls the world can deal with the emergence of truth in so many fields is to make a very powerful and concerted effort to divert these discoveries into a framework that will continue to serve the agenda of the Control System Matrix.

Picknett and Prince rightly notice that the "alternative history" that is being proposed by the current spate of books, gurus, New Age mass market workshops and symposia, utilizes ideas and concepts born in the "occult world". Unfortunately, they fail to distinguish the fact that what is "occulted" comes in two flavors: truth and just more and trickier lies.

In the past several years we have indeed been deluged with a tidal wave of books about ancient mysteries that have enthralled the world. The most widely promulgated of these books are by authors such as Henry Lincoln, Graham Hancock, Robert Bauval, John Anthony West, Robert Temple, Laurence Gardner, and a supporting cast too numerous to mention. Picknett and Prince astutely note that such writers may not be conscious participants in the Damage Control system, but that they are most definitely being provided with the grist for mills of a massive cover-up operation – a shell-game of reality with moves so dexterous that unless the reader understands from the beginning that the hand is, indeed, quicker than the eye, they will be lulled by the obvious truths so that at the point the lie is introduced, they will swallow it at once without noticing that it is a lie. And make no mistake about it: these lies are intended to be a deadly poison, slow acting, but 100 percent lethal.

Picknett and Prince are right about the fact that there is a lot of so-called occult, psychic, New Age channeled material that is purely evil – part of this conspiracy to cover up the failures in the old belief systems. But they are wrong to believe that the system that is in place, the beliefs that have been promulgated on humanity for millennia, are the benevolent results of natural human evolution, or a benign and omniscient God who has our best interests at heart. In fact, Picknett and Prince do not even seem to notice the fact that the present Matrix of beliefs is crumbling, and this is what has necessitated this co-opting and perversion of truth. If there was no failure of the old system, there would be no need for a new one. Picknett and Prince recoil in horror at the Conspiracy they have uncovered, but they do not realize that the old system is exactly the same, and that they have fallen for the oldest of Machiavellian tactics: create an enemy by demonizing your opponent, and then step in as a savior to do exactly what you have accused the opponent of planning. P & P do not seem to be fully cognizant of the subtle nature of disinformation tactics and how cleverly it has been used throughout the millennia to deliver lies wrapped in truth.

Meet the new boss, same as the old boss.

Giving them the benefit of the doubt, we do understand the position of P & P. It's one thing to pursue conspiracy theories and to find them and track them and think that there are some very naughty folks here on the Big Blue Marble. It's an altogether different thing, after one has tracked enough of these theories, to come to the realization that they are all just different parts of the same elephant, and that the critter is really thousands of years old. When that fact smacks you in the face, either you run screaming in denial, or you begin to step back from the truly BIG picture, the global-millennial picture, and you see that there is a very stinky rat somewhere. Having arrived at that point, you realize that such a conspiracy could not be created or sustained by human beings – at least not alone. And then you have to face the most difficult task of all: asking yourself who or what could be behind it?

Having asked that question, you realize that you simply cannot answer it unless you open your mind to a whole constellation of possibilities that you would formerly never, ever, in your wildest dreams have considered. Then, if you work very, very hard, you may discover the "truth" that *they want you to believe.*

However, if you continue to work very, very hard and are very, very lucky, you will realize that you need help, and you will seek this help based on the knowledge you have acquired that such help can and does exist – only we generally do not have access to it because we are too easily duped and manipulated – and then you might begin to learn the rules of communicating with higher minds than our own. At such a point, following such an approach, there is some hope of sorting out the mess. But it isn't easy, and it can't be easy. If it was easy, it would have been done hundreds or thousands of years ago, and the world would not be in the state it is in today.

Returning now to the disinformation campaign incepted by the Secret Cult, even if it is true that their goals are negative to humanity, the likelihood is that those negative goals are wrapped in layers of truth about humanity and human history – for a reason. And P & P missed that one. The fact is, if many of the ideas and teachings of such groups about human history prove to be correct, how easy will it be for them to claim that since they are right about those things, they are also right about their political, social, and economic aims? And that is how the most effective disinformation works.

By the same token, if P & P are proven wrong about their claims *against* the alternative history aspects of the conspirators, then their related claims that there is a conspiracy will likewise be ignored. And that would be a terrible mistake. Synarchist groups have been implicated in terrorism in the pre-WWII years. In the years leading up to the Nazi takeover of Germany, a Frenchman named Viven Postel du Mas wrote a notorious document, called the Synarchist Pact, which became their manifesto. In 1932, a society called the Synarchist Empire Movement was founded in France, which was described as "a secret society with very specific and limited membership, following a definite politico-economic programme". P & P discovered that this group was behind right-wing terrorist gangs such as the CSAR (Secret Committee for Revolutionary Action), and that most of the CSAR membership were also part of the Synarchist Empire Movement. In 1941, a police report in Vichy France exposed a plot by Synarchists to take over the government, noting a close relationship between the Synarchist movement and the Martinist Orders.

It seems that after World War II, the Synarchists went even deeper underground in order to work on Plan B, since Plan A (Hitler's agenda) didn't pan out. In recent years Synarchist groups have come out into the open both in Europe and in Britain, and this leads us to P & P's major research find: the connection between R.A. Schwaller de Lubicz and the Synarchist movement. Paraphrasing Picknett and Prince:

Given the nature of Synarchy one would probably never know the names of even the most powerful. But we do know quite a lot about one of them: R.A. Schwaller de Lubicz. It is curious that Schwaller de Lubicz has become the 'godfather' of Alternative Egyptology even though few have read his works first-hand. His ideas mostly come to us through the books of Graham Hancock, Robert Bauval and, of course, John Anthony West, all of whom have expressed their admiration for this scholar. They refer to him as a philosopher, or as a mathematician. What is interesting to us, however, is that, although Schwaller de Lubicz was those things, they never call him an occultist – which he was – and they never call him a Synarchist – which he was.

A leading figure in the Paris Theosophical Society, he broke away to form his own occult organization, which he called *Les Veilleurs* – the Watchers – specifically in order to carry his esoteric ideas into the political arena. Perhaps it will come as no surprise to discover that he has been described as a 'proto fascist.' He even claims to have designed the uniform for Hitler's SA ('Brownshirts'). Although it is not certain that his claim is true, Schwaller de Lubicz clearly had no problem with people thinking that it was. One of Schwaller de Lubicz's 'Watchers' was Vivien Postel du Mas, the man who wrote the Synarchist Pact of the 1930s. Through du Mas, Schwaller de Lubicz had a particular influence on Hitler's Deputy, the tormented and complex Rudolf Hess. Schwaller de Lubicz was anti-Semitic and racist – and, like the Nazis, thought that women were inferior to men. For example, he taught that women were intellectually incapable of understanding the *Hermetica*. All this is important, because it is impossible to separate Schwaller de Lubicz's political, Synarchist beliefs from his work as an Egyptologist, the work that certain authors so admire.

In the realm of cultural shaping, we find the *Holy Blood, Holy Grail* guys busy cooking up a "divine bloodline". This has now become the sensation of 2004 with Dan Brown's novel *The DaVinci Code*, taking the cultural programming to another level. This idea is supplemented by the work of Laurence Gardner who has connected the Holy Grail Bloodline to reptilian aliens. At the same time, we have a host of true believers around the planet preaching the gospel of those cute and helpful Grays, and the reptilian Lord who really loves us and never did anything to humanity except teach them all about how to be civilized.

As I wrote in my analysis of the Bible that can be found both on our website and in my book, *The Secret History of the World*, what seems to be true is that the writers of both the Old and New Testaments couldn't just toss out the oral traditions of the people. They used them in a very special way. With an awareness of how history can by mythicized and then historicized, and any combination thereof, we can look at the scriptures with a different eye. We can theorize that there must have been a real person around whom the legend of Jesus – the mythicized history – was wrapped. We can theorize that he was teaching something important and dramatic for it to have made such an impact. We can also theorize that this "impact" was seen as very dangerous at first, but later, after many twists and turns had been introduced, it was thought that the growing myth and popularization of Jesus could be utilized – with appropriate rulings on what was "holy writ" – as the centerpiece of a Control System. It often seems that whatever was positive was twisted and turned backward. What develops with a broad historical review, is the idea that whatever "Jesus" was really doing and saying, it was most certainly twisted, corrupted, and emphasis shifted in fairly predictable ways.

In other words, the Bible that we know, in its various parts, was declared to be "holy and infallible" to justify any of a number of political maneuvers.

Regarding the creation of the Bible as it really happened, in examining this process, we find nothing of the "Holy Ghost" in there. That's the plain fact. And a lot of people in the "business" of religion know it.

Nevertheless, in our current day, we find an astonishing state of affairs: our institutions of higher learning generally have a special faculty allotment for the teaching of theology, financed by the taxpayer, whether Christian or Jew!

One assumes that the students who study this theology are also given exposure to other studies, such as math, languages, science, and so forth.

The question then becomes: what kind of strange distortion, what incomprehensible corruption takes place in the minds of human beings, so that they can so completely separate their academic knowledge from what they hear preached at them from the pulpit?

What kind of brainwashing can so effectively cause the simplest of facts to be forgotten?

How does this happen? It is literally staggering to a logical, intelligent human being, that the fairy tale of the Bible – as God's word – has endured so long. There is nothing to which we can compare this in the entire seven thousand years of human history of which we are aware. Calling it all a "pack of lies" seems rather harsh, but it is increasingly evident that it is certainly intentionally misleading. And, in that case, what shall we call it?

How about COINTELPRO?

When researching religious matters, one always comes across prophecy and miracles. It seems that those who are to be kept in fear of the Lord need an unequivocal sign from time to time. Miracles and visions can sway whole armies. We can think of the battle cry "Great is Allah!" and the claim of the salvific blood of Christ that was held up as a shield against the Saracens. We should also be reminded of the mandate of Yahweh to "utterly destroy" just about everybody who wasn't hanging out with Joshua and his gang.

Such "visions" go back into our primeval past. Around 5,000 BC, the divine Ishtar was said to have appeared to Enme-Kar, the ruler of Uruk, telling him to overthrow the city of Aratta. But, at the moment, we are mostly concerned with visions in the context of the Bible since it is the Bible that underpins the beliefs of a staggering number of human beings on planet Earth at the present time, including their "revised forms" in the New Age and Human Potential movement, and most particularly George Bush and the Gang. That alone should give us pause to consider the company we keep!

Additionally, when we step back from the situation, the one thing that we see is that prophecy is at the center of the Judeo-Christian-Islamic tradition. The prophets of these religions claimed to be in direct contact with the Creator of the Universe, and this creator seems to have been singularly "personal" in the sense of having personal traits, whims, likes and dislikes. His prophets are, naturally, privileged messengers, receiving his divine revelations and these revelations divide mankind into those who believe them and those who don't. Naturally, those who don't are damned depending on who has the upper hand.

The Christian religion, and its New Age offshoots, is the chief proponent of the many End of the World scenarios with which we are most familiar. Scenarios about the end times originate mostly in the body of apocalyptic, eschatological writings of the New and Old Testaments. It is in the final book, Revelation, that most striking and symbolic representations about the end of the world are said by many to be depicted.

It is a difficult work to comprehend. Probably no other piece of writing in history has been examined more thoroughly and interpreted more widely. It is the end-of-the world legend, a doomsday tale on moldy bread with virtual reality special effects in abundance. It is the inspirational fountainhead for mad prophets, spittle spewing pulpit-pounders, apocalyptic Enochian magicians, fanatical true believers, grade-B movie makers, and knaves and snake-oil salesmen of every form and sort.

In William Bramley's book, *The Gods of Eden*, he noted that when we consider history, we can clearly see that the drive of human beings to have peace is as strong, if not stronger, than the drive to have war. But, when the issue of war is examined, one realizes that, most often, the "trigger" for war and related "inhumanity to man" is that *the drive for spiritual freedom is twisted by manipulation.*

It's easy to look back on history and see where this or that group was "misled" in their beliefs and thereby fell into errors of thinking that led to the perpetration of unspeakable horrors. We can point to the genocide advocated by the God of the Hebrews, or the religious-zeal-run-amok of the Catholic church when it instituted the Inquisition. We can see the twisted version of the "genetic superman" that led to the holocaust of World War II. It's easy to discern these errors of the past, because we "know more now". Well, isn't that an interesting thing? We *know* more now. How much more can we learn?

It almost seems as if the game has just gotten more and more complex, but the same essential errors keep getting repeated. What is at the root? (Aside from the fact that we notice the above examples all relate to monotheistic exclusivity.)

Human beings have a sort of built in drive to be "insured" or "underwritten" regarding any choices they may make. This is due to a fundamental condition of our reality. This condition seems to be a sort of "randomness" or lack of control of our lives. Our observations of reality tell us that there is "something out there" that we need to know about because having this key can "make or break" us. We adopt religions because we are anxious. We are anxious because we realize, from our observations, that at any moment, this "randomness" which manifests as destruction, will fall upon us either physically or psychically. It would be oh so helpful if we could see the future in advance, be informed of the respective consequences in the choices confronting us in every moment

Over and over again we can see that this need to be "insured" is what is used to manipulate human beings. What we see is that a scientific view of spirituality is discouraged while at the same time, the inner desire for "salvation" is constantly being stimulated by various religious teachings. As a consequence, a great many people can be led into doing a lot of cruel and stupid things. The perceived need to "save souls" is a prime example of how such a seeming positive polarization can be suddenly shifted to do the exact opposite of what the religious teachings explicate. And this is an important point to remember!

Zecharia Sitchin and William Bramley, following Von Däniken, have postulated that the ancient evidence demonstrates the actual, physical presence of an extraterrestrial race who came to Earth to set up "controls" over humanity, with possible plans to return and "harvest the fruits" of their efforts. In both cases, their studies have indicated strongly that this "extraterrestrial race" does *not* have humanity's best interests at heart! Both of them did a lot of work, gathered a lot of *facts*, and were certainly not listening to some bug eyed Gray alien who was trying to convince them that "this is for *you*! We are here to help!" Yet, somehow, both of them did not deal with a crucial element of the problem.

The fact is, we find today those same "aliens" zipping about, sliding in and out of our reality like slippery eels, gazing and probing and "communicating" all kinds of excuses and scenarios to explain what they are doing based on how gullible or ignorant their victims are. This factor has to be considered. In other words, what Von Däniken, Sitchin and Bramley fail to factor into their arguments is the *continuing* evidence of "interaction" and "domination" from another "realm" of existence. The Annunaki, as defined by Sitchin, and the "Custodians" as defined by Bramley, may not be *physical beings*, (in our terms), who occupy, dominate, and then leave for some obscure reason. The evidence of those people, now numbering in the multiples of thousands, claiming "alien abduction" and "contact with aliens" and even "visions of the Virgin" and other miracles throughout history, seems to contradict this view. It seems far more likely that the ancient stories indicate a cultural openness that *permitted perception* of such beings, *acknowledged their reality*, and merely made the distinction between them and ordinary human beings by referring to them as "gods".

William Bramley also chronicled considerable historical evidence of a relation between the sightings of UFOs and the sudden onslaught of deadly diseases or plagues. We have similar concerns in the present time which indicates that this is not a "new thing", but merely part of a cycle. The Annunaki have never left, and the Brotherhood of the Serpent is still with us, active and growing stronger by the day.

Considering religion as COINTELPRO, during my reading, I came across a curious remark by the medieval Jewish commentator, Rashi, saying, in effect, that the Genesis narrative *was written to justify what we now call genocide!* The God of Israel, who gave his people the "promised land", had to be unequivocally supreme so that no one, not even the dispossessed, could appeal against his decrees.[9]

In Umberto Eco's *The Search for The Perfect Language*, the idea is suggested, though subtly, that the development of the Hebrew Bible, even if there were some ancient texts involved, (though not nearly as ancient as most believers suppose!) was primarily a *"promotion" to validate Judaism*. This validation was necessary in order to then "validate" Christianity as the "one true religion". In other words, the "rights" of the Jews, the unappealable decrees of Jehovah/Yahweh, could be "inherited" by the Christian Church as instituted for political reasons by Constantine!

What we finally observe about Christianity can be summed up by saying that it is clear that it was taken over by a sort of

---

[9] See B.S.J. Isserlin, *The Israelites* (London: Thames and Hudson, 1998).

COINTELPRO to be used as a control system. The Egyptian religion became the model of Christianity, and the "Stargate Conspiracy" – substituting essentially Synarchic ideas for the original Christianity – was a great success. It has been used to kill more people than any other ideology in recorded history. It is, as it happens, the foundation of the Bush Reich Agenda – agents of the Apocalypse. Christianity – and other monotheistic religions – are basically Draconian. They are the well from which much in our society – our mores, ethics, judgments – is drawn. It has been the justification for the greatest series of bloodbaths in "recorded" history.

Could there be a reason for this?

Simultaneously, there are those that claim there is a "gradual revelation" plan going on via the government and its space program, juxtaposed against a big push by George Bush and the Fundamentalists of both Christian and Zionist tendencies to institute a One World Government. So, we have a right to ask: what the heck is really going on? What does it mean when Christian Fundamentalists talk about the "New Jerusalem" when, in point of fact, the evidences shows that anything and everything that had to do with the Old Jerusalem was lies and disinformation swirling around that crafty Yahweh/Jehovah with control issues?

The reality seems to be that Judaism, Christianity and Islam were specifically designed and created just to produce a particular situation that is desirable to someone at a certain point in time, and again, we see the same operation being run on humanity in the present day as the New Age/Human Potential movement.

Interestingly, there are ancient texts that refer to this very problem. In the book of Enoch, Jesus is recorded as saying:

> From the time when the devil fell from the glory of the Father and (lost) his own glory, he sat upon the clouds, and sent his ministers, even angels flaming with fire, unto men from Adam even unto Henoch his servant. And he [the devil] raised up Henoch upon the firmament and showed him his godhead and commanded pen and ink to be given him: and he sat down and wrote threescore and seven books. And [the devil] commanded that he should take them to the Earth and deliver them unto his sons. And Henoch let his books down upon the Earth and delivered them unto his sons, and began to teach them to perform the custom of sacrifice, and unrighteous mysteries, and so did he hide the kingdom of heaven from men. And [the devil] said unto them: Behold that I am your god and beside me is none other god.

And therefore did my Father send me [Jesus] into the world that I might make it known unto men, that they might know the evil device of the devil.

Let me repeat that part again:

And Henoch let his books down upon the Earth and delivered them unto his sons, and began to teach them to perform the custom of sacrifice, and unrighteous mysteries, and so did he hide the kingdom of heaven from men. And he said unto them: Behold that I am your god and beside me is none other god.

This is the god of Judaism, today's Christianity – but *not* of Christ – and Islam: the Devil. By their fruits you shall know them.

Laura Knight-Jadczyk, August 2004

AUTOBIOGRAPHICAL BACKGROUND OF THE AUTHOR NECESSARY TO THE CONTEXT OF THE WAVE

I have certainly had a number of "High Strangeness" experiences throughout my life that might seem, at first glance, to "fit" into the popularized "alien interaction" scenarios. While I know that some people seem to glory in the idea that they have some sort of connection to "alien intelligences", I never felt that way, and I certainly wasn't going to accept such an explanation if I could find another that fit the data better. After all these years, and much study and research, I'm not so sure that the popularized interpretations are at all correct.

What is correct is that, beginning in 1985, the "High Strangeness Factor" of my life was bumped up a few notches. My grandmother had died in 1984, and it has taken years for me to be able to articulate what was going on inside me at that point in time. In retrospect, I find that my grandmother's death was a "gift", because it was the impetus for asking of deep and burning questions.

I was then 32 years old, and my grandmother had been an omnipresent part of my life. What I observed in myself, as I went through this period of grieving, led me to draw a number of conclusions. It seems that, after a time, even if a loss is deep and profound, one eventually becomes accustomed not to expect to hear a certain voice, to see a certain beloved face every day, and a new "history" becomes the new way of being; the loss is no longer acutely painful. This new "custom" becomes the reality, as though the universe in which one now exists is not the same universe as the former one where the loved one was present.

But then, one has to ask: what happens to the love between people when one of them dies? Where does it go? Even if the reality is a new one, so to say, does that mean that the old one has ceased to exist entirely?

How can it be that such a bond, one that may be assumed to exist in Platonic noumenal terms, yet which is expressed in physical manifestation, seems suddenly to end when the material body is sealed in the tomb? Why is there this dreadful veil that prevents our access to other realities in terms of certainty?

The *concept* of a chair or an apple or any concrete object seems to be the only truly lasting thing about it since, clearly, the object comes into being and "exists" for a certain period of time, and then passes out of existence. What about abstract things like love? Is love therefore no longer "real" as a physical object can be no longer "real" because the dynamic exchange – the period of its existence in reality – has ended? Some part of me raged at this idea. No! Love and kindness, existing only as ideas, are more "real" in some realm of abstraction. But we have no access. When the dynamic in which those abstractions exist in material terms ceases to be active, where does it go? In what realm does this world of ideas of engendered things exist, be they solid or only ideological?

In the simplest of terms, my thoughts were: my grandmother is dead; how can I know she still loves me? What am I to do with the love I have to give her? What is the medium of exchange? Is it over?

Is there no more?

If so, then what's the point, damn it?

The answers offered by the Christian faith in which I grew up suddenly seemed not merely unsatisfactory, but downright insulting to the memory of my grandmother and the bond that had existed between us. The ideas of Spiritualism and the concepts of reincarnation were only slightly helpful. As far as I was concerned, there was no proof. There was a lot of circumstantial or anecdotal evidence and conjecture; but there was also another side: such evidence was declared to be either psychologically unsound or a satanic delusion to lead us astray depending on whether you asked scientists or the church.

But the issue remained. For *what purpose is love engendered*, and *where does it go* when the dynamic interaction in this reality comes to an end?

It's cheap and easy to say that "love never dies", and that love continues to exist between us and our loved ones who are no longer with us in some "astral" plane or place of the dead; or that we will meet the dear departed at some end-time resurrection. I was not satisfied with "The Lord gives and the Lord takes away; blessed be the name of the Lord". Even worse was: "It's not for us to understand God's ways; it's a Mystery!" And I most definitely wasn't going to have a séance and try to talk to my grandmother. To attempt to resurrect her that way felt blasphemous to the love I had for her, even worse than the idea she was "lost to me" until some final "end time" resurrection.

I was pregnant at the time my grandmother died, and the baby was born in the Spring of 1985. As a result of injuries I suffered during the delivery, I was bedridden for many months after.

Since I could no longer maintain my very active participation in life in a physical way, I was forced, by the universe, as it were, to find other outlets for my energy. I decided this would be the perfect time to not only catch up on my reading, but also to master the art of meditation which might assist in my investigation into this question of Eternal Life.

Several years earlier I had found a book on a "bargain table" in a book store entitled *In Search of the Miraculous* by P.D. Ouspensky. The blurb on the cover said: "The noted author of *Tertium Organum* combines the logic of a mathematician with the vision of a mystic in his quest for solutions to the problems of Man and the Universe". Since it was a bargain and promised to reveal secrets about our world, naturally, I bought it immediately. When I got home and tried to read it, it proved to be rather dry, and I gave it up. It had lain on the shelf ever after.

But now that I was bedridden, the door was wide open to reading as much as I liked. In that sense, it was a blessing. So, I remembered this book that I had put aside; it seemed that a book that promised insight to the issues I was struggling with – even a very dry book – didn't seem like such a bad idea when I could do nothing else. I asked for it, and soon it was located and brought to me.

I realized pretty quickly that this book would go to the top of the list of "forbidden works" according to the elders of the church, but I didn't care. After my experiences with the church over the past few years, the teachings were rapidly declining as the standard by which reality ought to be measured. I was still "on guard" against "evil ideas", but I was sure that I could filter out anything too "dangerous" in a work that promised insight on the issues for which I was seeking answers.

Everything was fine for about 17 pages, and I was getting "into" the style of writing and found it to be deeply interesting and then – well – then this mysterious "G" (about whom I knew nothing), made a remark that completely knocked the wind out of my still mostly Protestant sails. In response to Ouspensky's speculation that, in the industrial age, humans were becoming more "mechanized" and had stopped thinking, Gurdjieff said:

> "There is another kind of mechanization which is much more dangerous: being a machine oneself. Have you ever thought about the fact that all people themselves are machines? ... Look, all those people you see are simply machines – nothing more. ... You think there is something that chooses its own path, something that can stand against mechanization; you think that not everything is equally mechanical."

At this point, Ouspensky raised the very argument that was forming in my own mind:

> "Why of course not! ... Art, poetry, thought, are phenomena of quite a different order."

> Gurdjieff replied: "Of exactly the same order. These activities are just as mechanical as everything else. Men are machines and nothing but mechanical actions can be expected of machines"

I was so enraged that I snapped the book shut and threw it against the wall!

How dare he say such a terrible thing about human beings! How dare he deny the reality of the spirit, the sublimity of music and mysticism and the salvation of Christ! I'm surprised that sparks from my eyes didn't set the bed on fire and steam didn't issue from my ears. I was hot with outrage!

But, it had been said. The seed of the thought had been planted in my mind. After awhile, my curiosity about such a concept came to the fore. I began to mull over the issue in an attempt to find ways to disprove it.

I mused over my own life, all my interactions with other people, and gradually, I began to realize that there was, indeed, something mysteriously "mechanical" about the interactions between human beings. I thought about the many people I had worked with therapeutically using hypnosis, and how "mechanical" the therapy was, and how the roots of most of their problems were rather like "mechanical" and conditioned reactions to their perceptions and observations. Generally, it seemed, these perceptions were erroneous, and it was the error of this "mechanical" thinking that created the problems in the first place.

But, over and over again I could see that such problems and the ways they formed and operated, as well as the therapeutic solutions themselves, were, essentially, mechanical. It was like a formula. With just a few "hints" from the person, I could almost immediately see the whole dynamic of their past and the formation of their problem, as well as the "mechanical" way to solve it. I applied the technique, and just like changing the wires and spark plugs in a car, it made them start "firing on all cylinders" again.

Okay, so the guy has a point. But clearly, those people who were "saved" were saved from being mechanical, right? I wanted to find out if he had anything to say about that! I called one of my children to retrieve the book for me and I continued to read. The question was asked: "Can it be said that man possesses immortality?"

Gurdjieff's reply was fascinating:

> Immortality is one of the qualities we ascribe to people without having a sufficient understanding of their meaning. Other qualities of this kind are 'individuality,' in the sense of an inner unity, a 'permanent and unchangeable I,' 'consciousness,' and 'will.' All these qualities can belong to man, but this certainly does not mean that they do belong to him or belong to each and every one.
>
> In order to understand what man is at the present time, that is, at the present level of development, it is necessary to imagine to a certain extent what he can be, that is, what he can attain. Only by understanding the correct sequence of development possible will people cease to ascribe to themselves what, at present, they do not possess, and what, perhaps, they can only acquire after great effort and great labor.
>
> According to an ancient teaching, traces of which may be found in many systems, old and new, a man who has attained the full development possible for man, a man in the full sense of the word, consists of four bodies. These four bodies are composed of substances which gradually become finer and finer, mutually interpenetrate one another, and form four independent organisms, standing in a definite relationship to one another but capable of independent action.

Gurdjieff's idea was that it was possible for these four bodies to exist because the physical human body has such a complex organization that, under certain favorable conditions, a new and independent organism actually can develop and grow within it. This new system of organs of perception can afford a more convenient and responsive instrument for the activity of an awakened consciousness.

> The consciousness manifested in this new body is capable of governing it, and it has full power and full control over the physical body. In this second body, under certain conditions, a third body can grow, again having characteristics of its own. The consciousness manifested in this third body has full power and control over the

first two bodies; and the third body possesses the possibility of acquiring knowledge inaccessible either to the first or to the second body. In the third body, under certain conditions, a fourth can grow, which differs as much from the third as the third differs from the second, and the second from the first. The consciousness manifested in the fourth body has full control over the first three bodies and itself.

These four bodies are defined in different teachings in various ways. The first is the physical body, in Christian terminology the 'carnal' body; the second, in Christian terminology, is the 'natural' body; the third is the 'spiritual' body; and the fourth, in the terminology of esoteric Christianity, is the 'divine' body. In theosophical terminology the first is the 'physical' body, the second is the 'astral,' the third is the 'mental,' and the fourth the 'causal.'

In the terminology of certain Eastern teachings the first body is the 'carriage,' (the body), the second is the 'horse' (feelings, desires), the third the 'driver' (mind), and the fourth the 'master' (I, consciousness, will).

Such comparisons and parallels may be found in most systems and teachings which recognize something more in man than the physical body. But almost all these teachings, while repeating in a more or less familiar form the definitions and divisions of the ancient teaching, have forgotten or omitted its most important feature, which is: that man is not born with the finer bodies. They can only be artificially cultivated in him, provided favorable conditions both internal and external are present.

The 'astral body' is not an indispensable implement for man. It is a great luxury which only a few can afford. A man can live quite well without an 'astral body.' His physical body possesses all the functions necessary for life. A man without 'astral body' may even produce the impression of being a very intellectual or even spiritual man, and may deceive not only others but also himself.

When the third body has been formed and has acquired all the properties, powers, and knowledge possible for it, there remains the problem of fixing this knowledge and these powers. Because, having been imparted to it by influences of a certain kind, they may be taken away by these same influences or by others. By means of a special kind of work for all three bodies the acquired properties may be made the permanent and inalienable possession of the third body.

The process of fixing these acquired properties corresponds to the process of the formation of the fourth body.

And only the man who possesses four fully developed bodies can be called a 'man' in the full sense of the word. This man possesses many properties which ordinary man does not possess. One of these properties is immortality. All religions and all ancient teachings contain the idea that, by acquiring the fourth body, man acquires immortality; and they all contain indications of the ways to acquire the fourth body, that is, immortality.

The book went flying again!

I was outraged. But this time, my indignation lasted only a very short time. Again, in thinking over the many clues about human beings I had been collecting all my life, including those derived from observing myself, I saw something very deeply true being said here. As much as I might not like it, I could not deny the fact it was certainly a hypothesis supported by observation.

Hints of these matters did occur in the Bible, though they were among the most obscure references. Preachers and theologians generally tended to leave them strictly alone. At least 17 times in the New Testament, it's noted that Jesus taught his disciples in "secret", yet the teachings of Jesus in the Bible itself consists only of his purported public discourses. There was a lot missing, and Gurdjieff spoke as one with authority. What's more, it rang of truth.

The book was retrieved again. I was curious to see what further remarks might be made about Christianity. Ouspensky asked the same question I would have asked myself:

"For a man of Western culture, it is of course difficult to believe and to accept the idea that an ignorant fakir, a naïve monk, or a yogi who has retired from life may be on the way to evolution while an educated European, armed with 'exact knowledge' and all the latest methods of investigation, has no chance whatever and is moving in a circle from which there is no escape". Gurdjieff answered:

Yes, that is because people believe in progress and culture. There is no progress whatever. Everything is just the same as it was thousands, and tens of thousands, of years ago. The outward form changes. The essence does not change. Man remains just the same. 'Civilized' and 'cultured' people live with exactly the same interests as the most ignorant savages. Modern civilization is based on violence and slavery and fine words...

What do you expect? People are machines. Machines have to be blind and unconscious, they cannot be otherwise, and all their actions have to correspond to their nature. Everything happens. No one does anything. 'Progress' and 'civilization,' in the real meaning of these words, can appear only as the result of conscious efforts. They cannot appear as the result of unconscious mechanical actions. And what conscious effort can there be in machines? And if one machine is unconscious, then a hundred machines are unconscious, and so are a thousand machines, or a hundred thousand, or a million. And the unconscious activity of a million machines must necessarily result in destruction and extermination. It is precisely in unconscious involuntary manifestations that all evil lies. You do not yet understand and cannot imagine all the results of this evil. But the time will come when you will understand.

Gurdjieff was right. He was speaking at the beginning of the First World War, in the opening rounds of a century of unprecedented warfare.

My copy of *In Search of the Miraculous* flew across the room at least a dozen more times. I fumed and raged inside each time I was confronted with an idea that, upon reflection and comparison to my observations and experiences, seemed a far better explanation of the dynamics of human existence than anything I had ever read in my life.

As for this "unconscious evil" that Gurdjieff mentioned, he explained in the Tale of the Evil Magician:

A very rich magician had a great many sheep. But at the same time this magician was very mean. He did not want to hire shepherds, nor did he want to erect a fence about the pasture where his sheep were grazing. The sheep consequently often wandered into the forest, fell into ravines, and so on, and above all they ran away, for they knew that the magician wanted their flesh and skins and this they did not like.

At last the magician found a remedy. He hypnotized his sheep and suggested to them first of all that they were immortal and that no harm was being done to them when they were skinned. On the contrary, it would be very good for them and even pleasant. Secondly he suggested that the magician was a good master who loved his flock so much that he was ready to do anything in the world for them. In the third place he suggested to them that if anything at all were going to happen to them it was not going to happen just then, at any rate not that day, and therefore they had no need to think about it. Further, the magician suggested to his sheep that they were not sheep at all; to some of them he suggested that they were lions, to others that they were eagles, to others that they were men, and to others that they were magicians.

And after this all his cares and worries about the sheep came to an end. They never ran away again but quietly awaited the time when the magician would require their flesh and skins.

Ouspensky wrote that "theoretically, a man could awaken. But in practice this is almost impossible. As soon as a man awakens for a moment and opens his eyes, all the forces that caused him to fall asleep in the first place begin to act on him with tenfold energy. He immediately falls asleep again, very often dreaming that he is awake."

I also thought about my study of the history of man in my search for the answers to why things are the way they are, and how I had come to see it as the biography of Satan. I was beginning to realize that something was very wrong with the picture of the world that we are taught from the moment we are born, and that is further implemented in our culture, our society and most especially our religions.

I thought back over my life and realized that all the events that had gradually maneuvered me into my present position could most definitely be perceived as the "forces that act to keep a person asleep". It was a certainty that some tremendous pressure had been applied to stop me from observing, from analyzing, and most of all from thinking and learning.

The question was: who or what was the true nature of the "Evil Magician"?

***

Reading *In Search of the Miraculous* "jump-started" my thinking processes, which had lain fallow during the years when my first three children were small. Without really planning it, during this period of forced physical inactivity, I was establishing a regimen of deep and intense thinking, alternating with the deep contemplation and stopping of the chatter of meaningless thought that was achieved during meditation. My meditations seemed to progress quite rapidly. I later read that achieving just a few minutes of deep contemplation was difficult and often took years of practice, but it seemed that I rapidly achieved that point, and soon was able to enter a rather "timeless" state for what proved to be somewhat extended periods of time.

After my regular meditation exercises, I would sit up in bed, surrounded by piles of books and notebooks, reading and writing notes on what I read. As I did so, I would often stop and think about questions that occurred to me as I read. The instant these questions were framed in my mind, thoughts would simply pour into my head so fast that I was mentally leaping and jumping just to follow them. These thoughts always and only came in response to questions that I would pose mentally about whatever I was considering at the moment in my studies. The urge to write these thoughts down was so overwhelming that I spent literally hours a day, filling page after page in longhand. I still have boxes full of these notebooks. It didn't occur to me that I might be doing something called "channeling" at the time. In fact, such an idea would have horrified me. I was just "asking interesting questions" in an open way, with no attempt to impose any pre-conceived answers. What entered my mind in response to these questions just seemed like "thinking".

But, there was something curious about this particular "thinking". If I didn't write the thoughts down, they would stay there, backing up like dammed-up water. As soon as I started to write again, it was as if there had been no break in the flow of thoughts whatsoever. They picked up right where they left off.

At some point, I decided that I must find out if these ideas that were coming to me had any basis in fact whatsoever. Just because a thought "came to me", didn't mean I intended to accept it as a valid answer to my question. I most definitely needed more data! So the answers that "came to me" actually served to point me in the direction of certain studies that otherwise might not have been part of my experience. I was compelled by my rational and reflective nature to research each idea that came to me in order to discover if there was any way it could be supported scientifically and objectively.

Getting more data was a problem. I subscribed to a library service by mail, and soon began ordering and reading book after book on subjects that ranged from geology to physics; from psychology to theology; from metaphysics to astronomy. As I read, I found many pieces that not only supported the ideas that came to me in response to my questions, but also expanded on many of the concepts in dramatic ways, leading to more interesting questions, more answers, and more data collection. I was both surprised and energized to find that the ideas I was getting weren't so crazy after all!

I began to systematically assemble my notes and ideas, including the notes from "mainstream" sources that supported what I had written, or expanded the idea, or, at the very least, gave it plausibility. If the "idea" I had was not supported by observation or scholarly opinion, I discarded it. These notes and commentaries became a manuscript that I entitled *The Noah Syndrome*.

As I pulled on the thread of Ariadne, it seemed the entire fabric of my religion, as it was taught, unraveled, and there, concealed behind the metaphors of the Bible, supported by facts and ideas of science, was a concept so amazing that it took my breath away.

The idea was Macro-Cosmic Metamorphosis in Quantum terms.

How did I come to this when I started out trying to discover the noumenal existence of love and good and evil?

Well, actually, it's quite simple. As I followed the thread through the labyrinth, going from the very large to the very small, it became clear to me that the search for the true meaning of Love was the same as the search for Salvation and Faith and, ultimately, the search for the meaning of Eternal Life.

In Matthew 24, Jesus gives a discourse on the "End Times" – that period in which the last trumpet will sound and the Mystery of God will be revealed – which includes:

> [A]s were the days of Noah, so will be the coming of the son of man. For just as in those days before the flood they were eating and drinking, marrying and being given in marriage, until the day when Noah went into the Ark, and they did not know or understand until the flood came and swept them all away, so will be the coming of the Son of man.

This event, the End, was compared to the "Days of Noah" – the Deluge.

Well, what's so "mysterious" about a flood? What's so happy about most of the population of the planet being wiped out of existence? How can you call that "glad tidings?"

The key seemed to be held *in the concept of the Ark*. My search for the true meaning of Love, Salvation, Faith and Eternal Life was, essentially, a search for the *meaning of the Ark*. Metaphorically speaking, there is no better expression of this search than the story of Noah and the Ark. All quests of life and love and existence can be expressed in this story of a man, faced with the destruction of his world – and in this case, it was literally destruction of the entire world, or so the story goes – and he set about building an Ark.

The next question was, of course, exactly what is this process of Metamorphosis, and exactly what constitutes an Ark of safety?

At this point, a friend of ours died, and we fell heir to a trunk full of books. Among them was a small paperback. I will never forget the feeling that came over me when I read *None Dare Call it Conspiracy*, by Gary Allen. Everything in this book just slotted into place with the teachings of Gurdjieff and Ouspensky that Man is asleep and under the control of an "Evil Magician".

I realized that the Evil Magician was a metaphor, at least in part, for political and historical control systems. This realization was, once again, devastating to my illusions. As Gary Allen suggests, without any intelligent control, 50% of the time events would occur in social, cultural and political spheres leading to great benefit for all. Factoring in intelligent decisions to do good would bring this average even higher. I could clearly see this wasn't reflected in our reality. Man hasn't stopped killing his brother; he has just developed more efficient and mechanical means of doing it.

Why? Who or what is influencing events to the negative?

Putting Allen's ideas together with Gurdjieff's, it seemed merely the result of certain "mechanical" laws of the Universe that humans refer to as "good" and "evil". These laws were cyclical and could be better expressed in terms of physics. That is one of the threads I followed to the idea of Cosmic Quantum Metamorphosis.

I finished the research and notes for *The Noah Syndrome* on December 16, 1986. I went out and bought an old manual typewriter and began to type up my book from notes in longhand. By the time I was done with the manuscript I was a real hot-shot on that old manual typewriter!

As I typed, I began to have some very strange impressions. I could "sense", or "see with the mind's eye", a couple of very funny old men looking over my shoulder as I wrote, consulting with each other, telling me where I needed to make corrections or additions, and even chuckling with glee when I wrote certain comments. They were hysterically funny in their remarks to one another as they oversaw my project, and they jovially clapped one another on the shoulder when I would finally "get it" in regard to a particular point.

I knew that one of them somewhat resembled Albert Einstein, but it wasn't until quite a number of years had passed that I saw a photograph of Immanuel Velikovsky and recognized the other old gentleman.

To this day, I consider this experience a sort of figment of my imagination. But, on the other hand, as I understand things now, it could also have been a "bleed-through" from another reality, or universe.

After *Noah* was finished and duly rejected by a literary agent, I put it away for many years. When the Internet became available to people around the world, and I had learned so much more myself, I brought *The Noah Syndrome* into a new form. Now it has undergone a third metamorphosis. It became the starting point for an expanded work that has taken me far from my original quest.

It is truly strange, in retrospect, that my efforts to "find my Ark" ultimately led to being "found by my Ark" – my husband, Arkadiusz.

***

Several years and a number of very strange events went by. In 1991 I met a young man, Frank, with whom I had many conversations about metaphysical and philosophical subjects. Very early on, I shared the manuscript of *Noah* with Frank.

"It's fascinating", he said. "Brilliant. I couldn't put it down."

"Great!"

"But there's only one problem".

"What's that?" I asked.

"You failed to include the UFO and alien phenomenon."

"No I didn't", I insisted. "It's right there in the chapter about the Rapture!" In *Noah*, I had alluded to the New Age belief, shared in part by some fundamentalist Christians, of miraculous rescues off the planet during some End Time event.

"There is nothing on the planet more important and worthy of study than the alien problem. Trust me, I've been studying it for years!" Frank intoned with great import.

"Nonsense!" I snorted.

Frank responded with a long monologue about aliens that gave me serious doubts about the stability of his intellect. It was so hard to reconcile his brilliant expositions on so many subjects with this silly, childish belief in "little green men!"

I was, I admit, a flaming skeptic about aliens. I had spent so much time poking around in people's heads in therapeutic ways, that, with only a cursory examination of the issue, I'd decided that sightings and claims of abductions were strikingly similar to past life dramas. After reading Whitley Strieber's Gothic book *Communion* and Ruth Montgomery's patently ridiculous *Aliens Among Us*, I refused to give any serious consideration to the subject. The stories were so crazy I simply could not consider them to be real in any context other than as useful metaphors of psychological struggles. I was trying to keep an open mind from a clinical and scientific viewpoint. I wasn't sure that our whole existence, as we perceived it, wasn't simply a series of chemical reactions in the brain of the Cosmic Dreamer.

In short, stories of aliens and abductions seemed an archetypal drama of the subconscious mind. I called it the Millennial Disease and saw it as a form of mass hysteria. I attributed the physical scars and traces of abduction to stigmata-like effects, or poltergeist type events. Clearly, there was very little about UFOs and aliens that couldn't be explained by these theories.

So, when Frank wanted to discuss the "alien business" as a reality, we fell into disagreement. We were at an impasse on this subject. I even became contemptuous and sarcastic when referring to it as The Alien Rapture Theory. I held it to be about as reasonable as the various Pre-Tribulation, Mid-Tribulation, and Post-Tribulation Rapture theories of the fundamentalist Christians. Frank was not deterred by my rejection of the subject.

Frank frequently asked me to use hypnosis to help him "channel". He would say, "The one thing I *can* do is channel. I do it all the time."

I didn't have a very high opinion of "channeling", having read reams of it while writing *Noah*, but I decided it wouldn't be scientific to discard Frank's claims to be an "exception" without at least a trial. I suggested he just simply go into a relaxed state and try automatic writing. My opinion of channeling was not changed. Frank produced the same "cosmic word salad" that's been around for years. Nevertheless, in discussing the matter with Frank, I began to think about my own experiences in "getting answers", as well as the historical fact that "channeled" material can often be so close that it is clear that something other than just chance is operating. The little glimpses of truth intrigued me. So, Frank and I continued to discuss it and a theory began to take shape in my mind in response to the question.

Part of the theory I hammered out was that the reason other sources proved, in the end in case after case, to be so human and fallible, was because an initial error was made in the thinking of the various individuals who acted as channels or mediums. They assumed that a higher source could just be dialed up on the phone, so to speak, and that was that. I theorized, from the few flashes of light I could discern in the vast body of material, that an occasional truly higher source would manage to connect momentarily, or in a skewed or corrupted way, but that, for the most part, it was either discarnates who didn't know a whole lot more than humans did, or that the phenomenon was produced by psychological pathology. I studied the matter from a number of directions trying to discover a clue as to what the obstruction was, if higher sources did, in fact, exist.

The chief obstruction seemed to be this very cloud of theoretical lower level beings and/or thoughts that apparently surrounded our realm like a curtain. My research into this area led me to the work of Dr. William Baldwin, Dr. Edith Fiore, Dr. Carl Wickland, and others who had worked directly with possession and exorcism and related therapeutic techniques. Since studying these matters had long been on my agenda of "things to do", it seems that it manifested in my life at precisely the right moment.

There are many half-baked hypnotherapists who write lengthy books describing the afterlife as a place of great beauty and spiritual delight. The "journeys" and "destinies" of souls are explicated by recounting the most blatantly leading hypnotic sessions I have ever read. I would be ashamed to present material that exposed me as such a mind manipulator! Nevertheless, such books become wildly popular because they cater to the human need for existential comfort.

Aside from leading questions and mind manipulation by the hypnotist, it most certainly seems that there are a lot of "dead dudes" – or personality fragments – who will come forward in various ways, including using the vocal instruments of a medium, who make such pronouncements, and who describe things in glowing and ephemeral terms. Upon deeper inspection, it seems that there is a very great deal more to the matter than that.

The numbers of texts that have been written on the subject of the problems with the positivist channeled messages are considerable, most of them produced by research and not "channeled" information itself, nor philosophical conjecture. Many of the researchers in the field have been psychologists, psychiatrists, medical doctors, or priests with medical and/or psychological training.

I began my own experimental work in this area with a major attitude of skepticism. That was good because, as it turned out, having started as a skeptic, I was quite taken aback to discover the reality that the so-called astral planes are a veritable jungle. Even though I conducted my sessions with extreme care to avoid any possibility of contaminating my subjects, over and over again, I discovered that all was not well in the "higher" realms. It seems that there are "powers" in these realms that are most definitely *not* beneficial to humanity and do not have our best interests at heart.

That led, of course, to the question as to why so much nonsense is propagated by so-called channeled sources that are, clearly, in many instances, lying? In other cases, they are, at the very least, guilty of a serious lack of attention to crucial details. In my opinion, at this point in time, the lack of knowledge about this single issue is one of the chief reasons that it continues to build and perpetuate, increasing and amplifying the sufferings of humanity. How "good" are channeled sources that do not inform us of the truth of the "higher realms"? If anything, the so-called "New Age" movement has been so heavily inculcated with the idea that one must not ever think about negative things, that they, above all other people, are most subject to its predations. If you don't know about something, you cannot defend yourself against it. The consistent deflection from the truth of the state of the so-called higher realms by masses of published material over many years, suggested almost a program of disinformation. It was beginning to look as though there was something or someone "out there" who didn't want us to know something.

Yes, I know that this just flies in the face of most religious doctrine, and most definitely it contradicts standard "New Age" philosophies. But let me just say that, over and over again, this has been proven to be so in clinical experience of a sufficient number of trained researchers that before anyone dives into denial, they ought to give it consideration as a working hypothesis to be tested. If it's wrong, no harm can be done by having considered it. If it's right, it could save our lives.

> With limited, if any, knowledge and distorted perceptions of the nature of the spirit world, the non-physical reality, many people leave themselves open and create their own vulnerability as part of creating their own reality![10]

This remark contains within it the description of the trap into which millions upon millions of human beings have been imprisoned for millennia. I would like to point out that lack of true knowledge of the spirit worlds is, essentially, the philosophical foundation of "faith" as taught by the three major monotheistic religions, as well as the New Age religion. In other words: Faith, as understood and practiced by most human beings, is merely another word for denial, and denial constitutes living a lie, and a lie, by the definitions of those very religions involved, is "Satanic".

It is fashionable today to channel "my higher self" or "spirit teachers", to send love and light without having a specific request to do so, (thereby opening a bi-directional portal where the negative energies one is seeking to "transform" can rebound on the sender),

---

[10] William Baldwin Ph.D., *Spirit Releasement Therapy: A Technique Manual* (Human Potential Foundation).

and so forth. Without knowledge and an ability to discern, one is then subject not only to the vagaries of any passing entity who hears the call, but also to cosmic laws of which most of humanity are abysmally ignorant.

Some surround themselves with light, or pray and specify "for my highest good" in their invocations. What they do not realize is that this actually constitutes permission and invitation to any discarnate spirit who truly believes that it is acting "for your highest good" in its realm of wishful thinking and earth-bound ego fixation.

Keep in mind that we are not talking about demonic possession here. That is an entirely different kettle of fish, though it follows the same rules. We are talking about your garden variety, well-meaning dead dudes wandering in the lower astral planes due to ignorance or some sort of affinity to the Earth. As Edgar Cayce remarked: a dead Presbyterian is just that – a dead Presbyterian!

In coming face to face with all of this material and experience, I have to admit that I attempted to formulate a rationalist theory to explain it all. I could see that the jungle-like nature of the astral realms might be merely another psychological drama invented by the endlessly creative mind as a means of sorting through some current life issue. But, in the same way that I have never really cared if reincarnation was real or not, I didn't really care if the fact that there seemed to be higher level negative beings on the astral planes was real or not; I only cared that the therapeutic applications worked.

And work they did; consistently, and remarkably. One of the most amazing things about it was the consistency of the symbolic or archetypal language of the subconscious. Subject after subject, from all walks of life, with all different levels of education and intellectual development, from different religions and belief systems, all of them, when asked the same series of questions, responded with the same types of symbols relating to similar issues and relationships.

Whether they were actually discarnate beings, or some split off aspect of human personality, or energy constructions of an etheric sort, which could be detected and symbolically assigned personality and history, didn't matter to me; I knew that the mind is infinitely creative, and I was reluctant to take a hard and fast position on the subject. I continued to work with the concepts, constantly on the lookout for new data that might help me to refine, prove or disprove my theory. To remain as open as possible for new information, my working hypothesis was that it was very likely that all that existed was an artifact of consciousness; the only thing I was giving a high probability to was that consciousness could and did exist independently of matter. Consciousness could be positive or negative. Whether it was, in all cases, or even in most cases, consciously aware, I didn't know.

Part of the difficulty presented by this work with exorcism type activities, (though that is a misnomer for the procedure which amounts to "discarnate counseling"), indicated that most activity that passed for "channeling" could be immediately dispensed with as being merely the production of the so-called "astral realms", (leaving aside the issue of whether the astral realms were artifacts of consciousness). I began to wonder if there was anything truly "higher", and if so, what it was and how "high" could one really go?

This led to the formulation of the idea of the second obstruction to achieving possible high-level contact; I called it the "transducing factor". This hypothesis suggested that it was evidential that a truly higher level source simply could not make a full and secure connection with consciousness that was embodied in the physical state because it would be like trying to run a 110V appliance on 220V current. If it were a "higher" source, by definition, its energy would so overwhelm any human recipient that it could not be sustained.

Actually, I formulated this idea based on reading case histories. There were many that supported this hypothesis, and there were even examples of people who clearly had lost their minds after contact with "higher sources". Like meteorites, they flashed across the sky of our collective psychological and spiritual domains, brief illuminators of the landscape, only to crash and burn in ignoble descent. For the most part, it was clear that such efforts posed many dangers as explicated in extensive readings in ancient literature, occult writings and various Eastern mystical teachings.

There was another reason that I formulated this idea, and it was based on the observations of Nature. The one thing we observe consistently in the world around us is growth. What's more, we observe that growth occurs in cycles. Human consciousness begins to grow from the moment of conception. Whether or not this is the result of a merging of an external consciousness with a developing neurological/physical system, or whether it is merely the result of the "ghost in the machine" effect, consciousness grows. Let's take that as an observable given principle.

At the beginning of life, when there is less apparent consciousness, the being sleeps a great deal. In the prime of life, when the consciousness is most apparent and active (within wide variation which may depend on richness of consciousness), the body sleeps less.

At some point, consciousness begins to recede from the body in old age (again, with wide variation depending on unknown factors, possibly richness of consciousness), and the body again reverts to longer periods of sleep. The important thing is: we might think that this sleep and consciousness ratio is evidence of merging, emerging, and receding stages of consciousness. In other words, a "seed" consciousness is planted in a newly conceived/born human being; it grows according to the richness of the environment and the potentials of the DNA parameters that are present in the body. When it reaches optimum growth, it begins receding. The important thing to understand is that consciousness apparently recedes because it has grown to the maximum and it no longer "fits". It has achieved its fullest expression in that body, utilizing the available neurological/physical construct. We might conjecture that when this upper limit, or critical mass, has been achieved, then movement "out of the body" proceeds by stages.

This movement into the body by stages, and movement out of the body by stages suggested to me that the death process was a sort of "birth" into a "higher" or richer and denser state of being that was not sustainable by the physical construct! Had it been sustainable at a higher level, or at greater density and richness, the death process might not have been stimulated to begin at that point. That this might have something to do with genetic considerations occurred to me. Just as different plants and creatures have certain and definite genetic parameters that determine not only their configuration, function, learning potentials and life expectancy, so do individual humans, within certain ranges, have similar configurations, functions, learning potentials and life expectancy. That these potentials could relate in a symbiotic way to consciousness occurred to me as a strong possibility. In other words, consciousness can only grow to a certain limit that is determined by the genetic constraints of the body it occupies.

Thus, it seemed that it was logical to pursue this line to the conclusion that a truly "higher being", or one that has achieved great density and richness of consciousness, could not, by the very constraints of the genetic configurations of function and potential in the human body, actually enter into the human consciousness energy field and put on somebody else's body like a glove, for the purposes of direct interaction, unless it was of similar configuration and potential as the host body itself. It had grown and would no longer "fit".

The logical deduction then would be that, if a consciousness that was external was, in fact, able to enter or merge with a human being, or connect in a direct way, it could only be one that was not any more advanced than the normal consciousness potential of that human being, though without the constraints of space and time. This last consideration might give a different perspective to such a consciousness, but that didn't attest to its advancement in philosophical or spiritual terms.

In other words, a dead Presbyterian is just that: a dead Presbyterian. If the consciousness can use your body, it can't be much different from your own.

I noted in going through the literature on channeling and spirit mediumship that there were certain very interesting cases where it could be thought that the "possessing entity", (because, despite claims to the contrary, trance channeling *is* possession), was, at the very least, a consciousness a small order of magnitude more dense and rich than the medium him or herself who may or may not have achieved their consciousness/genetic potential. The curious thing about such cases was that there seemed to be a direct relationship between such potentials and body mass. In other words, mediums who seemed to be capable of making limited connection to seemingly higher (though only slightly) beings, were rather large. Not only that, but when subjected to scientific controls and measurements, as some of them were in the 19th and early 20th century, it was learned that such mediums could lose up to 15 pounds of body mass in an hour or two of such contact. Eusapia Palladino[11] is a case in point.

Considering such things made me think, naturally, of the very ancient Goddess images found all over the world, where She is nearly always represented as a very fat woman! Well, I was definitely a qualified applicant for the job! The only thing was, I was not at all satisfied with the levels of contact achieved even in those cases described above.

There were also stories of yogis and shamans who, in states of meditation or shamanic ecstasy where they claimed to have made some sort of "cosmic connection", lost incredible amounts of weight due to the "heat of the state". That this was a heat that did not necessarily register on a thermometer was clear, but heat of a certain

---

[11] Eusapia Palladino (1854-1918) was an Italian medium, well-known for her séances.

kind was definitely present in these cases, as well as significant fluctuation in body mass.

This led me to the idea that, in terms of channeling truly higher beings, the mode itself presented significant problems. Relative to the theorized "high voltage" of such higher sources, I proposed that the only way to make such a contact was to combine the energies of two or more people as a "receiver", and then to attempt to "tune" the receiver with repeated acts of intent.

As I puzzled over the problem, I realized that the only real way to combine energies as a human biocosmic receiver was to use some form of communication that required more than one person and which also provided an immediate feedback checking mechanism. The obvious answer was a board type instrument.

Well, in my younger days I most definitely had experienced modest success "playing" with such an instrument, though I had given it up as possibly "dangerous" or just merely childish. It was slow, tedious, and I wasn't exactly sure of the source of the replies, never mind how accurate they were. Nevertheless, now I was looking at it in a different way and considering the possibilities that it was a potential means of coordinating focus and intent as well as proximity of energetic biopsychic fields, with the added feedback loop for "tuning". I knew that I needed to research it to discover if, theoretically, it would suit the purpose.

There are two main theories about how the Ouija board is supposed to work. The first is called "automatism". Automatism is also supposed to be the means by which dowsing, pendulums, table tipping, automatic writing and other movement of physical objects by purported spiritual forces is supposed to take place. What this means is that the participants may not realize that they are responsible for the movements of the indicator, but they are still doing it themselves. Conscious or unconscious expectations can signal nerves to fire thereby causing tiny, imperceptible motions of the fingers which produce the "answers". In this theory, the use of the "talking" board is similar to theories of automatic writing which claim that such messages originate in the conscious or unconscious mind of the medium. Defined within this context, the talking board is merely a bypass of the conscious mind, and a shortcut between the unconscious mind and the neuromuscular control system. "Collective automatism" occurs when more than one person is operating the board.

So we see that, psychologically speaking, automatism allows the subconscious mind temporary control of some part of the body without the interference of the conscious mind. At the same time, it leaves the conscious mind conscious for checking the feedback, monitoring the activity, and basically balancing the effort within the controls of experimental protocols.

Some "experts" claim that having a healthy unconscious mind is the key to protection since opening such a door without due care could most certainly trigger psychosis in certain individuals. I have a slightly different view. I don't think that bypassing the conscious mind in this way can "trigger" psychosis. What I do think is that it can open a door to reveal psychosis that already exists within the mind and which, if careful analysis is undertaken, will be seen to have been present all along, manifesting in many symptoms of the body and life of the individual.

The issue of whether or not using a board, or any other type of unconscious accessing tool can "invite" possession is rather like asking which comes first, the chicken or the egg? Dr. Baldwin brings this issue up in an interesting way. Even though he has reasonably assessed so many other things, on this issue, he demonstrates that he, too, has fallen under the spell of the movie *The Exorcist*, and draws illogical conclusions. The evidence, as Baldwin describes it himself, tells us that the state of "possession" probably already exists in any given individual and the use of the conscious bypass only allows it to "speak" and reveal itself. But that presents its own set of problems. Obviously, anyone who is not trained in the techniques of Spirit Release should never open such a door. By the same token, based on reasonable assessment of the situation, an individual who has no knowledge of these techniques, who has not spent a considerable period of time learning about them and working with them, ought never to attempt to channel either in any context! To do so is to invite disaster. And that, of course, brings up the obvious question as to why "channeling" has become such a popular sport?

The Spiritualist Theory, of course, declares that the messages that may come clearly originate from "outside". Spirits or forces are contacted and channeled through the board. The Spiritualist Theory posits that the communicants are discarnate spirits or other ethereal beings who have a purpose for contacting the living. Nevertheless, even the Spiritualist Theory depends upon the theory of automatism for actual operation. The discarnate spirit is able to connect to the operator via the subconscious or unconscious mind and take control of the ideomotor responses, bypassing the conscious mind, and generating movement of the planchette via stimulation of nerve impulses. Naturally, this theory posits that, as soon as the communication has ended, the spirit leaves, and all is well and good. The evidence, however, indicates that if certain knowledge is not available, and certain actions are not taken, the spirit does not leave! It merely withdraws into the "interstitial" spaces of the energy field of the host and becomes quiescent, continuing to drain life force for its own sustenance.

One of the more interesting theories I came across was developed by Barbara Honegger who was said to be the first person in the United States to obtain an advanced degree in experimental parapsychology. Honegger suggested that automatism was the result of "stimulation" of the right hemisphere of the brain so that it could overcome the suppression of the left hemisphere. It was never entirely clear what was doing the stimulating, however, and I could obtain no further information on her research.

The Chinese seem to have been the first to use Spiritual Automatism in the form of a "writing planchette". The Chinese device was called a chi, and it was a sort of divining or dowsing rod used to write. It was said that the spirits came down into it, moving it, and the object of the activity was to use it to spell out the gods' messages on paper or in sand.

It seems that all "primitive" or preliterate cultures had some form of codified communication between spirits and the living. This phenomenon seems to be universal in the ancient world, and only came under condemnation with the inception of monotheism around 1000 BC. When Yahweh spoke through his channels, they were called prophets and the activity was "divine inspiration". When anybody else did it, it was necromancy or demonic possession, or even just out and out deception. This was because, obviously, since Jehovah/Yahweh was the only god, those other "gods" did not exist; therefore, anyone who claimed to be channeling them was lying. Of course that begs the question as to why people were put to death for lying about communicating with gods that were claimed not to exist. And, if they did actually exist, and were actually communicating, as Yahweh was also, then what status does that suggest about Yahweh, since he was the one who claimed to be the only god and that this was true simply because Yahweh said so via channeling? Most curious.

In the sixth century BC the Thracian Dionysiac cults were known to be using shamans as trance channels to communicate with the spirits, or what were then known as *theoi* or gods: discarnate immortal beings with superhuman powers. Some scholars suggest that rationalist philosophy was born out of the Dionysiac, Orphic, and Eleusinian mystery cults devoted to the channeling of these gods; certainly much ancient Greek philosophy, especially that of Pythagoras, Heraclitus, and Plato, was saturated with these mysteries.

This brings up the question, of course, as to how "channeled" information could have been the basis of the Rationalist philosophy that there was nothing to channel? Could it be merely a progression of the idea of Yahweh/Jehovah that there was only one god, and he was it? Just another step in stripping away any spiritual support from the lives of human beings?

In Plato's *Theagetes* Socrates confesses, "By the favor of the Gods, I have since my childhood been attended by a semi-divine being whose voice from time to time dissuades me from some undertaking, but never directs me what I am to do."

The Greek oracles at Dodona and Delphi and other sites would prophesy by sinking into a trance during which they were possessed by discarnate spirits; some of the famous ones by a single spirit, or what we would today call a "spirit-guide". Oracles often lived in caves and thought of the spirits they channeled as coming up to them from the underworld through fissures in the rock.

The most interesting item of all is the fact that Pythagoras used something like a Ouija board as early as 540 BC: a "mystic table" on wheels moved around and pointed toward signs that were then interpreted by the philosopher himself, or his pupil Philolaus. Even down to the present day, the mysteries of the Pythagoreans are subjects of intense interest to scientists and mystics alike. And here there seems to be evidence that the advanced knowledge of Pythagoras may have been inspired by a Ouija board!

By the time the Romans had conquered Greece, the rationalist movement was turning against spirit-channeling. Cicero, the Roman rationalist whom the early Church Fathers highly revered, railed against spirit-channeling or necromancy on the grounds that it involved ghastly pagan rituals. But, as noted above, eventually, rationalism bit the hand that fed it and began to devour its father, monotheism, by further extending the argument to the idea that there is no god, there are no spirits, nothing survives the death of the physical body, therefore there is really nobody for us to talk to on the "other side", so why bother? Science took the view that the whole thing was a con game, and that's pretty much the current mainstream scientific opinion of the phenomenon today.

After working with spirit attachment issues, I had a lot of questions. As I have already said, there was an open possibility in my mind that such "spirits" were merely fragments of the personality of an individual, sort of like little broken off circuits in the brain running in repetitive loops, created by trauma or stress. Perhaps an individual, when faced with a difficulty, entered a narcissistic state of fantasy, created a "dream", which was imprinted in the memory of the brain. If they then emerged from this state back into dealing with their reality, but not having dealt with the issue itself, it might become locked away in a sort of cerebral file drawer, sitting there, waiting to be triggered by the electricity or neurochemicals of the brain in some random unconscious scan. The same could be said for so-called past life memories; they were merely self-created memory files generated in a state of narcissistic withdrawal due to stress. Such neurological files could then be downloaded and read by using the conscious bypass method of either automatism or simply allowing the conscious mind to "step aside" as in trance channeling. For that matter, simple psychotherapy could be considered channeling in these terms. Conscious channeling is more problematic because it suggests a definite pathological condition in which spirit attachment or multiple personality may play a part. In such cases, the "alter" ego, as either an alternate personality or an actual attached entity, is strong and well entrenched enough to establish a far stronger hold on the body of the host than those which can only manifest via automatism or trance.

Professor Douglas Robinson at Ole Miss (The University of Mississippi) suggests that an analogy can be drawn between the function of a translator and the channel or medium. It is their purpose to step aside and allow the original author of a work in another language to speak through them. It is their profession to convey the fullest intention of the original author to a new audience that otherwise, not knowing the language would not have access to the material. In the ordinary sense, translation is done merely across linguistic or cultural barriers. In the sense of channeling, it is done across temporal, consciousness, or even hyperspatial barriers.

The crucial thing about both translating and channeling is the necessity for the mediator to not convey to the target audience his or her own ideas, meanings, arguments, or images. The translator must be a neutral conduit to the target audience of the ideas and meanings of the original author.

> The analogy suggests both (a) that the source author has the power to initiate communication with the target audience through the translator (the author is active, the translator is passive, or at the very most active only in the act of surrendering his/her activity to that of the author), and (b) that the translator possesses some means of gaining access to the author's voice and meaning, of reliably "opening up" to the intentional speaking of a person who is almost invariably other. Sometimes translators translate source texts they wrote themselves, but usually the source author is another person, most often distant in time and place, and not infrequently dead.[12]

In the present day, under the influence of rationalist Western technology, the idea that anyone can just sit down and begin to channel is very similar to the idea that translation can be done by machines with no human interface. This is a very subtle point. In terms of a computer program that translates from one language to another, and most channels, we see that the program attempts to execute an algorithm, or series of algorithms that consist of gathering intelligence, charting a course of action, giving a series of commands, and carrying them out. The results are only as good as the algorithms. And we see, from the literature, that the "channeling phenomenon" as it is widely practiced, omits reason from the algorithm. There is no feedback mechanism, and thus no possibility of accurate tuning. This means that it does not allow for an algorithm that can handle the fact that there may be competing forces inside the channel's head. Excluding reason and the possibility of competing forces results in the algorithm: "I am the Lord your God and there is no other because I said so! And if you don't believe me, then it will be all the worse for you!" Not very productive, to say the least.

The fact is, machine translation researchers despair of ever programming a machine to produce a translation of professionally usable quality without human assistance. In the same way, it is likely impossible to produce channeled material of any usable quality without full consideration for the competing forces as well as the application of Reason in dealing with them. Without application of knowledge and direct, rapid feedback, there is little possibility that anything other than useless psychobabble will emerge. And such seems to be the case. But of course, that excludes the narcissistic delusionals, the deliberate frauds, and the pathological cases of multiple personality. They are all out there in New Age Land, and it's a jungle!

---

[12] Professor Robinson's webpage. http://home.olemiss.edu/~djr/index.html

In the end, those machine translation systems that do work are, effectively, cyborg translation systems: they all require a human-machine interface.

In science fiction movies, we often see a "machine translator" that enables the space traveler to just plug himself into a gadget via some brain electrode, and open his mouth and automatically speak in the language of the planet he is visiting. The words may start out in his brain in his own language, but by the time the come out of his mouth, the machine has altered the nerve impulses to the organs of speech causing them to produce correct words in the unknown tongue. Apparently, the machine also works in reverse, and the space traveler may hear words spoken in the unknown language, but he "experiences" them in his own. What is interesting to me is the fact that it is a prosthetic device that turns the space traveler into a sort of cyborg translator who becomes able to "channel" foreign speech.

The point I am trying to make in this funny "reverse analogy" is that by the use of prosthetics, we are in a position to employ an algorithm that includes reason and feedback! Reason, when properly employed, posits an entire army of what Adam Smith called "invisible hands", which shape, direct, regulate, and control translation. And that leads us to the most interesting conclusion that reason, itself, can be an "invisible hand".

"Reason is an internalized form of ideological mastery". Just as the spirit seizes or possesses the channel and speaks – or otherwise operates through the channel's willing body – in the same way a text in a foreign language is fed into a computer to be translated, (often quite ineptly), so too does ideology and its agents – including reason – seize or possess the ideological subject and wield that subject's body as virtually its own. And in this sense, we discover that the channel, as a "translation machine", can become something far more interesting.

An individual who, via long and intensive study, comes to the idea that there is a possibility of communicating with higher consciousnesses, formulates a hypothesis of how to do it, and then experiments with that hypothesis, adjusting and modifying throughout the process, is, in a sense, being guided by invisible hands, or forces of the cosmos. But it is clearly a source of some greater complexity and deep need to communicate complex and new concepts that prepares such a translator. In terms of ordinary lower level channeling, we find that the spirits of such activities "hail" the channel through whom he or she wishes to speak by appearing before the clairvoyant; or welling up like verbal pressure inside the head begging to be released for the clairaudient. Sometimes the channel falls into unconsciousness and wakes up to find that something or somebody else had been using their organs of speech.

In the same way does the Cosmos at Large, via Reason and Knowledge and a questing spirit planted in a human form "hail" a potential channel/translator of truly higher realities. The words "translate", "transfer" and "transduce" all have the same Latin root. And it is in the role of translator that we discover that just "plugging in and turning on the machine" is not enough.

Translators must be trained; they must not only know the other language, they must know how to regulate the degree of fidelity with the source text, how to tell what degree and type of fidelity is appropriate in specific use contexts, how to receive and deliver translations, how to find help with terminology, and so on. All of this suggests a long period of training and preparation.

A translator-channel is someone who has studied these things, who knows these things, and who, most importantly, governs their channeling-translating behavior in terms of this knowledge. This knowledge is ideological. It is controlled by Cosmic ideological norms. To know, via reason, what those Cosmic norms prescribe and act upon them is to submit to control by them. To become a translator-channel of truly Higher Cosmic Consciousness is to be hailed as a translator by "invisible hand" of the Universe.

If you want to become a translator-channel, you must submit to the translator's role of learning the language in an expert way; you must submit to being directed by what the Cosmic ideological norms inform you is the true spirit of the source author, and to channel that spirit unchanged into the target language.

Thus it was, with all of these considerations in mind, I finally settled on the board type instrument as being the best mode of dealing with the issues. It is a prosthetic device that allows constant feedback between the algorithm of "machine translation" of the subconscious/ unconscious, and the human interface of the conscious mind which must constantly employ reason for "tuning". This is possible only with a board due to the fact that the "channel" is using both the conscious bypass for reception, while at the same time is able to maintain constant conscious integrity. By being, at all times, in full possession of their own mind and having the ability to observe, control and direct acceptance or rejection of any material or sensation at any time, reason is brought in as part of the algorithm. In other words, used correctly, by an individual who is knowledgeable in the subjects under discussion, as well as the clinically demonstrated realities of "other realms", this is one of the finest tools available for developing contact with the subconscious, the higher self, and/or benevolent entities which wish to make telepathic contact. And that is the key word: telepathic. This type of device allows one to create a "separate line", so to speak, a "switchboard" where a new circuit is established through a minute thread of consciousness without giving up control in anyway.

Due to the influence of the movie *The Exorcist*, the device has acquired a negative reputation. Yet, this was not always the case! Funny how an entire "doctrine" can be created by Hollywood which people then accept is as gospel.

Some so-called "experts" will claim that being a "medium" is okay, but that using a board or automatic writing as a medium or even "trance channeling" can only bring in "lower level" entities. They base this wholly illogical statement on the claim that "no spirit of an advanced degree of spirituality, no ascended master or guardian spirit, would ever stoop to abusing the writing or speaking talents of another person, living or dead". Let me get this straight: it's okay to do any of the above as long as you call yourself a "medium". If you call yourself a "channel", or if you establish protocols whereby you are in constant, conscious control, you are, by definition, only in contact with "lower level entities?" Most peculiar; also most abysmally ignorant.

Contrary to the above "expert" opinion, one part of my hypothesis, based on years of research, was that sustained contact with true higher-level sources had rarely, if ever, occurred in the entire history of channeling! At least not the type of sources I theorized to exist at truly higher levels of existence. Thus, no one really "knew the language". It was absurd to think that one could just sit down, from their present human condition, download and translate something that, evidentially, had almost never been encountered before.

At this point in time, I hypothesized that the "Universe at Large", or the "source" I wished to contact, did, in fact, have the power to initiate communication with the target audience – humanity – because it was evident, through all the experiences of my life up to that point, that the universe speaks to us via the events of our lives. The many remarkable synchronicities in evidence, as well as close observation of the dynamics of my life itself, as well as the lives of other people I had observed, could only be interpreted as deliberate actions from some ultra cosmic reality attempting to teach me the language of symbols. I felt that I had, most definitely, been "hailed" by the Universe which was asking me to undertake the task of learning the language and acting as translator-channel. Whether or not a more direct mode of communication could be established via myself as such a Translator, I was not entirely certain. But I was most definitely anxious to make the attempt to gain access to the Voice of the Universe by "hailing" back via a long process of building a circuit into and possibly even through, the deep unconscious mind.

Since it was clear that these interactions involved some level of being of which most of us are unaware, and to which we have little access, I realized that this amounted to the fact that I had to "learn the language" at some as-yet unknown level of my being. Not only was I proposing to learn this language that had never before been systematically studied, I knew that I had to learn how to "regulate the degree of fidelity with the source text, how to tell what degree and type of fidelity is appropriate in specific use contexts, how to receive and deliver translations, how to find help with terminology, and so on". This was the reasoning, or "ideological state apparatus" I was setting up as the protocol for the return "signal".

Reading through the literature on channeling, it was evident that the most respected and trustworthy material in the history of channeling had either come through a board type instrument, or had been initiated by a board type instrument. That it was a means of learning a new language in some internal place in the mind, like plugging in a translation matrix device, was evident. With the added information at my disposal regarding spirit attachment, multiple personality disorder and other pathological conditions, as well as the means of dealing with them effectively, I realized that, if I was correct in my hypothesis, I could possibly take channeling to a level never before achieved – or at least, only very rarely – maybe once every thousand years or so.

Of course, it all depended on a long period of "training" and applying the algorithm. And this meant a possibly very long period of using a board type instrument to "channel" not only one's own subconscious fragments through their series of dramas, but possibly an endless number of frequency related discarnates before all the "loops" had been played out and dealt with and brain synchrony was achieved.

In the end, I decided that even if that was all that we accomplished in the process, it was still a worthwhile activity. Purifying the mind by healing its fragments in whatever terms they manifest could only be good! The important thing I realized was to not give up using the board too soon. That would be like assuming one had a good mastery of a language just because one could use it for everyday purposes. To be a true translator, one must master a new language at the most subtle and refined levels imaginable.

At this point, I thought I had a pretty good theory, and it was time to put it into the test phase; so, we began. Frank and I met every week to sit and "Hail the Universe". I have notebooks which record every motion of the planchette for over two years. In the end, this material does, indeed, support my theory. We waded through endless loops of the unconscious mind, endless purported "discarnate" entities or past life scenarios; endless lost souls wandering in the astral realms seeking release into the light. At one point I realized that if any of this material had any factual basis, the board was an excellent tool for effecting spirit release, contrary to the opinions of Dr. Baldwin.

As our experiment in channeling proceeded, we discussed the many possible ways that a "true higher source" might be identified. We both thought that a higher source, by virtue of greater and more inclusive Cosmic Perspective, would be able to make absolutely stunning "predictions" that would "hit the mark" every time. The problem was, in a short term feedback loop of testing, how to validate such a hypothesis?

Frank came up with a solution: Lottery. Well, that seemed reasonable enough. We could ask for a lotto prediction from every entity, then "grade" them based on their ability to predict. Since there were daily games, we concentrated on these.

Now, while I have been known to buy a lotto ticket or two based on a dream or just an impulse, and to win when I do, I have never been a real gambler. If I had the money to buy a soft drink and, instead, decided to give up the drink in favor of a lottery ticket, I felt that this was no more than I would spend on junk food or a movie, and for me that was all it was: entertainment. If I won, it was fun; if I didn't, I hadn't lost any more than I would have wasted otherwise. I never considered buying a lottery ticket as a way of getting out of any financial difficulty. If I was in a situation where I could not justify buying even a candy bar because money was that tight, I didn't buy a lottery ticket either.

For me, the "lotto test" was theoretical. I wasn't going out and buying tickets, but I discovered that Frank was. Not only that, he seemed particularly devoted to this aspect of the experiment. Doing it as a test was one thing, but doing it with intent to profit was somewhat disturbing to me.

In actual fact, we did have a few hits in that regard. They usually came up on a different day than predicted, sometimes even as long as several weeks after they were given. Frank claimed to have made money this way, but I reminded him that his overall expenditure on tickets ought to be deducted from his winnings to get a real picture.

But "testing" by getting lotto numbers was only part of what we were doing. We were also "chatting" with the various entities that came and went by, asking for details of their alleged lives and experiences, trying to get checkable data. In the end, Frank and I and other participants in the experiment were quite fascinated with the parade passing before us, and we joked that it was better than going to the movies, watching television, or going to parties. In full consciousness, we could peer into endless realms of otherworldly activity – dramas of tragedy and hope, despair and joy – and do it all while drinking coffee, eating cookies, and taking time out to chat. But what was really going on at other levels of being would prove to be more fascinating and mysterious than anything I had hypothesized.

***

In February of 1993, I became ill and was again bedridden. After I began to recover, I called Frank and asked him to please bring me something interesting to read. Frank arrived with a big grocery sack full of UFO and Alien Abduction books!

I was furious!

"Frank, I am *not* going to read them so you just take them back!"

He set the bag down. "In case you change your mind, I'll just leave them anyway". He gave me an impish grin.

"I assure you that I am not that desperate!"

"Suit yourself", said Frank, and left me with the bag of lurid paperbacks.

After awhile, the boredom became pretty severe.

I reached into the bag and pulled out a book. Hmm. *Missing Time*, by Budd Hopkins. I was pretty amazed as I read. While the writing style left much to be desired, and the focus on hard facts was a bit sketchy, this was not the fluffy entertainment of Ruth Montgomery or the Gothic Existential Angst of Whitley Strieber. It was actually an attempt at "serious research!" I was surprised.

More disturbing to me, however, was the fact that I recognized many events that I'd shoved under the rug in my own life, clearly evident in the lives of the people interviewed for this book. They had reached a point of exploring these anomalies and talking about them and retrieving memories under hypnosis.

After some consideration, however, I brushed their "alien abduction" explanations away. I could think of a dozen other solutions. Besides, it was too soon to draw conclusions – I needed more data.

I read on. Book after book. *The Interrupted Journey. The Andreasson Affair. The Alien Agenda.*

With some amusement, I realized that there were people claiming Earth had been being visited by aliens since archaic times. There were others who claimed we had been visited a few times, but they were gone now, nothing to worry about! Another group claimed that we had "let them in" by setting off the atomic bomb; they were here to make sure we didn't blow ourselves up along with the rest of the universe. Some claimed they were good guys who were just a little weird because they had followed a different path of evolution, or were further along than we were. Others claimed they were demons from Hell, and we had better get ourselves back to church if we expected to survive the invasion.

Sheesh! The only thing certain was that people were seeing and experiencing something singularly strange. Secret government projects? Secret aliens-in-cahoots-with-the-government? By the time I finished I was sure of one thing and one thing only: there was a *lot* of smoke! Was there a fire? It was hard to tell if the whole alien abduction thing was a "manipulation" by the government to make people think aliens existed, or if aliens did exist and were trying to make the government look guilty and stupid.

What a morass of confusion!

Not to be intimidated by unexplained phenomena of any sort, I started working on a new theory to explain the UFO/alien abduction phenomenon. There was little in these stories that could not be explained by mass hallucination and hysteria, psycho-kinesis, stigmata, repressed memories of physical or sexual abuse, psychosis, schizophrenia – heck, just a whole cornucopia of tricks of the mind to choose from!

I worked on the problem, discussed it with Frank, and demonstrated how every event in every case he cited could be explained by some aspect of my new rationalist theory of UFOs. He was practically foaming at the mouth in frustration with my stubborn refusal to see anything other than what could be classified, categorized, and explained by any number of currently established scientific perspectives, even if some of them were a little far to the left of "normal". I was actually pretty proud of my fiendishly clever solution! Pride goes before a fall, you know. This was in March of 1993.

Not long after I had been released from my sickbed and the inundation of UFO books, I went to the supermarket one morning, and saw a stack of pink flyers with "flea-market" type ads just inside the door. I was looking for some additional computer equipment, so I picked one up and tucked it in my pocket. When I got home, I read over it and noted an ad for exactly what I wanted.

I called the number and talked to the woman named Patricia. We began to chat about computers and she asked, conversationally, what programs I used. I mentioned my astrology programs, which piqued her interest. This led to more questions which led to more answers, including some remarks about my work in hypnotherapy. As often happens, one thing led to another, and after an hour or so on the telephone, Pat asked to meet me so that she could consider scheduling a hypnosis session. It seems that there was something really strange that had happened to her back in 1987, and it *still* bothered her and she wanted to know why, or at least get relief from the internal anxiety it had caused.

The story was that she had been to the funeral of an aunt, accompanied by her 16-year-old son, and they were returning home to Maryland, driving on the Pennsylvania Turnpike. It began to snow, and she saw a very bright light ahead, off to the side of the road, sort of bluish white, and she thought that it was a light that had come on to illuminate a billboard since the snow had made things a bit dark. She then said that what happened next was so strange that, even in remembering it, she felt strange and uneasy. She said that she felt a paralysis come over her hands and arms as though someone had taken control of the car.

Having just read a grocery sack full of books on UFOs and "missing time" and all that, I immediately recognized the purported prodromal signs of a "missing time" experience as described by Budd Hopkins. It was rather creepy to be having this conversation right after having read those books. I managed to stay cool, however, and I casually asked, "what happened next?"

Pat said that this was the crazy part because she couldn't remember! After seeing the light and feeling the paralysis, the next thing she remembered was sitting at a traffic light 50 or 60 miles down the road. She did not remember making the turn off the main highway, and her son had just cut his finger on a tin of cookies he was trying to open. He was bleeding, and she "came to herself" saying, "there's a towel in the back seat". To further add to her dismay, she arrived home much later than she should have, but, at the same time, still had an almost full tank of gas.

She was sure that it had been her aunt attempting to contact her psychically, and she really needed to have an answer. What had her aunt been trying to tell her?

Well, the fact that she made no mention or claim about aliens made the whole thing far more interesting to me because if she had claimed to have been abducted by little green men, I would have ended the conversation. Of course, I did not want to even suggest anything about "aliens", because I wanted to try to prove my theory about alien abductions being "psycho-dramas" in the same manner as past lives. I just told Pat that we could certainly clear the problem up quickly with hypnosis! She made an appointment.

It was the night of Thursday, April 15, 1993. At the time of the appointment (Pat was caring for an ill husband and needed to come at a time when her kids would be home to look after his needs), it began to storm terribly. I was sure she would not come out in such rain and expected a cancellation; but surprisingly, she showed up.

We went through the normal pre-session interview, and then talked a bit about the event again. I wanted to get the times and details down about her general life situation, so I would have clues about areas of possible family conflicts that might be at the root of such a drama.

Pat was a real estate agent and also owned a medical reports business working under government contract to transcribe social security records. She talked a bit about her children and her disabled husband, who was dying. I was sure the stress of caring for him was an exacerbation of her problems.

Nothing was said about "aliens" at any point whatsoever. I carefully inquired about her interests. She had never been interested in metaphysics, much less aliens. She was a formerly devout Catholic who was now in a state of doubt about her religion. She was sure that I was not going to be able to hypnotize her. I decided to make a videotape of this session rather than the usual audiotape. I wanted a record of my "proof" that the "alien abduction phenomenon" had another explanation!

She was a good subject and quickly went under.

I instructed Pat to go back to the time when she was driving the route of their return from the funeral. It was snowing so hard that they turned onto another highway, trying to find better driving conditions. She described seeing the light in front of what she thought was a billboard. She described it as iridescent blue, a pale oval of baby blue, and the oval is hanging there in front of the billboard. It made no sense to her, and she began to rub her eyes – firmly in the memory – saying that she must be imagining it.

But, the light wouldn't go away and, still fully in the memory, she asked her son if he could see it. He couldn't, and she was confused even more. What was more, as she continued to describe it, the light just kept getting bigger.

At this point, Pat was alarmed because she felt something taking over the control of the car. She claimed that she wasn't driving anymore, something was driving the car, and the light was getting bigger.

Then the skip. All the drama and build-up to some dramatic climax just ends and she said, "I wish that damn light would change."

"What?" I asked.

"I'm just waiting for the light to turn green", she said. At this point, her voice became panicked. "Oh my God, Patrick! What did you do?"

It was clear that something was going on in her memory. Something was wrong.

"Oh my God, Patrick!" the woman was saying. "What did you do? There's a towel in the back seat. Get it."

I reassured Pat that everything was alright, and asked her to explain to me what was happening. She told me that she was sitting at a traffic light in a small town waiting for the light to change, and her son had been trying to open a tin of cookies someone gave them after the funeral. He couldn't open them, and she told him to get the penknife out of the glove compartment. Somehow he managed to cut his hand, and she was panicked by the copious amounts of blood. So, there they are, sitting at a traffic light all of a sudden, and Patrick's hand is bleeding – a lot.

Pat was agitated and upset all out of proportion to what was happening. Something was upsetting her, and not just the cut on her son's hand. She was breathing very fast and had raised her arms to her chest and crossed them, as though she was trying to protect herself. I reassured her that she and her son were safe.

I realized that we needed to understand how she skipped from the approach to the blue light to a little town fifty miles down the road. I asked her about this, and she was distressed to not know how she suddenly arrived at this traffic light. How did she travel 50 miles without being aware of it? What happened to the blue light?

I stopped her, and suggested that we start over again. I directed her to go back to the beginning, back to the turnpike, and start over. "Let's go through it again, a little more slowly this time", I said.

But it was futile. Every time we went through it, it skipped from the approach toward the blue light, and skipped to the traffic light 50 miles down the road, and her son was opening the tin of cookies with the knife and cutting his hand.

I was pretty determined to find out what happened during those 50 miles.

Frank was pretty excited and kept whispering to me that this was a "real alien abduction". I was just as insistent that "real abductions" might be something other than aliens. Indeed, I was open to a lot of ideas, but for some reason, I had drawn the line at aliens.

Since I considered it a real possibility that such scenarios were symbols of some sort of psychological drama, I decided to take my subject even deeper, for another replay. I planned to use my "secret weapon" for getting in the back door of the subconscious.

Well, it worked – partly. This time Pat managed to remember a parking lot. She could see the blue light growing, and she could feel the car leaving the highway. She described how she and her son stopped in the parking lot of a closed diner, just off the road, not far from the "billboard" from which the light emanated.

"What happened next?" I asked.

"I wish that damn light would change", said the woman.

Another skip, back to the traffic light 50 miles away. To say that I was surprised is putting it mildly. Whatever it was, it had something to do with an event somewhere between the parking lot and the traffic light: from a blue light to a red light.

I tried again. I spent a few minutes deepening the trance even more. I also decided to take Pat out of the event and have her view it at a remove, on a screen. In cases of very traumatic events, this often works to get a description of what happened, and then later, the emotional trauma can be dealt with. I asked her to see herself in a safe place, inside a room, sitting in a recliner, resting peacefully, and in front of her was a television on which she could view the events from that night without emotional attachment. I then told her to visualize a TV remote control in her hand with which she could control the "movie" on the television. She could fast forward, rewind, turn it off; whatever she needed to do to feel safe and in control. I asked her to go to the beginning of the story again, and push the "play button" and describe what she saw.

She was back on the highway driving through the snow. Along came the billboard and the light. I instructed her to use the remote and slow the action down, use the button that will advance the action one frame at a time.

She saw the blue light in front of the billboard. She saw it growing. She felt some force taking control of the car. She felt the car leaving the road, turning into the parking lot while she was fighting the wheel. The car parked itself, and they were sitting there in the car, in the parking lot, outside the closed diner. They didn't know why; they were waiting for something; someone was approaching the car.

I asked her to describe who it was.

"I can't", she said. She was twisting and fluttering her hands in agitation again. She began to hyperventilate. Her arms were twitching and jerking. She was rubbing them frantically with her hands as though she were in pain.

"What do you mean, you can't?" I asked.

"Because *THEY* won't let me". The word "they" was pronounced with such terror that a chill ran up my spine.

"What do you mean? Who is it stopping you from seeing, from speaking, from remembering? Who is they?" I asked, hoping she would blurt it out before the skip came again.

She just shook her head mournfully.

"I can't tell", she said. "I can't."

If ever there was proof that a hypnotherapist with a pre-formed belief cannot influence the recall of a subject, this case is a classic in that regard! I am ashamed to admit my assumptions now, and I freely admit that it may not have been the proper approach to the problem, but then again, the subject was not claiming to have been abducted by aliens – at least not consciously. What's more, I *was* very careful not to "lead" in any way, so the "experiment" was, essentially, uncontaminated.

To say that I was puzzled and frustrated is an understatement. I had never encountered a blocked memory that I could not find some way to access. This was one of my specialties. I could find the "back door" of the mind, ease the pain, and get to the root of the problem. With Pat, try as I would, nothing worked! She repeated, "I can't! I can't!" In frustration I asked, "Why?" and her answer had raised the hair on the back of my neck and chilled me to the bone: "Because *THEY* won't let me!"

For a few moments I was completely nonplussed. I had never encountered a "They" who could so effectively block memory and cause pain and suffering when attempts were made to access it. I quickly theorized that I was dealing with a deeply repressed trauma. I wanted to believe that it related to something in childhood, or perhaps even a past life, but I couldn't shake the eerie sensation that washed over me when she cried "THEY won't let me!"

I knew that I could not lose the professional "control", and I decided that it was not wise to push any further at this moment. Sometimes a subject must be "conditioned" over time. So I started the suggestions that would make her feel good, make her like hypnosis, make her want to do it again, and help her to go into a trance more easily in the future so that a deeper state could be achieved and we could "deal" with this thing. Then, I brought her out.

We discussed a future appointment and she agreed that she would like to try again and that was that, except for the fact that she called and cancelled on the day of the next appointment.

In considering the implications of this session, there were just too many unknowns, too many things that didn't make sense. What could happen on the side of a snowy highway that could be so dreadfully traumatic that it induced pain to even approach it? I could think of no scenario whatsoever that was so bad that it would not be remembered with emotional distance techniques in place. Even if the subject had just turned off the highway to rest, and a gang of psychopaths had grabbed them and forced them to participate in some bizarre Satanic ritual, that didn't compute because it could not explain why, against all laws of probability, they would let them go on their journey with only a cut hand. Was Frank right? Had this woman and her son been abducted by aliens? Did they have some technology that could implant a "pain block" to memory of the event?

That was just too far-fetched. I didn't buy it. There had to be something else, but what it was I simply could *not* imagine.

In the following weeks, a series of events occurred that really upset my self-assurance that all of this was just psychological suppression of ordinary human trauma. The newspapers and TV news shows began reporting multiple sightings of UFOs in the area. From the middle of April until the end of the month, more than a dozen people in Pasco, Hernando and Pinellas counties in Florida claimed to have seen a large, boomerang-shaped craft moving across the sky. The witnesses included a Hernando County sheriff's deputy, who said the craft carried no markings, had a row of blue lights and he estimated the wingspan at around 200 feet. He had observed it for several minutes before it accelerated to a speed that was impossible for any man-made craft.

Something about these stories bugged me. After the whole affair died down, I assembled the reports in chronological order, since some people gave their reports only after seeing that someone else had done so before them, and the order of the reports in the news was not the order of the sightings. I realized that the very first sighting of the black boomerang shaped objects had had been made by a person who lived only a few blocks away from my home on the evening of Thursday, April 15, at the exact time I was conducting my hypnosis session with the woman who lost 50 miles between the blue light and the red light. What was even more upsetting was that the witness's description seemed to place the black boomerang hovering directly over my neighborhood, maybe even right over my house.

The reports of the black boomerangs that came in conjunction with this session did not make me happy. In fact, it gave me the absolute creeps!

It also made me think.

If we conjecture that this "alien phenomenon" is part of some deep government conspiracy designed to experiment on people – perhaps to make them think that they are being abducted by aliens so that they will assiduously seek greater controls and protection from "Big Brother" – we have a curious problem with this case. The problem becomes: how could such a hypothesized group engineer the response to this session that did, in fact, manifest?

I was very careful not to mention the word "alien" or "abduction" to the woman on the phone prior to the session. If phone conversations are being monitored, how did this one get selected for special attention? Such monitoring, even for "key words" that would trigger a need for personal attention, suggests a conspiracy of such vast and complex proportions that the logistics of it stagger the mind.

Well, suppose it is a government conspiracy. Suppose that they do have such monitoring capabilities, that they are monitoring my phone, Pat's phone, or the phones of everybody by computer. As a result, suppose they knew I was going to hypnotize her and sent out a flotilla of stealth type aircraft to beam some wave at her (or something like that) which would prevent her from talking to me.

Why would they go to all that trouble?

It seems to me that it would be easier to just send one of those nice white panel trucks we see in the movies to park a block away from my house for their "wave beaming" activities.

Well, okay; maybe they just thought it was a handy time to create a UFO flap at that moment for general purposes: to get everyone all excited, to reinforce the "alien phenomenon" scenario they are creating.

We are still looking at logistics that stagger the mind.

The next question we have to ask is this: since this woman "appeared" in my life at precisely the moment I had been familiarized with the phenomenon sufficiently to recognize the symptoms, how do we deal with that synchronicity? If it is a government conspiracy that was aiming at taking me in by gradual degrees, by creating a series of events in my life that would lead me to give up my "rational explanations" of the phenomenon, what kind of surveillance and "human resources management" does that suggest?

Again, it boggles the mind.

My conclusion was that it couldn't be human engineered, but I wasn't ready to seriously consider that it could be "otherworldly" either. In other words, High Strangeness was everywhere. Thinking these thoughts produced a strange feeling in me of being "watched" in ways hard to describe. It was so strange a synchronicity that I couldn't help but think that the appearance of these craft related to our activities with the superluminal communication experiment. I tried to sweep this thought under the rug, but it kept coming back.

There was a final article in the *St. Petersburg Times* about this series of sightings and this last article was designed to put it all to rest; it was a suggestion that what had been seen was a "stealth bomber". It was all just a strange coincidence. My comfort zone was reestablished and I could rest at night.

For a while.

Frank, of course, was ecstatic with this event. It was proof that Pat knew things that were dangerous to know – something the aliens – or someone – didn't want her to reveal. He theorized that the presence of the UFOs was an effort to reinforce a pain block, or even induce it remotely, and that this was what she meant when she said "They won't let me [tell what happened]".

Even though this was a reasonable deduction, based on the observable evidence, I was not ready to buy Frank's theories. I was so determined to deny the evidence of so-called aliens, and to prove that the alien phenomenon was nothing more than a psychological aberration, that I decided that the rash of sightings was just another outbreak of millennial disease. As soon as one person claimed to have seen the giant boomerang, the public became excited and "infected", and everybody was imagining that they were seeing the same thing. After all, if there were so many aliens out there snatching people, where was the proof?

"Where's the evidence?" I asked Frank. "Show me a damned alien, for God's sakes. Habeas Corpus!"

***

At this point, again, health issues moved to the forefront. All my life, it seemed when I recovered by sheer force of will from one assault, another would arrive seemingly out of nowhere.

My ability to keep going was rapidly falling short of the challenges presented. I was able to walk limited distances no longer than five minutes. Standing soon became excruciatingly painful. Meanwhile, the numbness, tingling, and bone-deep aching in my left arm nearly drove me crazy. The doctor diagnosed it as angina, related to heart damage I had suffered during an illness in 1981. He suggested that I lose weight and get exercise.

Well, how do you get exercise when you can neither stand nor walk for more than a few minutes? Thyroid medication I had taken for years seemed to have no effect on my weight and only exacerbated the heart problem. I truly could eat very little and still gain weight. I joked that I could just look at a glass of water and get fat.

But it wasn't a joke.

I needed to be able to work for the sake of the children. At this point, I was seeing three or four hypnotherapy clients a week. This was so draining that the entire day following a session was employed in recovery. Each day I had to make a choice on how to engage my limited ability to function. Each choice meant a whole list of other things I couldn't do.

The obvious solution was swimming. The only place to swim therapeutically was a stressful 30 minute drive away, and my legs swelled terribly after just ten or fifteen minutes of riding in the car.

I began to think about how helpful it would be to have a swimming pool in the back yard. I spent some time visualizing a pool and myself in a healthy condition splashing in the water. I realized that there was just simply no way that we could manage such a project. It was a hopeless fantasy in terms of our present situation. I would have to think of another way; perhaps the beach or the public pool. But, just in case, I said out loud to the empty room, "God, a swimming pool would help!"

One night, my number two daughter asked her father if she could pick the numbers as he was going out the door to buy his lottery tickets. He laughed and said, "Sure!"

She picked them, and we won. Fifteen grand. We had the pool.

The pool wasn't ready until August. I thought it was appropriate that the children and I could "baptize" the pool by floating on our rubber rafts and watching the Perseid meteor shower.

August 16, 1993: In the subtropics, it gets dark about nine o'clock in the evening, so it would not be until a couple of hours later that meteor viewing conditions would be optimal. The children were excited to stay up late and watch a meteor shower in the pool. They had rushed out at about 10, while I stayed in and struggled to clean up the kitchen before going out to join them at eleven. Three of the five children were out there with me. My eldest daughter was on a date, and the baby was in bed.

I slid into pool for the very first time, and was so happy and grateful to have it! I moved to the far side to lean my head against the ledge and float, looking in the direction the meteors were supposed to be found. The viewing conditions were favorable: no moon, clear sky with only a slight upper level haze from the humidity, and the ambient light was minimal.

Suddenly, my twelve-year-old daughter cried out, "Look! Up there!"

This was no meteor. It was a 300 foot wide black boomerang, emanating a faint reddish glow, moving so slow and low that I knew if I had been standing on the roof of my two-story house, I could have reached up and touched it! We had plenty of time to observe it and note the "brushed matte black metal" appearance of its underside.

We watched as it moved ever so slowly overhead, utterly silent, seeming to float more than anything else. It continued south, seeming to skim the treetops.

We were looking at each other and all saying at once, "What was that?!" when my son shouted, "Another one!" And, sure enough, just to the west of the path of the first one, there was another. Every detail was identical: altitude, speed, reddish glow, and utter silence! I was, at this point, in sufficient possession of my senses to try to hear something! Dead silence. And that struck me as odd, since there are normally all kinds of night sounds: crickets, night birds, frogs and so forth. But there was no sound, no vibration, no hum. Nothing.

We stood there in amazement for a few frozen moments and then the kids began to shout for their dad to come out. He came to the door.

"What's all the excitement about?"

The kids were saying, all at once, "We saw a UFO!"

"That's nonsense", he said.

I will never be able to explain why I said this, but what came out of my mouth was, "Oh, it was just a flock of geese! I guess we are going to have bad weather because the geese are flying South early this year!" I laughed as I shoved it under the rug.

My husband looked at me like I was an idiot. "Geese", he said sarcastically, "do not fly South in August. And anyway, we are South!"

Hearing a logical refutation had a strange effect on me: I became very upset and confused all out of proportion to the event. The only thing I could think of to do was to go inside and call Frank.

Frank was absolutely ecstatic, crowing with delight.

"Finally you'll believe me! You saw a real UFO!"

"Now look, Frank! Just because something is a UFO doesn't mean it's an *alien* UFO!"

Frank's enthusiasm was not to be dampened. He had an ace to play. He had just gotten home a short time before I called and there was a message on his answering machine that he wanted me to hear. He rewound it and played it for me over the phone. Another friend had called him to describe having seen the exact same thing an hour earlier! He had been out in his driveway at 10 o'clock to see a few meteors and was also overflown by the big black boomerang, with his neighbor as a witness. Frank asked, if it was a secret government aircraft, why was it cruising our neighborhood so repetitiously, and why was it that *he* happened to know two of the very people to whom it had "shown" itself?

Well, that didn't seem like a great mystery to me. No doubt many people had seen it.

Nevertheless, there were certainly questions that were not being answered by my logic no matter how I tried to explain things away. At this point, I became so upset that I had to go in my bedroom and sit and consider the matter. It was clear to me that if I could not find a rational explanation for this thing, there was only one thing to think: either they were real, or I had contracted the "Millennial Disease" and was losing my mind.

This was certainly not a stealth bomber. The newspaper article had described them pretty thoroughly when the previous flap had occurred several months earlier. The writer had assumed that when people say they are seeing a "boomerang" shaped object, that they are really saying a "triangular" object. The description of the stealth bombers included a fuselage that the object we had seen simply did not have. It had been a boomerang shape. Not a triangle, not a diamond, a boomerang without any sort of "body" behind the bow shape. But how could I know this for sure? Maybe there were stealth bombers that were newer or different models.

Did anybody *else* see it besides Frank's friend and his neighbor and the kids and me? I wanted to get a consensus of descriptions. I wanted to know that I was not crazy. I wanted an explanation. That meant, of course, that with the weight of evidence from others, I would be able to consult with authorities and confirm that it was, indeed, easily explained as an experimental – but terrestrial – craft. Problem solved, case closed.

So, the next day, trying to act very casual in spite of my embarrassment at even asking such a question, I called a couple of the local television stations to inquire if there had been any reports of "strange objects" in the sky. One woman was very nasty and informed me that, of course there had been strange objects in the sky, it was called a meteor shower! Well, I was not talking about lights flashing across the sky, and I certainly knew a meteor from a 300 foot wide black boomerang, but damned if I was going to even utter those words! All I wanted to know was if there had been any reports of anything from all the meteor watchers that could not be explained.

The results were less than helpful. I was treated like a lunatic for even asking the question. That only served to heighten my dismay. But I wasn't ready to give up yet.

I received similar treatment from various other media sources I contacted in my effort to get some information. I was not comfortable enough to make a report of my own, so I was really trying to talk about the subject without even using the term "UFO". In retrospect, my reluctance to even say it is comical!

There didn't seem to be any information to be obtained until Frank called and told me that the weatherman on one of the television stations had mentioned that one of the "community weather observers" had reported several "flocks of geese" the previous night. Since I had tried to explain it to myself in these same terms, I thought that this might be a "hit". But that was all I was going to get from the "standard" sources.

I was frustrated at being blown off and treated like an idiot. This frustration only added fuel to the fire burning in me, driving the need to discover what it was I had seen. As I considered my options, I remembered an organization that collected reports of such things: MUFON (Mutual UFO Network). Maybe they would know. Even if they were somewhat to the left of rational in their belief that some sightings of strange craft were "alien", they were said to be trying to sort the real ones from the false reports. Perhaps they could help me confirm that I had seen an aircraft that was known, or conjectured to be, part of a secret government project?

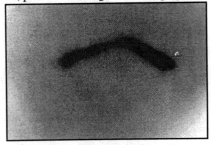

I looked in the back of one of Frank's books and found the phone number for the national headquarters of MUFON. The person who answered gave me the number for the local chapter. An answering machine picked up. The director was going to be on vacation for the next two weeks. I hesitated, but finally left my name and number and the fact that I wanted some information about a "possible UFO sighting". I was using "UFO" in the literal sense of the word: it was unidentified, and I was seeking identification in a rational sense, not a confirmation of alien visitations and more mumbo jumbo.

It was well into September before anyone from MUFON called me back, with an apology for taking so long. Since the monthly meeting was the next day, perhaps I would come and give the report in person. Well, that was pushing me just a bit too far, too fast. I was not ready to hang out with geeks who believed in little green men and who probably wore plastic pocket protectors, coke-bottle glasses, and kept Mad Magazine rolled up in their back pockets!

I mean, get real!

The day of the MUFON meeting, I was definitely not going to go. I was going to drop the whole subject. But, as the clock rolled around, the kids disappeared to various activities, the baby went off with her father, and I was left at home alone. The need to know had not lessened one bit, and I tried to come up with any rational excuse not to go. Surprisingly, my usual state of exhaustion was at a minimum and, with no other apparent reason to hinder me, I thought that maybe, just maybe, I would go and check this MUFON bunch out. If it was creepy, or if I became too tired, I could always come right home.

I was surprised. There were no geeks. Not a single pocket protector. And these folks were certainly too old for Mad Magazine!

I entered quietly, took a seat at the back of the room and listened to a discussion in progress. I was amazed at how extremely intelligent and rational these folks were; more so than average, in my opinion; and certainly brighter than the run-of-the-mill "New Age Groupie". No one was ranting a spittle flecked monologue about being visited by Venusians, taken aboard their craft, and transported to Looney-Land. Nobody was talking about aliens-as-God, here to "serve mankind" (on a platter). In fact, it was a rather technical discussion of possible propulsion systems of UFOs, based on observed behavior by credible witnesses whose stories were cited, along with some impressive documentation and credentials.

At the break, I was asked to sign a guest sheet. The director recognized my name and asked me to talk about my sighting.

After the break I stood in front of the group and, with extreme embarrassment, began to tell my little story about the Black Boomerang. As I was getting warmed up, the door opened (this was a public meeting room in a local library), and a big, burly, bearded man came in. I stopped talking while he got seated and the director introduced him to me. I was surprised at his name, which is an unusual Welsh one that happened to be my grandfather's middle name and had been his mother's maiden name. As I finished, all sorts of questions were asked. I made a drawing on a blackboard and that was that. I had said my piece and I sat down.

A discussion followed. The earliest sighting of the Black Boomerang type object, as I had drawn it on the chalkboard, was in Albuquerque in 1951. They were also seen in Lubbock, Texas, and became famous as the "Lubbock Lights" in the photo to the left.[13] It was noted, as a point of interest, that these early sightings also occurred in the month of August, which I thought was peculiar.

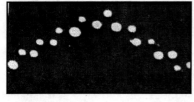

What was most interesting to me was the fact that the same design was seen over 40 years previously. That sort of cancelled out my idea of a new design. No change in model in 40 years? Those boys in Black Ops are really slipping! No imagination at all!

There were also extensive reports of these types of craft being sighted repeatedly in the Hudson Valley[14] of New York in a famous series of events that included all kinds of anomalous phenomena among the thousands of witnesses. A scientist had been involved in that situation, a Dr. Hynek. I had never heard the name before, but I was soon to hear it quite a lot.

---

[13] One of five photographs taken by student Carl Hart in Texas, August 1952.

[14] The Hudson Valley Sightings actually comprises of a number of incidents which took place between 31st December 1982 and 10th July 1986. These truly remarkable sightings have never been explained and even "arch-debunker" Philip J. Klass admitted to being baffled by the whole series of incidents.

Beginning in Putnam County, New York, the series of sightings eventually involved approximately 5,000 witnesses and covered the geographic area from Peekskill and Ossining, New York, in the west to New Haven, Connecticut in the east and from Brookfield, Connecticut in the north to Westport in the south.

Many of the objects observed were described as V-shaped or "boomerang-shaped" but later triangular craft were also witnessed.

A very large majority of witnesses claimed that the objects were truly colossal, at least 300ft. in size and, in general, most of them were travelling much slower than a plane. On the whole the UFOs were described as being silent, although a hum was sometimes heard.

All of the sightings were experienced at night and observers remarked that the objects showed between five and 15 lights of a number of colours, sometimes the lights changed colour and turned off and on. On occasions these lights were bright enough to illuminate the ground below the craft.

I would also come to respect his work and opinions.

Long after these events and discussions, I did more research on the "Black Boomerang" matter and discovered some very disturbing connections in an article in the book series *Mysteries of Mind, Space and Time*, written by Hamish Howard and Toyne Newton, edited by Peter Brookesmith:

> Clapham Wood is a small densely-treed area nestling in the shelter of the South Downs in West Sussex, England. ... [T]his is an area of mystery and intrigue and UFO sightings... Stunted trees, a large crater where nothing grows, and mysterious little clearings containing ruins of old cottages [are found there.]
>
> Several hundred years ago, an aged resident of Clapham reported that she had seen a "bright round shape like the full Moon" float down into the woods and disappear into the bushes. The woods were "filled with fumes that stinketh of burning matter" and the people of the town were afraid to go there afterwards. Since that time, there have been many more UFO sightings in this small area.
>
> In October 1972, a telephone engineer saw a large saucer shaped object in the sky above the woods. It hovered for some time before making a circle of the area, then veered off. At the same time, a couple were walking near the main road and thought they saw Jupiter or Venus low in the western sky – until it started to move very quickly due north, keeping in line with a ridge as it came toward them. Suddenly, when the object was over Clapham Wood, a beam of light descended vertically from it, and then rapidly withdrew, and the object shot away north-eastward at great speed.
>
> Paul Glover of the British Phenomenon Research Group was walking with a friend along the downs toward Clapham Wood one clear starlit night in the summer of 1967. At about 10 p.m., both men suddenly became aware of a huge black mass low in the sky blotting out the stars as it moved very quickly toward them. The object was boomerang shaped and made no sound. As it passed overhead the displacement of air was so great they ducked into the bushes for safety. They vehemently denied it could have been a cloud, for it retained its shape, was on a definite course, and there was no wind to drive it. Minutes later, they saw two bright objects high in the sky, which they watched for several minutes. One of the UFOs released a smaller object that traveled across to the second object, seemed to enter it, and then re-emerged and veered off, disappearing from sight. An hour later, on their return in the opposite direction of their walk, [apparently] two yellow lights descended in the region of the woods, followed just a few seconds later by two more, and then a final pair, making a total or three groups of two. Then at the point where they seemed to have dipped

down into the woods, two white beams of light shot out horizontally – quite unimpeded by the contours of the downlands – followed by the next two beams and then the final two, all traveling very fast, before disappearing into the night sky. No craft of any kind could be seen behind the lights.

During that same year, in the village of Rustington a few miles westwards along the coast, two schoolboys, Toyne Newton and John Arnold, who had never even heard of Clapham Wood, had a strange story spelled out to them *on a Ouija board*: that Clapham Wood was a base for spacecraft,[15] and that one had landed recently to fetch supplies of sulphur and other chemicals.

No one believed the boys, of course, but nearly 10 years later an investigation was carried out when soil samples were taken from the woods. From the report given in BBC-TV's Nationwide program at the time, it seems there was more than a grain of truth to the sulphur story. The investigation had been triggered by reports of dogs disappearing in the woods in 1975.

According to a local paper, the *Worthing Herald*, Wallace, a 3 yr. old chow belonging to Mr. and Mrs. Peter Love of Clapham, disappeared, as did a 2 yr. old collie belonging to Mr. John Cornford. Apparently the collie, although normally obedient,

---

[15] I found this reference to a Ouija board warning about UFO bases in conjunction with a sighting of a black boomerang to be quite coincidental considering my own sighting of a boomerang type craft, followed 11 months to the day by the "arrival" of the Cassiopaeans.

> suddenly rushed off into a small copse between two trees in an area known locally as the Chestnuts, and was never seen again. The mystified owner searched thoroughly!
>
> Mrs. H.T. Wells, who lives at nearby Durrington, said that when her collie gets near the woods, it becomes "desperate", and a golden retriever belonging to Mr. E.F. Rawlins of Worthing ran into the woods one day and returned "very distressed". Shortly afterwards it became paralyzed and had to be destroyed".
>
> Another dog owner, who wished to remain anonymous, reported that when she took her dog to this area it ran around in circles, foaming at the mouth, with its eyes bulging as if in great pain."

The account goes on to say that a horseman (who also wished to remain anonymous, but his report was said to have been verified) tied his horse to a tree and stepped back a ways to have a pit stop. When he stepped back out of the bushes, he was amazed to find his horse missing. Although he searched the area extensively and made exhaustive enquiries, the horse was never found!

Several people have reported the feeling of being "pushed over by invisible forces" in this area and others have had spells of faintness. Two men walking through the wood reported that both were afflicted at the same moment: one doubling over in internal agony and the other clutching his head and screaming that his eardrums were "being pulled out of his head". They both staggered about 50 yards further and the effects ceased.

The body of a missing man was found two weeks after he went missing, but in an extremely advanced state of decomposition. Forensic evidence showed that the rate of decomposition had been greatly accelerated due to "unknown factors". This article continues:

> A skeptical investigator, Dave Stringer of the Southern Paranormal Investigation Group, visited the area with a Geiger counter in August [there is that month again] 1977. The woods were silent and the air still. Everything appeared normal, but, as he pushed through heavy undergrowth, he had to lift the machine above his head. When he did so, it began to register an alarming high level. Mr. Stringer stopped and looked back at the area he had just passed through. He saw a dark shape about 12 feet in height; while not being distinctive in outline, it was very definitely not smoke and he could only describe it as a "black mass". Seconds later a large white disk shot out from behind nearby trees at a 45 degree angle and disappeared into the sky. Simultaneously, the dark mass disappeared. Stringer retraced his steps [braver than I!] and found at the spot where the form had appeared, an imprint of a four toed

footprint similar to one found at a place called Devils' Dyke near Brighton, where there was known to be a black magic "coven".

Stringer made a quick sketch of the footprint. It was unknown to him at the time, that it matches a footprint reproduced in Collin de Plancy's *Dictionaire Infernal* published in 1863, and that this footprint is supposed to be that of the "Demon Amduscias".

UFO sightings continued at Clapham into 1978 and 1979. The spate of strange reports at that time concluded with the disappearance of the Reverend Neil Snelling, vicar of Clapham Church, pictured previously. One morning after shopping at Worthing, he decided to walk back to his Steyning home through Clapham Wood. He has not been heard of since and an exhaustive search of the area revealed nothing.[16]

Paul Glover and Dave Stringer and another man went to Clapham to see if they could spot any UFOs. There was no activity. They decided to go home and as they were walking out of the woods, all three of them simultaneously had a feeling of intense cold. They hurried on and the feeling ceased. They decided to go back and check it out again. They did this three times, and each time experienced the sensation of a sudden and unnatural drop in temperature. Glover pointed his camera at the area of the cold, even though nothing was apparently visible. When the film was developed, it showed an uncanny white mass in the unmistakable image of a goat's head.[17]

All in all, I was coming to an awareness that this phenomenon was not only strange, it was possibly dangerous. Just how strange and dangerous I would discover soon enough. Back to the account of the MUFON meeting. It seems that synchronicity was rapidly becoming my middle name.

A gentleman who had arrived late was, apparently, well known by the group as an "expert", which interested me as much as his name. He talked at length about the theories of Zecharia Sitchin. I was intrigued by the historical connections to UFO sightings, though I discounted the precise interpretation put on the Sumerian writings by Dr. Sitchin.

At the end of the meeting, I asked this gentleman where he came from and told him that his uncommon surname was the same as my

---

[16] The retired Clapham vicar's remains were not discovered until three years later in August 1981 near Wiston Barn on the Downs and an Inquest subsequently declared an open verdict.

[17] Hamish Howard & Toyne Newton, *Mysteries of Mind, Space & Time,* Volume 4 (Westport: Stuttman, 1992).

great-grandmother's. He recognized her name and told me that his father had been her younger brother. The only reason I had never known of him or met him was, according to him, there had been a "religious" schism in the family. My great grandmother had abandoned the Baptist church and became Methodist.

Nevertheless, here I was, talking to a "long lost cousin" because I had seen a purported UFO!

We decided to have lunch. It was completely strange to meet this man who had so strong a family resemblance to me, and who was intelligent, articulate, informed, and clearly a scholar of some considerable prowess. Let's call him Sam.

I told Sam about our channeling experiment and joked about the "lotto number test" that clearly wasn't working, though we had won a decent prize completely without a prediction from the board. This item seemed to interest Sam a great deal, and I ended up inviting him to join Frank and me for our next session.

Meanwhile, two most disturbing things were taking place that are mirrored in the report about the Clapham Wood Black Boomerang and its effect upon animals. My collie, Danny-boy, went into a decline that nothing could reverse. The vet was completely baffled, and everything we tried, failed. In the end, he could only suggest a congenital heart defect leading to cardiac insufficiency. Within three months of the Black Boomerang, he died with his head in my lap on the kitchen floor. Danny was only 3 years old, a gentle and wonderful dog. I was heartbroken.

At the same time, my own physical condition, instead of getting better, had gotten worse from that first night in the pool. I was constantly sick. I had a terrible rashes, hives and welts. All the mucous membranes of my body kept swelling to the point that my throat and nose would almost shut completely. The undersides of my eyelids were so irritated they oozed yellowish, sticky fluids constantly. My ears itched deep inside which nearly drove me crazy.

These symptoms were always the precursor to a sort of "attack". This began with severe nausea. I felt as though a fence post had been driven through my chest. My breathing was labored and painful; I broke out in a cold sweat. My doctor finally suggested that I was suffering allergies which exacerbated my already compromised cardio-pulmonary system. It was decided that I must have reached a sort of "critical mass" of allergen exposure at some recent time. I had some relief from Benadryl and other allergy medications, but that was not a long-term solution. My body simply did not seem to be able to handle the toxins anymore. The doctor wanted to run extensive allergy tests and begin a course of treatment designed to more or less desensitize me to whatever was affecting my system.

The symptoms were worse at night, starting at about 11:00 p.m. I reasoned this must be the time of "critical mass" of the day's exposure to whatever allergen was active at the moment.

One night, around this time, a close friend of mine, Sandra, had come by to visit. We were just chatting when my eyes started burning, and I felt the slight tingling sensation in my lower lip which presaged the whole syndrome. I had told Sandra about the problem, trying to figure out what it might be I was allergic to, and I don't think she really understood how it worked. As she sat there watching, before her eyes, my lips slowly swelled until they were almost inside out; my eyes became slits, oozing fluid that I had to constantly wipe away with tissues and welts were raised on my arms and legs.

Sandra was completely shocked. "We need to get you to an emergency room right now!"

I laughed it off, went to the kitchen to get some Benadryl, and told her that there wasn't much the doctors could do. They'd observed the swelling, the hives, and the inflammation of my eyes. The "fence post" in the chest part just simply did not cooperate with being put under a microscope. If the doctors couldn't catch it in the middle of manifesting, they couldn't know what it was. Tests done when there were no symptoms told them nothing.

I explained to Sandra that, on two occasions when the symptoms began to manifest, my husband had driven me to the hospital, and by the time we arrived, the heart symptoms had gone away entirely, leaving only the skin manifestations. This was puzzling in the extreme, and it was taken as proof that there was absolutely nothing wrong with me except in my mind.

I, on the other hand, was thoroughly frightened at what was happening to me.

However, as long as I was sitting still and didn't try to move around too much, I was fine. Moreover, my brain hadn't died, so I continued to read and study to divert my mind. I also kept a schedule of hypnosis sessions. Without reading and my work, I would have felt completely useless. I would have had no life at all.

I began to concentrate on gathering every bit of data on the subject that I could get my hands on. What I found was that, down through the ages people have been visited by all sorts of strange beings. Some of these creatures have been utterly fantastic in description as well as activity. By far the most common type, however, have been

humanoid – having some semblance to the human physical configuration – although their powers have been distinctly super-human.

I read stories going back hundreds of years that told stories of these humanoid beings, but the fact is, there are images of them that are many thousands of years old. In the picture at left, we see a 6 meter high figure with a large round decorated head. The massive body, the strange clothing, the folds around the neck and on the chest suggest some ancient astronaut. The image is from Jabbaren, in the Tassili mountains, Algeria, south of the Hoggar, dated to about 6,000 BC.

Notice the disc like object over the shoulder of the figure on the right side of the image.

The image above is a 12,000 year old cave painting from Val Camonica, Italy. It appears to depict two beings in protective suits holding strange implements.

The small image to the right is an enlargement of a portion of the image below which is a wall painting located in the cave of Pech Merle near Le Cabrerets, France. These images date to around 17,000 – 15,000 BC. The scene depicts a landscape of wildlife along with a number of saucer shaped objects. In  the enlargement of the section above, right, it even looks like there is some sort of exchange of energy between two of the objects. A "War in the Heaven" perhaps?

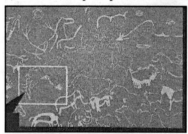

There are many, many more prehistoric images that suggest some kind of interaction between human beings and strange craft in the sky. In general, they seem to suggest a non-benevolent relationship and that the artists were "hiding."

The image below is from a 12th century manuscript *Annales Laurissenses* and refers to a UFO sighting in the year 776, during the siege on Sigiburg castle, France. The Saxons were besieging the castle when suddenly a group of discs described as flaming shields appeared hovering over the top of the church. The sign was interpreted as divine protection of the French and the Saxons fled, post haste!

The next two images are of tapestries created in the 15th Century. The one on the top is titled *The Magnificant*, and they are both housed in Notre-Dame in Beaune, Burgandy. The issue of the relationship between UFOs or other "unworldly visitors" to religious experiences will be discussed further on.

The next painting is entitled *The Madonna with Saint Giovannino*. It dates to the 15th century, though the Palazzo Vecchio lists the artist as unknown. It is generally attributed to the Fra Lippi school.

Above Mary's right shoulder is a disk shaped object. Below is a blow up of this section and a man and his dog can clearly be seen looking up at the object.

The painting below was executed on wood, on a piece of furniture to be precise, owned by the Earls D'Oltremond, Belgium. Moses is receiving the tablets and several objects in the sky are seen nearby. The date and artist are unknown.

Consider also the following report from the Gazette of the town of Nuremberg, Germany, written in 1561:

> At dawn of April 4, in the sky of Nuremberg, a lot of men and women saw a very alarming spectacle where various objects were involved, including balls *"approximately 3 in the length, from time to time, four in a square, much remained insulated, and between these balls, one saw a number of crosses with the color of blood. Then one saw two large pipes, in which small and large pipes, were 3 balls, also four or more. All these elements started to fight one against the other"*.

The events lasted one hour and artist, Hans Glaser, commemorated the event in a woodcut. Looking at the woodcut above, it seems that it depicts some of the objects crashed on the ground outside the city.

Mr. Matthew Hurley, author of *The Alien Chronicles*, has collected many images of artwork that appears to depict UFOs. He writes:

> The artwork in my collection consists of frescos, tapestries, illustrations, oil paintings and early photographs... One can only guess at why these artists chose to insert UFOs into their artwork. Did they have UFO sightings in their day and decide to add them in ? Perhaps they had an inner urge to insert them. Maybe they had some arcane knowledge about the relationship between UFOs and certain religious events. Whatever the truth is, there are UFOs in these pieces of artwork and one can ponder and reflect on this truth.

Dr. Karla Turner, professor of literature at North Texas University, and vocal alien abductions researcher, wrote extensively about so-called abductees who did not fit into the "Gray alien scenario" of abductions promoted by Budd Hopkins and Whitley Strieber. Dr.

Turner addressed such issues as military abductions, reptilian aliens, relationship manipulations and general deceitful tactics of so-called aliens. Karla authored several books including *Into the Fringe*, *Masquerade of Angels* and *Taken*.

The issue of "reptilian aliens" is certainly problematical, but in the image at right, we see humanoid type reptile images from Iraq, dated to about 5000-4500 BC. You can see them in the British Museum. We will return to this issue several times, so bear with me.

In 1995, Karla contracted a very dangerous form of breast cancer almost immediately after what she claimed was an abduction. She died at the age of 48. I really valued our internet friendship, and when she wrote me for the last time, telling me that she was too weak to continue our correspondence, I wept.

Looking back, of course, it's easy to speculate that Karla's death on January 9, 1996, might be an example of how "forces" might deal with someone who was getting entirely too close to the truth. She wasn't "martyred" in any obvious way. I will discuss some of her work in more detail further on, but for the moment, I want to just make a few important points. What she had been saying can be summed up in the following:

> It is a myth that alien abductions of humans follow a set pattern or agenda. Perhaps the best-known proponent of this theory is Budd Hopkins, who in his books made the genetics and other cross-breeding scenario familiar to the public. Yet when you read back through those books, you'll notice that several of the alien encounters seem to have very little apparent connection to an

interest in breeding of DNA. And even Hopkins, in the past couple of years, has had to expand his theory to include a definite alien interest in some other things, such as pleasure and pain in humans.

Other well-known UFO researchers also harbor restrictive theories about the abduction phenomenon. Jacques Vallee, David Jacobs, Whitley Strieber, Brad Steiger, John Lear, Raymond Fowler, Jenny Randles, Kevin Randle, John Keel and other writers hold a diversity of intelligent, often ingenious theories, yet each makes the same error. They ignore parts of the abduction evidence – whatever details don't support their ideas.

Yet it must be clear that any present theory which cannot account for all the known evidence is not acceptable. At best, it can be misleading, especially for victims of abductions who turn to these prominent researchers seeking answers...

As to researchers who claim that the ETs are here to help us evolve some higher consciousness or that they are here for some other positive purpose-saving our planet, promoting world peace, etc. – I challenge those researches to incorporate anomalous data in this view.

What about those people who suffer total breakdowns after their experiences? What about those who undergo wild personality changes, who find themselves obsessed with deviant sexual behavior they never had before, often leading to the breakup of marriages and friendships? These things have happened numerous times, but no researcher has yet explained the higher purpose behind such results.

Particularly disturbing are those cases where previously healthy individuals have an ET encounter and then develop debilitating or terminal illnesses. It is well known that many women suffer gynecological problems after their experiences, often leading to hysterectomies. But other instances have shown the development of severe fatigue, horrible swelling and itching, and even cancer. Where are the positive effects in these cases?

Theories are starting places for research, not proven conclusions, and UFO researchers must be willing to expand and alter their pet theories according to the data they uncover. It would be wonderful if we could shape ET experiences into something positive, but until the details of abduction encounters – all the details – are given serious consideration, I think it's dangerous to cling to theories that ignore data that will not fit. We owe it to ourselves to seek the whole truth.[18]

---

[18] *UFO magazine,* Vol. 8 No. 1 January/February 1993

Karla's husband, Elton, later published the following remarks, published in *Contact Forum* (September/October 1994), which are more timely today than ever:

> "186,000 M/Second – it's not just a good idea, it's the law", the bumper sticker read. Something about that statement irritated me. Here we were in the midst of a UFO conference and someone was selling an old reality!
>
> The mixture of our notions of physical reality and our concept of law are keeping us in the dark ages of human thought. Modern science has brought us many new ideas about the nature of the universe, but those ideas are constantly being challenged and changed as our powers of observation sharpen and equipment improves. I thank our scientists for their contributions; I love air conditioning, airplanes, and the television waves that travel our air. What bothers me, is that we have not stopped to consider, "The Law."
>
> What laws do the invaders (and I use that term intentionally) of our world abide by? I posit that we have no idea of the rules of the navigable universe by which these otherworldly entities operate. We continue to develop ideas of their intentions based on our own social rules and written laws. I asked a prominent author and researcher of the UFO phenomenon the other day why he thought the aliens could be trusted – why we should believe what they tell us. His reply was sincere, I think. He said they have demonstrated their truthfulness by predicting some future events, and, lo and behold, what they said came true. He said they have told us our planet is in ecological crisis and we know that is true. And, although they seem to have been here for thousands of years, they have not invaded us. What wonderful creatures they must be!
>
> In the few years that I have been studying my own personal invasion by these creatures, I have come to understand that the invaders do not tell the truth unless it serves *their* purpose. They play on our fears, using pollution, war, nuclear holocaust and greed as backdrops for their warnings. But every day since I was a small child, I have been aware that those things are part of our world. We all know these things. It does not take a zillion-plus-IQ creature from the planet Orlon to make me aware that we have problems in our world that we must face. We have very human problems to deal with – problems that we can deal with.
>
> The problems we cannot yet overcome is that of outside interference in our affairs. Some people may call it "benevolent intervention" and point to positive results. I respect the scientists and laymen of all disciplines who have been studying the alien phenomenon and artifacts for the past 50 or 60 years. It appears that they have made

some progress, as witnessed by the rapid developments in the aerospace industry, medicine, communications, etc., a great deal of which seems to have come from such research. What is missing is a thorough and public study of the mission and rules of engagement in the war for our world.

I believe that our very thoughts and consequently, our behavior as a race of sentient beings are being *undermined* through the power of insinuation and the implantation of controlling devices in our bodies by non-human (most of the time) entities. This is truly the most effective way to invade and conquer. I do not trust such creatures no matter what I have been told about their altruistic motives.

Karla Turner's work takes us directly into turbo-charged High Strangeness. *An Encyclopedia of Fairies* (Katherine Briggs, 1978) gives many examples of fairy abductions. The similarities between fairy abductions and UFO abductions is also interesting to note. People who claimed interactions with fairies generally reported marks on their bodies consistent with reports of alien abductions. Fairy abductions and UFO abductions also exhibit striking similarities to activities of incubi and succubi. Almost always a thick drink is given to the abductee. The victim is paralyzed and then levitated away. The fairies traveled in circular globes of light which is also commonly reported in UFO abductions. Another similarity to the UFO abduction scenario is the Bigfoot-type creature which was called a "bogie" in fairy lore. Many so-called fairies and aliens look and act a lot like what have been described throughout history as demons.

In his classic study *Passport to Magonia*, French scientist, Jacques Vallee presented many examples of similarities between fairy and UFO sightings. Jean Bastide, in *La memoire des OVNI* (1978) went further and said the "modern contacts established with extraterrestrials respect precisely the same rules as contacts in the past with beings more or less human in form".

A fairly classic example of an alleged succubus interaction is presented in the book entitled *The Haunted*, by Robert Curran. The following is a transcript of a taped interview with the victim:

Q. How did you first know something was wrong?

A. The way I came awake, I guess.

Q. There was something different about it?

A. Yes, it was like I'd been – oh, thrown off a cliff or something. You know, as if some violent action woke me up.

Q. Can you describe what you saw?

A. At first I didn't see anything at all. I just felt this tremendous sort of panic – I wasn't sure if I was having a nightmare or not.

Q. What convinced you that you weren't having a nightmare?

A. Her scales.

Q. Her scales. You mean by that serpentine – snakelike – scales?

A. Yes.

Q. You said "she". These scales were on a woman?

A. Yes.

Q. Would you describe her?

A. To be honest, I even hate to think about her. Her skin was paper white, but it was covered in some places with the scaly surface I mentioned, and then in other places with open sores, the kind you'd think a leper would have or something, And these sores were running with pus.

Q. How old was she?

A. I would estimate around sixty-five or seventy. I can't be sure.
Q. What else did you first notice about her?

A. She had long, white, scrabbly hair and her eyes were all red and the inside of her mouth and her gums were green. Some of her teeth were missing but those she had were very long and vampire-like.

Q. What about her body?

A. That was the weird thing. Her body itself was firm, you know, like that of a younger woman. Q. What did she do? A. She paralyzed me in some way. I saw her walking out of the shadows to our bed and I sensed what she was going to do but I couldn't stop her.

Q. Then what?

A. Then she mounted me in the dominant position and she started riding me. That's the only way I can describe it.

Q. Was it pleasurable?

A. No, no. In fact, I don't remember feeling anything at all, other than panic and complete terror.

Q. What was Janet doing during all this? A. Only after I'd been awake for a time did I realize that Janet had earlier gone downstairs to sleep on the couch, which she occasionally does in the hot months.

Q. What was the being doing next?

A. Coming to sexual climax. She just looked at me and smiled showing those incredible teeth. I tried to look away but something held my eyes to her. I could tell when she was having orgasms because she would give little jerks and her smile would broaden.

Q. She was having orgasms?

A. Oh yes, you could tell that by her expressions and her movements.

Q. Then what happened?

A. Then she vanished.

Q. Just like that?

A. Just like that. Just vanished. And that's when I noticed the sticky substance all over me.

Q. Sticky substance?

A. Yes. I suppose you'd have to compare it to semen, the texture of it, anyway. It was emitted from the creature's vagina. And I was sore, too.

Q. Sore?

A. Yes, as if I'd had prolonged sex, even though it had been only a few minutes. But then I began to wonder if I hadn't passed out during it or something because, as I said, my genitals were extremely sore.

Q. What happened next?

A. I went into the bathroom and looked myself over. The fluid on my body had a very pungent odor. I took a shower and washed it off as quickly as I could. I had to scrub very hard.

The belief that these are supernatural beings is to be found in every society around the world. This is a common theme in all religions as well as folklore. It seems that, in the guise of the UFO/alien abduction phenomenon, the reports are as frequent in our own day as they have ever been. An incident with startling parallels to the above was reported in one of Karla Turner's books:

> This time, as he lay on the table, after having been made to drink a cinnamon smelling liquid, he saw a white haired woman walking over to him. He said she seemed gentle and perhaps caring. She got on top of him, initiating sex, and when it was over she left.
>
> He remembered once when he was thirteen waking up to see a strange woman, dark-eyed with white wispy hair, approach him in unfamiliar surroundings. She got on top of him and engaged in sex, yet it was not at all erotic for Casey.[19]

The point is that there is a tradition stretching back *thousands* of years of beings abducting humans and their offspring; these beings fly in globes of light, can paralyze their victims, induce amnesia about the event, force strange drinks on their victims, have sex with them and, in many cases, ultimately drive them to madness, physical ruin, or even take over their bodies for their own use.

Legends of the vampire have persisted since the beginning of recorded history. The problem lies in sorting fact from fiction. The fact is that reports in *Eastern Europe* tell us that something called vampirism reached almost epidemic proportions in the 18th century.[20] The stories are quite lurid and many of the details must be attributed to the terrified imaginations of superstitious peasants, yet much of the documentation is so detailed and the witnesses so reputable that it seems impossible that there was not something going on there. The question is, what was it? The idea of a corpse coming out of their coffin at night to suck the blood of the living seems pretty irrational, and I think we can discard it as confused reports of a phenomenon of an entirely different nature: perhaps an interaction with what we, today, refer to as aliens?

From beyond recorded history the ritual drinking and spilling of blood has been the vital element in sacrifice, gaining power and appeasing the gods. For life, one must have blood. This is the centerpiece idea of both Judaism and Christianity. We have a right to ask: From what has this idea arisen?

---

[19] *Into The Fringe,* by Karla Turner, Ph.D., 1992

[20] We note that this was the century of the American and French Revolutions.

For many years occultists have talked and written about demonic bloodsucking materialisations. Dion Fortune believed that the astral body can escape from a person's living body and assume another form such as a bird, animal or vampire. Vampirism is believed to be contagious; the person who is vampirized, being depleted of vitality, is thought to be a psychic vacuum who then draws energy from the people they encounter in daily life. This energy is then available for the vampirizing entity on their next call to collect.

The cultic vampire, created largely by Bram Stoker in 1897, carries overtones of sexuality that may be more than mere accident. The combination of violence, psychic seduction, sex and giving up of life force made vampirism very popular. There have been numerous individuals who have been called or have called themselves vampires; none of these perverts actually rose from the dead though they have committed murders and/or drunk blood. They were not vampires in the supernatural sense of the word. Nevertheless, the connection between supernatural vampirism and sex is profound. We have to wonder what is the extraordinary fascination that vampirism has on the subconscious minds of many people? It seems to be the blend of sexual excitement, surrender to possession with the promise of immortality and thrilling evil. Sex and the supernatural: an unbeatable combination.

British actor Christopher Lee explained the appeal of the vampire by saying, "He offers the illusion of immortality ... the subconscious wish we all have of limitless power ... a being of tremendous brain and physical strength..."

The illusion of immortality! That is very similar to what has been offered to many UFO abductees. "Frank and James ... both of them had been told that new bodies were somehow being made or prepared for us" (Turner, 1992).

One of the most common effects of vampiric activity is physical exhaustion without explanation. This phenomenon occurs frequently in UFO abduction scenarios as we see in the following:

> Throughout the fall and winter, we felt literally under siege from forces and entities we couldn't fathom... the next morning, I simply

> couldn't wake up. No matter how hard I tried or how much tea I drank, I was in a daze the entire day, yet I had no reason to be so exhausted...
>
> [B]ut just as suddenly as she'd been exhilarated, she was drained of all her energy and almost fell to the ground in a faint... Megan collapsed on the couch, unable to speak or even open her eyes for almost half an hour. (Turner, 1992)

Another of the most common of all psychic phenomena is that of the poltergeist. An allied phenomenon is that of the invisible attacker. Raised scratch marks appear on the bodies of some poltergeist victims and on one occasion an investigating police officer saw cuts spontaneously appearing on the legs and chest of a screaming poltergeist victim. An example containing elements of sex, poltergeist stigmata and possible vampirism also appears in Karla Turner's accounts of UFO abductions:

> [H]e woke up in his bed with a strange female alien being beside him. " She was trying to get me worked up", he said. "She got on top of me and tried to make me respond, you know, sexually. But I kept refusing, I pushed her away and begged her to leave me alone... she was naked, though, and she felt really cold when she touched me" ... "I found these marks this morning", he pointed... three large puncture marks on the skin on the back of his calf arranged in an equilateral triangle...
>
> He was staying alone in a friend's apartment, collapsing in bed after hours of walking the streets alone, and when he awoke he was covered with bruises and scratches all over his back...
>
> "I was sitting on the couch, and it was late at night. And all of a sudden, the couch started hopping up and down, and then this footstool started hopping, I mean, really hopping. It was shaking me!" ...
>
> "The whole bed started to shake, and when I tried to move, I found I was paralyzed. I couldn't even speak, but somehow I finally managed to whisper a prayer, asking the god of truth and love to make this frightening force go away. I repeated the prayer again and again, until the paralysis broke, but the bed shook even more violently as my strength increased... I tried to rouse Casey and tell him what had happened, but he rolled over sleepily without responding... at that point, three women came in and approached me. They held me comfortingly and told me, 'You did the right thing, You passed the test.'" (Turner, 1992)

There are certainly striking parallels between the above events of an alleged alien abduction case and poltergeist phenomena.

This High Strangeness is part and parcel not only of the UFO and so-called alien encounter scenarios, but also of mythical vampire encounters and alleged cases of possession. When possessing entities have been questioned during exorcism about how they selected a target for possession they often reply that the subject was chosen before he was born. In most cases, the line of contact and the gradually building assault can be traced back to childhood. It could be said, in general, that the process of possession has already begun before either the target or those around him are aware of the signs. The same may be true of so-called alien encounters.

In most cases there is a sensation of the presence before an actual encounter takes place. The Betty Andreasson alien abduction is a classic. The scenario described is quite common in many abduction cases. For the sake of comparison, let's look at a condensed version.

A light appeared outside the window. The rest of her family appeared to go into a state of suspended animation. Four small creatures entered the room passing straight through a door. One of them communicated with her telepathically and led her outside where an oval craft was waiting.

On board she was subjected to a painful physical examination. A probe was pushed up her nose. Another probe was inserted into her navel and she was told she was being measured for procreation.

Next she was made to sit in a glass chair where she was enclosed by a transparent cover and immersed in fluid; she could breathe through tubes attached to her nose and mouth. A sweet liquid oozed into her mouth. When she was released from the chair she found that she had traveled to the alien's planet.

Two of the creatures took her along a tunnel and through a series of chambers. The first was full of small reptile-like creatures; the second was a large green-colored space where they floated over pyramids to a city of mysterious crystalline forms. She was taken into one of the crystal shapes where she was confronted by a giant bird that burst into light and then collapsed into a pile of embers. A voice told her that she had been chosen for a special mission which would be revealed to her. When Betty stated she believed in God, the voice told her that that was why she had been chosen. The leader, *Quazgaa*, told her that secrets had been locked in her mind. She was then escorted back to her home where she saw the rest of her family still in a state of suspended animation. The aliens put the family to bed.

Now, consider the following condensed account of a case of alleged demonic infestation, obsession and possible ultimate possession which has been thoroughly documented and described in *The Demon Syndrome* by Nancy Osborn:

> The room was bathed in a hazy, luminous glow. A strong scent of ozone... a gust of cool wind burst through the open window... It seemed peculiar to Ann that the moon shone so brightly on a cloudy night.
>
> She started to get up. Three dark silhouettes materialized as if entering through the open window... her husband ... slept on, oblivious... Two of the figures stayed in the background but the third drew nearer... he was taller than the other two... As the leader advanced the two smaller creatures seemed to float in the background, chattering unintelligibly... the mysterious intruder did not have a complete body... It was clothed in a black flowing shroud with two arms and hands extending from the edges ... but they were not human appendages. Not normal, regular arms and hands, but cloven ones like those of a pig. The teeth and mouth seemed inhuman. Four fangs protruded where incisors should have been, and rough, thorn-like projections were the closest semblance of human teeth. Its face had an almond shape and the skin was tinted pink. But it was the eyes that frightened Ann most, for they burned crimson... The creature had only a small amount of wiry hair that stood straight up, and the ears were pointed... there were no feet... the thing moved by gliding and floating...
>
> [The entity speaks] 'I have come to take you with me, Ann Haywood. You have been chosen to be one with us. Turn to me and I will give you peace and comfort.' ... a sense of euphoria overcame her. It was a warm, calm sensation... she exerted effort and began to pray again... 'You and your damned God! He's no use to you anymore. Can't you understand? I have come for you. Relax and let go. You will never be sick or worried again. It is a place of peace and warmth such as you experienced minutes ago. So let go, let go!'
>
> As the monster cajoled, it came closer and closer to Ann. Finally its mouth opened wide and it began to cover her face with its sticky maw. The heat of its breath and the unbearable stench emanating from it seemed to weaken Ann. The being's saliva felt hideously cold and slimy as the monster sucked her life force out... Ann began to struggle violently... the creature hissed in disappointment: 'I am your peace, and I am your strength. I will take care of you from now on. There is no god.' All three entities left through the bedroom wall and into the night... (Osborn, 1982)

In a chilling similarity we find certain images in common which have also appeared in other cases of both alien abduction and demonic infestation.

> An astral trip to some unknown, exotic place was standard fare. She saw the Egyptian pyramids... it was then that Ann felt that she was a part of eternity... immortal... safe, happy and free from pain.

In an interview with a member of the press, Ann Haywood was trying to explain how "the Lady" transported her in time to distant places.

> "She puts the robe around me and then my mind separates from my body. I can look back and see it lying there. Then we go up through the ceiling, pop out the roof, and fly into space. One night the Lady took me back in time. We were in a foreign country and the people wore old-fashioned clothes. The Lady took on the appearance of a beautiful woman in a blue robe. She performed miracles for them..."
>
> Suddenly Ann's face turned ashen and she asked to be excused. Her scream of pain was heard from the bathroom where she had taken refuge. When Ann came out, she was sniffling and holding her abdomen. The Lady had savagely attacked her for revealing that down through history, creatures like the Lady have taken the form of saints. They then use the gullibility of humankind to misguide and misinform people so that they believe they are seeing miracles performed. Ann begged the newsman to delete that portion of the interview. (Osborn, 1982)

And, reminiscent of the vampire and the Karla Turner case, Ann Haywood suffered too: contact with the 'Lady' was always physically draining. Ann felt used each time the creature took her, and her health deteriorated with each attack. The demon was slowly killing her both physically and mentally. If she wanted to make love with her husband the 'Lady' would tell her, "Ann do not waste your time in senseless copulation. I need your strength. You are mine..."

Ann's demon is also quite talkative, and we should pause to consider whether her talk is factual or more lies and deception. In the cases of alien abduction the scenario follows the demon infestation syndrome up to a point: the aliens are rarely, if ever, forced to admit their nefarious intentions. The demons, when queried under certain circumstances, will become quite verbose.

The 'Lady' transformed itself into a leopard and then a wolf-like beast. "We can take any form we choose... My kind rules this world. Destiny is changed forever when one of us appears... *Soon, not just you, Ann, but the whole world will know us*. Before the year two thousand, no one will deny our existence. But before your soul returns to spirit, another must replace you. There is one now who is being influenced."

Mechanical failures have been prevalent whenever Ann is present. Eugene Wyatt conducted the original interview before assigning a reporter to the feature article that was prepared for publication in the *Tennessean* (June 4, 1978 issue). The recording was taped on professional equipment. Yet, the machine tore up the tape. Mr. Wyatt said on record, "The computer failed immediately and had to be reset twice. When we tried to edit the story on a video-display terminal, it also failed. The whole power-supply section had to be replaced. It just burned out."

When a local television station did some footage with Ann at her home and later ran it through a monitor at the station, the film came out a dazzling red. The technician said he'd never seen a similar anomaly.

This is a condensation of Ann's remarks from several interviews:

> I'm saying that there are invisible worlds and beings that populate them. Just because we can't see them doesn't mean they don't exist... Every animal has a natural enemy. And so does mankind. It's not disease or death, but terrible creatures that watch us all until we become weak. Then they hover around us like vultures picking at a corpse. When this happens, we become broken in spirit. That's when people do terrible, unspeakable things. They commit suicide or kill others and just create misery for everyone. Often, the victims end up in mental institutions...
>
> One of those monsters lives inside of me... she only hurts me when I defy her. I try to stay on her good side. She's very temperamental and has a terrible temper. The Lady doesn't like religion, either. She doesn't believe in God as I do... the Lady doesn't communicate directly with anyone but me. Some have seen her, and she's left her voice on cassette tapes, but she's never spoken directly to anyone but me.
>
> I can speak to her aloud or in my thought. She knows everything you and I are saying and thinking. When she speaks, she has a woman's voice. When she's angry the tone is deeper.
>
> The Lady seems to know everything... sometimes we talk about the place she wants to take me to. She says I'll find peace and rest, no worry, no sickness and that I won't have to die a painful physical death like everybody else... I have never gone all the way to the place she wants to take me because I was afraid I wouldn't come back...

When I am with her it's usually a very pleasant feeling – when she's in a good mood – it's warm and peaceful... all my problems are blotted out... it's just a complete silence and we're together...

One thing the Lady doesn't like is that I pray a lot. She thinks I should never do that. If I don't stop when she asks me too she gets angry... my praying interferes with my relationship with her...

I don't think she's afraid of God. When I do go to church, she won't let me concentrate on what the preacher is saying... she distracts me somehow and she waits just beyond the church property line for me to come out... I thought at first that she was of the Devil...

I cry about it a lot... when I get depressed about it, the Lady snaps me right out of the bad mood... she tells me something about her side of the world – where I would go and what I would do and that changes my outlook and I just perk up... no suffering, no worrying, no death, a land that's filled with promise, where the idea that you can make something of yourself doesn't exist – you already are something... it feels like a tug-of-war and I'm in the middle. If I didn't love my family, I might have already gone with her. A lot of times I am tempted to give in...

She's also trying to convince me that I can't help anybody else who has a problem like mine. She says mine is not a mental illness... It's a reality conflict...

In the beginning I was really terrified. I would turn around and she would be there. I was afraid to go to sleep ant night, because she would come mostly at night, when everything was quiet, or in the daytime when I was at home alone. But usually she appears at night, when I settle down.

She comes, and we go away together. She puts the cape around me and it seems like I go off into a dream world. The Lady takes me to beautiful places here on this planet or to other planets, and sometimes into the far, far past. Occasionally we even visit the future, but I don't understand any of it...

I still can't get used to the way she looks... she's not like we are. Not at all. She doesn't even seem to have the same body composition as humans. When she touches me with her hands, it's like touching dry ice... her hands just stick to my skin, and they leave red marks wherever she touches... The physical contact stings from the coldness and also burns a little...

When she wants to she can control my thoughts. If she wants me to say something about her while she listens to a conversation, she'll let me remember things. But if she doesn't like a person, all information about her is erased from my mind as if she doesn't exist.

> She says it's time for me to talk about her. Also, she says that soon the whole world will know about her kind... she told me I was chosen... she needs people... she needs my breath. The Lady needs that in order to survive in the human world. She has to have it on a daily basis in order to exist on our plane. I supply her with the breath of life every day, sometimes as often as three or four times a day. More energy output on her part and mine requires more feedings of breath... its the same sensation as you get when you hyperventilate... the Lady has to have breath in order to stay down here...
>
> I know that I'm going to have to give up my family because they're Christian. I was saved at one time until the Lady came into my life. She says 'I don't know why you believe in old books that tell about a God that you must worship. That God belongs to other people and not to you. Have you ever seen God? You see me and you know that I am real, that I exist.'... it seems as if there's something like an army buildup. A forceful thing on both sides... she said that she will convince me sooner or later that there is no God ... she thrives on wickedness. (Osborn, 1982)

Considering the matter in depth, I could see a tradition stretching back thousands of years, of otherworldly beings abducting humans and their children.

Along with most rationalists, I had always considered these stories to be "psycho-dramas", or "artifacts of consciousness". The study of anomalous experiences, the paranormal, and related psycho-spiritual fields has occupied many of the brightest minds of our race for millennia and in the past two-hundred years or so, the explanations have tended to emphasize a particular reality as being the arbiter of all that exists, and anything that does not fit into that materialistic and anthropocentric reality is discarded as either irrelevant or pathological.

It's clear that strange things have continued to happen despite the fact that they do not conform to the rationalist scientific reality construct. However, what is distressing about that is the fact that it seems, for the most part, such events may be behind most of the world's religions. This is worrisome because of the fact that in those cases where the religious trappings are stripped away, the phenomena does not seem to be favorable toward humanity. Jacques Vallee's control system hypothesis is interesting in this regard. He writes:

> I believe there is a system around us that *transcends time as it transcends space*. The system may well be able to locate itself in outer space, but its manifestations are *not spacecraft in the ordinary 'nuts and bolts' sense*. The UFOs are physical manifestations that

cannot be understood apart from their psychic and symbolic reality. What we see in effect here is not an alien invasion. It is *a control system* which acts on humans and *uses* humans. (Vallee, 1979)

In other words, what Vallee was suggesting was something very similar to The Matrix, as represented in the movie by that name. However, I was looking at this and considering it long before the movie was made and the idea popularized. The very idea that this might be a reality that dominated or controlled our own was staggering. What made the problem so terrifying was the fact that my studies and experiences in "spirit attachment" and demonic possession were also reflected in the so-called UFO and alien phenomena.

The fact that modern alien abductions mirror demonic infestation and vampirism is part of a historical pattern. A pattern implies a pattern maker. What we are concerned with is who or what that pattern maker is, and for what purpose is it operating the control system.

The first thing I noticed in deeply studying this phenomenon was that some encounters with entities seem accidental, but others clearly are directed at a specific person. This led me to wonder whether the seemingly accidental encounters were as accidental as they appeared to be. In such cases, I had to ask: did the manifestation occur in response to some hidden need, a psychological state that calls for outside intervention of some kind?

French UFOlogist Jean-Francois Boëdec, in his book *Fantastiques recontres au bout du monde* (1982), suggests that UFO sightings start long before the actual experience. He noted many cases in which the witnesses had premonitions that something was about to happen, or for some reason they went home by a different route, or took an unaccustomed walk. Somehow, it seems, the witnesses were being prepared for the experience they were about to undergo. In many cases, the abductee claims there is a sensation of a presence before an actual encounter takes place.

I can't say that any such "premonition" occurred in my own experiences. I walked out to that swimming pool thinking of nothing but floating, relaxing, and maybe catching a meteor or two streaking across the sky. But that may simply be due to a lack of sensitivity or awareness to certain subtle clues. Perhaps my rational approach acted as a barrier?

However, Boëdec has a point. In my work with Spirit Release Therapy (which I should mention was a therapy I used because it worked, not because I "believed" in it) many so-called "attached entities" I "conversed with" during spirit release hypnosis sessions claimed that their host was chosen "before he was born". As I pointed out above, in most cases, a line of contact and the gradually building assault can be traced back to childhood. It might be said, in general, that the process of possession has already begun before the target or those around him are aware of the signs. But this flies in the face of many religious and philosophical teachings that tell us that we have "free will".

In any case of psychic vampirism or actual possession, there is usually a point at which the entity enters into a relationship with the individual. A decision is made by the victim to allow that contact. This often occurs simply *because the victim is not aware of the significance of the event.* It seems to be a minor event and may come as the result of tiredness, mental excitation, frustration, or pain.Another disturbing factor that emerged from my research was that these beings, whether demons, vampires or aliens, seem to have the ability to control our thoughts to a certain extent, our physical bodies, the weather and even events in our lives, to the point that we can be worn down under such attack and give in to their control almost by default. In the case of alien abductions, these may be the events staged as "alien abductions" which could be designed for the very purpose of wearing down the victim and inducing acquiescence.

Another element that is historically evident is the "physical exam". The famed Betty and Barney Hill case describes a simulated medical test in which a long needle is inserted into the navel. A fifteenth century French calendar, the *Kalendrier des bergiers*, illustrates the tortures inflicted by what were being called "demons" on the people they have taken. The demons are depicted piercing their victims' abdomens with long needles.

Jacques Vallee has expressed doubts that a material civilization with space and time travel capabilities would come in such numbers to do "stupid" things like abduct people and perform primitive experiments or examinations on them.

Many people report that their abductors are benevolent beings, but when we consider all the factors of the big picture of the phenomenon, it seems that such stories of benevolence may be misleading.

Kenneth Ring discovered that a large sample of people who reported near-death experiences (NDE) also tended to have had other, prior, "unusual experiences", including UFO sightings and/or abductions which were interpreted by them in a positive way. After their NDE, they generally reported a remarkable change very similar to a religious conversion. They also often reported the sudden acquisition of a new talent or interest. Ring tested his subjects in different ways, and most of them had high scores on what is called the *dissociative personality scale*. Such people are easily hypnotized and tend to  daydream a lot. So, there does seem to be a direct connection between thinking that ET is "good" and dissociation.

The skeptics jumped for joy at this news. They leapt onto the idea that Ring's experiencers were all simply inveterate fantasizers, or if they had in fact been abused, this "traumatization" led to a "need for attention and self-esteem" which led them to fantasize these experiences. Since there was a clear correlation between those who had experienced "positive alien interactions" and clearly pathological states, the label was slapped on everyone who acknowledged the possibility that the alien reality was more than just a meme infection.

Ring suggested that childhood dissociation might be a technique that an abused person could develop to adapt to a difficult situation. Because these people become strongly dissociative from an early age on, they find it easier to enter altered states of consciousness. Ring then proposed that since people in such altered states might have a wider range of perception than ordinary people, they might be more "prone" to experience paranormal events than a control group who might also be exposed, but unable to perceive them.

There is another way of looking at Ring's findings: it may be that people who are *not* able to perceive more subtle realities, might very well be the ones who are viewing reality in a dissociated state: dissociated from what *is*, the objective world. Whether they are promoting the "alien reality" as a positive experience, or the SETI reality, or any other reality that does not take into account the broadest range of observable facts, such individuals may be operating in pathological states of dissociation. In this sense, the idea that "God is in heaven and all is right with the world" is as much a fantasy as the idea that mankind is the result of mindless evolution.

A very simple way of looking at it is in terms of what is popularly called Stockholm Syndrome. A person who is not aware of the subtext of the play of forces in our world, a person who, as I had done, compartmentalizes things so they do not have to see the implicatory connections, may be the one who has dissociated and identified with the rationalist, materialistic interpretation of reality. In other words, if there is a control system as Vallee suggests, an Evil Magician, as Gurdjieff called it, it very likely promotes this view in order to conceal itself.

The term Stockholm Syndrome was coined in the early 70's to describe the puzzling reactions of four bank employees to their captors. On August 23, 1973, three women and one man were taken hostage in one of the largest banks in Stockholm. They were held for six days by two ex-convicts who threatened their lives but also showed them kindness. To the world's surprise, all of the hostages strongly resisted the government's efforts to rescue them and were quite eager to defend their captors. Indeed, several months after the hostages were saved by the police, they still had warm feelings for the men who threatened their lives. Two of the women eventually got engaged to the captors.

Psychologist Dee Graham has theorized that Stockholm Syndrome occurs on a societal level. Since our culture is patriarchal, she believes that all women suffer from it – to widely varying degrees, of course. She has expanded on her theories in *Loving to Survive: Sexual Terror, Men's Violence, and Women's Lives*, which is well worth reading.

The dynamics of Stockholm Syndrome directly address the issue of those who view their "abductions" as "desirable". Victims have to concentrate on survival, requiring avoidance of direct, honest reaction to destructive treatment.

When there is a socially imposed mandate to "think nice thoughts" and view the world in a positive light, even in the face of evidence to the contrary, people find it necessary to become highly attuned to the approval or disapproval of the "social norms". As a result, they are motivated to learn how to think in social norms, and do not examine their own, honest experiences. As victims of Societal Stockholm Syndrome, we are encouraged to develop psychological characteristics pleasing to the system. These include: dependency, lack of initiative, inability to act, decide, think; strategies for staying alive, including denial, attentiveness to the system's demands, wants, and expressions of approval of the system itself. We are taught to develop fondness for the system accompanied by fear of interference by anyone who challenges the system's perspective. Most of all, we are conditioned to be overwhelmingly grateful to the system for giving us life. We focus on the system's kindnesses, not its acts of brutality. Denial of terror and anger, and the perception of the system as omnipotent keep us psychologically attached to the Matrix Control System. High anxiety functions to keep us from seeing available options. Psychophysical stress responses develop. Such persons might even think that ET would land on the White House Lawn to "serve mankind".

This materialist reasoning applied to our reality reduces *ideas about other realities* to what are becoming popularly known as memes. A meme is a self-propagating idea, a unit of cultural imitation that, much like a biological or computer virus, effectively programs its own retransmission. They spread through motivating their "hosts" to create novel presentations of old ideas, and to proselytize. In this way it is suggested that ideas and beliefs are created by a specific combination of physical and psychological factors, and spread like contagions – cognitive viruses.

"Experts" will tell us that the concepts of alien invasion are merely memes, or metaphors, for penetration by forces we perceive as originating outside of ourselves. They suggest that such ideas are pathological contagions that contaminate our conscious and subconscious lives the same way a computer virus invades an operating system. It is then suggested that such a "virus" can destroy what is orderly and leave only fragmentation and disintegration. Some of them even suggest that the very idea of aliens is like the movie, "Alien", where the creature breeds inside the human, and at some terrible moment, erupts in blood and gore. We are assured that this idea "eats at us from the inside out".

Whoa! That's a heavy image!

One person in ten says that they have seen a UFO. According to a recent survey I read, about ninety percent of us believe Earth has been visited by extraterrestrials. But it is the strangest thing I have ever observed that these statistics will lead ordinarily intelligent people to suggest that this is a "psychosocial phenomenon of huge magnitude", rather than addressing the broader "reality" of UFO-ET phenomena. Talk about Stockholm Syndrome! I know whereof I speak because I tried that approach myself.

I had spent years studying psychic and psychological phenomena, and had come to the firm idea that any and all of it was simply a matter of understanding the nature of consciousness, perception, beliefs, memory, dreams, memory of dreams, the formation of images and its philosophical counterpart – it was all mind, and nothing else. I was convinced that our beliefs created our reality, and that "you spot it, you got it". If we didn't believe it to be possible, we don't see it.

In early 1994, as I was going through the research, and after another series of strange events which I have chronicled in some detail in my autobiography, *Amazing Grace*, I had a conversation with Frank that was extremely distressing. Frank began by listing the string of strange, synchronistic and even somewhat miraculous events that had brought me to this moment. He cited point after point through my life history, right up to the past few years when the strangeness of events, including bizarre synchronicities, had multiplied to the point that I felt like I was living in a madhouse where normal reality no longer held sway. The effect of having all of these things brought together in a sweeping view of my life history was overwhelming. It's one thing to have things happen sequentially, over a period of time, in more or less in isolation, which you can then shove under the rug and try to forget until the next incident, and quite another to have to look at it all in context. I had to admit that it certainly appeared that there were forces at work in life, in my own life particularly, that are not generally accounted for in the normal systems of explaining the order of the universe. In the face of the evidence, presented more or less as witness testimony in a courtroom might have been, I felt the formerly solid earth of my reference system slowly crumbling beneath my feet. With each point he made, I felt like another wave was washing over my foundation of sand. I seemed to be sinking into the mire of complete lunacy.

How can you deal with a life that has gone completely over the edge in terms of strangeness that you neither wish to experience, nor perpetuate?

As Frank pointed out, even though I was most definitely a "non-believer", as soon as I had been exposed to knowledge about the alien phenomenon, I encountered my first "alien abductee" case. Didn't I think this was unusual? And wasn't it a fact that UFOs had accompanied that first "abduction" session I'd conducted? Didn't I think this was an unusual phenomenon? Not everyone who might be an abductee under hypnosis attracts a whole flap of UFOs.

The question was, of course: was it the abductee or the therapist in whom the denizens of UFO-land were interested?

I didn't like the way the conversation was going.

Frank then pointed out the obvious (to him) connection between my deteriorating physical state and my own UFO encounter. When I protested there may be no relation at all, he pointed out how my dog had suffered and died within a very short time after this "exposure", and how my symptoms always seemed to peak at exactly the time of night the UFO had come along. What was my explanation for that little item?

I had none. I was distressed for him even to put it in words. As long as it was unspoken, I could continue to ignore it.

He kept pressing his points described in *Amazing Grace*: what about the Face at the Window? What about the kidnapping when I was a child by an individual who had been connected to the Navy in some mysterious way? What about the light outside at boarding school? What about the incident when I awakened reversed in the bed? What about all the gynecological mishaps I had suffered? On and on he went. And as he ticked off each item, I felt more and more nauseated.

Frank's theory was that the whole drama of recent times – a series of events spread across several counties, including dozens of witnesses, most of whom I didn't even know – was "staged" to get my attention; to wake me up. What was more, even our meeting was obviously a "destined" event.[21]

I did not like what Frank was saying. Like the incidents of the wet nightgown and the strange lights, I was really struggling to ignore the

---

[21] There was a bizarre series of synchronicities surrounding this that I have also recounted in *Amazing Grace*.

anomalies in my life. I did not like the connotation Frank was putting on my experiences. In the first place, I had studied too much, seen too much, and worked with too many troubled people to overlook the dangers of ego and subconscious tendencies to distort. When anyone starts to think they are "special", that God is "talking" to them, it's a sure sign of descent into delusion and "magical thinking".

Nevertheless, I had read many cases by now of strange events similar to my own that were attributed to "aliens", and that was the problem. If it wasn't "aliens", who or what was it? If it was what people were calling "aliens", did this mean they literally visitors from deep space? Or were so-called aliens merely artifacts – induced perceptions – of victims of some vast government mind control experiment? Most terrifying of all: were aliens what had been known as demons throughout history?

Of course, in my own mind, there was an additional twist to this line of logic: Why would anyone or anything go to so much trouble to set up so many bizarre things to get my attention if I wasn't supposed to do something about it? If I was supposed to do something, they had certainly picked the wrong person, because it was becoming pretty clear that I was probably not going to live a lot longer.

Considering "this UFO business" had another effect on me: I was grieving. I mourned the years I'd spent studying and digging for answers, only to have it all trashed in one night by a stupid black boomerang.

"Why me?"

"That's what you need to figure out", Frank said.

What I was figuring out wasn't very pleasant. Because of my experience as a hypnotherapist, I could detect the "signature" of a malevolent intelligences working in my life and my experiences in an effort to either destroy or divert me from something. If these evil beings had the power to interfere in my life with malicious intent, even when I was deeply involved with positive thinking and meditation – which one would suppose should act as a defense – what protection did anyone have? Were we, the human race, defenseless against these creatures?

The words of Gurdjieff came back to haunt me. Were the belief systems of metaphysics and religion useless drivel promulgated by an Evil Magician to convince people they were Lions, Men, Eagles or Magicians instead of sleeping sheep?

What kind of madhouse had I opened my eyes to see? Was the fact that I had seen it the very source of its existence? Was I, by noticing evil, more vulnerable to attack? Surely not: The evidence of the presence of evil threaded its way through the lives of others who denied all the clues. I saw clearly the "mechanical" or "accidental" nature of the Universe that Gurdjieff talked about. I realized that our own programmed refusal to see reality, our ignorance, was the chief door in our lives through which Evil entered.

Was it possible, as Gurdjieff suggested, to become free of this? To awaken? To see the projector behind the slide show of our lives? And, more important, to see who was running the projector and why?

I struggled with my thoughts and emotions for days. I was truly passing through the valley of the shadow of death. I had thoroughly convinced myself that UFOs and aliens could not possibly exist. In fact, even after the flap surrounding the hypnosis session with Pat, I had contemptuously declared that the "Millennial Disease" was spreading. Upon seeing the thing itself with my own eyes, I had pronounced it to be a flock of geese, in the same way I had rationalized the wet nightgown and grass seeds on the night I woke up reversed in my bed.

All those times, including the night I saw the strange light in the snow at boarding school, the events had been followed by protracted illnesses. If there were other incidents preceding any of my other physical disturbances, I certainly didn't remember them. But by now, from studying the literature, I was aware that many people might remember nothing at all.

After reading almost 15 hours a day for months – everything on the subject I could get my hands on – I began to realize: Some sort of "alien presence" on our planet *is real*, and everybody is telling lies about it. I was terrified.

If there is a psycho-spiritual or even literally physical "invasion" taking place before our very eyes, under our very noses, represented in the symbol system of our lives and experiences, interacting with this "control system" at some deep level, what kind of protection do we have?

Well, in thinking about it deeply, it does appear that these beings – whatever they turn out to be – can plunder our world, our lives and our very minds at will. But I also have observed that they seem to be going to an awful lot of trouble to conceal their activities and to confuse observers with hundreds of crazy stories of different "races" and groups of semi-mythological "good guys and bad guys".

After spending some time attempting to prove that the ET hypothesis was essentially a psychic contagion, a meme, a "Millennial Disease", and failing, I came to the realization that the reality of the phenomenon of psychic contagion was an important part of the process, but in a completely opposite way of what was being suggested by the "experts". What I noticed was the fact that "memes" seemed to be significantly present *in the context of obscuring the issue*. What seems to happen is that false ideas about what is really happening spread from core "authorities", such as the authors of popular books about UFOs, alien abductions, and so on, and this is seemingly designed to create "attitudes", perceptual controls, "reinterpretations" of personal experiences *by the act of implanting ideas about oneself and about the nature of experiences* which, due to their hyperdimensional nature, are ambiguous. In short, "memes" are the essence of Societal Stockholm Syndrome!

As it happens, in spite of the many claims that only those who "believe in the phenomenon" tend to experience it, the fact is that those who report the most intense involvements frequently never "believed" in the phenomenon at all, and confronted with the traumatic nature of their experiences, do *not* want to even consider that it might be real.

Considering people who, as Hynek described them, "through a long exposure to the subject, or motivated by a haunting curiosity to work in the field and to get our hands dirty with the raw data, came to know there was a signal", such individuals begin to view the world as it is, defying the memes that are generated and released on society like a form of bio-semiotic warfare. Of course, there is a special type of "meme" that is propagated to "reduce" or macerate those who suggest a reality to the UFO phenomenon as were typically used historically against anyone who perceived a higher reality, including great saints and mystics of all kinds. In such cases, a connection between sexual life and religious emotions is often drawn; conversion is a "crisis of puberty"; devotion is just the parental instinct of self-sacrifice run amok; the search for meaning to it all is merely a hysterical starvation for a more earthly object of affection, and so on. All of these are tactics of discrediting states of mind that produce nonlinear shifts in the psychic landscape.

St. Paul had an epileptic seizure on the Road to Damascus, Saint Teresa was a hysteric, George Fox suffered a disordered colon,

Carlyle had an ulcer. Those who are looking for a materialist explanation for everything will find all sorts of disordered glandular functions, and voila! All spiritual verities will be successfully disposed of and skepticism and the Blind Watchmaker will reign supreme!

The problem with these reductionist explanations is this: even if it is true that St. Paul had epilepsy, and that is the "materialistic account" of his vision on the road to Damascus, does that then negate the spiritual significance of the event? Because, in point of fact, every single "spiritual condition" – positive or negative – probably does have an expression in physiology.

We would also like to note that the hard-core skeptic is as likely to be skeptical because he suffers liver disease as the born again Christian is likely to be converted because his ulcer drives him to seek relief. The evil magician can have a dirty colon and the psychic vampire can have false teeth. In short, raptures and rants can be equally represented by organic conditions. And if this is taken *as the model of verity*, then none of our ideas, our thoughts, feelings, scientific doctrines, beliefs or disbeliefs, have any value at all. If such an idea is the theory upon which we are to evaluate our reality, then we must theorize that *every* idea emanates from the state of the body of the originator. That is to say: what is sauce for the goose, is sauce for the gander.

As I continued my examination of the standard religions as well as the many and varied New Age teachings, I saw these systems being used as the very means of propagating memes. I could see individuals with no extensive knowledge of historical metaphysics being fooled by a belief in the "benefits" of alien abduction. We repeatedly see terms describing "light" or related phenomena. This tends to make the percipients regard the experience as "good". Gurdjieff was right: mankind *is* asleep and one of the conditions of this sleep is the absence of an active "B.S. meter".

Many people reporting "abductions", when the surface or screen memories have been probed in a competent way, reveal memories of events so chilling in their implications that the first interpretation must be looked at carefully. The fear evoked in these experiences is tangible. Yet, these other beings somehow convince their victims that all they do is for "the good of the planet" or "the enhancement of our race". Even the esteemed John E. Mack, M.D., professor of psychiatry at Harvard, seems to have been taken in by such a view. He writes in *Abduction*:

> The idea that men, women, and children can be taken against their wills from their homes, cars, and schoolyards by strange humanoid beings, lifted onto spacecraft, and subjected to intrusive and threatening procedures is so terrifying, and yet so shattering to our notions of what is possible in our universe, that the actuality of the phenomenon has been largely rejected out of hand or bizarrely distorted in most media accounts...
>
> My own work with abductees has impressed me with the powerful dimension of personal growth that accompanies the traumatic experiences ... especially when these people receive appropriate help in exploring their abductions histories...
>
> Let us suppose that [Cosmic Intelligence] ... is not indifferent to the fate of the Earth, regarding its life forms and transcendent beauty as one of its better or more advanced creations. And let us imagine that the imbalance created by the over growth of certain human faculties ... were diagnosed ... as the basic problem. What could be done as a corrective? The two natural approaches of which we can conceive would be the genetic and the environmental. Is it possible that through a vast hybridization program affecting countless numbers of people, and a simultaneous invasion of our consciousness with transforming images of our self-destruction, an effort is being made to place the planet under a kind of receivership?

This view is rooted in emotional beliefs that cling desperately to any straw offered that those more powerful than we are "good". If they are not, what are we to do?

As I waded through the literature, I came across many controversial accounts said to originate from military intelligence officers, physicists hired to work on secret projects, and others claiming inside knowledge of a vast government cover-up. Some of these revelations match the reports of other individuals who claim to have recalled, either consciously or under hypnosis, scenes of unparalleled horror and abuse at the hands of some of the so-called alien visitors. This is generally taken as corroboration of one by the other. But we have to ask: why would participants in a cover-up be motivated to come forward? Is it that such individuals, having penetrated deeper into the veil of secrecy, have become horrified witnesses whose consciences prompted them to talk? Perhaps those in power began keeping their arrangements secret, only to discover they had a tiger by the tail and couldn't let go? Maybe they began sending "agents" out to "reveal" fragments of the truth, while the possibility of forced exposure looms ever closer? Or, perhaps, such individuals are part of a vast mind-control experiment designed like a monstrous crazy-making drama, where the government secretly promotes a belief in aliens while publicly denying it?

The book *Clear Intent* by Lawrence Fawcett and Barry J. Greenwood provides evidence based on the government's own documents that the highest-ranking public officials and the elite of the U.S. security and intelligence organizations have deliberately and persistently lied about aliens and UFOs for the last fifty years. That is raw data. Interpretations ought to be made rather carefully.

One thing I became aware of as I proceeded with the research was that there are quite a number of people who claim to be psychic, who have prophetic "dreams" or visions, or who channel "space brothers", claim that they are being contacted by beings who are here to "help" us or to "save us" if only we will let them, or have other psychic experiences may, in fact, be victims of quite different processes. These stories are spread around, increasing the level of confusion.

The bottom line seems to be that the idea that negative forces do not exist, and even if they did, there's no need to worry, is the greatest deception of all. We are repeatedly told: if we just think nice thoughts, or meditate regularly, or get saved, or repeat our affirmations, nothing icky will ever enter our reality. The facts seem to be that, as Vallee says:

> [T]here is a system around us that *transcends time as it transcends space*... What we see in effect here is not an alien invasion. It is *a control system* which acts on humans and *uses* humans.

We are not dealing with materialistic, Earth-based technology here! These guys walk through walls, float people out of their bodies and control minds – the abilities we have historically attributed to angels or demons or vampires. In the past, we dealt with ghosts and "gods" and demons. We are dealing with the same entities now, only we are calling them "aliens". They probably always *were* "aliens!" And maybe they want to be "gods" again.

One thing I knew for sure from doing the spirit release work, evil insinuates itself into our lives in the guise of goodness and truth. This problem is made even worse by the acceptance of the New Age teaching that "evil" simply does not exist unless an individual creates it in their reality. Evil follows the line of erosion of our spirituality *through the erosion of knowledge*. What better way to protect evil activities than to deny that they exist?

The New Age types say that putting one's attention on these ideas "gives them energy". This is true only if one focuses in this way with the intention of participation. However, a comprehensive understanding of these forces is absolutely necessary in order to know how to give them less energy.

It was a stunning and grotesque prospect for me to consider that humanity, as a whole, has been used and cunningly deceived for millennia. I realized that the UFO and alien business was truly nothing new. We have historical records of these phenomena stretching back thousands of years. If these beings could get what they want simply by moving in and taking it, would they spend so much time creating terror and confusion? Alternatively, perhaps the terror and confusion is exactly what they want to generate because they feed on it. That makes me also wonder why they are going to so much trouble to persuade us to accept their total control if they could take it at will? These guys would not be spending so much time terrorizing us and trying to sneak in the back door if it were possible for them to walk in directly. There is something we have that they want. There is some power we have that they don't want us to discover.

The act of facing the "pattern of activity" behind the events of my own life that bespoke such a hidden reality was absolutely soul searing and mind numbing. It acted as a conflict between my internal integrity, intellectual acuity, and all my emotional beliefs in a kind and loving god.

Well, I was most definitely learning, but I didn't like what I was learning. As I have said, of all people who never wanted to know anything at all about UFO's and aliens, I deserve a place at the head of the line. Yet, there it was.

To consider the idea of malevolent beings in control of our world that could prey on us at will, behind our ordinary reality, was utterly soul shattering.

I began to see the possibility of an interpenetrating reality of more or less physical solidity that interacted with humans as we may interact with wildlife in a forest: the hunters and the hunted.

Standing back from my life in overview, there were the hints of some sort of pattern maker, and it wasn't God in any sense that I had ever conceived of Him. Yes, I could see both positive actions and negative actions; a dynamic interplay of forces that related in some direct way to my own thinking, seeking, and growth. But exactly what it was, and precisely how it operated, I couldn't tell yet. It was like a shadow show where the shadows are produced by certain angles of light behind objects which, when finally revealed, may bear no resemblance whatsoever to the form of the shadow. A balled up fist could as easily be interpreted as a bird or a dog, or – when expanded to its full shape – a hand. Just what was I seeing? What's more, why did it seem that I was being challenged to see it? Why me?

I struggled until I was exhausted in my soul.

***

All through the early months of 1994 we had continued our weekly sittings. We had a number of participants who came and went, hoping to use the experiment to win the lottery. Most of them didn't understand that asking for lottery numbers was the smallest part of it. We also regularly "tested" various entities with questions about weather, politics, news items of various sorts, asked for predictions about this or that person and, admittedly, asked all kinds of snoopy questions just to see what would bounce back.

The point was to establish a "feedback" loop designed to access deep levels of consciousness at the least, or to "tune" the bio-cosmic receiver, at most. Most part-time participants had neither the patience nor the motivation to continue in anything that did not provide instant gratification. They wanted to be able to just "turn on, tune in and channel now!" Working at it was too much like – well – like work!

There was one individual who was a regular participant for almost half a year: Candy. I had met Candy through another series of truly bizarre events, and when she learned that I worked with hypnosis, she immediately wanted to be hypnotized because she was convinced that she had been abducted by aliens.

After dealing with Pat the night of the Flying Black Boomerangs, I wasn't too anxious to dive into that arena again. Just because I was a good hypnotist and had good techniques and ideas, didn't mean that I knew beans from apple butter about handling an alleged alien abductions. All the reading I was doing wasn't going to give me the technical education I needed to handle it, either.

Well, naïve bozo that I sometimes am, I thought it would just be a matter of making some calls to find who to go to for advice or training. I started at the logical place to begin: call the local psychologists and psychiatrists for guidance.

It wasn't a very good idea. Nobody in our semi-backwater area would even consider such an idea, much less touch it with a ten foot pole!

Okay. I called a couple of people at MUFON. Some names of psychologists in distant cities weren't going to do me any good. There also were MSW's (Masters of Social Work) specializing in "experience counseling", and even more with diploma mill Ph.D.'s or Th.D.'s (Doctorate in Theology) offering their services for nice fees.

Didn't anybody in the legitimate scientific fields think this phenomenon deserved investigation? Even if the phenomenon was bogus, what about the people claiming such experiences? Weren't they human beings deserving of counseling?

As I continued to make calls on Candy's behalf, the enormity of the problem began to overwhelm me. From what I could determine, many, many thousands of people – a cross section of humanity – were coming forward and saying that they had experienced contact with aliens from other worlds. In all my reading of history and social phenomena, I had never encountered anything quite like this. The general response that they get from others, including professionals who are supposed to be providing help and support, is *ridicule*.

In reviewing the cases available to me, I noted that the typical victim was almost frantically worried about a "loss of time", and some vague memory of being restrained or trapped. The person becomes hyper-irritable, suffers from loss of concentration and short-term memory. An "abductee" is generally hypersensitive to loud noises, claims to hear things no one else can hear, and to see things no one else can see, including getting "feelings" about others that are impossible to explain or quantify in any way.

One of the more disturbing aspects of the phenomenon is that there are often physical traces – scratches, puncture wounds, bruises – and even missing segments of skin, generally in perfectly round configuration as though removed by a cookie cutter.

Candy was obviously suffering. She was almost hysterical in her desperation to find an answer to what was going on in her life. It was clear that she felt almost abandoned by her husband and friends in this matter, because it was so strange and out of keeping with the other, utterly normal, aspects of her life. It was clear that she was suffering from severe anxiety, and a very real fear of being alone for even a short while.

No matter what the explanation for their experiences, these people needed to be taken seriously; they needed to be validated; and most of all they needed a support system.

Basically, I had three choices to consider in regards to Candy.

1) She was creating a hoax, no abduction occurred, and she knew it did not occur.

2) An abduction really occurred by persons or beings unknown.

3) No abduction occurred, but Candy believed it did.

I was rapidly giving up the idea that abduction stories were concocted for fame and glory. For most people, the event was one of great shame, and they most certainly didn't want anybody to know about it. That they were so desperate for help that they overcame tremendous reluctance indicates how severely they were traumatized.

The question of the sanity of people claiming to have been abducted was also rapidly being answered in the negative. If millions of people believed that a guy, 2000 years ago, died on a cross and arose three days later, and were considered sane, then people claiming abductions, with far more direct experience and evidence, were undoubtedly sane also.

I realized, however, that each individual case had to be considered separately. To assume anything from the beginning was not ethical. To begin an investigation of such an event meant that the only thing I would be dealing with was Candy's memory – either conscious or unconscious. Thus, a consideration of her life history was necessary. I was going to be far more thorough with Candy than I had been with Pat.

Candy was about 35 years old, the wife of a doctor, owner of her own fashion boutique, and mother to two girls. She had been born and raised in a very strict religious family, but, chafing at the restrictions, had left home at an early age to stay with a brother who worked in a designer clothing shop. There, she also began working in the same business and ended up marrying the owner. This man died, leaving her with a small child and a large inheritance.

A beautiful young widow with a baby and a lot of money does not remain on the marriage mart very long. With her new husband, the doctor (the spitting image of Dudley Do-Right), she moved to Florida where they had a second child together. The object was to get away from the unhappy memories of the loss of her first husband and start a new life. The boutique she left in the care of her brother, who managed the business on her behalf.

After her youngest child started school, Candy became bored and decided to go to work for a different doctor in the large medical complex where her husband also had his offices. She took an administrative position and settled into her role with ease. She was very intelligent, charming and attractive.

At the same time, Candy began to attend a Metaphysical/Spiritualist church, probably more out of curiosity than anything else, but soon became deeply involved in the spiritualist beliefs and practices. At this point, strange things began to happen. She claimed that strange things had happened to her all her life, but she just had managed to suppress most of it. I certainly understood this approach!

First, she kept encountering a man in the building where she worked. He was employed by a practice on a different floor, so she only saw him in the elevators, the parking lot, and the local cafes. Every time she did encounter him, she was conscious of a strange electricity between them. Soon they were exchanging brief pleasantries.

One evening, Candy and a co-worker, her friend Edith, went out for drinks together when Candy's husband was at a medical convention. The man she kept running into coincidentally appeared in the same bar and stopped by their table. They invited him to sit down and soon were involved in a conversation on metaphysical topics. Candy said that she could not recall how the subjects followed one after the other, but what was true was that in a very short period of time, the three of them were discussing deeply held beliefs, feeling intense rapport, and it was somewhat "magical". The man said he knew the location of an old Indian mound, apparently a place of great power. He offered to show both ladies where it was. Feeling secure with a female companion, Candy wanted to see this Indian mound, and they all went together in the man's car. Keep in mind that it was well past dark when they made this plan. When they arrived at the location, a swampy, wooded area on the Gulf of Mexico, they all got out and proceeded to hike through the underbrush to this purported Indian mound.

Now, aside from the absurdity of the picture presented here, three adults in their business clothing, hiking out in the muddy swamps after dark, there is the consideration of what, in the name of all good sense, would have sent anyone off on such a hike?

Nevertheless, that is, apparently, what they did. Three professional adults of impeccable good sense decided to go stomping in the tidal swamps on the Florida coast at night. At some point, Edith was left behind and lost and something happened to frighten Candy, but afterward she couldn't say what it was, only that she was very confused. She demanded to be taken home. The man cheerfully obliged, they located Edith wandering in the bushes, and he drove them back to their cars, and off they went home.

The only problem was, when Candy got home, it was almost midnight. She had "lost" well over two hours.

I went over this point with her carefully, going over the exact chronology of that night. She should have been home no later than 9:30 at the outside, yet, it was just a few minutes before midnight when she made it home. She was surprised because her children were already in bed sleeping, and the house was quiet and dark. When she saw the time, she became almost hysterical at the very thought that she had been gone so long. What might her children have thought?

At that point Candy's life began to fall apart. She was suddenly so emotional that she couldn't stay on an even keel from one minute to the next. She became almost uncontrollably obsessed with the man in the building, believing he was her "soul mate" one minute, and that he was a government spy the next. This was related to her belief that, somehow, the government was "watching" her. She felt that somehow she must find ways to be with this man because the government was using him against her, and they were really meant to be together. Then she felt he was watching her, and she had better avoid him.

Immediately following this event, her husband was in an auto accident with another woman in the car. Any reservations she might have had about the break-up of her marriage dissolved, and the relationship disintegrated rapidly. It was at this point that I first met her. In other words, she must have made her trip to the swamps at almost the exact time the series of synchronous events began to manifest in my own life that led me to meet Candy!

Candy apparently knew the abduction encounter scenario from reading or other sources. She thought she had experienced some sort of encounter with "Space Brothers". She was convinced that she had been given a message during her encounter, and that it was important for her to remember it to share with mankind.

Trying to get the story out of her in a linear way was like pulling teeth. The subject was so laden with emotion that it was difficult to make anything out of it without stopping her repeatedly, backing her up, and having her describe things in a sequential way. I didn't want to jump to any conclusions because I still held out for the possibility of other explanations. Based on the series of events, I thought it was also possible that she had been given some kind of "date rape" drug by this man who took her to the Indian mound with rather more ordinary – if reprehensible – intentions.

But Candy held firmly to the idea that the man had hypnotized her, that he was a government agent, and that the government was watching her because she was "chosen" by the aliens to deliver a message. Why or how he would be involved in her abduction if he were a government agent wasn't exactly clear, and certainly didn't make any sense. Candy knew it. She agreed with a rueful laugh that she knew she sounded crazy, and it was clear that she was close to the edge. She most definitely needed help, and if I couldn't find someone competent to send her to, or to instruct me, we might have been on our own with this one.

It also seemed to me to be important to find out how much Candy had read about alien abductions. She claimed that she had never read anything about it, that what she knew was just gossip and word of mouth, but I wasn't too sure. If she had spent a lot of time reading about the subject she was, in my opinion, "contaminated" as a true "test" subject. I could help her to deal with the trauma, but I could never consider her statements under hypnosis to be evidence of anything. After trying for weeks to find competent help without success, I finally agreed to do an "exploratory" session.

As might be expected, in Candy's subconscious mind, there were abductions galore. Candy was a veritable "chosen child" of the friendly Gray aliens. However, certain elements came up in her sessions that startled her. The abduction process was decidedly not as friendly as she'd thought. The following are extracts from a series of sessions done over a period of several months:

Q: Okay. What's happening to you next?

A: I see this bright light and I'm alarmed... I see fingers like suction cups on the end of them...

Q: What do they do?

A: They're like touching my face...

Q: How many individuals are there with you?

A: Oh God, this is weird. (Sigh.) It's almost like I see a dinosaur or something. With little short arms... and its, um... it's got funny skin... it's like, it's like... brownish, slickish... it's got a real funny face... it's like a skull but the front of the skull is like going out, real far out...

Q: Like a snout?

A: Yeah.

Q: How tall was it?

A: Um...

Q: Taller than you?

A: Oh yeah, it looked bigger than me. It's just funny.

Q: What's funny?

A: Nothing, it's gone.

Q: Where did it go.

A: I don't know. It disappeared.

Q: What do you mean it disappeared?

A: I don't know, it's almost like an image. And then it just vanished.

Q: How many other beings are there with you?

A: Um... they're all busy all over.

Q: About how many are there?

A: Um... five or six.

Q: What do they look like? Do they all look the same?

A: Oh, they're funny looking... they're almost like, um... they remind me of the baby dinosaur... how puffy his face was with the eyes were like... smaller... not big eyes like him... like squinty eyes...

Q: What color are their eyes?

A: Um... I don't know... when I look at their eyes I see a green circle that keeps swirling... [...]

Q: What is happening to you?

A: Um. (Sigh.) It's hard to breathe.

Q: Do you smell something?

A: No. I see a little... it's almost like a little gold scorpion. It's right by my nose... my face...

Q: What is it doing?

A: I don't know. They have it on the end of some tweezers.

Q: Where is the scorpion going?

A: (Signs of distress.) Uh, this is weird... it's almost like it goes in my mouth... the back of my... my, um, throat...

Q: How does it get there?

A: They put it there.

Q: How do they put it there?

A: Um... it's almost like I see a machine with an arm on it. Almost like a dentist's arm... I don't know...

Q: What is it for?

A: I don't know... television comes to my mind...

Q: Did they tell you what it was for?

A: No, they don't tell me.

Q: Is it in place now?

A: Um.. They're working on it. They're moving my head... I hear ringing in my ears

Q: What happens next?

A: Um... the back of my neck hurts!

Q: Why does the back of your neck hurt?

A: I don't know, its like... I have these headaches...

Q: Where are you now?

A: I'm on the table.

Q: What are they doing to you?

A: They're rubbing my arms.

Q: Has the scorpion been put in?

A: Um hmm.

Q: Did it hurt?

A: Um hmm.

Q: It did?

A: I don't know... it's just... I got a headache now...

Q: Where did they put it into.

A: Well, you know, it's like... in the back of my neck... its through my mouth into the back of my neck... and my ears... I hear my ears ringing... they're like clogged up... and I feel... I don't know... like shh... shocks or... I don't know...

Q: Shocks?

A: Pain shooting through my head.

Q: Pain? What is the pain from?

A: It's like nerve something... I don't know...

Q: Okay. You have a small mark above your ear... where did you get that mark?

A: I don't know, it's like, um... I don't know... I see this... I see a little tiny, um... metal box... I'm just gonna say what I see... I don't know...

Q: That's connected to the mark above your ear?

A: Yeah. It's almost like I feel like I'm being bit by an ant or something...

Q: Well, were you being bit by an ant?

A: Hm. When I thought... When you said that I see uh, um, it's almost like an ant made out of metal...

Q: Okay.

A: With the stingers.

Q: What does it do?

A: What, the ant?

Q: Um hmm.

A: It has... I'm seeing a needle on it...

Q: Long needle, short needle...

A: Uh, I see a needle... its like it connects to something...

Q: What does it do?

A: Goes in and it connects to something... I don't know...

Q: Did this happen at the same time that the scorpion was put in your neck through your throat?

A: No... (Distress.)

Q: Let's go back to where you are on the table and they have just put the little scorpion in the back of your neck through your throat... Now, you said this hurt... Did it hurt when they put it in? Or did it begin hurting after they put it in?

A: After they put it in. I had a headache... I have a headache... [...]

Q: Okay. How long have you been connected with this group?

A: Um... I just see a face in front of me...

Q: What does the face look like?

A: Um...

Q: Is it one of them?

A: Um hmm... it has real sad eyes... it doesn't want me saying anything... [...]

Q: Do they have any future plans?

A: I hear something saying yes.

Q: Do you know when?

A: No.

Q: Do you know what's in store... what will happen? Are you in cooperation with them?

A: Umm... I don't know... I don't feel good.

Q: What are you feeling right now...

A: I don't know... I'm feeling kind of sick to my stomach.

Q: Take a real deep breath and the nausea will pass.

A: Oh, God! (Sigh.)

Q: Now, Candy I'm here and I'll take care of you. You know we discussed beforehand that we want to know at the deepest level we can understand. Are these beings working with you with your permission?

A: Umm... No.

Q: Is there action you can take, or that you can perceive in a broad way, to prevent this kind of action or activity?

A: Umm... I don't know what this is I'm seeing... a tunnel...

Q: You're seeing what, a tunnel?

A: A tunnel with like webs all on it... I don't know what it is... its... (Long pause, signs of distress.)

Q: A tunnel with webs in it?

A: Yeah... it's not a nice place... (Signs of extreme nausea and distress.) Mmmm...

Q: If the tunnel could speak, what would it say?

A: You don't want to be here.

Q: Where is here?

A: It's almost like "where we can put you if we want you".

Q: What is there?

A: Bad stuff.

Q: What kind of bad stuff?

A: Ah... this is weird... it's almost like see a crayfish eating like a red glob... but the crayfish has a mouth...

Q: If the crayfish could talk, what would it say?

A: They don't talk. (Signs of nausea and distress.)

Q: What is the red glob?

A: I don't know... (Gagging.)

Q: Alright, take a deep breath now...

A: I don't like this...

Q: Alright, I am going to count from five to one, and on the count of one you are going to move to your highest level of consciousness... a place of pure light and knowledge. (Countdown.) How do you feel now?

A: Okay.

Q: Now, do you see the light?

A: Um hmm.

Q: Alright. I want you to merge with the light and the knowledge that is in the light. Is there any means by which you can stop these events or protect yourself? The knowledge will be there, you can access it easily.

A: (Long pause) It's almost like I'm hearing a voice say that we have something beautiful that they will never ever have.

Q: We as humans?

A: Um hmm.

Q: Is this what they wish to acquire?

A: Um... I don't know... they're just like, I would guess, parasites, or something like that. [...]

Q: What's going on around you.

A: I'm just going to tell you what I see... it's kind of weird. Umm... I see all these little white guys, they're like children... they're running around... a bunch of 'em... umm... I see this woman with gray umm... I don't know if I can see her... (Distress.) You know, it's like I'm trying to see and it's slipping. She's there but I can't see her.

Q: Take a real deep breath. I am going to count to three and on the count of three any blocks to your memory, any impediments, any distortions will dissolve away and you will see clearly and completely everything that occurred to you at that point in space time and forward. (Countdown.) What do you see? Look at this woman. What does she look like?

A: Umm... I'm in a different room. This room is a round room and it has almost like a glass dome over the top of it... ummm... I'm, uh... it's like a city I'm seeing. This is strange...

Q: Stop a minute... stop and take a real deep breath. Back up. Back up to the woman you couldn't see. On the count of three she will appear on the screen and you will be able to describe her clearly. (Countdown)

A: Umm... oooh... I see this woman... she's got long wiry white hair...

Q: What about her eyes?

A: I'm just going to tell you what I see. When I look in her eyes they are like circle green... circling green... spiraling... on one picture I see her as ugly but then I see a beautiful woman's face... I see her one way and when I look there is like a shadow over the face... it looks like a beautiful woman but when I first looked at her it wasn't but... when I look at it again it looks like a beautiful woman...

Q: What sensation do you get from this woman?

A: I just want to say she's hateful.

Q: Does she say anything to you?

A: No. It's like she's watching me real careful.

Q: What does her body look like?

A: Umm.. real thin and tall... really thin, thin, thin arms and long fingers.

Q: How many fingers?

A: I want to say four. She's real, real tall. Real skinny. But this big head with this wiry hair.

Q: Describe the head.

A: It's a triangle but kind of rounded on the edges.

Q: Does she have big ears or little ears?

A: No, I'm seeing little curves on the side of her head.

Q: What about her mouth?

A: Rows of teeth.

Q: What about a nose?

A: I'm seeing two little curves, real small... two holes, just holes.

Q: Does she say anything to you?

A: No. She's watching me though. Watching me as I'm walking by with these, these... she dislikes me for some reason.

Q: Okay, you're walking by, what happens next?

A: We're sitting down.

Q: We who?

A: I'm sitting down and there is a small woman next to me and there's a man next to me. And this woman's like, right around behind me, standing up.

Q: Which woman is behind you?

A: The one with the, uh, the woman I don't like. She's bossy.

Q: Is she in charge?

A: Unh uh. But she's got, I don't know... she has a certain function or something... But, umm... I don't know, she's just not nice.

Q: You're sitting on a bench and there's a woman next to you.

A: Yeah. This is a person. A human.

Q: Do you recognize her?

A: Unh uh.

Q: Do you recognize the man?

A: I can't see him very clear.

Q: As you're sitting on the bench, what happens? Why are you sitting on the bench?

A: They're showing us a big screen.

Q: Tell me what you see on the screen.

A: (Sigh.) Umm... What we are looking at is the Earth and they are showing us different places on the Earth.

Q: What about those places?

A: Bases I guess is what they are.

Q: Bases?

A: Um hmm.

Q: Anything that you would recognize?

A: Unh uh. Just spots, just showing different areas for some reason.

Q: What is the reason for showing you this?

A: (Sigh.) They are preparing us.

Q: Preparing you for what?

A: Departures to these different bases.

Q: Departures to these different bases?

A: Um hmm.

Q: Has anybody told you anything? Details as to why?

A: They're showing us.

Q: What else do you see on the screen?

A: Umm... Well, its, its... it's like they show us this... oh, that's weird... (Long pause.)

Q: Describe it.

A: They show us different spots... they show it to us and then all this information comes into our heads like all about it and where it is... all the information about what it's about and what's going on and...

Q: Well, what is the information?

A: Umm... (Sigh.)

Q: Tell us what is coming into your head as you watch these pictures on the screen.

A: They are training us for a job or something. They want us to know how to do things.

Q: What kind of things?

A: Well, how to run things.

Q: Run what kind of things?

A: Things that, umm... how things work.

Q: What things. How what things work?

A: How these bases work. Where they're located. And they are training us to live there.

Q: Are these bases on the planet Earth?

A: Um hmm.

Q: Can you name any specific ones?

A: Umm... The Amazon jungle, umm... the North Pole... they're all over.

Q: This knowledge, this information is coming into your mind as you watch these visual images on this screen, can you determine how to access it?

A: (Sigh.) I would say, umm... continuous hypnosis and peeling away the layers...

Q: Okay. Continue to describe what you are seeing on the screen. Anything else?

A: Umm... the only thing I see is that we're sitting there and it's like, umm... thought transfer, you know what I mean? It's like symbols and musical notes...

Q: You are seeing symbols?

A: Um hmm.

Q: And you are hearing music? Or sounds?

A: Well, I'm seeing the music.

Q: You are seeing the music?

A: Um hmm.

Q: Can you freeze frame any of these symbols and recall them and when you are awakened could you draw some of these symbols?

A: I don't know. They go real fast.

Q: Do they remind you of any kind of symbols you have seen at any place or time?

A: Um hmm.

Q: What do they remind you of?

A: Well, the crop circles.

Q: Okay, what's happening next?

A: We're just learning.

Q: Can you tell us any more of what you are learning?

A: All about these bases. And what we need to be doing.

Q: Do you get any sense of when you are going to be doing this?

A: Umm... 1998 comes up for some reason. It's an important time for something... the countdown begins then...

Q: Okay, do you get any sense of why it's going to be necessary to know how to do these things at these bases?

A: Oooh... we're in trouble...

Q: We're in trouble?

A: Um hmm.

Q: What do you see, what do you hear, what do you know?

A: I don't see, I feel... I just feel really sad.

Q: Why do you feel really sad?

A: I don't know, I just feel real sad. (Begins to cry.)

Q: Why do you feel sad? Talk about what you know.

A: It's just... I don't know... so much destruction...

Q: There's destruction, what kind of destruction?

A: I don't know. It's almost like wars or something.

Q: Is it wars? Or something else?

A: (Sigh, distress.) It's like somebody's coming.

Q: Somebody's coming? Who's coming?

A: I don't know. It's like an army of ships or something I see.

Q: An army of ships is coming?

A: Um hmm.

Q: What kind of ships?

A: Spaceships. All I see is a group small discs flying in big squadrons or something.

Q: Are these...

A: Not nice.

Q: Not nice? Can you tell where they are coming from? Do you have that information from your screen?

A: Unh uh.

Q: Somebody's coming, and you see that there is going to be a war. Between who?

A: It doesn't make sense. It's almost... there's... these aliens are working with the government to prepare, plan for this upcoming... whatever these other people, these other beings that are coming. I know that doesn't make sense but that is what I am seeing or feeling or hearing.

Q: Okay, are the beings you are with, would you judge them to be of positive or negative polarity.

A: Umm... they're nice... I think... Except that woman... I don't like that woman...

Q: Are the beings that are coming, do you think they are of positive or negative nature in relation to humans? Or, is it just what they are telling you, that they are nice and the ones who are coming are not nice?

A: It's just what they are telling me.

Q: Could it be possible that the beings that you are with are the negative beings and the ones that are coming are the positive beings?

A: (Sigh.) I don't know. I don't feel bad with these, these little white people... I don't like this woman, though.

Q: I want you to try a little experiment. I am going to count to three and on the count of three I want you to try to read her mind and see what she is thinking. (Countdown.) Connect and describe what she feels and thinks. How does she perceive what's going on?

A: (Distress.) What I'm feeling right now is really hungry.

Q: Is that how she feels?

A: Um hmm.

Q: Hungry for what? What is she hungry for?

A: (Sigh.) She feeds off of us.

Q: How does she feed off of us? What does she do when she feeds? What is it she is wanting to do?

A: She feeds off of us... I don't know.

Q: What does she do physically to feed?

A: It's like she puts her mouth over you and sucks something... like your air out or something... and her eyes, you know what I mean? It's, you know... she drains you.

Q: And she is one of this group that you're with?

A: She's like lurking in the back. She isn't in charge, but she's, um, in the background. She's watching me. She's one of them.

Q: Let's move forward. They are continuing with the showing of the videos or the images. What happens when they finish these images?

A: I feel sick to my stomach.

Q: Why do you feel sick to your stomach?

A: I don't know. I just feel really bad.

Q: Talk about why you feel really bad.

A: They told us things that hurt us. I don't know, I just feel really bad. I hurt.

Q: Let's back up. Stop where you are and let's back up... They are telling you things that are hurting you. What are the things they are telling you?

A: They are showing us all kinds of destruction. Cities of mangled iron... things aren't going to be safe...

Q: What's not going to be safe?

A: The planet's not going to be safe.

Q: From what?

A: This destruction.

Q: Who is causing the destruction?

A: I don't know. I just see a wave generated.

Q: A wave that's generated?

A: Um hmm.

Q: What generates the wave?

A: I can't see anything.

Q: What does this wave do when it is generated?

A: Throws the axis off. The magnetic axis. It's magnetic and we have magnetic axis. Somehow it throws it completely out of harmony. It does something to it and throws it out of harmony.

Q: And what is the result of this throwing out of the axis?

A: I see the Earth spinning. Not normally, but out of balance.

Q: Okay. And what it the result of this out of balance spinning?

A: Destruction.

Q: Okay. And you can't detect from where this wave originates.

A: Can't see anything.

Q: Is it a natural wave? Or is it unnatural?

A: I don't know what this means. Somebody is causing... they're disrupting something. All those ships I saw...

Q: Are the ships causing this wave?

A: They are disrupting something. There's a disruption.

Q: Are the squadrons of ships you see coming, do they come before this destruction or after?

A: The only thing I can say is that they ride the wave in.

Q: They ride the wave in? And you can't see where the wave is coming from?

A: All I can see is we have to get prepared.

Q: How do we get prepared?

A: They are preparing us.

Q: Do we have to do anything ourselves?

A: We are programmed.

Q: How can one tell if one is programmed?

A: Things will be triggered. You are set up to do certain things... movies, books, different things trigger things that are in your subconscious... I see a key, or a wheel... how a wheel fits together... two wheels fit together and it clicks in...

Q: Okay. This wave you speak of, do you sense that it is a wave coming from deep space or is it a wave coming from within our solar system?

A: It's on its way! We don't know about it but somebody knows!

Q: Who knows, does the government know?

A: Yes.

Q: Do they plan on telling anybody?

A: They are setting things in motion. This is why more and more information is being released.

Naturally, after reviewing these experiences, Candy had a whole different perspective on the abduction phenomenon. She became obsessed with reading everything about it she could find. In this respect, we were certainly on the same "path".

When we talked on the phone, there were strange clicks and buzzes on the line. I laughed at the thought of anybody tapping my line to see what we knew about "aliens", because it was a certainty that we knew very little. But Candy was convinced that she had "something" they were after – that the objective of any surveillance was herself. Her conviction that the man who had taken her out to the mounds was a government agent being intertwined with that bizarre conviction that he was also her soul mate led to her theory that he was being used to "lure" her into some kind of government conspiracy, and it was her job to "rescue" him in some way.

I knew that it was going to take a lot more work to peel away the screens and false memories, not to mention the emotional programs that were still driving Candy.

Nevertheless, it was in the hypnosis sessions with Candy that the subject of The Wave first came up. This item stuck in my mind, but until more data was available, it was just hanging there. We continued with our weekly sessions which had become as much a social event as anything else. Some people play bingo, some people go to clubs, we liked sitting around the board with our fingers on the planchette while we discussed the nature of our reality.

Interspersed with the "dead dudes" we chatted with during the experimental sessions, there were also "space brothers". One identified himself as "Jordan", and claimed to be on a ship near Mars, having just arrived there from an orbit around Neptune. He then went on to answer all kinds of questions that confirmed many of the theories of Zecariah Sitchin, claimed that he was a member of a "sister race" to mankind, and just generally performed like your standard "space brother". I was not impressed.

Jordan seemed to want to be a regular visitor, but after applying some tests by asking questions that could be checked, I decided he was just wasting our time, and I sent him on his way. The notebook for that period is full of "Earth Changes" and disaster prognostications, the kinds of questions everyone was interested in asking. Just skimming through the notes, I find many things that were typical nonsense such as the following:

Earthquake in the Bahamas.

Tsunami east coast – 200 feet high.

Raising of Atlantis April 23 1994. (That one was a loser for sure!)

Hurricane 8/21/94 barometric pressure 21.00, winds gusting at 600 mph, landfall Boston (another loser).

Earthquake California, 10/23/94, the big one, 8.9 Richter (another loser).

Economic collapse stock market drop 500 points in one day on 12/4/94.

Pole Shift 9/9/99.

Extraterrestrial contact.

AIDS will mutate to airborne virus, will be also transmitted by fleas; and so on and on.

Obviously, like the many prognostications about photon belts and Hale-Bopp from so many popular sources, it was just nonsense piled upon nonsense. I don't think the entities were deliberately lying to us, nor do I think that they were "evil". I just think that Cayce was right: a dead Presbyterian is just a dead Presbyterian. If a person dies with strong beliefs formed in the crucible of life on Earth, they take those beliefs with them. And it seems that souls congregate with other souls of similar "frequency" or belief. In this way, they support one another in their illusions and become convinced that what they experience is the whole banana. In this way, they can communicate with the living, absolutely convinced that what they are saying is truth, with the best of intentions; and in the end, it can be all lies.

I didn't want lies, however well-intentioned the source. I didn't want to hear the same tired old illusions that humankind has been fed for millennia that have never done anything to help us change our status on Earth and in the cosmos. I wanted one thing and one thing only: the objective truth, *if* it existed. I wanted to know how to "go home". Like a person playing blind man's bluff, I was groping for answers.

As I studied, the question inside me grew larger and larger. By this time I had read a few dozen books on UFOs and aliens, but their arguments were so contradictory and confusing that I despaired of ever making any sense of it all.

Frank and I had watched several videos starring Al Beliek and Bob Lazar, and all their supposed "answers" raised more questions. Sure, it was fine and dandy for Bob Lazar to say that he worked on alien craft at Area 51 and that endless reports of the phenomenon existed from thousands of years ago. But were the "lights in the skies" and the stories of fairy abductions the same phenomena that happened here and now in our world? The claims of cover-up and conspiracy had a certain appeal. I really got the creeps thinking about alien critters with bug eyes and B.O.

One anonymous writer claimed that until he had hard evidence that it was not the CIA or some maverick secret government experimenting on human beings, he would continue to deny that it could be aliens. This person wrote:

> Until someone kills a real alien and lays its cadaver on my doorstep, I will continue to believe 'Gray Aliens' are USAF or CIA personnel dressed up in funny costumes. I will continue to believe that our comrades are being abducted and murdered by government agencies [and] that telepathic contact experiments are being conducted by the same government agencies. If aliens are not humans in costumes, they are at least darklings built by human DNA tinkerers in some of those secret underground laboratories.
>
> I have a great deal of trouble accepting the story that aliens have been conducting genetic experiments on humankind for 10,000 years. That would suggest that we are really little more than their livestock, they actually 'own' us, just as we believe we 'own' beasts of the field and fish of the seas and birds of the air. It also suggests they have an extremely long attention span unless they are moving through time and aren't really 'going anywhere!'
>
> We tag sea turtles in the North Atlantic and track them by satellite to see which way they go. We tag birds and fish and elephants to follow their migrations. Are we supposed to believe creatures from Zeta Reticuli are doing the same to humans?
>
> Friends! Why would beings who can travel sixty-six zillion light years through space and time in any direction at any time, want to concern themselves with something as stupid and boring as tagging and following the migration and sexual behavior of humans (who would be the equivalent of primeval slugs to them)? What is the point?
>
> To capture, examine, impregnate and tag human females to carry their crossbred children? If they are as wonderful and advanced as some say, they should be able to grow their children in canning jars on their own planet!
>
> To cultivate us as food? If they are twenty billion years more advanced than we, why haven't they figured out how to grow synthetic protein in culture dishes in their own labs on their own planet in their own star cluster?

If we are nothing more than experiments of an advanced race of beings, no more than bacteria on a cosmic glass slide, that means there is no God, no law, no rules, no leaders, no followers. ...There should be no trials or punishment for 'crimes' because the concept of crime and punishment would be null and void if we belong to funny-looking Gray creatures from Zeta Reticuli.

If we have no more rights than a common housefly, then we'll have to do away with ownership of property as well. If we believe that, we'll have to do away with governments and public minions, dismantle the military and let anarchy reign supreme, laying about until one of the owners comes round to lop off an arm or leg for dinner or grind us into sausage and stir us up in a big vat somewhere in Nevada, USA.

But wait! Why would creatures who can jump from Earth to Zeta Reticuli in a heartbeat keep their food supply in Nevada? Why don't they take it with them? If you were able to jump from one town to another or one state to another by thinking it, and you wanted to paint a house in say, Texas, would you keep the paint bucket in New York and jump back and forth every time you had to load the brush just because you could jump back and forth? If you could jump to the grocery store, would you jump forty times to buy forty items or would you get everything in one jump so you wouldn't have to bother?

People! That's why we have refrigerators and pantries! So we don't have to get in the car (flying saucer) and drive to the store (Nevada) every day! I can't believe we're more intelligent than our Gray owners! They must be humiliated.

But if all this nonsense is being orchestrated by an agency of Earthlings who wants you to believe in UFOs and funny-looking Gray aliens, then it all makes sense, doesn't it? Humans are being abducted for medical experiments. Humans are being contacted telepathically to sort out the ESPers. Human females are carrying the seeds of a future race of cosmonauts. They may be producing embryos which are sent into space aboard the shuttle to see if they live or die in a weightless environment, the evidence of which will be applied to the technology of future manned excursions to the planets of this solar system and beyond.

The above is, in a nutshell, the view of the hard-shell skeptics. Putting aside the hyperbole and evangelistic style of writing, the guy has a point.

Such an argument sounds pretty reasonable at first glance. It was only when I thought about it a bit longer that I realized the problem with such an idea. If the government is behind all the abductions, surely they would have screwed up at least once in 45 years and we would know that fallible human beings were doing it! The fact that not one single incident, not one single abduction, not one single purported kidnapping event has ever resulted in a screw-up that led to anyone seeing the "man behind the curtain", not one. That should give us pause to think.

This guy expects me to believe that the US government can pull off an enterprise of this kind, with evidence of world-wide activity, for over 50 years, involving possibly millions of individuals, the logistics of which make the machinations of WWII look like the planning for a picnic? I'm sorry, I can't buy that. And so, even though he has many points about the phenomenon that beg for explanation, I think that we have to look for a hypothesis that explains and predicts the phenomenon better than what he has suggested. And part of that hypothesis may be that the ideas he is proposing are deliberately planted in the mind of the public for the very purpose of hiding a dreadful and sinister secret.

We can also see that, if the government is not involved, then public officials would be most interested in maintaining the cover-up. As the guy pointed out: to admit certain possibilities could lead to worldwide chaos and anarchy. If we are, as Charles Fort was wont to say, "property", if we "belong" to some race of advanced beings who use us for food and resources, then there is no point to anything we believe in at all. It is all a lie; a sham; a grand illusion; an enormous cosmic fraud. Who can live with that thought?

So there was no answer. Only clues to be followed.

But following the clues, based on my work with spirit release and exorcism, I had an idea about why the purported aliens really wanted human beings. It had nothing to do really with regenerating their race by stealing embryos or using human beings in their version of Hamburger Helper. From reading the cases, from the information about Candy's supposed alien abductors, I had the idea that their food was a type of energy: the energy of emotion.

The stories told about a "gazing process", where the abductee was subjected to a sustained and intense eye contact that generated a form of "life review". This drew forth extreme emotional response as the chief feature of the experience, and afterward, the victim often became ill, feeling drained or depleted in a significant way.

But this did not explain certain other reports filtering out here and there about aliens feeding on human blood, or bathing in ghastly vats of body fluids and parts to "absorb" nutrients. If they were creatures that fed on energy, what were they doing partaking of material nourishment, no matter how the process was accomplished?

Again, there were more questions in my mind than answers.

***

On July 16, 1994, at our weekly Saturday evening sitting, we were all a bit excited at the latest news from space. Fragments of Comet Shoemaker-Levy were soon to begin a series of collisions with the planet Jupiter, an extremely rare cosmic event. The impacts were supposed to continue for the next seven days, and I was very interested to see if this would have any noticeable effect on Earth.

We were just sitting there with our fingers lightly on the planchette, the "question" inside me growing larger and larger as it had been doing for months, when suddenly the planchette began to move in slow, deliberate circles in a way we had never before experienced.

We jerked our fingers away!

I asked Frank, "Did you just do that?"

"No", he replied indignantly. "Put your fingers back. Let's see what's going on!"

A funny pinching feeling and a tingle started at the back of my head that ran down my arm. The planchette began to move again slowly in a spiral. Spiral in and spiral out. We did the usual thing and said, "hello!"

Slowly, the planchette precisely and deliberately spelled "Hello."

That was not exactly usual. The usual response to "hello" was for the planchette to go to "yes". It always took a bit for each entity to get "warmed up" and be able to move comfortably around the board.

As unusual as that opening was, we were not prepared for what was about to happen.

We were not recording either. In the transcript that follows, the questions are reconstructed from memory. The answers, however, were written down as received.

Q: Do you have any messages for us?

A: Keep doing what comes naturally.

Q. (L) In what respect?

A: Study.

Q: (L) What is your name?

A: Mucpeor.

This was an unusual name. Up to this point in time, the names we had been given had all been, more or less, familiar. Names like "Dave" or "John" or "Mary" were not uncommon with the "dead dude" crowd. Some of them even used archaic, but still familiar names like "Agamemnon" or "Aquila". So, a completely unfamiliar name with no known connection was another first. Since we had already been visited by a spate of "space brothers", the next logical question was:

Q: (L) Are you an alien from another planet?

A: Alien from your perspective, yes.

That was a funny answer. They were not "aliens", but were "alien from our perspective"? Well, Jordan and the other space brothers had belonged to one "alien" group or another. The Cosmic Confederation or the Galactic Brotherhood or whatever. So the next natural question was:

Q: (L) What is your group called?

A: Corsas.

Q: (L) Where are you from?

A: Cassiopaea.

Q: (L) Where is that?

A: Near Orion.

Q: (L) I heard that the Orions are the "Bad guys". Are the Orion group bad?

A: Some bad.

I had read so much about different purported groups of "aliens", most of whom pointed the finger at a slew of them from somewhere in Orion who were here to do all kinds of nasty things. So this was certainly a "test question". The fact that the Cassiopaeans did not jump on the Orion bashing bandwagon was significant.

Candy had recently read a book on the channeled *Ra Material* which explained a concept of determining "good guys" from "bad guys". This consisted in asking if the entity served self or others. So, that was the next logical question:

Q: (L) Do you serve self or others?

A: I serve both.

Q: (L) Are you bad or good, in our terms?

A: Good.

Q: (L) What is your philosophy?

A: One.

Q: (L) What are you here for tonight?

A: Prophecy.

Q: (L) What prophecies?

A: Tornadoes Florida – several.

Q: (L) Where else?

A: Also Texas and Alabama.

Q: (L) When?

A: Sun is in Libra.

Q: (L) What planet are you from?

A: Carcosa. [Misspelled in the notes, scratched out and re-written.]

The term "Carcosa" was one of the first signs we were dealing with something a bit different here. Up to this point, none of the discarnate entities we had dealt with had been able to read our minds. But here, there was a funny reference to a word that had been playing through my mind all day. I was a bit startled by this remark. It was from Jacques Vallee's book, *Revelations*. At the beginning of each section, there are quotes from Cassilda's Song in *The King in Yellow*, Act 1, Scene 2, by Robert W. Chambers. After the session, I opened the book to re-read the quotes. The Song goes:

> Strange is the night where black stars rise,
>
> And strange moons circle through the skies,
>
> But stranger still is... Lost Carcosa.
>
> Songs that the Pleiades shall sing,
>
> Where flap the tatters of the King,
>
> Must die unheard in ... Dim Carcosa.
>
> Along the shore the cloud waves break,
>
> The twin suns sink behind the lake,
>
> The shadows lengthen... In Carcosa.

More interesting still, to those already familiar with the Cassiopaean material, is the reference to the "twin suns". Referring to Carcosa, I asked:

Q: (L) Where is that?

A: 2 D I L O R.

The planchette had begun to move very fast and we were not able to keep up. The last remark was lost and only a few of the letters written down.

Q: (L) What was that again?

A: You pay attention.

Q: (L) What else is going to happen?

A: Seattle buried; Japan buckles; Missouri shakes; California crumbles; Arizona burns.

Q: [Unknown question.]

A: Go to Denver airports.

Q: (L) When is all this going to happen?

A: Scandal – Scandal – Denver Airport.

Q: (L) What about the Denver airport?

A: Scandal.

Q: (L) I don't understand.

A: New Denver airport.

Q: (L) I don't understand.

A: Pay attention.

Q: (L) Okay, we are paying attention. What are you trying to tell us?

A: Denver new airport big big big big scandal.

Q: (L) What kind of scandal?

A: Government.

Q: (L) Specifically what?

A: You will see Dallas airport is secret base Orlando too Miami too.

Q: (L) What about Denver airport and how does it relate to prophecies?

A: Denver reveals the government Look for it Pay attention.

Q: (L) What else do you have to tell us?

A: Montana: Experiment with human reproduction. All people there – rays – radon gas.

Q: (L) How are they doing this?

A: Compelled – Don't trust Don't ignore too strong urges sinister plots.

Q: (L) What do you mean? I don't understand?

A: Strong urge is directed by sinister plot.

Q: (L) Plot by whom?

A: Consortium.

Q: (L) Who are the members of the consortium? Aliens? The government?

A: All.

Q: (L) All who?

A: Government and other.

Q: (L) Who is the other?

A: Unknown.

Q: (L) Why can't you tell us who is the other?

A: You know who.

Well, all this was very interesting. Finally, an entity that could spell and didn't spend any time wandering around looking for the letters. Now was my chance, so I decided to ask the question that had been bugging me all day as a sort of test.

Q: (L) Bob Lazar referred to the fact that aliens supposedly refer to humans as containers. What does this mean?

A: Later use.

Q: (L) Use by who? How many?

A: 94 per cent.

Q: (L) 94 per cent of what?

A: Of all population.

Q: (L) What do you mean?

A: All are containers 94 per cent use.

Q: (L) I don't understand.

A: Will be used 94 percent.

Q: (L) Used for what?

A: Total consumption.

Q: (L) What do you mean by consumption? Ingested?

A: Consumed for ingredients.

Q: (L) Why?

A: New race. Important 13 years about when happens.

Q: (L) Why are humans consumed?

A: They are used for parts.

Q: (L) We don't understand. How can humans be used for parts?

A: Reprototype Vats exist. Missing persons often go there and especially missing children.

At this answer, I was in shock. What kind of entity would tell us such things? What kind of awful reality must such information proceed from? I was torn between terminating contact that very instant, and working my way through it to find some resolution.

Q: (L) Do we have any protection?

A: Some.

Q: (L) How can we protect ourselves and our children?

A: Inform them. Don't hide the truth from children.

Q: (L) How does truth protect us?

A: Awareness protects. Ignorance endangers.

Q: (L) Why tell children such horrible things?

A: Need to know.

Q: (L)I don't know how knowing this helps. This is awful. Why tell children such things?

A: Must know – ease pain with meditation.

Well, the very suggestion of frightening my children with such horror stories practically sent me into a fit! But, again, I was torn. More than anything I was curious as to what kind of being would be saying such dreadful things. The negative entities I had encountered most definitely had never said such things; in fact, they always presented themselves as really good but misunderstood and persecuted. Finding excuses for their evil was the hallmark of beings of darkness. Were we now addressing a different kind of dark being, one that was so dark it didn't care how many awful things it said? Or, were they telling me things designed to galvanize me – me, the mother of five children – to ask more questions designed to protect our children?

Q: (L) Why are you telling us this? It's awful!

A: We love you.

Swell. But what kind of love would tell us such awful things, I wondered. And then, immediately I realized that I was always warning my children about dangers. Even if I didn't like to admit that the world was a dangerous place, I knew that I had to tell them such things in order for them to be aware – to preserve them.

Q: (L) Are we supposed to tell others?

A: Don't reveal to public. You would be abducted.

That was a reasonable answer and certainly didn't suggest that they had an agenda for us to go around scaring people. I was curious about the so-called "project" mentioned as being completed in about 13 years, (2007) for which this being was saying so many terrible human sacrifices were made. Even if it was an evil being, maybe I could get enough information in a hurry that I could tell others and maybe it would make sense to some of those who were more familiar with such details.

Q: (L) What is the purpose of this project?

A: New life here.

Since I had formulated my idea that the aliens feed on human emotion, I decided on this for a test question. An alien who fed on us would very likely deny it unless, as I already thought, we were being addressed by a being of such insouciant darkness that we had never encountered its ilk before.

Q: (L) Are the aliens using our emotions and energies?

A: Correct; and bodies too. Each earth year 10 percent more children are taken.

They weren't going to let that missing children issue alone. It was too horrible to contemplate. Why did they keep saying something that upset me so? I was a bit distraught, as a mother, and in a shaking voice I asked:

Q: (L) Do they suffer?

A: Some.

Q: (L) Do they all suffer?

A: Some.

Q: (L) What happens to souls? Is this physical only?

A: Physical – souls recycled.

Q: (L) Where do the souls go?

A: Back here – most.

Q: (L) Do some go elsewhere?

A: And go out of planet human.

Again, just in case this monstrous story was true, I wanted details – something I could check.

Q: (L) Who is responsible for this?

A: Consortium.

Q: (C) This is totally sick! I don't want to do this any more!

A: Sick is subjective.

Q: (L) But what you are telling us is so awful!

A: Understand, but all does not conform to your perspective.

With that answer, I realized that what we were being told, as crazy as it sounded, just might be the truth. But again, what kind of being tells such truths?

Q: (L) Why is this happening to us?

A: Karma.

Q: (L) What kind of Karma could bring this?

A: Atlantis.

Q: (L) What can protect us?

A: Knowledge.

Q: (L) How do we get this knowledge?

A: You are being given it now.

Q: (L) What knowledge do you mean?

A: You have it.

Q: (L) How does the knowledge of what you have told us help us?

A: Gives great defense.

Q: (L) What knowledge gives defense?

A: Just gave it.

Q: (L) What specifically?

A: Don't ask that not important.

Q: (L) We don't understand.

A: Knowing about it gives psychic defense.

Q: (L) How do we tell other people? And who should we tell?

A: Inform indirectly only.

Q: (L) How?

A: Write.

Q: (L) Should we use hypnosis to uncover such memories?

A: Open.

Q: (L) Have any of us been abducted?

A: Yes.

Q: (L) Who of us sitting here?

A: All.

Q: (L) How many times?

A: Frank-57; Candy -56; Laura-12.

Q: (L) Why has Laura not been abducted as much? (Laura laughs)

A: It is not over.

Q: (Candy laughs.)

A: Candy was abducted last month. Laura – 33 – [years of age or years ago?]

Q: (L) Who is abducting us?

A: Others.

Q: (L) What is the name of the group?

A: Different names.

Q: (L) Are we all abducted by the same group?

A: Mostly.

Q: (L) What did they do to us?

A: Gave false memories. Made you inhibited child – headaches – sick at school.

Q: (C) Where is my implant?

A: Head.

Q: (L) Frank?

A: Same.

Q: (L) Laura?

A: Same.

Q: (L) What are the implants for?

A: Study device.

Q: (L) To study what?

A: Soul composition.

Q: (L) Do any of the rituals we perform provide protection against further abduction?

A: Don't need protection if you have knowledge.

Q: (L) How do we get this knowledge?

A: Deep subconscious.

Q: (L) When did we get it?

A: Before birth.

Q: (L) Is there anything else we can do for protection?

A: Learn, meditate, read.

Q: (L) Are we doing what we need to be doing at the present?

A: So far. Need awaken. Must go now. Out of energy. I must go.

I didn't know what to think. Indeed, again there was that injunction to learn.

I was traumatized by the information given; that was a certainty. How was I supposed to process that? Over the years I had become so sensitive to the sufferings of others that I had to look away if we were forced to pass an auto accident. I had to leave the room if there was a sad story on the news. If a movie became sad, I couldn't continue watching it. If I read a story about an ill or abused child, I would become depressed for days afterward.

I had five beloved children of my own, and I was a sort of vicarious mother to every child on the planet. I didn't see grubby little boys as bratty kids, I saw them as the beloved child of their mother; and I identified with all mothers. I would take as much care for the child of a stranger as for my own; and would be grateful for any other mother to feel the same about my children. My children were my life. So why did they push this issue about children being taken and experimented upon? Was this designed to hurt me specifically so that I would feel bad and the entity, whoever he was, could feed on the energy of my suffering? Or was I being driven to learn something important; something crucial for all humanity?

There was only one thing to do: get some facts.

I thought it would be a relatively easy thing to buy a world almanac and discover what the statistics on missing children were: how many were missing, how many were successfully returned to their families.

Nothing.

Okay, Plan B. I made calls to local law enforcement agencies. What government department kept track of such statistics? I was passed from one to the other and back again.

How about Plan C? I called agencies and said I was a freelance news reporter doing an article. In this country, that's a fair way to get public information. No special credentials are required.

But it didn't matter. No one knew much about missing children.

There are now dozens of organizations and agencies that are devoted to "missing and exploited children". The only problem is, you still can't get a straight, single answer to a simple question: how many children go missing every year and how many are returned safely and where's the proof? Everywhere you look you get a different figure, though, over time, a sort of "standard" figure has evolved. But getting any kind of hard copy on hard statistics with data to back it up is, as far as I have been able to tell, impossible. Nobody wants to talk about it in those terms.

And I began to ask myself, why?

What's more, during that week of trying to get answers to this one particular issue, I began to get a feeling that something was definitely not right with our world. Something was horribly wrong and nobody was admitting it, much less talking about it. I had no proof that what the communication from the board had told me was true. Yet I most definitely had been obstructed in trying to prove it to be false.

Maybe he or she was telling a simple truth. And wasn't that what I was after? Even though I was asking for Truth, like everyone else, I still had the idea that Truth ought to be "nice". The fact that Truth might not be all sweetness and light was not lost on me even if I still had that prejudice that "higher beings" would say only "lofty" things.

The next session, on the last day of the Comet Shoemaker-Levy impacts with Jupiter, the barrier between realms collapsed, quite literally with a thunderous crash. It was July 22nd.

We were a bit curious whether the strange communicants from the previous week would return. I had recently taken a Reiki course, and Candy and I were experimenting with utilizing the words and symbols that Reiki teaches to increase one's energy flow. There is one particular word and symbol that is supposed to assist a circuit in the frequency of the body to open an "etheric connection". I had drawn the symbol on a sheet of paper which I slipped beneath the board, and Candy and I were repeating the words over and over again. Suddenly, the planchette spelled out: "Frank say it too". So, Frank joined us in the gentle repetition of these "energy words."

Suddenly, we heard three very loud and very close thunderclaps directly above the house. These booming sounds were so strong they actually made the building shake. It sounded like a plane exploding right over the top of us. Fearing imminent destruction, we jumped up, throwing our chairs down backward behind us, and dashed madly to the door to see what was happening in the skies overhead.

The sky was completely clear, the moon was shining, stars were twinkling.[22] After looking around and listening for a bit, we decided this must be one of those "out of the blue" lightning strikes we had heard about, even if there had been no flash of lightning accompanying it. We would have noticed the light with the windows open.

We returned to the table in a state of extreme puzzlement and began to sit again, talking about this strange thunder and paying little attention to the board at all. Again, the planchette began to move in slow, deliberate spirals. And again, I said, "Hello!"

A: Hello.

Q: (L) Is anyone with us?

A: Listen, Look. Learn. Stop eating.

(Candy was having a snack.)

Q: (L) What is the problem with eating?

A: Not good connection.

Q: (L) What is your name?

A: Ellaga.

Another unusual name; I was intrigued.

Q: (L) Are you discarnate from Earth?

A: No.

Q: (L) Are you from the same group we communicated with the other night?

A: Yes.

Q: (L) Are you from another galaxy?

A: No.

Q: (L) Where are you from?

A: Cassiopaea.

Q: (L) Is this the constellation we know as Cassiopeia?

A: Yes.

Q: (L) What can we do for a better connection?

A: Less noise.

---

[22] The moon was in Capricorn, and Jupiter was between the claws of the Scorpion, now known as Libra, and Virgo. Aquarius had just risen in the East, and Cassiopeia had been up for about half an hour or so.

There was activity in the next room. We shut the door.

Q: (L) Do you have information for us this evening?

With this question, the planchette took off, and I started calling out the letters for Candy to write, trying desperately to keep up. They were delivered in one long string with no word breaks so that we had to study them after to divide them into words. It was impossible to try to follow word by word, putting the letters together in the mind, so I gave up and just pronounced each one as the planchette dashed around the board.

> A: Space invasion soon. Four to six years. Battle between forces good and evil Wait near Look far Listen Mexico fall Ethiopia quake September both New Near January Paris bomb London Blizzard 109 die Plane down Tahiti Cholera Montana January 1995 government US behind California quakes Three soon Oklahoma political abduction February 95 Big news.

The curious thing about this last remark is that on February 25, 1995, we were given a warning of a terrorist bomb attack within a month. Connect that to Oklahoma "political abduction", the word February followed by "big news", and we find a curious relationship to the April 19, 1995 Oklahoma bombing of a federal building in which at least 168 people lost their lives. Later convicted in the bombing, Timothy McVeigh, a Gulf War veteran, told reporters he was under the control of an implant in his hip, and that he believed he had been abducted and programmed by the government.

It seems pretty clear that no "space invasion" has occurred on our planet within "4 to 6 years". At least, not in the terms we would understand a "space invasion". However, I was reminded of what Candy had said during one of her hypnosis sessions about 1998: "It's an important time for something... the countdown begins then..." I later came back to this point for clarification and the following exchange occurred:

Q: (L) Will there be a war in the sky with the aliens?

A: Yes.

Q: (L) Will it be between Orions and the Federation? (I had gotten these terms from the Ra Material.)

A: Yes.

Q: (L) Will it be visible on Earth?

A: Oh, yes.

Q: (L) When will this be?

A: It has already started. Will intensify steadily.

Q: (L) Why are we not aware that it has already started?

A: Disguised at this point as weather. Fighting part still in other dimension. Will go to this one within 18 years. Anytime within this period. Not determinable exactly when. Could be tomorrow or 18 years.

Q: (L) 18 years from now is 2012. Is there some special significance to that time?

A: By then.

I found it utterly fascinating that weather was being described as a mask for activities in higher realms. This idea is, in fact, very ancient. Continuing with that second encounter:

Q: (L) What is causing the Earth Changes?

A: Electromagnetic wave changes.

Q: (L) Can you be more specific?

A: Gap in surge heliographic field.

Q: (L) I don't understand.

A: Put Frank on processor channel open.

Q: (L) Do you mean that Frank can channel on the computer?

A: Yes. Do it now.

I thought then – and this was later confirmed – this was an attempt at side-tracking the process. I had the feeling that such a request was coming from Frank, who was not very enamored of the board process, though he patiently went along with me, or from some other source that would have very much liked to divert us from our controlled method. We had certain feedback loop tuning control. From wherever the request came, I was determined not to accede to any requests and just said "no" and pushed on.

Q: (L) Is a meteor or comet going to hit Earth?

A: Open.

Q: (L) What are the effects on us of the comet striking Jupiter?

A: Further field imbalance.

Q: (L) Was that comet meant for Earth as some psychics are saying?

A: Open.

Internet rumors at the time of the Comet Shoemaker-Levy impacts on Jupiter held that this comet had been meant to hit Earth, but a certain group of aliens, and I don't remember which one, had decided to "save" the Earth by redirecting these comets to strike Jupiter instead. Naturally, all of mankind was supposed to be grateful to this particular group for saving our buns from the fire!

Q: [Unknown question, probably relating to missing children. I think I had brought the subject up again to "test" and see if we couldn't get a more "nice-nice" answer. Well, if that was what I was expecting, that was not what I got!]

A: Bits children's organs removed while wide awake – kidneys crushed – then next feet – next jaw examined on table – tongues cut off – bones stress tested – pressure placed on heart muscle until burst.

Q: (L) Why are you saying these awful things?!

A: Must know what consortium is doing.

Q: (L) What children are they doing this to?

A: Done mostly to Indian children.

Q: (L) Why am I getting this horrible feeling while you are telling us this?

A: Because subject is distressing.

Q: (L) Why do we need to know these things?

A: Very big effort on behalf of Orions and their human brethren to create new race and control.

Q: (L) Where are you from?

A: Cassiopaea.

Q: (L) Where do you live specifically?

A: Live in omnipresence.

Q: (L) What does that mean?

A: All realms.

Q: (L) Can you tell us what your environment is like?

A: Difficult.

Q: (L) Well take a stab at it.

A: What stab?

Q: (L) Do you serve self or others.

A: Both. Self through others.

Q: (L) Candy wants to know the details of her abductions.

A: Do you?

Q: (C) Yes.

A: Are you sure?

Q: (C) Yes.

A: Soon, vibrations not right at this time.

Q: (L) Does this mean Candy's vibrations are not right to receive this information?

A: Right.

Q: (L) Why was information about our abductions given last time?

A: Was not I.

Q: (L) And who are you?

A: Ellaga.

This last response only became clear later. We were soon to learn that each session brought forth a different "entity". As each "moment" in space time was totally unique, so were the energies surrounding us and our questions. Thus a different name of the communicating entity designated a different frequency, though we were told that there were really no "separate" entities communicating. Each session was unique in its question-answer energy exchange.

Since my cousin, Sam, had been so devoted to the ideas of Zecharia Sitchin's *The 12th Planet*, I decided that a couple of questions along that line might be interesting. Sitchin claims in his books that a superior race of alien beings once inhabited our world. He claims that they were travelers from the stars, that they arrived eons ago, and genetically engineered mankind to serve as their slaves. He claims that the "Sons of Anak" mentioned in the Bible are the Annunaki, and also that they are the same as the Biblical Nefilim. They are a race of gold-seeking giants from a renegade planet in our own solar system, known to the Sumerians as the "Planet of the Crossing". This planet "crosses" the plane of the ecliptic every 3,600 years, and when it gets close enough, these beings make a "hop" to earth to check up on their creation. Supposedly, this will happen again soon. The title comes from the fact that Sitchin proposes 12 houses of the zodiac for 12 "planets". He includes the Sun and moon in his count because they are zodiacally significant. But, in actuality, it is really a 10th planet, excluding the Sun and Moon. He also fails to note that the Earth is excluded from zodiacal considerations due to the fact that astrology is geocentric. Since Sam was so "sold" on the Sitchin scenario of ancient astronauts, and I was equally convinced that it was a theory that was full of errors, I thought that this would be another good test question.

Q: (L) Is there a tenth planet as described by Zecharia Sitchin?

A: No. [Okay, no point in pursuing that!]

Q: (L) Was Venus ejected from Jupiter?

This was proposed by Immanuel Velikovsky as an explanation why ancient astronomers and mythmakers claimed that Venus was born from Jupiter.

The reader will most certainly wish to read *Worlds in Collision* because it is one of the most rational books ever written. Even if Velikovsky was wrong about some of the conclusions he drew regarding myth and legend, his observations and proposals of a new way at looking at the cosmos have yet to be fully appreciated. And, according to the Cassiopaeans, he was, at least, partly correct. But, in response to the question, was Venus ejected from the planet Jupiter, the answer was:

A: No.

Q: (L) Did Venus follow a cometary orbit for a time as theorized by Velikovsky?

A: Yes.

Q: (L) Did Venus appear in our solar system, from the area of Jupiter, coming from deep space as suggested by Velikovsky?

A: That is correct.

Q: (L) Was Venus the pillar of smoke by day and fire by night as seen by the Jews during the Exodus?

A: No.

Q: (L) What was seen by the Jews?

A: A Guideship.

Q: (L) Were Sodom and Gomorrah destroyed by nuclear weapons?

A: Yes and no.

Q: (L) How were they destroyed?

A: EMP

Q: (L) What is "EMP?"

A: Electromagnetic pulse.

This last remark about "Electromagnetic Pulse" energy was made long before any of us at the table were aware of anything called EMP. It was later described in some detail by Col. Corso in his book *The Day After Roswell*. But that was a few years ahead of us at this point in time.

Unfortunately, after the previous two years of mostly nonsense spirit interactions, we were not yet in the habit of taping, and we did not know if this communication was a fluke or not. So, we only have notes from the first half dozen or so early sessions. After a couple of weeks of repeated contact and apparent strengthening of the communication, I bought a special tape recorder to tape the sessions.

From this point on, we began what I intended to be a far more rigorous fine tuning and "testing phase" of the communication. This consisted in rapid questions that jumped from one subject to another across a broad range of categories. I was checking consistency, trying to confuse the source, and also trying to determine range and limits. I was most especially interested in questions relating to "unsolved mysteries" and spent days going through books looking for particular "mysteries" to ask about.

In one sense, this was a good thing, and in another it was not so good. One thing that became very evident during this process was that there was no way possible for any of the information to have been "beamed" into our heads from any human source. The questions were so random and the answers were so rapid, many of them checking out after later research, that it precludes the idea of being "beamed from a satellite" by human agents. If the information had been "beamed" via a satellite, whoever was there reading our minds in zero time, or tuning in to our questions via some listening device, would have had to have the fastest "look-it-up-quick" crew on the planet. We also had to really dig for the answers that invariably confirmed that the Cassiopaeans could tell us things that were most definitely not part of our own subconscious minds.

The Cassiopaeans were fast on the draw. And they soon began doing their own punctuation, accurately I might add, so that if anyone was "beaming info" into our heads, they were a stickler for grammar, as well as the fastest at looking up answers in the world's biggest library!

The very bad thing about my "testing phase" is the fact that there is almost no part of the material where the subjects do not just jump all over the place. Indeed, we would come back and ask follow-up questions at later times, but any one session could jump from higher cosmic realms to the perception of house cats.

Nevertheless, even though I was taking the experiment a bit more seriously, I still had no real idea what I had done. Even now, twelve years later, I try to keep an open mind, to always be aware of the fact that our own minds can fool us in myriad ways. We still research on a daily basis – often making amazing discoveries because we have been given a "clue" from the Cassiopaean transmissions. It is only in this context of hard research that the subject of The Wave can be approached.

CHAPTER 1
RIDING THE WAVE

The subject of The Wave has come up many times in the Cassiopaean sessions, and many people have written to me asking for more details about this mysterious event that is suggested to be a part of our future experiences. It is such a vast subject with so many references, that I have put off dealing with it until now. But, the time is right, I think, to talk about some of these things.

In one of the earliest contacts with the Cassiopaeans, being in the "test mode," I tossed a rather general question out one night:

07-23-94

Q: (L) What is causing the Earth Changes?

A: Electromagnetic wave changes.

Q: (L) Can you be more specific?

A: Gap in surge heliographic field.

I didn't make too much of this answer because it was more or less incomprehensible to me, and we were not yet at the stage of recording the sessions on tape, so I was pretty busy trying to keep notes of everything. But, as we proceed, this answer will become very important, so remember it!

Actually, I had first encountered the idea of some sort of strange "wave" in a hypnosis session with an abductee which I have described in the previous section which included the actual transcript of the hypnosis session.

There are a lot of extremely interesting things that developed during this hypnosis session, but we are going to focus on The Wave. Now that we have the first reference to it, and the context in which it occurred, let's zoom in on the specific remarks:

Q: Who is causing the destruction?

A: I don't know. I just see a wave generated.

Q: A wave that's generated?

A: Um hmm.

Q: What generates the wave?

A: I can't see anything.

Q: What does this wave do when it is generated?

A: Throws the axis off. The magnetic axis. It's magnetic and we have magnetic axis. Somehow it throws it completely out of harmony. It does something to it and throws it out of harmony.

Q: And what is the result of this throwing out of the axis?

A: I see the Earth spinning. Not normally, but out of balance.

Q: Okay. And what is the result of this out of balance spinning?

A: Destruction.

Q: Okay. And you can't detect from where this wave originates.

A: Can't see anything.

Q: Is it a natural wave? Or is it unnatural?

A: I don't know what this means. Somebody is causing... they're disrupting something. All those ships I saw...

Q: Are the ships causing this wave?

A: They are disrupting something. There's a disruption.

Q: Are the squadrons of ships you see coming, do they come before this destruction or after?

A: The only thing I can say is that they ride the wave in.

Q: They ride the wave in? And you can't see where the wave is coming from?

A: All I can see is we have to get prepared.

Q: How do we get prepared?

A: They are preparing us.

Q: Do we have to do anything ourselves?

A: We are programmed.

Q: How can one tell if one is programmed?

A: Things will be triggered. You are set up to do certain things... movies, books; different things trigger things that are in your subconscious... I see a key, or a wheel... how a wheel fits together... two wheels fit together and it clicks in.

Q: Okay. This wave you speak of, do you sense that it is a wave coming from deep space or is it a wave coming from within our solar system?

A: It's on its way! We don't know about it but somebody knows?

Q: Who knows, does the government know?

A: Yes.

Even at this point I didn't connect the wave Candy talked about with The Wave mentioned by the Cassiopaeans in the earlier session; which, I should make clear, Candy had no knowledge of that remark. So, at the next contact with the Cassiopaeans I brought up the subject of Earth Changes again, asking a question related to the ideas I have presented in my book *The Noah Syndrome*, and as the subject went forward I brought up the question of the wave as specifically related by Candy:

09-30-94

Q: (L) Is it true that at regular intervals the sun radiates massive amounts of electromagnetic energy, which then causes the planets of the solar system to interact with one another to a greater or lesser extent?

A: Other irregular pulsations determined by external vibrational events.

Q: (L) The sun is not the source of the periodicity of "dyings"?[23]

A: Sometimes. Many causes.

Q: (L) Well what is the cause that recurs like clockwork? Is there some cause that is a regular pulsation?

A: Cometary showers.

Q: (L) Where are these cometary showers from?

A: Clusters in own orbit.

Q: (L) Does this cluster of comets orbit around the sun?

A: Yes.

Q: (L) How often does this cluster of comets come into the plane of the ecliptic?

A: 3600 years.

Q: (L) What body were the Sumerians talking about when they described the Planet of the Crossing or Nibiru?

A: Comets.

Q: (L) This body of comets?

A: Yes.

Q: (L) Does this cluster of comets appear to be a single body?

A: Yes.

---

[23] Some scientists believe that the extinctions or "great dyings" that have been repeated many times throughout geological history are related to catastrophic events, perhaps asteroids hurtling into the earth.

Q: (L) Is this the same object that is rumored to be on its way here at the present time?

A: Yes.

Q: (L) Who were the Annunaki?

A: Aliens.

Q: (L) Where were they from?

A: Zeta Reticuli.

Q: (L) Do they come here every time the comet cluster is approaching to sap the soul's energy created by the fear, chaos and so forth?

A: Yes.

Q: (L) The two events are loosely interrelated?

A: Yes.

Q: (L) Is that why they are here now?

A: Close.

Q: (L) Is there a large fleet of space ships riding a wave, so to speak, approaching our planet?

A: Yes.

Q: (L) Where are these ships from?

A: Zeta Reticuli.

Q: (L) When will they arrive?

A: 1 month to 18 years.

Q: (L) How can there be such a vast discrepancy in the time?

A: This is such a huge fleet that space/time warping is irregular and difficult to determine as you measure time.

Q: (L) Are these craft riding a "wave" of some sort?

A: Yes.

Well, that was interesting, but it was late and we put off more questions until another time. But the issue of the big window of Estimated Time of Arrival really bugged me, so that is what I wanted to pin down. And, at this point, we started taping the sessions.

10-05-94

Q: (L) Assuming there is a fleet of spacecraft riding a wave, and approaching from the vicinity of Zeta Reticuli, what does it mean to say that the space time warp is indefinite in terms of arrival? Why is this? Please specify.

A: Mass affects electromagnetic transfer within gravity wave.

Q: (L) Can you help us out any more here?

A: Mass affects time cycle: small equals short cycle. Large or dense equals long cycle.

Well, I was completely out of my depth on that answer and didn't know how to go any further with it before thinking about it. As it turned out, I didn't come back to the subject myself – at least not on purpose – but it sure came up again in an unexpected way. I had been reading about Easter Island and was curious about the completely *ugly* heads represented by these statues. I really wanted to know what race or group they represented. I figured that whoever carved them must have been representing themselves, even if only as a caricature, and it might be a clue as to what groups were where on the planet in ancient times. So, I tossed in a question about Easter Island one night and got back a whole lot more than I had bargained for!

11-02-94

Q: (L) Who carved the stone heads on Easter Island?

A: Lemurian descendants.

Q: (L) The natives say the stones walked into position. Is this true?

A: No.

Q: (L) Well, how?

A: Tonal vibration.

Q: (L) And what did these stones represent?

A: Nephalim. [This is the Cassiopaeans' distinctive spelling]

Q: (L) Is this what the Nephilim looked like?

A: Close.

Q: (L) Does that mean that the Nephilim were present in Lemuria?

A: Close.

Q: (L) Where was Lemuria located?

A: Pacific off South America. Right near, all around Easter Island is remnant of Lemuria.

Q: (L) What happened to Lemuria?

A: Submerged close to time you refer to as Fall of Eden, approximately.

Q: (L) Well if the Nephilim were brought here 9 to 12 thousand years ago [as you have said previously]...

A: Last visit. Have been here 5 times. Will return.

Q: (L) The Nephilim are going to return? [I was pretty shocked, to say the least!] Where do the Nephilim currently live?

A: Orion.

Q: (L) They live in the constellation Orion? Where is their planet?

A: Don't have one. In transit.

Q: (L) The whole dad gum bunch is in transit?

A: Three vehicles.

Q: (L) How many Nephilim does each vehicle hold? [At this point I think my voice was shaking]

A: About 12 million.

Q: (L) Are they coming to help us? [I was hoping!]

A: No. Wave, comet cluster. All using same energy.

Q: (L) Using same energy to what?

A: Pass through space/time.

Q: (L) Does this mean that without this comet cluster they cannot pass through space/time?

A: No. "Slower."

Q: (L) So, it is slower for them to come here without this wave. Where is the wave coming from?

A: Follows cluster.

Q: (L) It follows the cluster. What does this wave consist of?

A: Realm border.

Q: (L) Does the realm border wave follow the comet cluster in a permanent way?

A: No.

Q: (L) Is the realm border associated with the comet cluster each time it comes?

A: No. Realm border follows all encompassing energy reality change; realm border will follow this cluster passage and has others but not most.

Q: (L) Is this realm border like a dimensional boundary?

A: Yes.

Q: (L) Okay, this realm border, do dimensions...

A: Pulsating realms. Fluctuating realms.

Q: (L) Is our realm fluctuating or pulsating?

A: No.

Q: (L) What fluctuates?

A: Residence. Your planet fluctuates between realms.

Q: (L) How often does this fluctuation occur?

A: About every 309,000 years. [It should be noted that this is almost exactly 12 precessional cycles.]

Q: (L) In other words we can expect to be in fourth density for about 300,000 years?

A: Yes.

Q: (L) Does this mean that the Edenic state existed for about 300,000 years before the "Fall?"

A: Yes.

Q: (L) You are saying that the planet fluctuates...

A: No, realms do; planet merely occupies realm.

Q: (L) What is the source in space/time of this other realm?

A: Too complex for present energies.

Q: (L) What is the generative source?

A: Part of Grand Cycle.

Q: (L) Is this the cycle understood by the Mayans?

A: They understood partially.

Q: (L) Their calendar extends to 2012... is that accurate as to the time of the realm border change?

A: Close. Still indefinite, as you measure time. Lizzies[24] hoping to rule you in fourth density. Closer to 18 years.

And, 18 years from the date of the above session would be December 2012. But, let's not get too focused on that since there is a lot more material to cover. The next mention of The Wave was in response to another "innocent" or seemingly unrelated question:

11-07-94

Q: (L) Recently I read an article about bursts of gamma rays in the upper atmosphere. What are these bursts of gamma rays?

A: Increasing energy with approach of wave.

And again, in response to another question about an earthquake, made its appearance:

11-24-94

Q: (L) Can you tell us about this recent volcanic eruption? What was the cause?

A: "Heating up" of earth.

Q: (L) What is causing it to heat up?

A: Vibrational frequency changes.

Q: (L) What is the source of these vibrational frequency changes?

A: Oncoming wave as we have told you before.

---

[24] "Lizzies" is a short-hand notation for those theorized denizens of hyperdimensional realities whose "essence" is "read" as reptilian. Many students of the UFO/alien subject tend to see the alleged hyperdimensional Reptilian race as physical like us and not, as we suggest, hyperdimensional creatures of variable physicality. Still other groups tell us that these reptilians are purely demonic, ethereal beings, who can "descend" into a person, or a human being can "host" a reptilian and "shape-shift" into this form (only if they have the genetics, mind you), and become temporarily reptilian themselves. The Queen of England and many of the leaders of the world have been listed as being of this latter type, with tales spun around them that pass the bounds of bizarre into lunacy.

Many physicists suggest that all that really exists are "waveforms" and we are waveforms of reality, and our consciousness is something that "reads waves." *We* give form and structure to the waves we "read" according to some *agreed upon convention*.

And so, certain denizens of hyperdimensional space are "read" as more or less "reptilian" because that is the "essence" of their being, the frequency of their "wave form." We actually have come to prefer calling them the *Overlords of Entropy*. They are not necessarily physical as we understand the term, nor are they necessarily "alien" as we understand the term either. We suspect that the perceptions of these levels of reality and their "consciousness units" are what is behind many religious conceptions and mythological representations of "gods and goddesses" and creatures of all sorts.

Q: (L) This oncoming wave, is this a wave which is so large or so vast that its effects are felt many years in advance of its absolute arrival point?

A: All waves in nature have a "contract" phase.

Q: (L) Does that mean like just before a wave comes up on shore it kind of sucks everything out?

A: Yes.

Q: (L) So we are in the sucking back phase [demonstrates with hand motion and sound effects].

A: Cute analogy.

It may have been cute, but I was starting to think seriously about this Wave business!

11-26-94

Q: (L) You have told us through this source, that there is a cluster of comets connected in some interactive way with our solar system, and that this cluster of comets comes into the plane of the ecliptic every 3600 years. Is this correct?

A: Yes. But, this time it is riding realm border wave to 4th level, where all realities are different.

Q: (L) Okay, so the cluster of comets is riding the realm border wave. Does this mean that when it comes into the solar system, that its effect on the solar system, or the planets within the solar system, or us, may or may not be mitigated by the fact of this transition? Is this a mitigating factor?

A: Will be mitigated.

So, that was a bit of a relief. What the Cassiopaeans seemed to be saying was that there was something about this wave that made it possible for it to be *utilized* according to the frequency of the individual. So, we asked a few more questions along this line in the same session quoted above:

Q: (L) Does any of this mean that the Earth Changes that have been predicted, may not, in fact, occur in physical reality, as we understand it?

A: You betcha.

Q: (L) Does this mean that all of this running around and hopping and jumping to go here and go there and do this and do that is...

A: That is strictly 3rd level thinking.

Q: (L) Now, if that is 3rd level thinking, and if a lot of these things are symbolic, I am assuming they are symbolic of movement or changes in energy.

A: Yes.

Q: (L) And, if these changes in energy occur does this mean that the population of the planet are, perhaps, in groups or special masses of groups, are they defined as the energies that are changing in these descriptions of events and happenings of great cataclysm. Is it like a cataclysm of the soul on an individual and or collective basis?

A: Close.

Q: (L) When the energy changes to fourth density, and you have already told us that people who are moving to fourth density when the transition occurs, that they will move into fourth density, go through some kind of rejuvenation process, grow new teeth, or whatever, what happens to those people who are not moving to fourth density, and who are totally unaware of it? Are they taken along on the wave by, in other words, piggybacked by the ones who are aware and already changing in frequency, or are they going to be somewhere else doing something else?

A: Step by step.

Q: (T) In other words, we are looking at the fact that what's coming this time is a wave that's going to allow the human race to move to fourth density?

A: And the planet and your entire sector of space/time.

Q: (T) Is that what this whole plan is about, then, if I may be so bold as to include all of us here in this. There are people who have come here into human form, to anchor the frequency, is this what we are anchoring it for, for this wave, so that when it comes enough of us will be ready, the frequency will be set, so that the change in the planet can take place as it has been planned?

A: Yes.

Q: (T) Okay, when the people are talking about the Earth Changes, when they talk in literal terms about the survivors, and those who are not going to survive, and the destruction and so forth and so on, in 3rd, 4th, 5th level reality we are not talking about the destruction of the planet on 3rd level physical terms, or the loss of 90 per cent of the population on the 3rd level because they died, but because they are going to move to 4th level?

A: Whoa! You are getting "warm."

Q: (T) Okay. So, when they talk about 90 per cent of the population not surviving, it is not that they are going to die, but that they are going to transform. We are going to go up a level. This is what the whole light thing is all about?

A: Or another possibility is that the physical cataclysms will occur only for those "left behind" on the remaining 3rd level density earth.

Q: (T) Okay, what you are saying, then, is that we are anchoring the frequency, so that when the wave comes, we move to 4th level density as many people as possible, in order to break the hold the fourth density STS have got on this planet, those who remain behind will not have enough energy left for the STS beings to bother with the planet any longer. There will be less of them so the planet will be able to refresh and they will be able to move on in their lessons without interference?

A: Close.

Q: (L) At this point of dimensional transition, is what we are doing, anchoring a frequency, that will literally create another earth in fourth density, which will then exist in fourth density, and the old 3rd density earth – almost like the splitting of a one celled organism, only in this splitting one half of it moves into another dimension and is energized and quite literally created by the anchoring frequency, while the old one remains and experiences 3rd density reality?

A: Step by step.

Q: (L) Are we anchoring frequency to create a split?

A: One developing conduit.

Q: (T) What is the conduit for?

A: You and those who will follow you.

Q: (L) This conduit. Is this a conduit through which an entire planet will transition?

A: You are one. There are others. Developing at this point.

Q: (T) These are conduits for us to move to fourth density in?

A: Knowledge is the key to developing a conduit.

Q: (T) We're developing a conduit to move us from 3rd density to fourth density. Once we have moved through the conduit does that mean we have completed what we came here to do, and that is anchor the frequency?

A: Partly.

Q: (T) Is the conduit kind of like an escape hatch for us?

A: Close.

Q: (L) Let me get this straight. When we move through this conduit, are the other...

A: You will be on the 4th level earth as opposed to 3rd level earth.

Q: (L) What I am trying to get here, once again, old practical Laura is trying to get a handle on practical terms here. Does this mean that a fourth density earth and a 3rd density earth will coexist side by side...

A: Not side-by-side, totally different realms.

Q: (L) Do these realms interpenetrate one another but in different dimensions...

A: Close.

Q: (L) So, in other words, a being from say, 6th density, could look at this planet we call the Earth and see it spinning through space and see several dimensions of earth, and yet the point of space/time occupation is the same, in other words, simultaneous. (J) They can look down but we can't look up.

A: Yes.

Q: (L) So, in other words, while all of this cataclysmic activity is happening on the 3rd dimensional earth, we will be just on our 4th dimensional earth and this sort of thing won't be there, and we won't see the 3rd dimensional people and they won't see us because we will be in different densities which are not "en rapport", so to speak?

A: You understand concept, now you must decide if it is factual.

Well, heck! What an assignment! But, on the other hand, how many choices are there? As you might expect, the subject came up again, and again the Cassiopaeans led us into it. On this occasion, they did something rather unusual – they gave a long string of "predictions" without stopping for questions. This was unusual because the overall Cassiopaean position on predictions is that:

> "The forces at work here are far too clever to be accurately anticipated so easily. You never know what twists and turns will follow, and they are aware of prophetic and philosophical patterning, and usually shift course to fool and discourage those who believe in fixed futures."

So, it was strange for them to make such a lengthy set of predictions even if they assigned no dates to them.

But, the predictions in this series seemed to be more like "marker" events – things that would begin to happen together in a sort of "group" as a marker that other things would then begin to happen like the falling of dominoes.

12-03-94

A: Ukraine explosion: chemical or nuclear. Hawaii crash: aviation, possibly involving military. More California seismic activity after 1st of year: San Diego, San Bernardino, North Bakersfield, Barstow: all are fracture points. Hollister, Palo Alto, Imperial, Ukiah, Eureka, Point Mendocino, Monterrey, Offshore San Luis Obispo, Capistrano, Carmel: these are all stress points of fracture in sequence. "Time" is indefinite. Expect gradual destruction of California economy as people begin mass exodus. Also, Shasta erupts, Lassen activity. Ocean floor begins to subside. Queen Elizabeth serious illness; blood related. Princess Diana suicide attempt. Gas explosions in NE United States, Texas and other. Supernova and unusual weather all over. Memphis feels tremors. Minneapolis banking scandal relates to mysterious Nordic covenant. Evangelical sexual tryst exposed. Gold is discovered in California after one of the quakes.

Regarding the mention of a suicide attempt by Princess Diana, there were revelations of *prior* suicide attempts though in actual fact, the probability that was chosen was that she died in an automobile crash at the same time as the "Flood of the Millennium" occurred in Europe.

The most recently publicized claims by the bodyguard who survived the crash is that he blames Dodi Fayed for Diana's death because Dodi was careless and made very bad choices about security.

I suppose, in a certain sense, Diana's acquiescence to Dodi's choices could be termed "suicidal."

What is even more interesting to me as I now go through *The Wave* to prepare it for book publication, is the fact that the so-called Project for a New American Century, otherwise called "PNAC", was formulated in June, 1997, two months before the death of the People's Princess. The current activities of George W. Bush and his neocon-artists are based on this plan. Part of the text of this pernicious document states:

> "The Project for the New American Century was established in the spring of 1997. From its inception, the Project has been concerned with the decline in the strength of America's defenses, and in the problems this would create for the exercise of American leadership around the globe and, ultimately, for the preservation of peace."

> "At present the United States faces no global rival. America's grand strategy should aim to preserve and extend this advantageous position as far into the future as possible."

> "Preserving the desirable strategic situation in which the United States now finds itself requires a globally preeminent military capability both today and in the future."

> "Although it may take several decades for the process of transformation to unfold, in time, the art of warfare on air, land, and sea will be vastly different than it is today, and "combat" likely will take place in new dimensions: in space, "cyber-space," and perhaps the world of microbes. Air warfare may no longer be fought by pilots manning tactical fighter aircraft sweeping the skies of opposing fighters, but a regime dominated by long-range, stealthy unmanned craft. On land, the clash of massive, combined-arms armored forces may be replaced by the dashes of much lighter, stealthier and information-intensive forces, augmented by fleets of robots, some small enough to fit in soldiers' pockets. Control of the sea could be largely determined not by fleets of surface combatants and aircraft carriers, but from land- and space-based systems, forcing navies to maneuver and fight underwater. Space itself will become a theater of war, as nations gain access to space capabilities and come to rely on them; further, the distinction between military and commercial space systems – combatants and noncombatants – will become blurred. Information systems will become an important focus of attack, particularly for U.S. enemies seeking to short-circuit sophisticated American forces… And advanced forms of biological warfare that can "target" specific genotypes may transform biological warfare from the realm of terror to a politically useful tool."

> "The current American peace will be short-lived if the United States becomes vulnerable to rogue powers with small, inexpensive arsenals of ballistic missiles and nuclear warheads or other weapons of mass destruction. We cannot allow North Korea, Iran, Iraq or similar states to undermine American leadership, intimidate American allies or threaten the American homeland itself."
>
> "HOMELAND DEFENSE. America must defend its homeland. During the Cold War, nuclear deterrence was the key element in homeland defense; it remains essential. But the new century has brought with it new challenges. While reconfiguring its nuclear force, the United States also must counteract the effects of the proliferation of ballistic missiles and weapons of mass destruction that may soon allow lesser states to deter U.S. military action by threatening U.S. allies and the American homeland itself. Of all the new and current missions for U.S. armed forces, this must have priority." [25]

Another, even more evil part of the PNAC plan which directly relates to the complicity of this group in the attack on the World Trade Center and the Pentagon, states:

> "Further, the process of transformation, even if it brings revolutionary change, is likely to be a long one, absent some catastrophic and *catalyzing event – like a new Pearl Harbor...*"
>
> "And advanced forms of biological warfare that can "target" specific genotypes may transform biological warfare from the realm of terror to a politically useful tool."

Even though we had a nagging suspicion that there was something terribly wrong with the circumstances surrounding the death of Diana Spencer, beloved icon of compassion and service, it was not until George Bush came to power by extraordinary and illegal means, that any of this series of predictions began to make sense. (My guess is that, due to the fact that they were given so far in advance, that there was some "blurring" of the facts.) Would Bush and the neocons have been able to pull off what they have, and continue to do, if there were unassailable Icons of Peace speaking out against them?

In October of 2004, we were already two years into our *Signs of The Times* project, and the editors of the page wrote a bit of commentary on this issue as follows:

> Where have all the Heroes Gone?

---

[25] *Rebuilding America's Defenses: Strategy, Forces and Resources For a New Century,* September, 2000. (http://www.newamericancentury.org/RebuildingAmericas Defenses.pdf)

Heroes and heroines are that rare caste of human being who, when faced with oppression or hardship, are unwilling to lie down and submit to the usually formidable forces pitted against them. Of course, heroes need not always be acting in a consciously altruistic way, but it is the spirit of resistance to tyranny and freedom of choice that moves them, or moves through them, that can shine as a light for all those with eyes to see it. One might have thought that the modern world, with all of its injustice and suffering, would provide ample breeding ground for a new breed of heroes and heroines of all types, yet we find that this is not the case.

Perhaps it is our modern, dumbed-down, unimaginative, mechanized civilization, with its emphasis on career, money and personal gain, that has severely limited the possibilities for their emergence – or perhaps it is more true to say that the oppression has become so complete, so all encompassing, that even those of a heroic disposition are no match for it. Yet the twentieth century has, nevertheless, produced a few notable examples of those people who, finding themselves in a position of influence and with a choice to make, in their own way chose truth over lies, justice over injustice, and heroism over pusillanimity.

Readers will note that we have used the past tense in the preceding sentence, for, sadly in the modern world, heroism, particularly when it is on a grand and public scale, is not appreciated by those who thrive on a lifeless, apathetic population. As a result, the life expectancy of the average modern-day hero or heroine, who threaten to awaken the multitudes by their example, can be sharply curtailed. While we can be forgiven for seeing only the tragedy in such a scenario, and while we might lament the naiveté of the heroes, their actions, and the process of containing their potentially "negative" effects – even when it involves the ultimate sacrifice – can sometimes expose the face of the anti-hero who, far too often, steals the show here on the BBM. For any readers of a heroic disposition, such knowledge is immeasurably valuable.

Let us take a look then at some of the modern-day heroes who, by their lives, have sought to inspire humanity to greater things, and by their deaths, inadvertently exposed the face of the anti-hero.

The list we came up with included the Kennedy brothers, Dr. Martin Luther King, John Lennon, Princess Diana, and others, whose untimely deaths deprived the world of any individuals in a position of influence who, in their own way chose truth over lies, justice over injustice, and heroism over pusillanimity.

So it is that we consider Diana's death, and her mention in this series of prophecies to be a true "marker" of the evil times that were coming. In another sense, as others have suggested, it was the "death of the feminine," the destruction of the goddess by the warlike male god, Jehovah, the victory of the Blade over the Chalice.

To continue with the series of "marker" events:

12-03-94

UFOs dramatic increase and Gulf Breeze gets swarmed, becomes massive "Mecca". Laura sees much more UFO activity. Huge wave of UFO activity. All manner and origins. Just you wait, it will give you chills and that feeling in the pit of your stomach. Many aliens[26] will appear and we will be visible too. Think of it as a convention. All must awaken to this. It is happening right now. The whole populace will play individual roles according to their individual frequencies. This is only the beginning. Just you wait "Henry Higgins," just you wait!(?)

Q: (L) Are you a Rodgers and Hammerstein fan?

A: Yes.

Q: (L) How do you relate to the Pleiadians?

A: Pleiadians are communicating with many others; we are bursting upon the scene with you, but we are essentially the same, just at slightly different focus points on the realm border.

Q: (L) Well, why is all this activity happening now?

A: The Grand Cycle is about to close presenting a unique opportunity.

Q: (L) Does this mean that this is a unique opportunity to change the future?

A: Future, past and present.

Q: (L) Well, that sort of makes me think that if things are not changed somewhat at this point on the Grand Cycle that things could get really direfully screwed up, is that correct?

A: But they won't. You have not grasped concept.

Q: (L) Yeah I have, I got you, I understand. It's just part of the cycle. It's all a cycle. I mean their being here is part of us being here...

A: You do??? [Inscribed giant question mark on board]

Q: (L) Do what?

A: You said you understood concept. Really? Learn.

Q: (V) I am just concerned about this "convention"...

---

[26] Keep in mind that "aliens" as used by the Cassiopaeans, has an altogether different meaning from the standard use of the term. This will become clearer as we proceed.

A: Convention is because of realm border crossing.

Q: (L) And why is there a convention attending this realm border crossing? I mean, is it just a "reely big shew!"

A: It is an opportunity, as in an opportunity to affect whole universe. Picture cosmic playing of "Pomp and Circumstance" AKA "Hope and Glory."

Q: (L) How can a convention with slews of different kinds and races of people, converging on a single little pin-point planet on the outer edges of an insignificant galaxy, at the farthest reaches of this enormous universe, affect the whole thing?

A: That is your perception.

Q: (L) Well, what is the correct perception? Are the planet Earth and the people thereon, and the things that are going on in this spot, the Earth specifically, more important than maybe we would ordinarily have thought?

A: The Earth is a Convergence point.

Q: (L) Was it designed to be a convergence point from the beginning?

A: Natural function.

Q: (L) Has it been a convergence point all along? Is that why so many weird things happen here?

A: That is difficult to answer because you have no understanding of "time".

Q: (V) Has this type of convention thing happened on other planets with other groups of beings?

A: Has, is, and will.

Q: (L) So, in other words, there are other planets, I don't mean similar in structure or occupation, but other planets that are convergence points. If these convergence points are scattered around the universe, is the convergence of this realm border crossing going to occur simultaneously at all points in the universe that are convergence points?

A: No.

Q: (L) It only happens at say one, or selected, convergence points at any given point?

A: Close.

Q: (L) So, do realm borders have something to do with location?

A: Realm borders ride waves.

Q: (L) And where do these waves come from?

A: They constantly cycle.

Q: (L) Does it have something to do with the movement of the planet Earth into it or does it move onto us?

A: Either or.

Q: (F) Does this convention or convergence have something to do with the fact that there are living beings on the Earth?

A: Yes. And because you are at critical juncture in development.

Q: (L) I would like to know in terms of prophecy if the prophecies you gave us in the first session are still valid and upcoming?

A: They are evolving.

Q: (L) Does that mean that they are evolving to the point that they are going to happen soon?

A: Fluid.

Q: (L) Does that mean that some of them may not happen?

A: Yes.

Q: (L) And the prophecies that you gave tonight, are they subject to change also?

A: Maybe.

Q: (L) When was the last time a realm border crossed as far as the Earth is concerned?

A: As you measure on Earth, 309,000 years ago.

Q: (L) What does this wave consist of in terms of energy?

A: Feeling. Hyperkinetic sensate.

Q: (L) What does that mean?

A: All. Too complex for this medium.

Q: (L) Okay. How many times has the wave come and involved the Earth, as we know it?

A: Infinite number.

I was completely nonplussed by that answer. Infinite number? How can the linear mind cope with such an idea? But, I was game to try. I started planning my "Wave Questions" in advance:

12-05-94

Q: (L) I would like to know what is the definition of, and would you describe for us, a dimensional curtain?

A: Self-explanatory. Think.

Q: (L) When we are talking about dimensional curtains we are talking about divisions at the same level of density, is that correct?

A: Maybe.

Q: (L) Can dimensional curtains be between dimensions at the same level of density?

A: Yes.

Q: (L) Are dimensional curtains also something that occurs between levels of density?

A: Yes.

Q: (L) So, a dimensional curtain is a point at which some sort of change takes place... what causes this change?

A: Nature.

Q: (L) In specific terms of the engineering of it, what defines this change?

A: Experience.

Q: (L) Is it in any way related to atomic or quantum physics or the movement of atoms?

A: Yes.

Q: (L) Okay. An atom is in 3rd density. What distinguishes it from an atom in fourth density?

A: Reality.

Q: (L) What distinguishes one realm from another?

A: Assumptions.

Q: (L) Okay, what you assume or expect is what you perceive about that atom depending upon which reality you are in, is that correct?

A: Close.

Q: (L) What determines your assumptions?

A: Experience.

Q: (L) My experience of atoms is that they congregate in such a way as to form solid matter...

A: Every thing that exists is merely a lesson.

Q: (L) Okay, so once we have learned certain lessons, as in experience of certain things, then our assumptions change?

A: Yes.

Q: (L) Okay, is this wave that is coming our direction going to give us an experience that is going to change our assumptions?

A: Catch 22: One half is that you have to change your assumptions in order to experience the wave in a positive way.

Q: (L) And what does this wave consist of in absolute terms?

A: Realm border.

Q: (L) Is that realm border as in a cut-off point between one reality and another?

A: Yes.

Q: (L) Is that realm border as in dimensional curtain?

A: Yes.

Q: (L) So the planet Earth is going to pass through a dimensional curtain?

A: Or *an* earth. All is merely a lesson, and nothing, repeat nothing, more.

Q: (L) Well, my experience with lessons has been that they are generally painful. Is this realm border crossing, or this merging experience going to be what we, or I, in the 3rd density, would perceive as painful?

A: Wait and see.

I pretty much felt like I hadn't gotten anywhere at all with the last series of questions. But, of course, it set me to thinking *very* hard about the subject!

In the meantime, I had a most distressing experience with a hypnosis subject. The issues of that session seem to be somewhat related to the matters at hand, so I had better tell you a little about it. Brace yourself.

CHAPTER 2
MULTI-DIMENSIONAL SOUL ESSENCES

The subject of the hypnosis session transcribed below was a woman, about 45 years old, who was a science instructor at one of the local high schools. She, too, had begun to experience some rather strange things in her life after becoming associated with a metaphysical church in Tampa, about 40 miles distant from our home at the time.

As with most cases of this kind, the initiating events are so lost in a confusing mess of contradictory details that it is difficult to sort out what exactly happened in what sequence. The person is usually in such a state of Post-Traumatic Stress Disorder (PTSD) that it is difficult to get them to make any sense.

(I would like to note as an aside that I have worked with many other subjects who have gotten into difficulties from erroneous teachings promulgated at various "Metaphysical Churches" which have popped up all over the country in the past dozen or so years. In one case, the individual was possessed by a really nasty entity that informed me that many of the teachings of the "New Age" are designed to turn on, or trigger "mind control programs" leading to enslavement by powerful STS forces which plan to "take over" or "replace" mankind completely. In all such cases, knowledge truly does protect.)

This woman, referred to me by the owner of a book store in Tampa, called and left a hysterical message on my answering machine saying that somebody was following her, she was afraid and could I please call her right away because she needed to find out what was happening in her life – it was a shambles! Familiar story, yes?

She had been married to a professor at USF and had divorced him when she became convinced that he was sexually abusing their daughter. Whether there was any truth to the abuse claims I don't know, because the evidence was that the courts must not have thought so because the father had liberal visitation rights.

After a couple of interviews, I scheduled a session, and I was *not* prepared for what came out of that one!

After the induction I did what I normally do in such cases, which was to direct the subject to mentally create a "sanctuary" from which to work. This is a guided imagery exercise in which many things about the individual can be learned by the ways in which they describe their "private retreat" from the world. The general procedure is to find some aspect of the "sanctuary" that can be used as a "bridge" to the regression part of the session. For example, if there is a mirror on the wall, it can be used as a "viewing screen" to other times and places. If there is no mirror, but there is a window to the outside, then that can be used instead. The available furniture is utilized for further relaxing the subject as he/she is instructed to get comfortable on the sofa/bed/chair that may be described, and the trance is deepened from that position. It's a particularly useful technique – sort of like hypnosis within hypnosis – because it gives deeper access to the subconscious mind while maintaining the "safety zone" for the comfort of the subject.

The subject (we can call her "Ruth," though that is not her real name), created a lovely cottage filled with pleasant symbolic mementos of her life, or her "desired life," which she wandered through and described in some detail. The first object she mentioned was a table of dark polished wood. There were shelves lined with beer steins and copper ale cups, a smell of warm cinnamon from the kitchen, and her feelings in regard to the cottage were so nostalgic that she became tearful several times during the description. Here, we will pick up the session verbatim. My questions are designated "Q", and Ruth's responses are "A":

12-06-94

Q: Are there any books or papers on any of the shelves?

A: On the table. There are a few.

Q: Can you see the titles on any of the books?

A: No. There are no books, just papers... looks like a map.

Q: Do you know what it is a map of?

A: Like a treasure map kind of...

Q: Why don't you walk over to it and have a look? Tell me about it.

A: It's a treasure map. And I see... first I see the directions up in the left corner.

Q: What does it say?

A: Celestial journey. It's got things moving on it!

Q: What's moving on it?

A: The lights coming from the little circles... or the ships. The lights keep moving around. It's down to the ground and they go 'round... and there's three ships... and the lights go down to the ground. They go around. It's like they take turns going around...and there's red and green...and the ground is down toward the bottom. That's where I'm walking.

Q: You are walking in the place on the map?

A: It's funny. I'm in the map! And I'm walking.

Q: Continue and describe what you are seeing.

A: I'm in the woods. And. I'm... ooooh... I see this ship... and it's glowing... pulsating. It's got lights! It's just MAGNIFICENT! It's round... the edge of the trees... I go around... I see it! I SEE IT!

Q: Who's on board the ship?

A: They're out on the ground.

Q: Describe them to me.

A: They are kind of far away yet... they are kind of like insects...

Q: What do you mean "kind of like insects?"

A: We're walking around, you know...

Q: What kind of insects do they remind you of?

A: Oh! Grasshopper! This is like... like... when I was in a past life... and I WAS a grasshopper! And I ate... I ate... something. Oh! I remember. I ate humans. And I had blood all over me. I think I must be one of them... but I'm not sure yet.

Q: So, they eat humans?

A: There's this little girl... with brown hair... curly. And she's dressed in a light colored blue dress. And it has petticoats in it. And this insect being... eats her.

Q: Is this one you are seeing as you are going through the woods? Or is it from another time?

A: Uhh... this is in the woods.

Q: And you see this insect being eating a little girl?

A: Yeah.

Q: How does that make you feel?

A: Oh...I don't have any feeling. I'm just watching it. It's like I'm detached.

Q: What does the little girl say?

A: She doesn't seem to mind.

Q: Okay. Stop the action for one moment. The whole scene you are observing is going to be projected onto a sort of movie screen. But, this is a very special movie screen that is really a curtain. Now, you have a little box in your hand like a TV remote control, and there is a button on that remote that makes the movie screen/curtain split and open and shows you the true essence of the scene you are viewing – it shows you the energy behind the events you are observing. All the masks and screens will be removed in one instant...

A: Excuse me... I'm eating that little girl!

Q: Okay. How does that make you feel?

A: It's food. I pull her hair back because the hair doesn't taste good.

Q: Do you look at her before you eat her?

A: Yeah.

Q: What does she look like?

A: Shirley Temple kind of...

Q: How does it make you feel now to look at yourself as that other being, that insect, eating that little girl?

A: It's a way of life. It's just what does happen.

Q: Okay, now. I want you to push the button on your remote control and split the movie screen. What do you see behind the screen?

A: [Subject begins to breath in short, gasping breaths.] Treacherous...

Q: What is treacherous?

A: [Whispers] It's like... it's *not* a grasshopper...

Q: What is it?

A: It's like an ant... it's an ANT... and it's DEVOURING... they're FEEDING... uh... uh... uh... they're FEEDING... they're FEEDING... [Gasping and choking] these kids... KIDS are being herded in and they're EATING THEM!

Q: How do you feel?

A: Horrified!

Q: What do you want to say?

A: Uh... UH... HUH... [Gasping and choking and sobbing] They're HUGE! I can't... there isn't anything I can do! They have NO understanding! They're CREATURES! Their EYES! HUGE! They're like Preying Mantises... that's it... They tear arms off like we would a chicken wing... look at the blood! It's running down!

That's why they grow these kids! This happens ALL OVER EARTH!

Q: Are you okay?

A: I knew that Earth was a terrible place... but I didn't know it was a feeding ground! [Coughing] We're in danger. RIGHT NOW! You and I are in danger. Because we know. It's scary. This is why there are so many lies and deceptions... the so-called "abductions" are lies... all smokescreen. Jesus Christ! Manipulation... [Laughs] WE are the manna! I SAW this in a past life... but it was left unfinished because the therapist got scared. It's what you call a "hot item." [...] Now I know why I'm here. It's penance... what I did in the past.

Q: As one of those beings?

A: That's right. But I'm not gonna lay myself down and let 'em eat me!

Q: Let's go back to the map. I want you to go back to your cottage, go to the table, pick up the map and look at it again and tell me what you see.

A: I see big... either... it's not snakes... it's more like tree roots. And they're slithering... kind of brownish green. I am ONE of them!

Q: You are one of these snakes?

A: I don't see heads... I just see bodies.

Q: What is happening to them?

A: They just kind of weave in an out like a whole big bunch of earthworms.

Q: Do you get any sense of where and when this is? Is it on Earth?

A: It's at the core... ohhh... I see! These ships go into the Earth and feed these big worms.

Q: What do they feed them?

A: People. That's the ships they talk about in Peru. The Arcturian book talks about the caverns that the ships go into... and how they exist inside the Earth.

Q: Are you one of these worms or are you just looking at them?

A: Well... I'm looking at the worms from a spaceship... it's got ... the window is kinda like a lid only it's in the middle. These are our *parents*! Isn't *that* wonderful! We all gotta come from somewhere! We're... the DNA from these worms is just part of it...

Q: What do they use the DNA from these worms for?

A: I'm not sure. Let me look. It's like there's a basic DNA... and it's a combination of the worms and the ants ... uh... and they can create whatever being that they want to depending on how much they take from where. It's kind of like a chemistry lab... the whole thing is like a scientific project.

Q: I want you to move to an event that impacted you with the feeling of being "prey" that you have wanted to address...

A: Oh! They're going to push me down! And feed me to the worms! I think that I'm there as part of the expedition... but they turn on me and... They're going to push me out of the ship... and down... to the worms.

Q: Do they do it?

A: It's like I'm hanging onto the door... and I plop... down... and they EAT me!

Q: How does it feel?

A: Crunchy.

Q: Okay. Go back. What do the others in the ship look like? Are you one of them? Do they look like you?

A: Yeah. Well... they've got clothes on. They have uniforms. The weirdest thing... they have on uniforms... but they're insects. Insect-like people! Insects with intelligence. More like ants that stand up and have human-like qualities. Now! Hang on just a minute! Their heads! I see the heads. And the eyes... they aren't really big on these guys. The head turns and... they're just... I don't know... Preying Mantis sort of... but their hands aren't like Preying Mantises... they're just a different kind of insect... more like an ant.

Q: Do they have fingers?

A: I guess it's more like a fly. They don't really have hands. It's just like it tapers off... kind of like a fly without wings. And they have on these uniforms. Huh!

Q: You were one of them?

A: Yeah. I guess I was. [Deep sigh.]

At this point, I took her back to her sanctuary, gave her suggestions for well-being and integration of what she had learned, and brought her out.

Needless to say, this was a pretty bizarre story and I definitely wanted to ask the Cassiopaeans about it at the soonest opportunity.

12-09-94

Q: (L) Now, I would like to know the name of the beings Ruth described as something like ants, flies or preying Mantises in her hypnosis session?

A: Her essence.

Q: (L) Well, you said that the Preying Mantis beings that V__ encountered were called Minturians. Are these the same?

A: No.

Q: (L) Is there a difference between essence beings and incarnate beings?

A: Yes.

Q: (L) And what were those snaky, slug-like beings that she saw?

A: Same.

Q: (L) Are you saying that all of this stuff is who she is? All of these creatures and these...

A: In some of the alternate realities.

Q: (L) Do all humans have creatures like that that are their essence?

A: Yes.

Q: (L) My essence is something that horrible and dark and icky?

A: Subjective.

Q: (L) Well, weren't those horrible icky beings eating little children? Weren't those real human children?

A: Yes. How do you think you are viewed by deer, for example?

Q: (L) Well, I can immediately see that. I saw that already. I mean that cows and chickens would have to view us that way. I mean, it's pretty gross.

A: Roaches, too.

Q: (L) Is that why the night before Ruth's session, I dreamed of ants that I could have stepped on and smashed, and for some reason I decided I did not want to take the life of even a single ant?

A: Yes.

Q: (L) Was that dream preparing me for what I was going to experience in that session?

A: Yes.

Q: (L) Well, what do we do about these essence parts of ourselves? I mean, I don't like it that there may be something of the predator in me. I would like to not have it, or get rid or it, or transform it, or whatever.

A: Wait and see.

Q: (L) Well, am I going to have to remember myself doing things like that in order to come to terms with it?

A: Yes.

Q: (L) Is that going to happen to me, that I am going to have memories like that surfacing?

A: Yes.

Q: (L) Well, I am having a hard time coping with it in someone else, how am I going to deal with it in myself?

A: You will.

Q: (L) Is this something we are all going to have to do?

A: All eligible fourth density candidates.

I came back to the subject again the following evening:

12-10-94

Q: (L) Were these in any way physical beings on the earth we occupy in space/time from where we are at this moment?

A: No.

Q: (L) This happened in a so-called alternate reality?

A: Is still.

Q: (L) So, in some alternate reality, Ruth is a preying mantis being eating little children?

A: And so are you. And all others.

Q: (L) Are these aspects of our being coming to earth as part of the realm border crossing?

A: Yes.

Q: (L) Are all of us going to have to face these aspects of ourselves as other beings?

A: Yes.

Q: (L) Are there other parts of us in all realms doing other things at this moment?

A: Yes.

Q: (L) And how is this going to be affected by the realm border crossing?

A: Will merge.

Q: (L) Do we need to do some kind of work such as hypnosis to bring these aspects of ourselves up and deal with these things a little at a time?

A: Will happen involuntarily. Will be like a thermonuclear blast. See the pattern. Orion, Pleiades, Arcturas, Cassiopaea; check distances from earth; progress locator for wave combined with earth references of space-time. For you to figure out. Cross-reference channeled messages printing dates and location. We are where we are. Cross-reference time and distance.

Q: (L) What book do we need to cross-reference?

A: Any star chart and Marciniak, Arcturas Channel, Orion literature and us. We speak from "crest" of wave, now, where are we?

Q: (L) You speak from the crest of the wave?

A: Yes.

Q: (L) You said in another session that you were 6 thousand miles...

A: Window of transmission. How far away is Cassiopaea?

Q: (L) Do we need specific distances?

A: General is okay.

Q: (L) So, if we just find the general distances... and does each of these star clusters represent a general area of the wave?

A: Each represents locator in space-time. You can judge speed and ETA by cross-referencing distance with publishing dates and these messages from us.

Q: (L) I got it! You mean that *you* are the Arcturians, the Pleiadians, and now you are the "Cassiopaeans" because you "are where you are"! And you are riding the wave. Is this wave a straight line connecting all these constellations?

A: Circuitous or cyclical route.

Q: (L) So, is it like a spiral?

A: Yes.

Q: (L) So we really need to set up a map so we can draw it?

A: Yes.

Q: (L) When we speak from Orion we are "Orions". When from Pleiades, we are "Pleiadian", and so on.

Q: (L) So, all of these channeled books you have mentioned are coming from the same basic source, through different channels, that they are able to connect with because of their different positions in space time and preparation level of the channels, is that correct?

A: Close. We have given you a Wave crest locator. We are from where we are and speak. Get it? We are where we are.

Q: (T) So, you are not really Cassiopaeans from the Constellation Cassiopeia?

A: We are Transient Passengers. When Wave reaches Earth, we merge with you.

Q: (L) When you were at Orion, did you merge with the Orions?

A: Not on same frequency for realm border crossing.

Q: (L) What effect did the wave have on the Orion sector?

A: None. Already at fourth density level.

Q: (L) Where did the wave originate?

A: Did not.

Q: (L) Has it always been cycling through the universe?

A: Close.

Q: (T) Okay, you are riding on the crest of this wave in 6th density, is this true?

A: Yes. We are you in 6th density.

Q: (L) Are you alternate selves extending into higher densities?

A: At your current reference point in space-time, we are you in the future.

Q: (L) You are not, by any chance, one of those weird ant or preying mantis beings are you?

A: Yes and no.

Q: (T) You are just another part of ourselves? You, us, the Lizards, the ants, the grays, the trees...

A: We are your whole self as you/we are in 6th density.

Q: (T) So, what we are working to become is you? You are us?

A: Yes.

Q: (T) So, when we move to fourth density and become whole with ourselves, we will know you also for a short time?

A: Not whole yet when at fourth density. Closer when at fourth density.

Q: (L) When Candy was under hypnosis she described seeing a fleet of space ships "riding a wave" and this unnerved her. She felt this wave was a fearful, invasion-type thing. Did she perceive you and your wave?

A: Wave is transport mode.

Q: (L) Is that transport mode for many beings?

A: Yes.

Q: (L) Are you coming to invade us?

A: No, merge.

Q: (L) Are others coming with the intention of invading us?

A: Yes. Wave is "crowded."

Q: (T) So, everybody out in the whole universe who wants a piece of the earth action is on this wave?

A: At realm border crossing.

This gave us the idea that this "Wave" business is a lot stranger than anything we could ever have imagined.

Another comment about The Wave was made a week later:

12-17-94

A: Always "Network." Networking is fourth density STO (Service To Others) concept seeping into 3rd density with upcoming realm border crossing. Coming from 4th level into 3rd because of influence of wave.

A follow-up question regarding the plotting of The Wave and ETA (estimated time of arrival) was asked:

12-31-94

Q: (T) Last session when I was here you were giving us information on how to calculate when the wave is going to reach Earth. I was able to plot two of the four for distance, but two were constellations. I cannot plot those distances.

A: Check third most distant star in Cassiopaea and middle "belt" star in Orion, closest star in Leo.

About a week later, a strange event occurred. The first inkling I had of it was when I awakened in the night with a very strange sensation that a loud noise had awakened me, though I could hear nothing. I went back to sleep and, later in the morning my daughter reported to me that she had experienced something strange at about the same time. The question she asked me startled me: "Mom, have you ever been able to see with your eyes closed?"

As a matter of fact, that was a common occurrence for me just prior to having an out-of-body experience, but I didn't want to alarm her even though I was, myself, a little upset that this sort of thing was happening to my 15-year-old child. Also, she was aware of some sort of "being" in her room with what she described as a "small, squeaky voice."

Then, later in the morning, a friend called to talk at some length about the sound that he had heard during the night and the peculiar effects he noted. That evening, when T & J arrived for the session, they were full of the story about a loud booming noise that had awakened J as well as T's father. It had been so unusual that they had discussed it at length. So, we asked the C's about it and again, a seemingly unrelated question led to more information about The Wave.

01-07-95

Q: (L) We have a few interesting questions tonight. I think the first thing on everybody's mind is the strange events during the night and early morning hours, reported by T and J compared with events that JW told me about by phone this morning. T's dad noted it, and also something woke A__ up with a start and she experienced some strange effects. I was awakened with a strange feeling that something very *loud* had just been heard, though it was more like an echo in my head than actually hearing it with my ears. We are a little bit curious about this event, this occurrence, and we would like to have some information on it. What exactly was it?

A: Thunder.

Q: (L) It seemed to be an extraordinarily massive strike, and it seemed to have been heard at a great distance in several directions. Where, in fact, did this lightning bolt strike?

A: Cell was uniformly structured throughout region.

Q: (T) So we all heard that particular blast because of that?

A: No. Each zone received similar EM profile, thus one particularly heavily charged event in each zone.

Q: (L) What is an EM profile?

A: Electromagnetic.

Q: (L) Was there any particular significance to this type of blast since it is not something any of us has experienced in our immediate memory. Is there any implication to this blast in terms of fourth density activity?

A: You have, and yes. As always.

Q: (L) Since this was such a boomer, what exactly was going on in fourth density that produced a boomer like this?

A: Overlapping densities, lasting approximately 1.3 seconds, as you measure time i.e.: for 1.3 seconds, you lived completely in fourth density.

Q: (T) So this was a significant event for us to have noticed?

A: The noticing was more significant than the event.

Q: (T) What about if you didn't notice? I didn't actually hear it, J did. So it was important that we were aware that something had happened...

A: You did at another level of consciousness.

Q: (L) Did this event have anything to do with A__'s experience this morning of being awakened by a rustling in her room and thinking that she heard a squeaky voice calling her name?

A: Yes. fourth density "resident."

Q: (L) And what kind of fourth density resident was this?

A: Om Type.

Q: (L) What is a type Om?

A: You would rather not know!

Q: (L) No, I would rather know. If something is going to be visiting my daughter in her bedroom, I definitely want to know who or what it is.

A: Who says this will be regular event?

Q: (T) This was just a one-time event?

A: Yes.

Q: (V) Was the reason A__ was so aware of this is because she is psychically open when she is asleep?

A: Yes.

Q: (V) Is there anything she needs to do to control her psychic openness in order not to be harmed?

A: Why control something beneficial? [...]

Q: (L) Going back to the event of this morning, when JW related his experience of it to me, he said that when he opened his eyes that the light looked yellow... (V) I noticed the discoloration too... (J) Was that related to the event?

A: Yes.

Q: (J) What caused the light to change color?

A: Leftover fourth density effects.

Q: (L) Is this something that is going to be happening more and more as we move to fourth density?

A: Yes.

Q: (L) Is this electromagnetic charging of the atmosphere, I am assuming that is what it is, and that it is occurring as part of the shifting of densities...

A: Yes.

Q: (L) If it is an electromagnetic charging of the atmosphere, is this charging coming about because of this oncoming wave and effects that we are beginning to feel more and more of, are they part of the wave, its presence or approach?

A: It is a buildup, similar to the early effects preceding the arrival of a sea wave.

Q: (T) Are the extremely high winds they have been experiencing in North Carolina and California and the earthquakes in Japan all related to this?

A: Yes.

Q: (T) Yes. 140 mile an hour winds up in the Carolina's and out in California they were hitting 160 miles an hour winds. (L) Well, they told us we were going to have really weird weather. (T) There was another earthquake in Japan today. This has been ongoing for the last couple of weeks. Japan is supposed to go. (V) Sylvia Brown was on a talk show. She had said that there was going to be a big earthquake in Alaska... a huge one... what can you tell us about this?

A: One of many events of the buildup lasting years, as you measure time.

We became aware of the fact that many anomalous things might be effects of fourth density "bleed through" as a result of The Wave. As noted in the previous section, an increase of UFO activity was indicated to be part of the "symptoms" of the approach of The Wave. We wanted to know more about this aspect:

01-07-95

Q: (L) You guys said that we were going to have a whole big, bodacious bunch more of UFO activity this year, is that correct? 1995

A: Bingo!

Q: (L) And I guess it has already started because some guy in Michigan filmed a UFO in broad daylight and they showed it on the news three days in a row and I don't think they were being snide in their comments... (F) Yes they were. I saw it on channel 13 and they were being definitely snide. (L) The fellow in Michigan, could you identify that craft for us and to whom it belonged?

A: It was the Grays.

Q: (L) Now, are the Grays going to allow themselves to be seen more and more in 3rd density in the upcoming years?

A: Yes. All of these events are related to that with which you are now familiar. All is related to approach of oncoming wave, what the details are will remain to be seen.

Not long after this, Susy and Barry Konicov, publishers of *Connecting Link* magazine, called and wanted to ask a few questions. Barry asked some particularly interesting questions about some other aspects of The Wave:

01-11-95

Q: (Susy) Why are you choosing Laura and Frank to transmit this information?

A: Because balancing fields are correct.

Q: (Barry) Maitreya... What is the destiny of this person in this lifetime?

A: Plays prominent role in disinformation process.

Q: (Barry) Is Benjamin Creme aware of that?

A: No.

Q: (Barry) Are the E.T.'s putting thoughts in Benjamin Creme's head?

A: Yes.

Q: (Barry) What is their purpose in this?

A: To cause confusion, diversion, and deception so that reality channels may be cloaked. Self-explanatory.

Q: (Barry) Does this mean so that what we think is real really isn't?

A: Close.

Q: (Barry) This must mean that the Aliens want to give us one person to focus on which is so spectacular, so that we cannot see the truth.

A: Remember warnings about false prophets in the "desert."

Q: (B) Does this mean that Benjamin Creme is an STS (Service To Self) person?

A: Yes, indirectly.

Q: (Barry) Is he the antichrist?

A: No. The "antichrist" is not an individual, but consortium.

Q: (Barry) Who is the Consortium?

A: Term refers to idea of large body of individuals.

Q: (Barry) Human beings?

A: Yes and others.

Q: (Barry) Are these people who have reincarnated for lifetime after lifetime and have kept the same memory to continue the same plan?

A: Only a select few.

Q: (Barry) Is this channeling going to go beyond the primitive method of one letter at a time, or is it going to go into the method of writing or typing or direct channeling consciously or unconsciously?

A: Can now, but there is less danger of corruption through this method.

Q: (Barry) What is the purpose of this contact?

A: To help you to learn, thus gain knowledge, thus gain protection, thus progress.

Q: (Barry) What do the Cassiopaeans gain from this contact?

A: By helping you, we are moving toward fulfilling of our destiny of union with you and all else, thus completing the Grand Cycle.

Q: (Barry) Is this the only probability open to you or is this the best probability open to you?

A: Both.

Q: (Barry) Are you a great distance from us in light years?

A: Distance is a 3rd density idea.

Q: (Barry) Light years is 3rd density?

A: Yes.

Q: (Barry) What do you mean by traveling on the wave?

A: Traveling on thoughts.

Q: (Frank) Our thoughts or your thoughts?

A: Not correct concept.

Q: (L) What is the correct concept?

A: All is just lessons. Thoughts unify all reality in existence and are all shared.

Q: (Susy) You travel on a wave of energy created by all thought forms?

A: Thought forms are all that exists!

Q: (Barry) Have those that are STS acknowledged that those that are STO are going to win in this race or conflict?

A: No, absolutely not! In fact, the STS cannot conceive of "losing" but instinctively feel pressure building upon them, that is the reason for the impending turmoil.

Q: (Barry) What happens to them when they lose, does this mean that they are degaussed, or does that mean that they have to go back and do the whole evolutionary process all over again on the other polarity?

A: Latter.

Q: (Barry) So, there is a nexus point coming up?

A: Close. When we said "close" we meant concept was "close" to reality. Not close in terms of time or distance.

Q: (Barry) At that point do they experience the pain that they have caused?

A: No. That is what happens on 5th level only.

At the time we asked about the "Essence Beings," the Cassiopaeans had given their "riddle" about "We are *where* we are." They had also said "We are you in the future." We were very curious about this idea, so we tried for some clarification:

01-14-95

Q: (L) You have told us in the past that you are us in the future and that you are moving this way to merge with us.

A: Yes.

Q: (L) As we measure time, how far in the future are you us?

A: Indeterminate as you measure time.

Q: (L) Does this mean that at the point in time when the wave arrives on the Earth in this upcoming event that you have given us the information to plot the ETA, is that the time at which you will merge with us and become us in the future?

A: No, that is not the correct concept.

Q: (L) You have said that when the wave arrives that you will merge with us. Is this the same thing that you are talking about when you say that you are us in the future?

A: No.

Q: (L) So, we are talking about two separate events or subjects, or two separate points in space/time, is that correct?

A: No. You are again slipping into trying to apply 3rd density logic to higher levels of density reality. We are trying to help everyone to advance.

Q: (L) So, we are not talking about the same event...

A: What is "future," anyway?

Q: (L) The future is simultaneous events, just different locales in space/time, just a different focus of consciousness, is that correct?

A: Yes, so if that is true, why try to apply linear thinking here, you see, we are merging with you right now!

Q: (L) I see. (T) So, what you are trying to say is that when the wave comes it is going to take us to fourth density, if we are ready, but we are not actually going to merge with you in 6th density at that point, but we may experience a "merge" at that point because all points of focus merge during transition from one density to another?

A: Partly correct, partly way off.

Q: (J) What part is right and what part is wrong? (T) The wave is going to take those of us who are, at that point ready, to move us into fourth density, is this part correct?

A: Open.

Q: (T) Which part of it is open?

A: You are a fourth density candidate.

Q: (T) So, we are fourth density candidates but that doesn't necessarily mean that we will make it into fourth density, true?

A: Partly.

Q: (T) As fourth density candidates, anyone that is, when the wave comes, if they have reached the correct frequency vibration, and have raised themselves up to the point that the wave will take them, they will, at that point, move into fourth density, true?

A: Close enough.

Q: (T) Now, when those who move into fourth density make the move, will they experience completeness or merge with all other densities of their being, at that point, even if it is for a short time?

A: For one immeasurably small instant, this is what is meant by "illumination"!

Q: (T) But, for that small instant, because there really is no time, maybe an instant or an aeon, depending on how any individual might measure it; we might experience oneness with ourselves?

A: It may seem to last "forever."

Q: (L) Is this what is known as the "rapture?"

A: Some have attempted to explain instinctive thought patterns this way.

At some point around this time, I watched a TV program about what is called the "Taos Hum," which is a humming sound heard in Taos, New Mexico, mostly, but has been heard elsewhere as well, and only by some people. Apparently it is quite annoying to a few of them. All sorts of theories were offered, but nothing really "fit" all the instances precisely.

01-21-95

Q: (L) I want to know what this humming sound is that people are hearing all over this country? I mean people have been reporting hearing this intense humming sound that literally drives them crazy. There was a TV special on about this the other night. What is this humming and where is it coming from?

A: Increased EM waves in preparation for oncoming wave.

Q: (L) What is the source of this sound, I mean, where specifically, location-wise, is it coming from?

A: Cosmic.

The following excerpt from the Cassiopaean Transcripts brings up a very interesting idea. The Cassiopaeans have suggested that there is a "soul evolution," that is facilitated by the works of higher densities. Apparently, souls "grow." After aeons as say, rocks, they evolve to become plants. After aeons as plants, they evolve to become lower animal life forms. After some period as this or that type of animal, they may "graduate" to a higher or more intelligent animal which has some sort of interaction with human beings, and after numerous incarnations of this type of interaction, they advance to become the "lower level souls" of humanity. At this point, they begin "incarnative" experiences through the human cycle in 3rd density until they come to the point of graduation to fourth density.

03-04-95

Q: (J) Is there any significance to the fact that one of our cats has been looking like she is really trying to tell us something?

A: One of your cats, no, make that 2 of your cats, are close to transition to 3rd level.

Q: (T) Sabrina's moving up in the world, she's going to get a promotion! (J) What's going to happen to her when she hits third? She's going to be a human?

A: Yes.

Q: (J) Wow. (T) When she moves from cat to human, her cat body will die?

A: Yes. We mean at next incarnation whenever that occurs.

Q: (T) Two of our cats? They are third density "candidates" like we are fourth density candidates?

A: Exactly.

Q: (L) Does that mean that when a person is a fourth density candidate that they have to leave their body to go to fourth density?

A: Yes, unless they are in the body when the wave arrives.

All of the above material illustrates some aspects of The Wave. We are beginning to understand that it is some sort of truly amazing Cosmic Event, which will be affecting our lives for some time to come. But, there is still more. Our curiosity about this event was just getting warmed up.

CHAPTER 3
DOROTHY AND THE FROG PRINCE MEET FLIGHT 19 IN OZ
OR,
"I DON'T THINK WE'RE IN KANSAS ANYMORE!"

The Myth of the Golden Age: a period when the Pole was "Oriented" differently; when the seasons were different; the year was different. It was a primordial paradise where time had no meaning.

The memory or imagination of a Golden Age seems to be a particularity of the cultures that cover the area from India to Northern Europe.

In the Americas, the most fully developed mythologies of history were those of the Mayas and Aztecs, *for whom there was no past era unclouded by the threat of cyclical destruction by fire of flood.* Nor does the philosophy of Buddhism have any place for nostalgia, although in practice it absorbed the idea of declining ages from its Indian surroundings.

But in the ancient Middle East there is an obvious relic of the Golden Age in Genesis, as the Garden of Eden where humanity walked with the gods before the Fall.

The Egyptians spoke of past epochs ruled by god-kings. Babylonian mythology, as reported by Berossos, had a scheme of three ages, each lasting while the vernal equinox precessed through four signs of the zodiac; the first of these, under the dominion of Anu, was a Golden Age, ended by the Flood. The Iranian Avesta texts tell of the thousand-year Golden Reign of Yima, the first man and the first king, under whose rule cold and heat, old age, death and sickness were unknown.

The most fully developed theory of this kind, and probably the oldest one, is the Hindu doctrine of the Four Yugas. A contemporary scholar describes the first of these ages:

> In the first Krita Yuga, after the creation of the Earth, Brahman created a thousand pairs of twins from his mouth, breast, thighs, and feet respectively. They lived without houses; all desires that they conceived were directly fulfilled; and the Earth produced of itself delicious food for them, since animals and plants were not yet in existence. Each pair of twins brought forth at the end of their life a pair exactly like them. As everybody did his duty and nothing else, there was no distinction between good and bad acts.
>
> After the Krita or Satya Yuga, things get progressively worse: each successive yuga sees the human race falling into increasing unhappiness and evil, until at the end of the Kali Yuga, the world is set on fire, deluged with water, and then reborn. (Godwin, 1996)

I have written elsewhere about the Cassiopaean story of the legendary "Fall" from Eden. Apparently, this was also the last time The Wave was here – 309,882 years ago.

As I mentioned previously, this is pretty much 12 precessional cycles, since there is some disagreement at present as to exactly how long a precessional cycle actually is. The figures vary, but if you divide 309,882 by 12 you have the figure 25823.5, which is right in the ballpark.

There have been many researchers in the past few years that have noted the seeming importance of the precession of the equinoxes in ancient myth and legend as well as archaeological implications. But, without the understanding of The Wave, none of the theories as to why this precessional cycle was so important have made much sense. For those who haven't read those articles on our website about the Lost Golden Age, I will present the material here before we go on with the discussion of The Wave.

10-05-94

Q: (L) What was the Fruit of the Tree of Knowledge of Good and Evil that was supposedly eaten by Eve and then offered to Adam?

A: Knowledge restriction. Encoding.

Q: (L) What did it mean when it said Eve ate of the Fruit of the Tree of Knowledge. What act did she perform to do that?

A: Consorted with wrong side.

Q: (L) What does consorted mean?

A: Eve is symbolic of Female energy.

Q: (L) The female energy did what when it consorted?

A: Lost some knowledge and power.

Q: (L) What was it that the fruit symbolized?

A: Limitation.

Q: (L) I want you to know that this does not make a whole lot of sense.

A: Yes it does. Think carefully. Laura you are missing the obvious.

Q: (L) In what sense would eating the fruit be limiting?

A: Believing that one source contains all knowledge is contradicting reality. If the concept was the eating of the Fruit of the Tree of Knowledge provides all knowledge, then one is being deceived, because no one particular source can provide all knowledge. Therefore, when one believes in the deception, one has now trapped oneself within parameters of limitation. And, forevermore, the human race, will be poisoned by the very same problem which is reflected in several different ways: one is always seeking the truth through one pathway or religion, instead of seeking it through a myriad of pathways; and also believing in simplistic answers to very complex issues and questions.

Q: (L) What was the flaming sword barring re-entry to Eden?

A: Symbolizes trap.

Q: (L) Where was Eden?

A: Earth.

Q: (L) The entire earth was Eden?

A: Yes.

Q: (L) Was the "fall" in Eden, or the loss of the Edenic state, also accompanied by a cataclysm?

A: Yes.

Q: (L) What was the nature of that cataclysm?

A: Comets.

Q: (L) The cluster you have mentioned before?

A: Yes.

Q: (L) And, how long ago did this occur?

A: 309882 years ago.

Q: (L) What was the true identity of the serpent in Eden?

A: Lizards.

Q: (L) Was the loss of the Edenic state also accompanied by a takeover of mankind by the Lizzies?

A: Yes.

Q: (L) Well, then how did mankind come to be here?

A: Combination of factors. Numerous souls desired physical existence then were altered by three forces including principally Lizards through Grays, Nephalim and Orion union.

Q: (L) About these three forces. You said numerous souls desired physical existence. When the numerous souls did this, how did physical existence come to be?

A: First was apelike.

Q: (L) And then what happened? Did these apelike beings just pop into the air? What did the souls do with these apelike beings?

A: Souls altered them by transfer into seeded bodies. Orion Union was first to put human souls in for incubation process thereby producing Neanderthal.

Q: (L) Are you saying that genetically altered ape embryos were put back into ape females for gestation?

A: No. Souls only.

Q: (L) They put the souls into the ape-like bodies?

A: Close. The soul's presence in the ape body causes its genetics and DNA to change.

Q: (L) So, human souls entered into living creatures on this planet to experience 3rd density reality and by entering in caused mutation?

A: Yes. Then were altered by Orion Union first. They resemble you.

Q: (L) Who resembles us?

A: The Orions. Orion Union. There are others in the Orion Community.

Q: (L) Are some of the Orions not good guys, as we would term it?

A: Yes.

Q: (L) Are some of them good guys?

A: Yes.

Q: (L) Where did the souls come from that entered into the bodies on the planet Earth? Were they in bodies on other planets before they came here?

A: Not this group.

Q: (L) Were they just floating around in the universe somewhere?

A: In union with the One. Have you heard the Super Ancient Legend of Lucifer, the Fallen Angel?

Q: (L) Who is Lucifer?

A: You. The human race.

Q: (L) Are you saying that the souls of individual humans are parts of a larger soul?

A: Yes. Close. The One. You are members of a fragmented soul unit. All who have fallen must learn "the hard way."

Q: (L) Are you saying that the act of wanting to experience physical reality is the act of falling? What is it about wanting to be physical that is a "fall"?

A: Pleasure for the self.

Q: (L) Did, at any time, the human race live for a long time in an Edenic state, where they were able to be in bodies and *still* had a spiritual connection?

A: Yes. But not long. No addiction takes long to close the circle.

Q: (L) So, mankind was addicted to pleasuring the self?

A: Became quickly.

Q: (L) How long from the time of the moving of souls into bodies until the "Fall" in Eden occurred?

A: Not measurable. Remember, Laura, there is no time when this event occurred. Time passage illusion did not exist at that point as well as many other falsehoods.

Q: (L) So you are saying that the Fall in Eden was also the beginning of time?

A: Yes.

***

11-26-94

Q: (L) What was the true event behind the story of the "Mark of Cain?"

A: Advent of jealousy.

Q: (L) What occurred to allow jealousy to enter into human interaction?

A: Lizard takeover.

Q: (L) Wasn't the Lizard takeover an event that occurred at the time of the fall of Eden?

A: Yes.

Q: (L) Was this story of Cain and Abel part of that takeover?

A: Symbolism of story.

Q: (L) This was symbolic of the Lizzie takeover, the advent of jealousy, and the attitude of brother against brother, is that correct?

A: Partly. The Mark of Cain means the "jealousy factor" of change facilitated by Lizard takeover of earth's vibrational frequency. Knot on spine is physical residue of DNA restriction deliberately added by Lizards. See?

Q: (L) You mean the area around the occipital ridge? The structures underneath?

A: Yes.

Q: (L) What was the configuration of the spine and skull prior to this addition?

A: Spine had no ridge there. Jealousy emanates from there. You can even feel it.

Q: (L) Do any of these emotions that we have talked about that were generated by DNA breakdown, were any of these related to what Carl Sagan discusses when he talks about the "Reptilian Brain"?

A: In a roundabout way.

Q: (L) Okay, at the time this "Mark of Cain" came about, were there other humans on the planet that did not have this configuration?

A: It was added to all simultaneously.

Q: (L) How did they physically go about performing this act? What was the mechanism of this event, the nuts and bolts of it?

A: DNA core is as yet undiscovered enzyme relating to carbon. Light waves were used to cancel the first ten factors of DNA by burning them off. At that point, a number of physical changes took place including knot at top of spine. Each of these is equally reflected in the ethereal.

Q: (L) Well, the question I do have is, how many people were there on the planet and did they have to take each one and do this individually? How did they effect this change on all of them?

A: Light wave alteration.

Q: (L) And light waves, actual light waves, affect DNA?

A: Yes.

Q: (T) What was the origin of the light waves?

A: Our center. Our realm. STO. The Reptilian beings used sophisticated technology to interrupt light frequency waves.

Q: (L) Well, what I am getting out of this that you are saying, from what you are not saying, is that it was almost like, well, was there a battle and you guys lost?

A: Yes. Now understand this: It is all part of natural Grand Cycle.

Q: (L) Is this natural Grand Cycle just part of the interaction between light and darkness, which just simply must be?

A: Yes. We are at "front line" of universe's natural system of balance. 6th density. That is where one rises to before reaching total union of "The One."

Q: (T) So we are but one battle in the universe in an overall, ongoing struggle?

A: Yes. Balance is natural. Remember, it's all just lessons in the Grand Cycle.

The year 2000 marks the 100th anniversary of the publication of *The Wonderful Wizard of Oz* by L. Frank Baum. Baum went on to write a total of 14 books about Oz before he died in 1919. Almost everyone is familiar with the story, which is archetypal in its nature, so I won't bore anybody with a recapitulation. If there *is* anyone who is not familiar with it, check it out of your local video store and make some popcorn. When you are done, come back and finish reading this page.

Dorothy's adventures follow the classical lines of the myths of the great heroes as outlined by Joseph Campbell in *The Hero with a Thousand Faces* (1949):

> The standard path of the mythological adventure of the hero is a magnification of the formula represented in the rites of passage: separation – initiation – return: which might be named the nuclear unit of the monomyth. A hero ventures forth from the world of common day into a region of supernatural wonder; fabulous forces are there encountered and a decisive victory is won; the hero comes back from this mysterious adventure with the power to bestow boons on his fellow man.
>
> The cosmogonic cycle is presented with astonishing consistency in the sacred writings of all the continents, and it gives to the adventure of the hero a new and interesting turn; for now it appears that the perilous journey was a labor not of attainment but of reattainment, not discovery but rediscovery. The godly powers sought and dangerously won are revealed to have been within the heart of the hero all the time. He is 'the king's son' who has come to

know who he is and therewith has entered into the exercise of his proper power – God's son. ...From this point of view the hero is symbolical of that divine creative and redemptive image which is hidden within us all, only waiting to be known and rendered into life."

In specific terms, Dorothy follows the pretty much "set" formula for the mythical hero(ine):

Receives help from a goddess-like being known as Glenda, the Good Witch of the North;

Meets several companion/helpers symbolizing knowledge, courage and love;

Undergoes tests of stamina, courage, and seeing through deception;

Defeats evil in the persona of the Wicked Witch of the West;

Returns to Kansas with wisdom she did not formerly possess.

There have been assorted political and pseudo-mystical interpretations of *The Wizard of Oz* popularized through the years. In one of them, the idea is presented that Dorothy, herself, is the *real* wizard because she is the only one who really accomplishes anything. In another, Toto is compared to Anubis, the dog-headed Egyptian guide of the dead. It is because of Toto's actions that Dorothy gets caught in the tornado to begin with. But, in the end, Toto exposes the Wizard as a "humbug." Then, when the Wizard is about to take Dorothy home, Toto once again discombobulates the action by chasing a cat, forcing Dorothy to miss her ride and use the Ruby Slippers instead.

In this line of thinking, my own ideas have tended in the direction of Sirius and Orion. I can't help but see Dorothy outlined in the constellation with the funny little Toto at her heels!

There is one interpretation that views Kansas as the "outer world" and Oz as the "inner world" and Dorothy's job is to integrate the two, symbolized by resolving the duality between the Wizard and the Witch. That one is a little lame, in my opinion.

The Hebrew words for the Tree of Life are *otz chaim*, and one interpreter gets into applying esoteric allegories based on Kaballah to the story. I wonder if he noticed that "Baum," too, means "tree?"

In Baum's 14 *Oz* books, Oz evolves as a utopian paradise where food and other needs simply grow on trees. It is a land without sickness, aging or death. More than that, it is ruled by a goddess: Princess Ozma.

But, Salmon Rushdie points out a certain "flaw" in the story that has not been satisfactorily dealt with, even by Baum himself in his later books, namely that in spite of the fact that Kansas is initially presented as a bleak and dreary place – monochromatic, in fact – Dorothy's only wish, once she has been transported to the lovely paradise of Oz, is to return!

One has to ask, 'Why?' Aside from missing Auntie Em and the rest, why in the world does she want to go back to that barren, treeless landscape? Why is the whole philosophy of the film expressed in the final words of Dorothy: "There's no place like home!"

In the following series of excerpts from the Cassiopaean transcripts, we encounter Dorothy, Oz and Kansas in a different context than we have heretofore considered. It is in this context that we begin to understand why "there's no place like home!" and furthermore, that The Wave may play a large role in activating our individual and collective Ruby Slippers!

03-11-95

Q: (L) At one point we were told that time was an illusion that came into being at the time of the "Fall" in Eden, and this was said in such a way that I inferred that there were other illusions put into place at that time...

A: Time is an illusion that works for you because of your altered DNA state.

Q: (L) Okay, what other illusions?

A: Monotheism, the belief in one separate, all-powerful entity. The need for physical aggrandizement. Linear focus. Unidimensionality.

Q: (T) Is separate the key word in regard to Monotheism?

A: Yes.

Q: (L) Can you tell us a little bit about how these illusions are enforced on us, or how they are perceived by us?

A: If someone opens a door, and behind it you see a pot of gold, do you worry whether there is a poisonous snake behind the door hidden from view, before you reach for the pot of gold?

Q: (L) What does the gold represent?

A: Temptation to limitation.

Q: (L) What does the door represent?

A: Opening for limitation.

Q: (L) Was limitation presented as a pot of gold when, in fact, it was not?

A: What is snake?

Q: (T) The Lizards? (L) Who was the snake?

A: Result of giving into temptation without caution: i.e., leaping before looking.

Q: (L) Does that mean we did not open the door?

A: Yes.

Q: (T) Who opened the door?

A: Lizards.

Q: (L) So what you are saying to us is that the story of the temptation in Eden was the story of Humankind being led into this reality as a result of being tempted. So, the eating of the fruit of the Tree of Knowledge of Good and Evil was...

A: Giving into temptation.

Q: (L) And this was a trick...

A: No! Tricks don't exist!

Q: (T) Okay, no trick, a trap?

A: No! Traps don't exist either. Free will could not be abridged if you had not obliged.

Q: (T) Now wait a minute. I am losing the whole train here. What were we before the "Fall?"

A: STO.

Q: (T) We are STS at this point because of what happened then?

A: Yes.

Q: (T) Okay, now, we were STO at that time. The Lizards opened the door, we are using this as an allegory, I guess; the Lizards opened the door and showed us a pot of gold hoping that we would reach in for the pot, or walk through the door, when they were waiting for us on the other side in order to take us over in some way. Am I on the right track?

A: Hoping is incorrect idea.

Q: (T) Okay, what was it they were trying to do by enticing us?

A: Trying is incorrect idea; continue to probe for learning opportunity.

Q: (T) We were 3rd density STO at this time. Was this after the battle that had transpired? In other words, were we on our own at that point, as opposed to before?

A: Was battle.

Q: (L) The battle was in us?

A: Through you.

Q: (T) The battle was through us as to whether we would walk through this doorway... (L) The battle was fought through us. *We were literally the battleground.* (T) Was the battle over whether or not we walked through that door?

A: Close.

Q: (T) Okay, we were STO at that point. You have said before that on this density we have the choice of being STS or STO.

A: Oh T, the battle is always there, it's "when" you choose that counts!

Q: (T) This must tie into why the Lizards and other aliens keep telling people that they have given their consent for abduction and so forth. We were STO and now we are STS.

A: Yes, "When" you went for the gold, you said "Hello" to the Lizards and all that that implies.

Q: (T) Okay, that was what I was trying to get at. You said that the Lizards, or the forces of STS opened the door.

A: No. Shouldn't say opened. We said "opened" only to introduce you to the concept, so that you would understand.

Q: (L) So, let's let go of the part that somebody "opened" the door. (T) The door was always there and always open. I was just trying to work with the analogy. So, the concept is that, as STO beings we had the choice of either going for the gold or not. By going for the gold, we became STS beings because going for the gold was STS.

A: Yes.

Q: (T) And, in doing so, we ended up aligning ourselves with the fourth density Lizard Beings...

A: Yes.

Q: (T) And by doing so we gave fourth density STS permission to do whatever they wish with us?

A: Close.

Q: (T) So, when they tell us that we gave them permission to abduct us, as many people have reported from their abduction experiences, it is this they are referring to?

A: Close.

Q: (J) Go back to what they said before: "Free will could not be abridged if you had not obliged." (T) We, as the human race, used our free will to switch from STO to STS. (L) So, at some level we have chosen the mess we are in and that is the Super Ancient Legend of the Fallen Angel, Lucifer. That is us. We fell by falling into that door, so to speak, going after the pot of gold, and when we fell through the door, the serpent bit us!

A: But this is a repeating syndrome.

Q: (L) Is it a repeating syndrome just for the human race or is it a repeating syndrome throughout all of creation?

A: It is the latter.

Q: (L) Is this a repeating syndrome throughout all of creation simply because it is the cyclic nature of things? Or is it as the Indians call it, Maya?

A: Either or.

Q: (T) We are working with the analogy. The gold was an illusion. The gold was not what we perceived it to be. It was a temptation that was given to us...

A: No temptation, it was always there. Remember Dorothy and the Ruby Slippers? Think of the Ruby Slippers. What did Glenda tell Dorothy???

Q: (J) You can always go home. (L) You have always had the power to go home...

A: Yes.

Q: (L) So, we always have the power to return to being STO? Even in 3rd density?

A: Yes.

Q: (T) Now, you keep referring to the movie, The Wizard of Oz. You have been saying...

A: 6th density inspired.

Q: (T) You have good filmmakers up there in 6th density. Okay, you keep referring to the movie, and that we have an ability within us that is something like the Ruby Slippers that can take us back to STO any time we wish.

A: Yes.

Q: (T) So, all this stuff we have been talking about, the realm border, the wave, raising the frequencies...

A: Realm wave is the "tornado."

Q: (L) In the analogy of Dorothy and the whole thing, the place where she started out was Kansas. Was going to the Land of Oz the STO state?

A: STS.

Q: (L) So Oz was STS. And Kansas, not necessarily the physical surroundings, but the state of mind of Dorothy prior to the Oz experience, was the STO state.

A: Yes.

Q: (L) So, we don't need necessarily to look at Kansas or the fact that it was filmed in black and white, it is just the state of mind. The going to Oz.

A: And Elvira Gulch.

Q: (J) The lady that turned into the witch. It was because of her that Dorothy ended up in Oz. She let her dog tease Elvira's cat, Elvira took the dog, which escaped, and Dorothy was trying to cover for the dog.

A: The witch is the Lizards.

Q: (T) Yeah, okay. (L) The moral of the story is: don't let your dog chase cats belonging to Lizards! (T) Tornado. Dorothy fell from the STO to the STS state through the tornado. Is this true?

A: Yes. Analyze more carefully, suggest break to do so.

[Break and Discussion]:(T) They are equating the tornado as the shift from STO to STS.

(L) Maybe it also is a shift from STS to STO.

(J) Yes, a shift from one to the other would be dramatic.

(T) Was it a density shift also? The realm wave is supposed to be a density shift: a window between densities. Is there also a shifting between STO and STS? Is there a gateway that you go through? A door?

(F) Oh God! There are so many possibilities here.

(L) And if you switch into STO do you find yourself on a different Earth?

(T) They said this tornado is representative of Dorothy going from STO to STS state. She also went from her reality to a totally different reality.

(F) That's true.

(J) But switching from one to the other is going to be traumatic.

(T) They have been talking about a realm wave...

(F) I don't think it matters which way, I just think that in that particular story it was laid out that way.

(T) But what they have been telling us so far is that the realm wave is a window to move between densities.

(J) Right.

(T) But they just said to us that the tornado is an analogy of a realm wave. But the tornado was a passage from STO to STS, not from third to fourth density.

(J) Two different things.

(F) True, however, a realm border passage may represent any kind of sudden shift?

(T) That is what I am wondering. Can it also mean that not only would we shift from 3rd to 4th, but also would we shift from STS to STO and start out in an STO state there? And then have, again, whether or not we shift back to an STS state in fourth density? Do you always start out in an STO state?

(F) No, because if a realm border is coming now, and they have told us over and over again that we are STS, and what they have actually told us is that the *realm border is a shift from 3rd density to fourth density, and they never said it was a shift from STS to STO, they have said that it is our choice.*

(T) Yes, but they just referred to the tornado as this realm wave, and, in The Wizard the tornado was the symbol of shifting from STO to STS. I don't know. I'm just trying to get a handle on what they are trying to tell us here because it is something extremely important.

(J) They have been saying "Ruby Slippers, Ruby Slippers," not "tornado, tornado."

(T) Yeah, they said that just now, that the wave is the tornado.

(F) I think that is a different subject, there.

(T) But now it is the same symbology. The tornado took her from one point to another and the Slippers took her back to point A again. Two different concepts.

(F) There are all kinds of intricate little things here; somehow there must be a way to connect it. You know what it is? "Remember the slippers," they said, meaning that the pathway was always there for her to go home. Don't you remember Glenda telling her "Ooh, no dear, you can always go home. All you have to do is say, 'there's no place like home.'"

(J) Yeah, but you had to be wearing those slippers...

(S) Now, you know what? The tornado or the wave could act a lot like going to 5th density. As she was looking out the window all these things passed by... like a life review...

(T) Yes, her life passed by her.

(F) Yes, but they have told us that the realm border passage itself is going to result in all kinds of hairy stuff going on. It's just totally bizarre in every one of the concepts we have come across so far!

(J) It is a radical change in reality.

(T) Yes, but for Dorothy, in the movie, it was violent in the fact that it was a tornado, though it did not physically hurt her.

(J) Yes, and that is what we have been told, too.

(F) She was scared...

(T) Yes, but that was a mental thing... it was up here [pointing to head] where the hurt was. She didn't get hurt physically.

(F) That is also another thing to speculate about: throughout the entire movie, she was never hurt physically. Through all the threats, she was never actually hurt. For some reason, the witch couldn't just grab the slippers off of her...

(T) It was also 1939. If the movie had been made in 1995 they would have had machine guns, missiles, chainsaws, and there would be body counts all over the place. And she still could have gone home anytime she wanted. You know, Dorothy Meets the Terminator.

(L) Dorothy and the Chainsaw Massacre.

(S) Dorothy goes to Elm Street. [Laughter]

(T) It's a cross between a children's fairy story and a Stephen King nightmare.

(F) You know, the fundamentalists have attacked the Wizard of Oz.

(L) They have? Why?

(T) Because it is Satanic.

(F) Yeah, they say it's Hollywood's effort to pull people away from Christianity and fundamentalism and all that jazz.

(T) The Wizard of Oz is evil, to the fundamentalists.

(F) Yes, because you don't need the blood of Christ to get back to Kansas.

(L) I guess that's why Cinderella is politically incorrect.

(T) Because she didn't sleep with one foot on the floor like all the sitcoms back in the 60's.

(J) Excuse me?

(S) We went from Oz to sitcoms?

(J) I think you are mixing your metaphors.

(S) That was Sleeping Beauty.

(T) Yeah, that was Sleeping Beauty in the box.

(J) And one foot on the floor.

(L) No, Snow White was in the box.

(T) Snow White was in the box. Yeah, Disney took all the things that had Beauty sleeping in them...

(L) Did you ever stop and think about that symbology: Sleeping Beauty, being awakened by a kiss?

(F) Who turns into a frog?

(L) No!

(F) Oh, that's right, the frog turns into a prince.

(L) That's another analogy. Being awakened from the illusion into which one has been put by the evil witch...

(F) And Cinderella...

(L) And also, in all of these fairy tales it is because of some choice and lack of knowledge...

(J) Rumplestiltskin...

(S) The Ugly Duckling...

(T) Yeah, all of Grimm's fairy tales were really pretty grim. They have been cleaned up a whole lot.

(L) Yeah, in the original Cinderella, the stepsister cut off part of her foot to get it to fit the slipper and the Prince found her out because of the dripping blood. (J and S) Ooooh! Yuck!

(T) Must have been the glass slipper, cut my foot!

(L) And there you have the imagery of a shoe that creates a transition... Ruby Slippers and Glass Slippers... hmmmm...

(T) Are we getting anywhere? We got the idea that when we fell from STO to STS we gave the Lizzies the right to do what they are doing. So, when they make the statement that we said they could, we did.

[End of Break]

A: Okay.

Q: (L) We are having a bit of a puzzlement here because we are wondering if the tornado which represents the realm wave is something that moves one from an STO state to an STS state while still remaining in 3rd density?

A: Okay, that is one way. Okay...

Q: (T) The realm border is not only a way of transferring from one density to another, but it is also a way of transiting from STS and STO and back?

A: Can be.

Q: (T) So, those who get hit by this wave can transit from third to fourth density and come out as an STO being even if they are presently STS?

A: In some of the passages that has occurred.

Q: (L) Okay, so people can either go from STO to STS in third or fourth density... any of these choices are open at this passing of the realm wave?

A: Any of the above according to the orientation of the wave.

Q: (L) And what is the orientation of the wave that is coming? Is it strictly to move us from 3rd density to fourth density? Is this a function of this wave?

A: Yes. We have told you this.

Q: (L) And they have told us that this is a wave from third to fourth density. Some of the waves, apparently, can move from STO to STS... (T) As this wave passes by, does the orientation of the wave depend upon the individual?

A: Compare to sea waves. Waves are a part of the fiber of all nature.

Q: (T) Is it going to depend on where on the wave you are, the crest or the trough, as to which way you transition on it?

A: No.

Q: (T) In other words, a wave that is going to transition from third to fourth density will do so no matter where you are on the wave when it passes?

A: Yes.

Q: (T) A wave that is aligned to transit people from STS to STO or vice versa will do that also?

A: Or you could "go under" instead.

Q: (T) Under the wave? Then you wouldn't move at all. (L) You could be pulled under; you could drown and become part of the primordial soup! (T) Is that Minestrone?

A: Chicken Noodle. [Laughter.]

Q: (L) If you go under you get sucked into the ocean and start cycling all over again?

A: It is not that simple.

Q: (J) I didn't think that was simple at all. (T) Let's not even start on that one. I'm still trying to work out this movement from STO to STS. You keep referring to the movie about Dorothy. In the movie she was told she could go home any time she wanted just by saying I want to go home, or whatever. That is a lot easier than going through all the conniptions and contankerations waiting out this wave that comes only once every so often. Is there a way for us to go back to STO that is easier and simpler than hanging out for 300,000 years waiting for this wave to come around?

A: Sure!

Q: (T) Okay, now we are getting somewhere. Where are we going? So, there is another way of doing this.

A: Now wait a minute, are you ready to just go to fourth density right now?

Q: (T) Yeah, I am ready. Right now. Let's rock and roll! J, feed the cats when you get home! (L) Well, don't you think that the idea of just taking off and leaving and abdicating your responsibilities and agreements is an STS thing? (T) Yeah, but I'd be fourth density STS! (S) You and the Lizzies! (T) Now, now! Calm down! I wasn't saying... I'm not ready to go now because I'm wanted here! Anyway, what you are saying is that the realm wave is not the only way to make the transition, is this correct?

A: One idea presented.

Q: (T) And we are here to set up some sort of a frequency to pull as many beings through the wave, when it passes, and that is the whole purpose of why we are here... Is that it?

A: That implies interference with free will.

Q: (L) So, we are here to set up a frequency so that others may join with us... IF they choose... Just out of curiosity, whom do the munchkins represent?

A: 2nd density beings.

Q: (L) Whom do the Witch's soldiers represent?

A: The Nephalim.[27]

Q: (L) If the Nephilim are coming 36 million strong as enforcers for the Lizzies, does the Confederation have a like amount for defense?

A: We don't operate that way.

Q: (L) Are we just going to have to fight them off ourselves?

---

[27] I have left the word exactly as the Cassiopaeans' spelled it. The reader will find that they have their own "spelling" of certain words, and in such cases, I leave theirs as is, but spell the word according to convention when I use it.

A: Remember Dorothy... Glenda is like us.

Q: (L) And who is the Wizard? Is that the Beast or the U.S. Government?

A: Close. Illuminati.

Q: And the monkeys are the Grays?

A: Close.

Q: (L) If water destroyed the witch, and the witch represents the Lizzies, can we destroy the Lizzies?

A: Knowledge.

Q: (L) But there are only a few on the planet who have the knowledge. Am I correct?

A: What do you mean? Against all when the time comes.

Q: (L) So the 36 million Nephilim will be against all on the planet when the time comes? Their arrival will wake everybody up?

A: Of course.

Q: (L) And those who have the knowledge and can dispense it to others... well... they may suddenly be heard...

A: Yes.

Now, let's look at the following extract from a more recent session that clarifies much of the information given above:

08-28-99

Q: (L) I have this book, this Marcia Schafer thing: Confessions of an Intergalactic Anthropologist, and its a bunch of channeled stuff; one thing she says: "The snake is associated with the sign of wisdom and higher learning, and is often regarded quite highly in mystical circles." I would like to have a comment on the idea of the snake as a "sign of wisdom and higher learning" as many people believe and teach nowadays, though the serpent is presented as the evil Tempter in older texts.

A: Snake is/was reported in context of the viewpoint of the observer. Maybe the observer was just "blown away" by the experience. If you were living in the desert, or jungle, about 7,000 years ago, as you measure time, would you not be impressed if these Reptoid "dudes" came down from the heavens in silvery objects and demonstrated techno-wonders from thousands of years in the future, and taught you calculus, geometry and astrophysics to boot?!?

Q: (L) Is that, in fact, what happened?

A: Yup.

Q: (L) Well, this is one of the problems I am dealing with in trying to write this history of mankind. As I understand it, or as I am trying to figure it out from the literature, prior to the 'Fall in Eden,' mankind lived in a fourth density state. Is that correct?

A: Semi/sort of. fourth density in another realm, such as time/space continuum, etc.

Q: (L) Okay, so this realm changed, as a part of the cycle; various choices were made: the human race went through the door after the 'gold,' so to speak, and became aligned with the Lizzies after the 'female energy' consorted with the wrong side, so to speak. This is what you have said. This resulted in a number of effects: the breaking up of the DNA, the burning off of the first ten factors of DNA, the separation of the hemispheres of the brain...

A: Only reason for this: you play in the dirt, you're gonna get dirty.

Q: (L) What was the motivating factor for playing in the dirt? What essential thing occurred? You said once that it was 'desire-based imbalance.' What was it a desire for?

A: Increased physicality.

Q: (L) What was the objective sought for in this desire for increased physicality?

A: Sensate.

Q: (L) How was sensate first experienced so that these beings had an idea that they could get more if they increased their physicality?

A: Not experienced, demonstrated.

Q: (L) Demonstrated how, by whom? The Lizzies?

A: Basically.

Q: (L) Demonstrated in what way? Did they say: 'here, try this!' Or did they demonstrate by showing or doing?

A: Closer to the latter.

Q: (L) They were doing things, experimenting, playing, and saying: 'look, we are doing this, it's so great, come here and try it?'

A: Not really. More like: "we have this, you could have this too."

Q: (L) What seemed to be so desirable about this increased physicality when they said 'you can have this?'

A: Use your imagination!

Q: (L) Was there any understanding, or realization of any kind that increased physicality could be like Osiris lured into his own coffin by Set? That they would then slam the lid shut and nail him in?

A: Obviously, such understanding was lacking.

Q: (L) Sounds like a pretty naive bunch! Does the lack of this understanding reflect a lack of knowledge?

A: Of course. But more, it is desire getting in the way of...

Q: (L) Okay. The 'Fall' occurred. It seems like, and some of the archaeological studies indicate, that for many thousands of years, there was a peaceful existence and a nice agrarian society where the goddess or female creative forces were worshipped. At least, this is what a lot of present-day books are proposing...

A: No. These events took place 309000 years ago, as you measure it. This is when the first prototype of what you call "modern man" was created. The controllers had the bodies ready; they just needed the right soul matrix to agree to "jump in."

Q: (L) So, prior to this time, this prior Edenic state...

A: Was more like fourth density.

Q: (L) But that implies that there was some level of physicality. Was there physicality in the sense of bodies that look like present-day humans?

A: Not quite. And we cannot answer because it is too complex for you to understand.

Q: (L) Does this mean that the experiences... that the bodies we possibly would move into or transform into, as fourth density beings, assuming that one does, would also be too complex for us to understand? You are saying that this 'sort of fourth density' pre-Fall state, in terms of the physical bodies, is too complex to understand. If going back to fourth density is anything like coming from fourth density, does that mean that what we would go back to is something that is too complex to understand? This variability of physicality that you have described?

A: Yes.

Q: (L) So, was there any kind of worship of God, or religious activity in this pre-Fall state, this Edenic, fourth density state?

A: No need when one has a clue.

Q: (L) What I am trying to get at here, what I am trying to understand, is the transition from the goddess worship to the god worship; the change from the understanding of cyclical time as expressed in the feminine cycles, and expressed as the goddess; to the concept of linear time, expressed as the masculine principle. It seems to me that these were stages of inversion of concepts which gradually led to the ideas that the Lizzies are imposing on us, and seem to have been working in this direction for millennia – the dominator experience which expresses as: believe in something outside yourself that will save you, otherwise you are damned because the world is going to end, and you are going to get judged. It's like all of these ideas have been planted throughout time in preparation for them to come in and act like the "Saviour" and take over. This is the concept I am trying to deal with here. I am trying to understand what was worshipped. Okay, we had these guys; they fell from Eden. Once they jumped into the physical bodies, as you put it, what was their level of conceptualization regarding the universe? Did they still retain some understanding at that point?

A: Kind of like the understanding one has after severe head trauma, vis-a-vis your normal understanding in your current state.

Q: (L) So, they were traumatized; they may have had bits and pieces of ideas and memories, but they may also have lost a great deal altogether. There may have even been a sort of "coma" state of mankind for many millennia. But, after they woke up, with the bits and pieces floating around in their heads, they may have begun to attempt to piece it all together. So, they started putting it all back together. What was the first thing they put together regarding the cosmos around them?

A: Sex.

Q: (L) What did they decide about sex? I mean, sex was there. They were having sex. Is that it? Or, did they understand the cosmos as sex?

A: More like the former. After all, that is what got you guys in this mess in the first place! Just imagine the sales job if you can: "Look how much fun this is! Want to try it? Oops, sorry, we forgot to tell you, you cannot go back!"

Q: (L) I really fail to understand – and I know it is a big issue that has been hinted at and alluded to in many so-called mystery teachings, and outright claims have been made regarding sex in all religions and mythologies – but I fail to understand the mechanics of how this can be the engineering of a 'fall.' What, precisely, are the mechanics of it? What energy is generated? How is it generated? What is the concept of the misuse of this energy, or the use of the energy?

A: It is simply the introduction of the concept of self-gratification of a physical sort.

Q: (L) On many occasions you have said that the ideal thing is to have perfect balance of physicality and ethereality. This has been said on a number of occasions. Now, I don't understand how it can be that gratification of a physical body can be the mechanics by which one is entrapped? Is it not gratifying to look at something beautiful? Is it wrong, sinful, or a form of a fall, to look at beauty, to hear something beautiful such as music, or to touch something that is sensually delightful such as a piece of silk or the skin of a loved one? These various things that the human being derives pleasure from very often elevate them to a spiritual state.

A: Possession is the key. In STS, you possess. If you move through the beautiful flowers, the silk, the skin of another, but do not seek to possess...

Q: (L) It seems to me that it is possible to experience all of these things, including sex, without the need or desire to possess, but only to give. In which case, I still don't understand how it can be a mechanism for a 'fall.'

A: If it is desired, then the mechanism is not to give. Do you eat a piece of chocolate cake because it is good to give to the stomach? In STS, which is your realm do not forget, one gives because of the pleasant sensation which results.

Q: (L) Could it not be said that, if everything that exists is part of God, including the flesh, that if one gives to the flesh, without being attached to the giving, that it could be considered a giving to the 'All?'

A: Explain the process.

Q: (L) For example: there are some people who like to suffer, because they believe that the flesh is sinful. That is a big thing that the Lizzies have instituted. For centuries they have wanted people to suffer, and they have made this big deal about sex and anything that might be considered pleasant or desirable should be denied, and that a person should suffer, and revel in their suffering. And, actually, making a person...

A: If one seeks to suffer, they do so in expectation of future reward. They desire to possess something in the end.

Q: (L) What I am saying is: if a person can simply BE, in the doing and being of who and what they are, in simplicity; to become involved in doing everything as a meditation, or as a consecration, whether they are walking down the street and being at one with the air, the sunshine, the birds and trees and other people; in this state of oneness, doesn't that constitute a giving to the universe as giving oneself up as a channel for the universe to experience all these things?

A: Not if one is "feeling this oneness."

Q: (L) We are what we are. Nature is nature. Progression is progression. And if people would just relax and be who and what they are in honesty, and do what is according to their nature without violating the Free Will of others, that this is a more pure form of being than doing things out of any feeling of expectation, or desire; to just BE, not want... just BE?

A: Yes, but STS does not do that. You are all STS. If you were not, you would not be where you are.

Q: (A) There are those who are happy in the STS mode; and there are those who are trying to get out of the STS mode...

A: STO candidates.

Q: (A) These STO candidates are not able to just simply BE, even theoretically, because then, STS would eat them.

A: No.

Q: (L) Why not?

A: STS does not eat according to protocol. STS "eats" whatever it wants to, *if it is able*.

Q: (L) That's what we said. If you are an STO candidate in an STS world, you are basically defenseless, and they eat you.

A: No.

Q: (L) Why? What makes STO unavailable or 'inedible?'

A: Frequency resonance not in sync.

Q: (A) But then, that would mean that all these people who are saying that we need just to love everything and everybody, are right. They just be, and love, don't do anything, just give everything to the Lizzies... they are right!

A: No, because motivation is STS.

Q: (L) How is the motivation to love everything and everybody, and to just give, STS?

A: Feels good.

Q: (L) So, they want to do it because it feels good?

A: Want is an STS concept.

Q: (L) So, you seem to be suggesting that the real trick is to just become non-attached to anything and anybody, do nothing, and just dissolve into nothing? No thought, no want, no do, no be, no anything!

A: If you are STS, that does not fit, but, if you did exactly that, you would reincarnate in an STO realm, where such energy does fit.

Q: (L) But, if you have become nothing, how do you reincarnate? And, when you say 'reincarnate,' that implies being in a body!

A: You do not become nothingness.

Q: (L) But, being incarnated means being in a body?

A: No.

Q: (L) You mean moving into a realm that does not necessarily mean being in a body?

A: Close. But fourth density STO is partially physical. Does not consume nor possess. You are confused because you seem to think you must be STO to be an STO candidate. You are STS, and you simply cannot be otherwise, until you either reincarnate or transform at realm border crossing.

Now, moving along to the next subject of discussion that brought out more aspects of The Wave, we find a strange correspondence to the general theme of *mythical archetypes*. In *The Hero with a Thousand Faces,* Joseph Campbell describes one of the preliminary stages in "The Hero's Journey" as "The Call to Adventure."

> Long, long ago, when wishing still could lead to something, there lived a king whose daughters all were beautiful, but the youngest was so beautiful that the sun itself, who had seen so many things, simply marveled every time it shone on her face.
>
> Now close to the castle of this king was a great dark forest, and in the forest under an old lime tree a spring, and when the day was very hot, the king's child would go out into the wood and sit on the edge of the cool spring. And to pass the time she would take a golden ball, toss it up and catch it; and this was her favorite plaything.
>
> Now it so happened one day that the golden ball of the princess did not fall into the little hand lifted into the air, but passed it, bounced on the ground, and rolled directly into the water.
>
> The princess followed it with her eyes, but the ball disappeared; and the spring was deep, so deep that the bottom could not be seen. Thereupon she began to cry, and her crying became louder and louder, and she was unable to find consolation. And while she was lamenting in this way, she heard someone call to her, 'What is the matter, Princess? You are crying so hard, a stone would be forced to pity you.'
>
> She looked around to see where the voice had come from, and there she beheld a frog holding its fat, ugly head out of the water. 'Oh, it's you, old Water Plopper,' she said. 'I'm crying over my golden ball, which has fallen into the spring.'
>
> 'Be calm; don't cry,' answered the frog. 'I can surely be of assistance. But what will you give me if I fetch your toy for you?'
>
> 'Whatever you would like to have, dear frog,' she said; 'my clothes, my pearls and jewels, even the golden crown that I wear.'

The frog replied, 'Your clothes, your pearls and jewels, and your golden crown, I do not want; but if you will care for me and let me be your companion and playmate, let me sit beside you at your little

table, eat from your little golden plate, drink from your little cup, sleep in your little bed: if you will promise me that, I will go straight down and fetch your golden ball.'

'All right,' she said. 'I promise you anything you want, if you will only bring me back the ball.' But she thought, 'How that simple frog chatters! There he sits in the water with his own kind, and could never be the companion of a human being.'

As soon as the frog had obtained her promise, he ducked his head and sank, and after a little while came swimming up again; he had the ball in his mouth, and tossed it on the grass. The princess was elated when she saw her pretty toy. She picked it up and scampered away. 'Wait, wait,' called the frog, 'take me along; I can't run like you.' But what good did it do, though he croaked after her as loudly as he could? She paid not the slightest heed, but hurried home, and soon had completely forgotten the poor frog – who must have hopped back again into his spring.

This is an example of one of the ways in which the adventure can begin. A blunder – apparently the merest chance – reveals an unsuspected world, and the individual is drawn into a relationship with forces that are not rightly understood. The blunder may amount to the opening of a destiny.

Thus it happens, in this fairy tale, that the disappearance of the ball is the first sign of something coming for the princess, the frog is the second, and the unconsidered promise is the third. ...

The frog, the little dragon, is the nursery counterpart of the underworld serpent whose head supports the Earth and who represents the life-progenitive, demiurgic powers of the abyss. (Campbell, 1949) [28]

How does this relate to our subject?

The herald or announcer of the adventure, therefore, is often dark, loathly, or terrifying, judged evil by the world; yet if one could follow, the way would be opened through the walls of day into the dark where the jewels glow. Or the herald is a beast representative of the repressed instinctual fecundity within ourselves, or again a veiled mysterious figure – the unknown.

...Whether dream or myth, in these adventures there is an atmosphere of irresistible fascination about the figure that appears suddenly as guide, marking a new period, a new stage, in the biography. That which has to be faced, and is somehow profoundly familiar to the unconscious – though unknown, surprising, and even frightening to the conscious personality – makes itself known; and what formerly was meaningful may become strangely emptied of value: like the world of the king's child, with the sudden disappearance into the well of the golden ball.

Thereafter, even though the hero returns for a while to his familiar occupations, they may be found unfruitful. A series of signs of increasing force then will become visible, until ... the summons can no longer be denied. (Campbell, 1949)

It seems that we have just such a symbolic herald of the Coming of The Wave...

03-18-95

Q: (L) J and I have a question. Hilliard mentioned to us the other day that the frogs are disappearing from the planet.

A: Ozone layer.

---

[28] This illustration came from Grimm, Jacob and Wilhelm, *Grimm's Fairy Tales*, Helen Stratton, illustrator (London: Blackie & Son, 1903).

Q: (L) They are getting fried because of the loss of the Ozone layer?

A: Fried? [Laughter]

Q: (L) Frog legs, anyone?(J) Where are they going? (T) The ozone layer is depleting and they are the first of the things we are really noticing as an effect of this?

A: Yes.

Q: (J) Where are they going? (T) They are not going anywhere. They are dying. (F) They are not reproducing.

A: Yes.

Q: (B) They have very sensitive skin. (T) Soon it is going to be affecting us all.

A: All part of the wave effects interconnecting realities.

Q: (L) Well, if it is having this effect on frogs, what is it going to do to us when it gets stronger?

A: Wait and see.

Q: (L) Now, come on! This doesn't sound like a real pleasant thing. Don't you think you ought to give us just a little more on this? A clue here?

A: No. [Laughter]

Q: (T) Are they saying that the loss of the ozone layer is a direct result of the approaching wave? (J) They sure did! (T) The loss is not due to the fluorocarbons?

A: Misinterpretation, review statement thoroughly.

Q: (J) Is removal of the ozone layer part of the frequency "fixing?"

A: Close.

Q: (L) It's keyed on interconnecting realities.

A: Yes.

Q: (L) Are you saying that the wave is causing the interconnecting of realities? (J) And the ozone layer is in the wave?

A: No "of." And causing actions, which affect third density in myriad ways, closing the circle.

Q: (L) It is a symptom?

A: Yes.

Q: (T) But, is the relationship of the ozone being depleted and the approaching wave, perhaps that the wave isn't directly causing the depletion, it's the Lizzies causing human beings to act in ways that deplete the ozone layer in order to create suffering, in order to feed on this negative energy because of the approaching wave? In other words, the wave is causing the destined actions to take place that are necessary for the closing of the Grand Cycle?

A: Close.

Q: (L) And the dying off of the frogs is part of this? Poor little frogs... I like frogs...

A: So are "Earth Changes."

Q: (J) Is the depletion of the ozone layer a part of the equation required for the wave...

A: In third density reality, it is important.

This last remark is most interesting. The Cassiopaeans seem to be saying that the depletion of the Ozone layer is *necessary* for some reason... that the "new state of being" will be, in some way, affected or even effected by this phenomenon. Remember the passage at the beginning of this section where it was said:

A: DNA core is as yet undiscovered enzyme relating to carbon. Light waves were used to cancel the first ten factors of DNA by burning them off. At that point, a number of physical changes took place including knot at top of spine. Each of these is equally reflected in the ethereal. Light wave alteration.

Q: (L) And light waves, actual light waves, affect DNA?

A: Yes.

Changes in the ozone layer certainly reflect a difference in the amount of radiation from the sun that passes through the atmosphere. But, to continue:

03-18-95

Q: (J) So, it is part of the natural progression of movement from third to fourth?

A: Let's try using the word "reflection," and see if that "rings a bell." Third into fourth and vice versa. Oncoming wave is a transformation from third density to fourth density; so events happening due to the approach of the wave are causing changes across densities and realities! *In third density, you will notice changes that will have third density explanations, but they are a manifestation of the approach; you see them as third density because that is your current point of reference!* Remember that all reflects in and across all density levels but also there is a merging upon arrival of the wave, it is realm border crossing!!!!!!

So, we possibly need to look at all of the things happening on our planet, the things we perceive as very negative and disturbing, as the "contract phase" of The Wave. Many of us have noticed that, very often, when negative forces put some action into effect that is intended to be very harmful, when it interacts with persons of certain frequency, or who are internally configured in the STO pattern, the negative action turns out to be of great benefit – though the sender of the energy certainly did not *intend* it that way! "Turning lemons into lemonade" comes to mind.

If we look at the situation in this way, and understand that the greatest weakness of the STS pathway is their illusory "wishful thinking" tendency, then perhaps we can understand that things are happening, as they ought to be. Some sort of critical mass of negativity has to be reached before sufficient Contact Potential Difference[29] can be developed to draw in the light!

And, when you consider that aspect, and the way negative energy can actually work for good when it interacts with individuals of internal STO configuration, even if the initial perception is that something terrible is happening (what doesn't destroy us makes us strong), then you have to also consider the opposite occurs when folks send love and light toward negative beings of internal STS configuration... it doesn't change them to "good guys," it merely is food for them to become stronger and meaner! As Michael Topper has written in his article, "Channeling, UFOs and the Positive/Negative Realms Beyond This World":

> The alternate convention to which a certain "New Age" mentality turns whenever the possible existence of actual, deliberate negativity approaches, is that of the vaguely "Christian" tactic: love-bomb the blighters until they see the error of their ways, by the point-scoring Good Example set. Such cheek turning is in practice, of course, a very selective espousal, since it rarely seems to constitute the day-by-day business attitude of the very same proponent. Even in the case, however, that this recommendation weren't outright hypocrisy it would remain fatally fatuous, for they (the STS) "do not want your love".

---

[29] When two metals contact, a voltage difference is established across the interface—the so-called contact potential difference—with a magnitude from a couple of tenths to a few volts.

If the metals are "well-defined" metals, the contact potential difference can be calculated from the work functions, i.e., the energy it takes to remove a loosely bound electron from the metal. It should be stressed, however, that this charge exchange between metals only gives rise to what we normally understand as static electricity when the two metals are separated extremely quickly, such as when a metal powder is blown against a metal surface.

The Negativity of the Higher Densities is ipso facto awake; it has chosen the rejection of other-love as a whole-being orientation, and therefore has no subconscious residuum of receptivity that might secretly "respond" to the good intentions of a positively-directed beam (even if such a beam proceeded from a sincere resolve which consistently applied its Samaritan counsel in all other avenues of life).

Indeed there is deeper implication than this. In the face of such uncommon or truly spiritual negativity the presumption of such conventional counsel might well result in consequences worse than simple "lack of success." It has to be understood that spiritual principles and religious precepts, have to be evaluated against an enlarged context, and modified according to the forms of information "unique" to the higher domains to which consciousness must adapt.

The principle to "love one and all alike," to bestow "blessings upon all beings" and so forth is not subject to abandonment at this stage; we are not to somehow understand that a reversion to hatred and warfare are suddenly "all right" due to the extenuating circumstance that "pure spiritual evil does indeed exist". Universal Love is and always remains the principle in some proper form; but the specific beaming of the "love-vibe" in the direction of the [STS beings] not only possesses the defect of wholly wasted effort; the philosophy informing it tends to contribute to a tremendous misreading of the elements actually involved…

What then are we to "do" with the counsel of the general Teaching thus far delivered to this density, such as that of "love thine enemy"? How are we to interpret such a precept or indeed understand the principle of Love altogether, when its application seems so susceptible to a sticky, spider web ambush from planes of reality actually eager with invitation for so innocent an approach?…

If then the first spiritual precept to "Love God with all your heart" is a familiar reference of 3rd density consciousness, how is it that such a framework possesses it? And how does such a reference coexist with corollary commandments and encomiums, i.e. precisely those such as "love thine enemies," "love your neighbor as yourself," etc?

When we learn the whole-being expression of Love as that spontaneous Love of the One Infinite Creator, the very essence of Love tends to emanate impersonally as a global value, spreading without effort or special address to all quarters where it's received or not according to the specific will of every form. In this way its Presence doesn't become confused with the conditional presence of the myriad beings "positive" or "negative." Nor does its Presence become confounded with the mechanics of "give and take," which are all relative identifications of the mind common to the complex of 3rd-stage psychology that accepts the teaching of Love according to its lights—in which love is understood as a conceptual miasma of "owes" and "oughts."

Now, before we close this section, there are a few more excerpts that I would like to present that tells us a little bit more about just how strange this Wave Event is going to be. Remember the ending of *Close Encounters of the Third Kind,* where the pilots that had been lost in the Bermuda Triangle emerged from the spacecraft as though being "returned" by the aliens? Well, that was a funny image that might have some small basis in fact. Witness the following from the same session just quoted:

03-18-95

Q: (L) What causes some planes, people and ships to disappear in the Bermuda Triangle? Where do they go and what happens to them? I know you have previously said that it was EM wave disturbances from a submerged Atlantean pyramid that kicks into action every now and then... but where do those folks and things go when they disappear?

A: Of course some are just crashes and sinkings, but when accompanied by unusual phenomena, it is because of irregular anomalies.

Q: (L) Where do they go?

A: To parallel reality.

Q: (L) Is this parallel reality like being on a parallel earth?

A: No.

Q: (L) What do you mean by a parallel reality?

A: Varies according to circumstances.

Q: (L) What happened to the infamous Flight 19?

A: They are still trying to get their bearings.

Q: (J) Oh! My God! Oh, how horrible! They are still out there trying to get back. (T) They are in a parallel reality... (L) Where time doesn't exist... (T) They are in a reality that holds them in frozen space/time over the ocean, am I getting this right?

A: In their thought reference, like being "lost souls."

Q: (L) Bummer! Does this mean that they are "stuck" in time? (J) You got it!

A: Bingo!

Q: (L) Is there any possibility that they could fly out of this place that they are stuck in and back into our reality?

A: Absolutely. Remember, the wave is approaching, and as it gets "nearer", more and more unusual events take place, witness crop circles, for example.

Q: (L) Is there anything anyone can do to release persons stuck in these parallel realities and bring them back into the reality of origin?

A: Yes, but the technology is a closely guarded secret.

Q: (L) Do you know the secret?

A: Yes, but you do too!

Q: (L) I do too?

A: Philadelphia Experiment.

Q: (L) Since you mentioned the Philadelphia Experiment, could you tell us in specific detail, how this was done? What kind of machine was used, and how can we build one? [General uproar and laughter]

A: Do you intend to sit here for a day or two?

Q: (J) In other words, it would take a day or two to give us the information? (T) Yeah, we got the time. Get some paper and a pencil. Let's start with a diagram... [Laughter]

A: In short, build an EM generator. [...]

A: Now, some more information about Flight 19. Do you remember a few years ago that a team of researchers claimed to have found the planes, and then retracted?

Q: (L) Yes, I remember. [All agree.]

A: Did you find this to be curious?

Q: (S) Yes, because the planes that they found were never reported missing. (T) Yes. (L) Is that why it was so curious? (J) Why did they publish a retraction later? (S) Where did the planes come from that they found?

A: Yes, if only you knew the details, and how three of the team have required massive psychiatric aid.

Q: (L) Well, tell us the details!

A: Patience, we are, but must do so slowly... What they found were five planes matching the description, and "arranged" in a perfect geometric pattern on the bottom of the ocean, but the serial numbers did not match. Now, first mystery: There were no other instances of five Avengers disappearing at once. Second: Two of the planes had strange glowing panels with unknown "hieroglyphics" where there should have been numbers. Third: When they tried to raise one of the planes, it vanished, then reappeared, then vanished again then reappeared while attached to the guide wire, then finally slipped off and fell to the bottom. Fourth: In one of the planes, on the bottom, *live human apparitions in WWII uniforms were temporarily seen* by three exploratory divers and videotaped by a guide camera. Lastly: Three of the planes have since disappeared. All of this is, naturally, being kept secret!

Q: (S) I wonder where the planes came from. (L) That is the obvious question!

A: Parallel reality, you see, when something crosses into another reality, it accesses something called, for lack of a better term, the "thought plane", and as long as that reality is misunderstood, the window remains open, thus all perceptions of possibility may manifest concretely, though only temporarily, as thought plane material is constantly fluid.

Q: (L) Does this mean that this was a "Flight 19" of a parallel reality that went through a window into our reality?

A: Close.

Q: (L) Was this part of, or connected to, the loss of our "Flight 19?" Did we exchange realities here?

A: *It is the thought patterns that affect the reality*, when that window is opened, all thought can become physical reality, though only temporarily.

Q: (L) Does this mean that the divers' and searchers' thoughts about this became reality?

A: And all others.

Q: (T) All others involved in the search?

A: All others on the planet.

Q: (T) Even those that did not believe that the searchers were going to find them?

A: Yes. Researchers found what they expected to find, but when others heard the news, other things started to happen according to which thought patterns dominated.

Q: (L) So, in other words, if somebody believed that it was Flight 19, it appeared, and if somebody did not believe it was Flight 19, it disappeared?

A: Yes.

Q: (J) Oh jeez! (T) Well, I didn't believe it to begin with... (L) So, I guess we won! (F) We sent some poor guys into the psychiatric ward. (L) No, I think the searchers went looking for this and because there was a window there... (T) The planes showed up exactly as they expected to see them, in a formation... But the planes would *not* have come down as described there, and they appeared *in a formation* on the bottom. That should have told the searchers something right there. When I heard that they had found those planes in a formation, that close together, that bothered me. (F) Even if something sinks to the bottom, it won't arrive there in the position it started at the top. (T) And what they *did* find after they started checking the records, was that there are about 200 of those planes crashed along the coast. And, there was another guy who said that he found one of those planes, only it wasn't one of Flight 19. I have a question... what happened to the PBY plane that went out searching for Flight 19?

A: Still trying to find the Avengers.

Q: (T) Is it in the same parallel reality with Flight 19?

A: Yes.

Q: (T) Will it ever find them?

A: ?

Q: (L) In the perception of the crew of Flight 19, how much time has passed?

A: None.

Q: (J) So, they have no idea. (S) I wonder if they will come back to our time or go back to their time?

A: Your perception.

I think we are beginning to get some idea of how truly strange, wonderful and "plastic" our reality is. Perhaps this Wave is a "facilitator" for that plasticity, and that different groups and belief systems will manifest certain realities at the point in time that it "hits," thereby "collapsing" the wave form of our macrocosmic reality? Just a thought, and maybe it has more to do with "belief" systems than what one thinks. But, that is a subject that we will deal with at another time. Suffice it to say: yes, we DO create our own reality; but not in the sense that is generally thought or taught by the standard "New Age" philosophies.

The next two small comments that relate to The Wave came from the same session:

03-18-95

Q: (L) We would like to know what the Christian Cross represents at a deeper level? Does it have anything to do with "Realm Border Crossing."

A: Part of the Lizzie disinformation campaign, sorry! Cross is "cross" in English only.

A therapist friend of mine was present and she had been experiencing very strange things while working on me subsequent to an auto accident I was in. So she asked:

Q: (S) Why, when holding acupuncture points on Laura, do I get the sweats so bad I feel like I am absolutely roasting? I can't even be in this room where they do the channeling without breaking into a heavy sweat!

A: Because you are undergoing changes relating to the approach of the wave.

I should add that I experience this rather frequently myself during meditation, communicating with the Cassiopaeans, and sometimes when I simply begin to think about some of the concepts the Cassiopaeans have talked about. It feels rather like having a raging fever, and I *have* taken my temperature during these episodes with nothing showing on the thermometer. Yet, anyone who touches me also begins to perspire. This last fact persuaded me that I wasn't just having a hormonal "hot-flash."

The next excerpts I am adding were not in the original version of this chapter of *The Wave*. However, since they add information to the data bank, I think it is important to include them here now.

06-22-96

Q: (V) A few weeks ago several of us began to suffer from internal heat, insomnia, and other things. What was this?

A: Image. Deep conjunction of fibrous linkage in DNA structure.

Q: (V) Well, I want to know if it is in my mind that I get so hot, or does my body temperature actually elevate?

A: Only on 4th.

Q: (V) I don't understand.

A: Bleed through, get used to those!

Q: (L) Does this mean we are actually experiencing a bleed through of fourth density?

A: Image.

Q: (V) Are the little flashes of light I see also a manifestation of this?

A: Maybe so, but try to concentrate on the ethereal significance, rather than the physical.

Q: (L) When you say "deep conjunction of fibrous linkage," does this mean that we are conjoining with a linkage to a fourth density body that is growing, developing?

A: Slowly, but surely. Now, get ready for a message: We have told you before that the upcoming "changes" relate to the spiritual and awareness factors rather than the much publicized physical. Symbolism is always a necessary tool in teaching. But, the trick is to read the hidden lessons represented by the symbology, not to get hung up on the literal meanings of the symbols!

Q: (L) You say that the symbology has to do with hidden meanings. The symbology that you used was "image" and "deep fibrous linkage" of DNA. Now, is that a physical, symbolic image?

A: Yes.

Q: (L) What is your definition of "image?" We have many.

A: Learning is fun, Laura, as you have repeatedly found!

Q: (L) Well, I am so hot now that I really want to know! And, how come I am always the one who gets assigned the job of figuring everything out?

A: Because you have asked for the "power" to figure out the most important issues in all of reality. And, we have been assisting you in your empowerment.

Q: (L) Image. DNA linkage. (V) "Power" was in quotes.

A: Leave that alone for now, you will know soon enough.

Q: (V) Is this fourth density body something that already exists so that we could communicate with it?

A: Habeas Corpus?

Q: (V) Well, they just said... (L) Well, what they must mean is that you ARE it – you are transforming little by little and all of the unpleasant little side-effects are just part of it.

A: Yes.

***

12-28-96

Q: (L) Okay, while we are waiting for Ark's response, I have a question. I am BURNING up! What is the reason for this unbearable heat I am suffering?

A: Heat means fourth density bleed through.

Q: I am about to die of heat, and I know it is cold in here. When you say fourth density bleed through, what do you mean?

A: Oozing of faint reflections of new reality.

***

01-14-95

Q: (L) You have said that when the wave arrives that you will merge with us. Is this the same thing that you are talking about when you say that you are us in the future?

A: No.

Q: (L) So, we are talking about two separate events or subjects, or two separate points in space/time, is that correct?

A: No. You are again slipping into trying to apply third density logic to higher levels of density reality.

Q: (L) So, we are not talking about the same event...

A: What is "future," anyway?

Q: (L) The future is simultaneous events, just different locales in space/time, just a different focus of consciousness, is that correct?

A: Yea, so if that is true, why try to apply linear thinking here, you see, we are merging with you right now!

This "merging" that produces such extraordinary heat was still a bit of a question in the back of my mind for quite awhile until one day I found a reference to the phenomenon in the work of the Sufi Shaykh Ibn al-'Arabi (*The Sufi Path of Knowledge*, by William Chittick):

> A State is that which enters in upon the heart without self-exertion or the attempt to attract it. ... [T]he State is the changing of the attributes of the servant...

> State signifies certain dimensions of spiritual realization, it denotes the special powers that accrue to the servant [...] the State is in conjunction with terms denoting extraordinary feats or miracles ... producing effects in the outside world through concentration...

> The possessors of the States engender things through resolve and throw secondary causes far from themselves.

Considering what the Cassiopaeans had said about "merging," the following points in al-'Arabi's discussion of the "states" take on considerable significance:

> When an angel brings a ruling or knowledge to the servant, the human spirit encounters the imaginal form and through the giving and receiving, which are two lights, the constitution becomes excited and inflamed.

In the two lights, the native heat of the constitution is strengthened and the magnitude of the light is increased. The color of the servant's face changes because of this and it is the most intense State that might be. The bodily moistures ascend in vapors and this is caused by the compression undergone by the natures when the two spirits meet.

When the possessor of the state regains his composure, the heat abates and the constitution increases in coldness and the cold overcomes the heat and the possessor of the state begins to shiver. All of this is the descent of a spiritual attribute upon the heart.

"The word *hal*, or State, is derived from the root from which we get '*self-transmutation*' or to change from one situation to another."

I came across the description of the "states" quite by accident, but very synchronistically, after a certain event that I described in still another session as follows:

08-24-96

Q: (L) Okay, I have two quick questions. Last Sunday morning, after the session the previous night, I had a very strange experience similar to what Al-'Arabi describes as being in a 'State.' It was like being taken up into a condition of near madness [like being *inside* a vision], Ark was there, [in the vision] and then, when it became unbearable, [the energy began] pulling back, and I was left so cold I was shaking and rocking. I was shivering like I would never get warm and I could *feel* my soul rocking in my body. I would like to know exactly what this was?

A: Balancing of half-self.

Q: (L) What is a half-self?

A: Your starter version, relating to birth karmic imprint.

Q: (L) What in the world does *that* mean?

A: What you were assigned with at the onset of this incarnation.

Q: (L) Do you mean that this was 'starting' something? Like a starter in a car?

A: No, what you started with. This must be periodically re-balanced at apex of significant junctures.

Q: (L) The next thing that happened was that a few days later, I went into another state. [I was almost unconscious, but I kept working on mastering this state, and trying to open my eyes, and all I could see was living light. Everything I looked at was light. After this continued for awhile, I heard my computer ping, and the visionary state was broken. After I recovered, I checked my email.

Ark had just sent an excited message.] He had just seen me come in the window. What happened?

A: Learning is fun!

Looking at this from a slightly different angle, there is the incident that is included in a later chapter but also ought to be included here. The session was one in which a guest had brought an "aura camera" and a couple of strange photos resulted. In the following excerpt, "AM" is the guest with the camera.

01-20-96

Q: (AM) Take a deep breath and hold... [aura photo of L is taken]

We waited a few minutes for the photo to develop and when it did, it was totally unlike the "aura photos" taken of all the other participants at this session. Since the camera is essentially taking a photo and superimposing another image on it, it should at least show the physical outlines of the subject. It didn't.

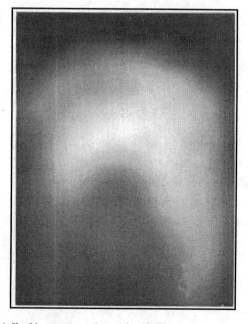

Q: (L) [looking at aura photo of self] This is very strange, guys. How come I am not in this picture and F shows up in his? Why have I physically disappeared?

A: Learning builds spiritual growth, and awareness "solidifies" knowledge.

Q: (L) Okay, guys, smile for the camera! [Aura photo of board is taken with L's and F's fingers on planchette.] (L) Okay, but that does not explain why I disappeared.

A: Because the energy field enclosure was unifying you with the conduit, as is usual during channeling sessions between third and 6th density level communications.

Q: [Photo of board develops, and geometric figure appears to sounds of amazement from group] (L) What is this geometric figure?

A: Was a visual representation of the conduit, indeed!!! The reason for such clear luminescence is that thought centers were clear and open in you at the moment of the photograph. In other words, there was an imbalance of energy coming from sixth density transmission point. So, what you are viewing is 100 per cent pure light energy of uncorrupted knowledge transmitted through you. This has never been seen in third density ever before. You do not completely realize the ramifications of this yet, but you will. We have made history here tonight folks!!!!!

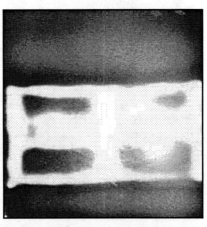

In the photo on the this page, you can see my hand at the right and Frank's hand at the left with our fingers resting lightly on the little plastic planchette.

As I have written at the beginning of this volume, I began writing *The Wave Series* and other articles as a way of collecting excerpts together in general subjects. As I published them, more and more readers asked questions. In my attempts to *give* answers to them, as the Cassiopaeans had given to me, I found that a truly extraordinary thing began to happen.

The Cassiopaean Experiment had resulted in transmissions from myself "in the future," and I realized that by doing the suggested research, by digging for the answers based on the clues given me, I was *becoming* myself in the future – a cosmic self. I began to see what I had been trying to convey to myself from this superconscious state. The years of experimental work had created a new circuit wherein it was possible to simply ask a question in my mind about the subject at hand, and the answer would flow through my fingers onto the keyboard. I was often as amazed at what came out as anyone.

I asked the C's (myself in the future) about it, and here was what they said:

09-23-00

Q: (L) I have to say that the writing of this [Wave] series has been one of the most educational projects I have ever undertaken. Because, in the writing, I have had to comb through the transcripts and have had to explain it to other people and before I can do that, I have to explain it to myself. It has become a profound mind expansion thing...

A: Good.

Q: (L) It's almost as much fun to be learning the things I am having to assemble as if I were reading it. And I'm the one writing it. It's really quite amazing.

A: In part you are [writing].

I finally understood what the Cassiopaeans meant when they said:

06-09-96

Q: (L) Al-'Arabi describes unified thought forms as being the "Names of God." His explication seems to be so identical to things you tell us that I wonder...

A: We are all the names of God. Remember, this is a conduit. This means that both termination/origination points are of equal value, importance.

Q: (L) What do you mean? Does this mean that we are a part of this?

A: Yes. Don't deify us. And, be sure all others with which you communicate understand this too!

Q: (L) What quality in us, what thing, enabled us to make contact. Because, obviously a lot of people try and get garbage.

A: You asked.

Q: (L) A lot of people ask!

A: No they don't, they command.

Q: (L) Well, a lot of people do ask or beg or plead, but they get all discombobulated with the answers.

A: No, they command. Think about it. You did not beg or plead... that is commanding.

So it seems that, by this time, I was truly merging with "Myself in the Future" and I had direct access to this awareness through my writing, showing me how to assemble and edit the material together after I had made such a mess of it in the original question and answer phase. It was as though the long period of working with the board had developed a circuit that bypassed my conscious mind and worked directly through my hands.

The idea of the "Names of God" as explicated by Ibn Al-'Arabi also assists us in understanding what the Cassiopaeans meant when they said "We are *where* we are."[30]

Certainly, this process of working with the material creatively has come under a great deal of attack from those who would like to "deify" the Cassiopaeans and declare that the material "belongs to humanity" and that I have no right to research it, examine it, correct it, or otherwise refine it. I find that attitude to be quite disturbing.

In any event, this discussion indicates to us, perhaps, something of a foretaste of the effect of The Wave upon mankind – or at least portions of mankind. Perhaps these experiences give us an inkling of what fourth density might be like?

I can verify that such a condition *is* followed by a coldness that cannot be alleviated for some time. I have alternately burned and shivered many times as a consequence of certain meditative exercises, not to mention participation in the channeling process. And of course, there is the very interesting "visionary" states that may include bi-location.

The important thing to note is that it denotes a "change from one situation to another," and is described as "self transmutation." I suspect that The Wave is an energy source that will interact with every individual according to his or her frequency resonance. To some, it may indeed be the End of the World. But for others...

> "Meantime, the world in which we exist has other aims. But it will pass away, burned up in the fire of its hot passions: and from its ashes will spring a new and younger world, full of fresh hope, with the light of morning in its eyes."
>
> -Bertrand Russell

---

[30] The subject of the Names of God and "Thought Centers" is covered in some detail in my book, *The Secret History of the World*.

CHAPTER 4
THE CASSIOPAEANS GET TAKEN OUT OF THE CLOSET AND GO FOR A "TEST DRIVE"

Now that we have talked about The Wave in more or less "philosophical" terms, things will get a bit more intense from here on out. Events began to move rapidly in our lives, which reflected in the channeling experiment in pretty remarkable ways in which I will describe as briefly as possible.

Two members of our group, T and J were also members of MUFON, the Mutual UFO Network, and, even though MUFON is pretty much a "nuts and bolts" operation, T and J thought that some of the material coming through the Cassiopaean experiment was worthy of being presented at a MUFON meeting. Thus, they arranged for me to speak to the group where they were members.[31]

The original arrangements that were made with the MUFON people were for an hour of time, which I figured would allow a little development of the background, some of the material, and a few questions and answers. At some point, however, for reasons that were never really made clear to me, the time was cut from an hour to *15 minutes* – 20 at the most. I was in a panic wondering what I could say in 15 minutes that would make any sense at all! I was given to understand, however, that MUFON rather frowned on channeling, per se, and was more interested in the "UFO Cadillac" – you know, like a used car on a lot where you can go up to it and kick the tires. The closest thing I had to that was my own sighting, so I tried to figure how I could work that into the talk and STILL get some words in about the Cassiopaeans.

On the day of the meeting, (the official "coming out of the closet"), after the various business matters of the MUFON group were dealt with, and a couple of recent UFO sightings were recounted, the "Main Attraction" that we had been "bumped" for

---

[31] This is the event Tom French wrote about in his article that I quoted at the beginning of this book.

began. It was a talk about the *Urantia Book*.[32] The gentleman giving the "talk" passed around 15 or more photocopied pages to each individual in the audience of about 200 or so people; everyone got their own copy of *Urantia* excerpts. While I was waiting for them to finish passing them out, which took some considerable time, I read all 15 pages. I just thought I would give myself a head start so when the man began to talk, I would have some idea of what he was talking about. Bad idea!

As it turned out, the photocopied excerpts *were* the talk. And for the next hour and a half the man at the podium read from the 15 pages, slowly and painfully, stopping periodically to fix the audience with a gimlet eye to make sure that no one was deviating from the program of following him word by word and line by line. Each time he reached the end of a page, he paused and there was the loud rustling noise of over 200 people dutifully turning their pages in unison! This mass turning of pages actually generated a draft in the room!

But, eventually it was over; the torture came to an end and we got up to stretch our legs. After the break, T and J gave a nice, short, entertaining introduction and I talked only briefly – almost exactly the allotted 15 or 20 minutes – about the experiences that had introduced me to the subject of UFOs, including the sighting of the Black Boomerangs over my house, and so forth. Then I tried to get in a quick synopsis of the kind of material the Cassiopaeans were delivering, and how closely it coincided with much of the research being done in several fields, including UFO investigations; the only difference being that the Cassiopaeans gave background and "inside" info, which tended to make the picture clearer and more comprehensible.

Another MUFON group leader was present at that meeting, and he thought that our material was of sufficient interest to deserve a longer presentation for his own group in a nearby city. So he arranged this with us and it was announced at the end of the meeting that we would do a "demonstration" at *his* upcoming meeting the following month.

We were a bit concerned about doing this in a group setting, because, up to that time, we had very carefully controlled the

---

[32] According to The Urantia Book Fellowship, *The Urantia Book* is an anthology of 196 'papers' dictated between 1928 and 1935 by superhuman personalities… The humans into whose hands the papers were delivered are now deceased. The means by which the papers were materialized was unique and is unknown to any living person.

environment of the project, and there were so many variables involved. So, just prior to this "demonstration" and talk, we asked the Cassiopaeans about it and their response was a bit curious:

> 03-04-95
>
> Q: (L) Will we be able to do a demonstration at the MUFON meeting on Saturday?
>
> A: Yes, because it is predestined.

That was certainly curious, but, as things turned out, more curious than we ever could have supposed.

At the second MUFON meeting and demonstration, one of the more skeptical participants brought some sort of gadget up to the table where we were seated – I think it was a gauss meter or an EM (electromagnetic) wave detector – and set it up beside us. He had adjusted it to the ambient EM of the room with a full occupancy and many people standing in the rear and around the sides.

J gave a short introduction where she explained that she was not a "believer," and even had many doubts about the UFO/alien reality. This was due, she explained, to her lack of having ever had any kind of personal "experience." However, because her husband, T, was very deeply involved in studying such phenomena (having had a number of his own experiences through the years), in solidarity with him, she had become involved in MUFON and was, at the time, the acting Secretary of their chapter. She and T also edited, published, and often wrote articles for the area MUFON newsletter.

But, even so, as J confessed, she was *not* a believer, though she found the ideas presented by the Cassiopaeans to be fascinating.

After J's few remarks, she turned the podium over to me and I went through a brief recapitulation of the long process we went through over several years before the Cassiopaean contact was established. I then began to try and explain what the material was imparting to us in the form of "explanations of the order of the Universe," so to speak. Do keep in mind that this was *very* early in the experiment – we had only been receiving the information about 9 months at the time of these talks, so the fact was that even *we* didn't know the full scope of what was going to come in the next few years! I will insert here the transcript of my talk from this point:

> 03-11-95
>
> In terms of accessing who and what you are in totality, one of the things the Cassiopaeans have said is that, originally, the human being was created with more active DNA than they currently

operate with. An event occurred that has been remembered by all the cultures around the world as "The Fall," or the loss of the Edenic state, and this was primarily due to, depending on the cultural myth being examined, a snake, serpent or dragon, whatever. But, it is generally a scaly, reptilian type of being. What the Cassiopaeans have said indicates that there may be more to this than mere mythical conceptualization!

The Cassiopaeans have talked about the fact that the DNA can be reconstructed or reconnected because it is still there, it is just broken up or "de-activated." The important elements of this process include oxygenation, spinning or centrifuging, as well as certain activities such as meditation, and gaining knowledge.

One of the things that I have experienced recently has been pretty interesting in terms of this idea. After my accident I began to have a lot of body work done, including different types of "energy work," and at certain points, this began to affect me in strange ways.

After one of these sessions of energy work, for about seven days or longer, it felt like a water main was attached to my solar plexus, and was pumping in memories and emotions from every lifetime I had ever lived; I mean hundreds and thousands of images!

Everybody says "oh, I want to remember my past lives!" but think again! I got to experience every emotion of entire lifetimes with this review! It was so bad that I thought I was going to drown in it and die! I would sit there – and everybody will tell you that I was a horror to be around during that time – rocking in my rocking chair saying "Oh God! Oh God! I can't stand this! Please let it stop! Let it stop!" Images of people, places, events, castles, knights charging into battle on a horse waving a battle axe; deserts, jungles, death, destruction, diseases, plague, pestilence; all these kinds of things just flashing by, like Dorothy in the tornado; all this stuff flying by!

Meanwhile, the emotion of every one of these images was hitting me full force!

I might have seen the image for only one second, but the entire emotion that went with it would hit me and I was gasping and choking from one incident to the next, one after another after another.

So, at one of the sessions we asked just what it was that was going on with me... I was about to collapse under the strain – and the Cassiopaeans said: "Oh, you just activated more of your DNA!" Well, fine! Stop it! Take it back! No more! I can't handle it!

But, apparently, that is what having this knowledge can do! It is a condition of being able to access universes of information! The

Cassiopaeans have said: "It's *fun* to access..." and I asked them: "Fun for *whom?!*"

After a few more remarks, I turned the podium over to T, but I do want to mention the fact that my description of the events of my state of "remembering" as being similar to Dorothy in the tornado is something that I had forgotten entirely until I transcribed the tapes.

T introduced himself and made several remarks about having attended some of the early experimental sessions *prior* to the Cassiopaean connection and that he and J had more or less given up on the project because nothing seemed to be happening during that time.

It was only later, after the Cassiopaeans came through, that I was able to persuade them to have a look at the material. I valued their insight and input because I knew that both of them were as skeptical as I was and I certainly felt in need of a "second opinion," not wanting to fall into the "true believer" trap that is so common nowadays. After his intro, T made the following remarks:

> You can tell by now that there is a *lot* of information here. I've been rambling on for the past 20 minutes here and there is more. It doesn't matter where you start with it, you end up having to explain the whole thing.
>
> At this point, there is nine months worth of material and in another three months we'll have to explain a whole year's worth because the Cassiopaeans continue to give new information – they add to it as we learn to ask the questions correctly.
>
> As my wife has said in her remarks, neither of us were great believers in channeled information and it took several months for Laura to get us up to her place to see what was going on. We had been up a couple of times before during the early experiment stage and had gotten nowhere. We live down in St. Pete and that's a long drive to make to come up for the evening, to sit around and have nothing come through.
>
> When we finally came up Laura told us, "You're not going to believe what this is doing." We came up in November – they've been receiving the Cassiopaean information since July – and I watched for a little while seeing this little thing move around on the board. I mean, it bounced around all over the place; I never saw anything move that fast! A mouse trying to get away from my six cats is about the only thing I've seen move as fast as that little thing moved on the board!

So, I sat down. They let me sit in for awhile just so I could put my hand on it. I wanted to touch it; I wanted to see what it was. And I sat there for about 25 minutes or so and my arm was tired!

I work with computers and I'm used to "mousing" (speaking of mice), on the computer, pointing and clicking and all that, all day long. My arm had moved around this board so fast for 25 minutes or so, that I actually had shooting pains in my shoulder from it because I wasn't used to that position for that length of time. I couldn't believe how quickly it moved. I couldn't believe the amount of energy I could feel running through that little section of the room.

Since then, I have noticed that it is not just one person; it's not just those people sitting at the board, it's a combination of all the people in the room; all the people in Laura's house, for that matter. The more people, the more energy, and the faster it goes. Twice the planchette flew off the board.

On New Year's Eve, there were a whole bunch of people there and there was so much energy – just loose energy, not directed energy because people were just milling around, it was a New Year's Eve party – and we couldn't keep the planchette on the board. It was flying back and forth so fast it flew right off the table and sailed through the air.

We picked it up, put it back down, and it was across the board again. It took about 20 minutes for the energy to settle down so we could get any kind of information. Then, the information may or may not have been that good because all the people in the room weren't concentrating. It was loose energy in the air.

A couple of weeks ago a couple people came up who are involved in UFO research and they understand energy flows and how to direct it. And, we had the same experience. The Cassiopaeans told us then that it would take time to settle the energy and direct it because there was just so much of it. That little planchette was sailing again... flew off the table a couple of times and through the air. It went off the table with so much force it just kept going... took us a good 25 minutes to get it settled down again. They told us: "you've fractured the channel." I guess that the "wire" that runs between here and sixth density got increased in size the other night. We rewired it for sure!

Q: (from audience) Is there any dizziness effect?

A: (L) No, no dizziness. It feels more like warm drafts of air against the skin, and then an elevated feeling.

Q: (Aud.) Is it like euphoria?

A: (L) No, it's more of an intense, mental sharpness... a focus to the nth degree... it actually energizes us. We've done sessions that lasted up to 8 hours, tape after tape, and no one was tired!

Q: (Aud.) Have you had other movements in the room during the sessions, like objects falling off shelves or something?

A: (L) No, we haven't. We've actually asked that question and the Cassiopaeans have said that if there were such movement, it would be strictly energy from the lower chakras. We aren't dealing with that level here. If you get poltergeist type phenomena, you can pretty well figure the level it comes from. But, of course, during the early phases of the experiment, we *did* get some of that type of activity. On one occasion, a candelabra flew off a shelf, and several other things went crashing around. It was real unpleasant energy. That is the sort of thing we worked to get beyond.

A: (T) We aren't even sure who or what the Cassiopaeans are. They say they are sixth density and that they are "us" in the future – but that may not be the case. We aren't going to sit here and believe it just because they say it. We are presenting it that way because that is *their* description. We don't make the mistake of believing everything that is coming through, we are just presenting the information. We are still wondering what it is we have tapped into. Is it some kind of universal, Cosmic Retrieval System? Is it some kind of universal computer? Is it the Jungian archetypal consciousness? What have we tapped into? We do not know.

What impresses me about it, even beyond the confirmations we have gotten on different material, is the consistency of the information. There are reams of material already, and it is consistent right across the board. It doesn't vary in level. It's not like a contact that is extremely intelligent one week and super dumb the next. It's consistent, uniform and has continuity.

A: (L) One exception, I would point out: if there are people in the room who would be upset by any particular information, the Cassiopaeans will more or less "hold back," and will suggest that we ask it later. It is rather like a courtesy to the person in the room who is not prepared to hear the answer. When it's just us, information comes through that might not come with new people present.

A: (T) They will also not permit children to be present as they have indicated that such activities can be detrimental because the energy levels that are generated are too much for the "young circuits," so to speak.

Q: (Aud.) Your sources are obviously champions of Free Will. Obviously, that is the way the universe is supposed to be. Have they given you any reconciliation as to why our density seems to have been interfered with in terms of Free Will? I know there are a lot of sources that say that we agreed to be abducted before we came here, but that's just a little bit too thin, in my opinion.

A: (T) What we have been told on that is that this universe was created as a Free Will Universe. It was created specifically to allow all souls to do whatever they wish to do; they have complete choice about what they wish to do. The Grays, the Lizards, whoever they are who abduct and put implants in people, have the right to do that because it's their Free Will to come here and do that to us. And, they have the right to tell us whatever they want to tell us to rationalize their behavior.

Our right is to *not* believe what abducting entities tell us. We have Free Will to believe or not believe them. If they tell us in one lifetime that they have the right to do this to us, and we choose to believe them then, and then, in this lifetime, they try the same tricks and we choose *not* to believe them, in each case, we are exercising our Free Will and so are they.

This is a Free Will Universe. We can change our mind. They are trying to convince us that we have no choice in that; whether we believe them or not is *our* choice.

There's more to it than that, of course, because interfering with us physically, obviously, goes on all the time. They have more power than us physically, or pseudo-physically. It is the same relationship between us and animals in our reality. Cows and sheep and chickens have Free Will, too, but we have more power than they have and we have convinced them (and ourselves), in our need to consume food, that "this is good for you, this is your purpose in life." Just as we consume animals, so do those in higher densities than ours consume us.

But for the most part it occurs in terms of energy and not specifically in terms of flesh, though that too occurs. We are part of a food chain, so to speak, and we are *not* at the top by any means!

Anyway, back to 300,000 years ago: there was a battle between the forces of Service to Others and the forces of Service to Self at all different levels of density. Unfortunately, the forces of Service to Self won the battle.

The Lizards are fourth density Service to Self beings. They can come to third density, but they can only sustain themselves here for a short time because their technology does not allow them to extend it any further.

At fourth density, they are still using technology, they are still learning para-physical things. They have subjugated us; they have implanted us; they have taken our DNA and manipulated it so we won't remember who we are and what we can really do...

Anyway, the Lizards have created the Grays. They are fourth density also. They have no souls; they are robots. The Grays were created in such a way that the Lizards could send them into third density as projections, so to speak. They can project some portion of their own energy into the Grays so that when they are in third density, they are not only a robot being controlled by them, they are actually "in it," so to speak, looking through it's eyes. It may even be that several Grays constitute the energy of a single Lizard portion. The whole purpose of the subjugation of humans by the Lizards is that they use us as food. The old John Lear/Bill Cooper stuff about the vats of body parts may have some truth to it. But, mainly, they take energy. They want our energy. That's what they feed on in fourth density because they are basically energy beings in fourth density. They feed on energy. There is positive energy, there is negative energy. Service to Self beings in fourth density feed on negative energy produced by third density beings, and even 1st and 2nd density beings on occasion.

They like us because we have emotions. Emotions generate energy. That's why you're always reading that the Grays seem to be "so interested in our emotions! Our love, our hate, our this and that." They control us and create situations that produce negative energy. The more negative energy they can create, the more food they have. That's what the whole purpose is.

There is another purpose also: they covet the idea of being third density physical/material beings. They haven't done it in a long time, and the physicality of it is just so attractive to them because they are so hung up in Service to Self, that part of the plan is to create a new race for themselves.

What you have to understand is that we have so much information here, and we are still trying to dig through it and understand what it is they are telling us. They have given us a massive amount of information. It's to the point now, that when we do a session, not only do we ask questions, but it turns into conversations. It's not like what you normally do with a Ouija board – you know "am I gonna get rich?" "Yes." "Am I gonna be poor?" "No." "Am I gonna get in a car wreck?" "Yes." And that kind of stuff. It's really like sitting around with a bunch of people and talking. We talk. They will talk to us. We can ask a question, get an answer, and then be talking about the answer amongst ourselves, and they will comment on our comments, interject remarks, agree or disagree with our analysis.

What we are trying to talk about today – and this is the first time we have done this in such a large group – is that we are still trying to work through all this information. When you sit around the house talking about something: say you say "we're gonna talk about politics" and you're sitting there talking about politics – and somebody says something and you say "oh, that reminds: did you see the sale down at the store?" and the discussion goes off on the subject of the sale, and you say "yeah, I got a hammer," and that leads to "I was working on the house," in the way that conversations do – going off in tangents all over the place. You may never talk about politics again after the first few remarks.

Well, our sessions are like that, too. We may start with a topic, and one thing will lead to another, which leads to another, which takes us out someplace else, so the information we have in the raw transcripts is all jumbled together that way – like a free-form, stream of consciousness type thing, and we have to go through this and piece it together again. It's like a big jigsaw puzzle of questions and answers and comments and information that's all mixed together.

We have to go through and transcribe all this information, it's all in notebooks and on tapes and Laura has spent a lot of time sitting there trying to transcribe the tapes and comparing what is on the tapes to what is in the notebooks. It's a long and tedious process because, when there is a large group, she has to identify the voices and put the right names in place so we know who is saying what. We have here 155 pages in 10 point type, and that's just up to over a month ago. We have to be able to sort all of it out and understand it ourselves so that we can go back and ask intelligent questions about points that have not been covered completely.

A: (J) Yes, and they always remember when they have already told us something. We may argue, but if we go back and look, sure enough, it's there!

A: (L) Yes, and if a question gets asked and then six months later, a different person asks the same question, the Cassiopaeans will tell us to go back and review. They will say "bring so-and-so up to speed."

A: (T) Yes, they will ask us to go back and look it up.

A: (J) One time they told us, NO! Stop! Listen! Wait! – trying to get our attention because we were off on a question spree – and they said: YOU have the answers! They told us specifically to stop channeling, sit there and talk the matter over. They told us that we could find the answers by "networking."

A: (L) Yes, so we spent an hour or more talking about the subject and by the time we got through, we realized that we did, indeed, know the answer.

A: (T) The bottom line of what they seem to be trying to tell us, which we are trying to "get," which "we" in sixth density are trying to help "Us" in the present to do, is to understand that, within the next 20 years or so, this Realm Wave, this window, so to say, is going to arrive. And, when it arrives, we will have the opportunity to move from third to fourth density as a group, as opposed to individually, one at a time through any number of lives.

If, and when, we are able to do this, the object is first: to get us to move, but second: this is part of the counterattack against the Lizards from the Service to Others beings who are trying to get us back in the realm of freedom. They can't interfere with Free Will, but if they can inform enough of us, and we can make a free choice to move back, it will break the Lizards' hold on the human race.

The object seems to be to break the Lizard hold on the human race. At that point, whether this works or not, whatever happens in third density, happens. And then, the whole focal point of the campaign moves to somewhere else in the universe, because they are doing this in other places. This is *not* the only place that this is happening.

A: (L) And don't get the idea that this is something terrible. Are you all familiar with the Yin-Yang symbol, the black half and the white half? This is really what this is all about. We don't need to look at it as though it is really an actual battle, though in some terms, expressed at this density, it displays that way as well as in Earth Changes. What it is is that for over 300,000 years we have been in the Service to Self realm, or the dark half of the circle. Now, the cycle is coming around. You have to remember that we are just doing this, as the Cassiopaeans say, "for fun!" [Laughter.]

Now, we are gonna take a break, and after the break we are going to try to demonstrate – I don't know if it is going to work – but we are going to try. We don't want any personal questions. Don't ask what house you are gonna buy next year. Try to come up with some good questions, write them down for us, and we will see what happens.

During the break we set up the board and arranged the chairs with everybody in their proper alignments according to the compass points. I sat at the East, Frank at the North, T at the West, and the South position was open. I was really nervous when we sat down because I had no idea if things would work in a different location or not. But, after a few seconds of contact, the planchette began to spiral around in large circles, finally going to the word:

A: "Hello."

Q: (L) Hello.

A: New location?

Q: (L) Yes, it's a new location, indeed. Where do you transmit through?

A: Cassiopaea.

Q: (L) Are you having difficulty operating in the new location?

A: Some but should stabilize.

Q: (L) We have questions from the audience. Shall we begin?

A: Sure!

Q: (L) The first question here is: "In which density is our astral existence?"

A: 5th, density of contemplation, you did not explain that one, did you?

Q: (L) Yeah, we forgot to explain that. Sorry.

A: Okay. Explain 5th now please.

Q: (T) 5th density, is where souls go when they die. When you leave your physical body in any one of the first 4 densities, your soul moves to 5th density. They call it the contemplation density. That's where you go, and you get to review the life you have had, and learn from it, and decide what it is you want to do next when you incarnate next. In the chain of densities, one through seven, the souls exist in 1 through 4 and in 6th, actively, and in 5th density passively. Did I get that right?

A: Yes.

Q: (Aud.) What energy are they using to create the conduit?

A: Open frequency EM wave.

Q: (Aud.) Is there a mathematical formula for creating the conduit? If so, what is it?

A: Create one at your leisure!

Q: (L) I guess if you want a mathematical formula, you are supposed to create one at your leisure! [Laughter] (J) That's humor, I guess.

A: Not totally humor!

Q: (Aud.) Is it beyond our current scientific level?

A: Yes.

Q: (Aud.) What exists in inner earth region as reported by Admiral Byrd? Well, I think we should add "allegedly" reported by Admiral Byrd.

A: Cross awareness "window."

Q: (L) So, a window exists in the inner earth region?

A: Did for Admiral Byrd at that instance.

Q: (L) So, he passed through an awareness window?

A: Yes.

Q: (T) What is an awareness window?

A: You have been told.

Q: (L) Yes. It's in the transcripts.

A: Realms can be accessed at will if awareness balance is proper.

Q: (L) If awareness balance is proper, "cross awareness window" means that you can cross over in awareness to another realm. Is that right? Let me break it down: does this mean that if your awareness is balanced, you create a "window?"

A: Close.

Q: (L) Can this happen to a person spontaneously?

A: Yes.

Q: (L) It is not something that you necessarily have to work for, it can happen to anyone, any time...

A: Unlikely.

Q: (L) So, it *can*, but without some preparation, is unlikely to happen. Okay, next question: "After seventh density is the Big Bang, and everything starts all over again?"

A: Close and partial. Grand Cycle access.

Q: (L) You mean that 7th Density is a "Grand Cycle Access?"

A: No, review.

Q: (L) Seventh Density is the Big Bang and it all starts all over again and that is the Grand Cycle? There is really no beginning or end, just an endless cycling?

A: No. Grand Cycle is self explanatory to 6 people here.

Q: (L) I guess I'm not one of them. (A member of the audience here gives an explanation, but it is impossible to decipher it from the tape as they were apparently in the back of the room. It sounds something like "at Seventh Density there is a window of Access to the Grand Cycle.")

A: Yes.

Q: (Aud.) What is the true age of the Great Pyramid? (L) That's already been given.

A: Yes.

Q: (L) I believe the figure that was given was 10,600 years ago, more or less. (Aud.) Where do alien craft go when seen going into water such as lakes, rivers, the ocean, etc. Where do they go?

A: Variable.

Q: (Aud.) Where did the one go that I saw at Longboat Key? Where are they going off Longboat Key?

A: Non-specific.

Q: (L) Different destinations? (T) Are some of them going to a base?

A: Not there, but remember, you are talking about dual density cross-transference, therefore "rules" for third density do not always apply.

Q: (Aud.) Are they using the ocean water as a conduit or window?

A: Maybe but not the only "method."

Q: (T) So, they could be doing about anything down there once they have entered the water.

A: Yes.

Q: (T) Including just sitting there waiting.

A: Why not?

Q: (Aud.) Did you ever ask them who built the Great Pyramid? (L) Yes, we did. The response was Atlanteans.

A: Descendants of same.

Q: (Aud.) Did they ever tell about the purpose for the pyramids?

A: (L) Yes, they did. First of all, the Atlantean civilization existed for a very long time and was quite extensive all over the globe, not necessarily confined to the semi-legendary "continent of Atlantis."

Apparently, interplanetary travel was as easy for the Atlanteans as it is for us to take a trip to the store. They had bases on the Moon, bases on Mars; the monuments of the Moon and Mars are Atlantean in origin; they also had some of their giant crystals on the Moon and Mars, and these were used to collect Cosmic and Solar energy as a power source.

We have talked about locations of such crystals on the Earth and why they were not destroyed in the cataclysms that destroyed Atlantis and the answer was that the engineered function of these crystals was such that massive amounts of energy interacting with them is absorbed and transmuted, so to speak. If you put an atomic bomb on one of them, it would absorb the energy and transduce it. It was the design function.

When we asked if our present technology could decipher how to use these crystals, and the response was "would a Neanderthal know how to fly a 747." [Laughter]

So, when we are talking about the Atlanteans, we are talking about a super advanced civilization and the descendants of them, after the destruction that occurred which destroyed this amazing culture, built these pyramidal shapes, which had a similar function as the pyramid shaped giant crystals, though much less effective. In other words, the Pyramids are simply gigantic machines. They were used to manipulate energy to control weather, power the many things that a civilization requires to be considered "advanced," to preserve and transmute or heal. Just a whole host of energy applications similar to what we do with electricity. But, still, it was a step down from the far more advanced Atlantean technology, and as time went by, other things occurred, and eventually this knowledge was lost.

Q: (Aud.) Is there a giant pyramid, or a step pyramid in China?

A: Yes.

Q: (T) Can you give us some information about this pyramid?

A: Yes.

Q: (L) Was it built by Atlantean descendants also?

A: Yes.

Q: (L) I think that the Atlantean civilization was much like our present one... it didn't really denote a specific place, though there may have been the equivalent of the "Western technological world" as is America, at the present time. In fact, when we asked about the population of the world at the height of Atlantis, the answer was that it was pretty much the same as it is now, over 6 billion. We then asked how many were left after the destruction and the figure was either 19 million or 119 million. I screwed up in the transcribing and will have to go back to the tape to get it right. Well, which was it?

A: 19 million.

Q: (L) That is a serious reduction from 6 billion.

Q: (Aud.) In all the varying transitions between 1st and 6th density, does any soul ever perish, or become extinguished?

A: No.

Q: (T) We asked about this at several points. Apparently all souls began at the same point in "time," and all will be returned to 7th density at the same time. No new souls are being created, and no souls are ever destroyed, they merely change from state to state according to their "lesson profile," or what they have learned or need to learn and experience. (L) Yeah. That's the good news; here's the bad news: those that don't graduate to fourth density on this pass of the wave get to do third density all over again, in its entire cycle. [Laughter]

Q: (Aud.) Have you ever asked about why there is so much suffering here on Earth?

A: (L) Yes, and it's not Eve's fault!

Q: (Aud.) Well, I don't know about others, but if there is a utopia out there somewhere, I'd rather be there and never come back here again! And what you are telling me is that, even though we go back to 6th density, we have to come back again.

A: (L) No, that's 5th density – contemplation level. You make the decisions there, and if you are here, it's because you chose to be here. But, the only way to get out of the cycle of the third density Service to Self level, the consumption level where you must feed on others – and that is really the bottom line there – you must transcend that issue, the physicality. You become an energy being who only gives conjoined with other beings that also only give, and in such symbiosis, no one ever lacks.

But, yes, there is a very definite reason for the suffering at this level and T touched on it a while ago – the dominance of the Reptilian beings that fed off of us for the past 300,000 years.

They dumbed us down, implanted control impulses in us such as jealousy, greed, avarice and so forth, so that we would constantly generate negative energy while they are sitting there in fourth density with a straw just slurping it up! "Yummy!"

So, when you feel yourself going into negative states, if you want to transcend it, all you have to really do is understand that it is not *yours*. You don't "own it." Yes, it is part of the physicality of this density, but it is a physicality that has been genetically tampered with so that such emotions will dominate. You can *not* act them out, you can refuse to be controlled by such states, you can *choose* to be other, even if it requires something of an inner struggle between the choice of the soul and the wants of the flesh which are pretty clever at being rationalized by the brain so that we don't see what is really going on very clearly at all.

Q: (Aud.) So, we actually chose to accept this state of being at some point, and now we can choose otherwise?

A: (L) That's exactly right. Each moment, we have the choice of accepting the Lizzie program, or to follow a different line of choices. The mass of humanity, the group – and we have been told that the Legend of Lucifer is the story of this choice and refers to the human race – made this choice. I don't know about you, but I've had enough. I think I changed my mind! [Laughter]

At this point, a member of the audience (referred to as "AB") has taken T's place at the board. This was the "skeptic" who, at the beginning of the session had set up his little meter beside the board on the table.

Q: (L) Okay, we have a new person at the board...

A: Yes.

Q: (L) We have a question here from somebody about Walk-ins, and before I ask it, I would like to ask a sort of "pre-question." My question is: how often does something along the idea of a "walk-in" occur?

A: Rare.

Q: (L) Yes, it was a very popular idea, and still is. I mean, how easy can it be to say "oh, I didn't do that! It was the former occupant of this body!" Or, "I can do *this* now, because I have just taken over this body. I'm not a trash man, I'm really a brain surgeon, so hand me a scalpel!" and that sort of thing.

People were creating all kinds of exotic and elaborate "backgrounds" for themselves, and as I heard these stories, they got wilder by the day! "I'm Prince or Princess So-and-So from the Planet Hoogabooga! Make obeisance, peasant!" How bizarre can it get?

Q: (Aud.) Have you asked about actual, physical life forms on other planets, or is it just us here in the Universe?

A: (L) Yes, we have, but let's get in this question we have already. It says: "Are any of those who claim to be Walk-ins really so?" And, we sort of answered that already. Yes, it *can* happen, but is very rare. The question continues: "If so, who are they specifically? My friend in Longboat Key, Gail ____, is she one?"

A: No.

Q: (L) Well, so much for that. (Addressing audience member who is nodding her head vigorously) Did you know that already? (AM) Yes. I just wanted to make sure.

Q: (AB) Given the amount of destruction the Reptilians have done to our DNA, what can we do to repair it? Is there a diet adjustment?

A: Maybe. It is open to the individual to experiment and discover.

I should note that the energy, at this point, was quite fractured with the new person at the board and the planchette was moving very slowly.

Q: (L) I think that the conduit has to be readjusted to the new energy.

A: Yes. Note light waves in device.

Q: (L) You mean the meter beside us? Turn it around so we can see it. (T) What is the bottom of the range? (AB) .1, .2 is the ambient. It's been hitting peaks of 5 at times before I sat down. That's microgausses. (J) What light waves are you referring to?

A: Near window.

Q: (L) A space/time window? [There was no physical window in the room.]

A: Yes.

Q: (L) I think that this is in response to your question about DNA. We are supposed to notice that the meter is measuring some sort of energy and that this represents light waves near the "window" or conduit that is established by the channeling, and that this is one of the things that can change DNA. I don't think that eating or drinking one way or another can make a difference, it is what is inside – which, in a sense *can* change what you eat or drink, but it is a change that comes from a different direction than a change that is done deliberately in order to alter DNA. They have said that light waves alter DNA. (AB) What specific light frequency?

A: 6 pt 5

Q: (AB) Angstroms?

A: Yes.

Q: (AB) That's actually the frequency of a medium red neon laser. A laser is a monochromic frequency. It's like one of those laser pointers. It puts out only one color, one exact frequency. 6.5 would be mid-orange?

A: Yes.

Q: (Aud.) What are certain people in our government and our military gaining by being more conspiring than lucid?

A: Open.

Q: (T) Many things. Is there one thing in particular that they gain from this?

A: As we know, answer is dangerous.

Q: (T) We've gotten several answers like that when we touch on sensitive questions.

At this point, the tape ended, and we ended the "demonstration session" that was supposed to have been "predestined." Was it? What were the ramifications aside from the fact that the small, local MUFON group had the largest attendance ever in its existence?

As it turned out, there were interesting developments shortly thereafter.

Two months following this session, we attended another meeting of the local MUFON group where a physicist, Professor Ruggero Santilli, was scheduled to speak. At that same meeting were many of the people who had attended our "demonstration," and some of them gathered around during the break to ask us further questions about the experiment in channeling. Prof. Santilli joined them, was given a brief synopsis of the situation, and was intrigued enough to ask to attend a session.

As it happened, we were planning one that very evening, so after the meeting, we all drove back to the house with Prof. Santilli and his wife following, and settled down to see what would happen.

05-27-95

Q: (T) We have some company this evening. Roger and Carla Santilli are with us. Roger has some questions to ask.

A: Hello, Roger.

Q: (RS) Hello. I want to know whether we can have any clues on the propulsion systems of UFOs?

A: Sure!

Q: (RS) What's the mechanism of the propulsion?

A: This is difficult to answer when posed in such a manner, as we are talking about multiple realities, density levels and various modes as well!!

Q: (RS) Is the gravity experienced by an anti-particle in the field of matter attractive or repulsive?

A: Repulsive when thought of in the way that is parallel to your studies, but, as we alluded to in the previous answer, there are more realms involved besides the one with which you are most familiar.

Q: (RS) The next question is: particles move, matter moves, in our direction of time, do anti-particles, anti-matter flow backward in time?

A: Think of it as merely one seventh of the equation, Roger!

Q: (L) Can we get an answer on whether this is the case strictly on the third level of density?

A: Backward.

Q: (RS) Yes! I am interested in the propulsion systems of UFOs, the only way that I can perceive traveling the long distances involved in interstellar space is to have what is called a "space/time" machine. We cannot move the enormous distances unless you can fold, somehow, time and space. You cannot fold space unless you join it and fold time. You cannot have interstellar travel unless you have a space/time machine. But, a space/time machine means to also have the ability to move forward and backward in time, to manipulate time.

(L) Yes, you would have to cross distances and simultaneously move backward through time so that you would end up arriving wherever you are going essentially at the same moment that you left.

(RS) That is why I asked whether we could use anti-matter as propulsion, because it would be repulsive in the right direction. The second question whether, when we use anti-matter, we would move backward in time. Because, some of those objects, you see them moving, and they can be moving in space but not in time, or they could be moving in time but not in space. If you see a UFO, it does not mean that it is in our time. It could be in a completely different time.

(L) And, they disappear sometimes right before the eyes of the observer, and the question is: where do they go?

(RS) They could be standing still in space, but moving time. Or moving backwards.

(L) And, there are a lot of abductions reported where there is seemingly no time lost at all. They come in, haul the victim out, do whatever they do, and then they slide them back in a fraction of a second away, if not at the identical second they took the victim out!

(RS) Yes! This article I presented is exactly about this point! If, indeed, anti-particles have lift, then necessarily they have to go backward in time. Then they manipulate this: you can have an abduction any length of time inside the craft, but in our time, in our level three, it is zero time!

(L) Yes, exactly! And not only that, there is the phenomenon of the craft that looks small from the outside, but inside is huge!

(RS) That is all tied up in it! This is very exciting. I am learning the language. In our third level, the motion in space and time occurs via the change of the unit of time and space, therefore, can we change the unit?

A: Yes, this is precisely what we mean when we speak of "transiting from 4th to 3rd."

Q: (RS) So, when they travel from fourth to third, they change the units. That is precisely what is in the article in the journal! [Holds up book.] This is published in the Ukraine, [turns to page and displays diagrams and equations] this is the experiment to test anti-gravity.

There is a two-mile long tunnel that is a vacuum inside. They suck the air out. The first measure is to shoot photons to identify, at the end of the two mile tunnel, the no gravity point.

The second measure is to shoot a neutron, and we know that a neutron is attractive. So, after two miles, the energy is very, very low. So, there is no gravitational effect when the neutron hits the point.

Then, the third step is to shoot an anti-neutron at the same time and see what happens. This experiment will resolve this issue that this board has answered very scientifically. We call it the gravity of anti-particles because we don't know. It can be down... Einstein predicts this as attractive as a neutron, anti-matter and matter have the same gravitational attraction. That's what Einstein says.

But, when Einstein's theory was proposed, in 1915, anti-matter wasn't discovered until 50 years later.

If now, theoretically, the only way a particle, in our theory, can go up, can have lift, is if time is reversed. There is no other possibility. So, if this experiment is correct, then the space/time machine is absolutely a consequence and can be tested in a laboratory. You can have a particle moving backward and forward in time. [Displays new diagram.]

This is the other experiment which is, in this case, is done by putting a particle which is neutral and subjecting it to... since we don't have a bunch of anti-matter – ideally we would have a pellet of matter and replace it with anti-matter – we don't have a pellet of anti-matter, at this point, there are ways to do it though and it can be measured as to which way it moves, up or down.

Now, the question of the units, it is very important, a fundamental question, because, say, you are outside a UFO, and you see the UFO as big as a car, say, and people go inside and report this enormous interior. There is no other way to do this than by changing the unit.

What is for us one inch, that unit is completely different inside. For us the unit is the same along the three directions. Now, if you are inside, they can have different units in different directions. This means that if you are outside a cube, and you go inside, the shape, not only the dimensions but the shape even, can be different.

At the third level, is it true that the value of the dimension is changed by the available energy, or the energy is used to change the value of the units?

A: This concept crosses the density barrier, not limited to level three.

Q: (RS) Goes up to level four. That's the means of propulsion of the UFO.

A: Reason for exponential awareness "explosion" is approach of wave. Now, concentrate on visualization. Answers are located there... After a period of contemplation, Roger to "hit upon" breakthrough question to solve puzzle currently occupying "center stage" of his psyche, with only one piece missing currently.

Q: (RS) I notice that if the question is not properly phrased...

(L) You don't get your answer! Be specific.

A: Careful not to confuse with too much data that is not connected in the same concept arena, as visitor is concerned primarily with one direction; in order to familiarize let data be absorbed on schedule comfortable to researcher! Like trying to learn mathematics in broken dosages!

Q: (RS) Two short questions and then I will stop...

A: Ask as many as you desire!

Q: (RS) In our level three, does the use of anti-matter change the sign of the unit? Does this imply the reversal of the sign of the unit of space and time?

A: Yes, but problem has always been for level three entities, that the "other" side is uncharted, therefore experimentation is not recommended, unless with assistance from level four through six STO.

Q: (RS) That is an incredible answer because this is traveling in time.

First they said that by using energy you can change the numerical value of the units, and from this (incomprehensible) you can make a (incomprehensible) show. Now the question: how you can go backward in time; by changing the sign of the unit: plus one second and we move forward, if that unit is changed to minus one second, we move backward. So the question is, by using anti-matter, can we move backward? But their answer was saying... precisely, that we are moving from level three to level four.

In Greece, at this time, at the University of Santia (?), the nuclear physics laboratory at the University, there is a potentially fundamental experiment going on based on my studies to search for fundamentally new source of energy by bombarding zinc 70 or molybdenum 100 via Gamma with 1.294 MeV energy. Will the experiment be successful...

A: All of the experiments you speak of share one thing in common: They all "touch the borderline" from the perspective of the third density side.

Q: (RS) Will you help us? (Carla) Yes, let's be practical! [Laughter]

A: It is possible to cross over into fourth density from third, using third density technology. In fact, various individuals and groups on a more or less accidental basis have already accomplished this; the problem is "what does one do when one reaches fourth density reality with only third density training and experience?"

Q: (L) Could you, if we spent the time, help us with this training and technology?

A: Yes, but what do you intend to use it for? This is not like going to Disney World for a day, you know! What is your knowledge quotient regarding following: electromagnetism, Einstein's "unified field theory." And did he ever complete said theory, or was it completed under the supervision of Consortium [i.e. the "powers that be," the "hidden controllers" or our world; the "secret government"], and suppressed. And if so, what are the ramifications!!! Also, Roger, are you capable of "filling in the blanks," we think so!

Q: (RS) From the third level there cannot be a unification of electromagnetism and gravitation because they are identical. There is an identity between electromagnetism and gravitation. So, there is no need of the unification because they are identical. Is this view correct?

A: Yes. What about fourth level?

Q: (RS) To my understanding to the third level, this is where the possibility to go up a level comes in. If gravitation and electromagnetism are identical, then anti-gravity exists. The origin of anti-gravity is not unification. Einstein was wrong, but the identification that they are the same implies the existence of anti-gravity.

A: Wrong when searching on level three density exclusively, but this is where the Consortium comes in, i.e. "Can of Worms."

Q: (T) It is considered known to the general public that Einstein did not complete his Unified Field Theory, but that may be a falsehood. Part of the disinformation campaign.

(RS) From what we know, Einstein failed to achieve the Unified Field Theory because the assumptions were not realizable. Can I ask a question? The origin of the mass of an elementary particle is primarily electromagnetic, therefore, the gravitational field of elementary particle must be primarily of electromagnetic nature. That's why the view at level three is, outside mass, the gravitation and electromagnetism are identical. This is our belief at this time, supported by experimental evidence. Why is this wrong? I need an explanation.

A: Not wrong at level three, wrong to limit to third level.

Q: (RS) Is it true that the universe has equal amounts of matter and anti-matter as seen from level three?

A: Yes, all others as well.

Q: (RS) Then it is true that the total time in the universe is null?

A: Yes.

Q: (RS) This is incredible!

A: But, Roger less pressure! [Roger lightens up, pause] Thank you. Now, remember, most important concept is balance. How is balance achieved?

Q: (RS) Matter and anti-matter. So, if matter is flowing in this direction of time, anti-matter is flowing the other way. They balance each other.

(J) This is my question of the total time of the universe, which is zero. If we flow this way, maybe others in another galaxy are flowing another way. The sum is zero.

A: Not galaxy, dimension.

Q: (RS) Yes. Another level. I always think at level three!

A: Not any more! [Laughter]

Q: (RS) How can we represent mathematically the identification of gravity and electromagnetism, including the fourth level that you suggest? How can this be done? How can the inclusion of the fourth level be realized?

A: We asked you to visualize for answers. It is always there for you to discover.

Q: (RS) It is not going to be easy, but I am going to give it a try.

A: What ever is?

Q: (RS) The question is how to represent mathematically the transition to the fourth level. I think that this can be done by isogeometry, the geometry that we discussed earlier, which is generalization of the unit of space and time...

A: Geometry is one key, but there is another.

Q: (L) What is the other key?

(L) Could you give us a clue. Just a little clue?

(RS) Give us the formula!

A: Have already... access...

Q: (RS) We should have a session... because this is confirmation of the only mathematical model we have of the UFOs... the only one that exists as far as I know. We have a computer model... we cannot build a UFO, we don't have the technology, but we can put the formula into the computer and get a model.

A: Merge geometry with optics.

Q: (RS) What?! It is the science of light.

A: Matrix.

Q: (RS) That is precisely what I have done. I've done a representation of light represented by a unit, which is a matrix. I have already done this! Years ago!

A: But you left out one important factor, remember, hypothesis does not theory make!

Q: (RS) I made a conceptual hypothesis in my mind. That's not a theory. It has to be formulated in a quantitative way, that's the mathematics, the formula, and then this has to be proven experimentally that it works. Hypothesis, formula, and experimental verification is the process for a theory.

A: Now, what factor was missing, Roger?

Q: (RS) I don't know. But how... I do not know how to express it mathematically...

A: Light waves... gravity... electromagnetism...

Q: (RS) I have to think it over. In isogeometry...

A: What role do waves play in third level understanding of physics?

Q: (RS) Transverse oscillation of the ether... the medium that fills up the entire universe. No wave can exist unless there is a medium to propagate it. Transverse oscillations fill up the entire universe.

A: Light, gravity, optics, atomic particles, matter, anti-matter... unify, please.

Q: (RS) That lists everything...

(J) What do they all have in common?

(RS) Oh! All of them are vibrations of the medium that fills up the universe! We perceive things, everything, even spaces between things. Reality is the opposite of this. Because light is a wave, like sound. If you remove the air, sound cannot propagate. Light is the same thing. Light is a wave and cannot propagate unless there is a medium that fills up the entire universe. So what we perceive as being solid and empty is not true perception.

The whole universe is filled with the vibration of this medium. So, without the medium, there would be darkness. So, light is an oscillation of this medium. A particle is also an oscillation only the wave propagates and the oscillation stays there. So when I move my hand from here to here, I have just moved the oscillation. The space is oscillating. We are completely empty, but space is filled up.

So, the answer is that what they have in common is that they are all oscillations of this medium that fills up the entire universe as perceived from third level and I think from fourth.

A: Now, what relation between gravity and light?

Q: (RS) I do not know. At this moment in my studies, I do not know. Light can be converted into matter, therefore there is gravitation.

(L) But, what could the relation between gravity and light be?

A: Access knowledge base and network.

Q: (RS) The only connection between light and gravitation... the photon and the anti-photon (?) produces a pair of electrons and positrons, particles and anti-particles, and those particles have gravitation. So, in this way electromagnetic waves... a photon can create matter...

(L) And matter has gravity...

(RS) And matter has gravity, so... it can be converted...

(L) But where does it come from?

(RS) That is a good question because it isn't known. It could come from a vacuum...

(L) But how does it happen?

(RS) In experiments in the laboratory, you shoot a photon at a nucleus and the nucleus spits one electron and one positron, and so you have conversion of photon into particles. Those particles have gravitation. I do not know if a photon has gravitation. I don't think so, it travels at the speed of light. There is no time. Time is suspended.

(L) Okay, is it true that at the speed of light, there is no gravity?

(RS) There is no gravity.

(L) Okay, then maybe the speed of light is the antithesis of gravity just as anti-matter is the opposite of matter?

(RS) That is a good point. A very good point!

A: Close.

Q: (J) Is it about balance?

A: All is.

Q: (L) If at the speed of light there is no gravity...

(RS) There is no time...

(L) Then gravity must be...

(RS) The clue... But is the missing clue... are we discussing the missing point to go from the third to the fourth density?

A: Yes.

Q: (RS) Then the point is valid. So, then if you go at the speed of light then you are in fourth density.

A: Now, what is missing factor, which allows third density and fourth density matter to achieve light speed without disintegration? Think...

Q: (RS) That is the fundamental question of nuclear physics... matter cannot reach the speed of light intact...

(J) Anti-gravity?

(RS) Even by using anti-gravity. At this moment, matter cannot do this...

(L) Okay, if you have some matter and this matter is speeding up, and it is approaching the speed of light and it is losing its integrity the faster it goes, what if, at some point you start incrementally adding anti-matter which...

(RS) Use the inverse process... take an electron and positron and put one inside the other and recreate the photon. But matter cannot reach the speed of light... if it does, time stops... there is no dimension...

(L) Maybe it is consciousness?

A: What is the missing link between matter and consciousness?

Q: (RS) Ah!

(L) If we knew these things we wouldn't be here! [Laughter]

(RS) It is supposed to be a field.

(J) Is it EM?

(RS) No, a bio-energetic field.

(L) What if consciousness creates gravity?

(RS) Gravity is created by matter.

(L) But isn't matter created by consciousness?

(RS) Yes, the mind can create matter...

A: There are no "gravitons."

Q: (RS) Not to my knowledge. They do not exist. They are in Einstein's theory, but I will never believe it... Does our consciousness create gravity?

A: Getting "warmer." Not "our."

Q: (L) Somebody else's consciousness creates gravity?

(RS) Fourth level.

A: Level Seven.

Q: (RS) Oh yes! That I can understand! The ultimate level. Is it true that the universe, as perceived from level three, which is expected to be made up of equal amounts of matter and anti-matter, is, in actuality, open? That is, is matter continuously created somewhere in the universe? Matter and anti-matter?

A: Better word would be: Recycled.

Q: (RS) Is it true that the same recycling occurs in the center of the earth. There is a theory that the earth is expanding. I heard this at a congress; that the earth is expanding in diameter precisely because the center of the earth is in process of the creation of matter. Is this correct?

A: Off base, but all concepts are valid within unified dimensionality.

Q: (RS) My biggest problem has never been new knowledge, but politics, particularly the politics on Einstein. Is the can of worms mentioned before, can you give me anything on this? As soon as you go beyond Einstein, there are all sorts of problems, political problems in our contemporary society. Any suggestions?

A: Political problems have root in effort to suppress knowledge already gained in limited quarters for purposes of control of civilization.

Q: (RS) That is the best answer I ever heard. Very, very good.

(T) While I was walking around outside smoking my cigar, I was getting the image that one of the reasons that Roger is here tonight is to experience this, but also to see and read what we give you. We are not making this up. It is coming from somewhere. There is substance to this information. Roger is going to Europe. You have colleagues in Europe who are working on these very same things. The Cassiopaeans have indicated that you are on the edge of opening this barrier. That this can be done, it has been done with disastrous results the few times that we know of and possibly other times that we do not know of.

What I am getting at is, part of the reason you are here and seeing this may be because you need to take this information with you because when they breach these barriers, they need to understand what they have done. Because, if they don't there is a possibility that what is transpiring naturally will be accelerated. Does artificial breaching of the barrier between the densities accelerate...

A: Yes.

Q: (T) That may be why when we ask how long this process is going to take, this oncoming density change, they answer "one month to 18 years." And we were thinking that maybe they can't tell how long it is going to take for this transition point, this realm border to come through our section of space/time and do whatever it does. Maybe what they are referring to is not that, but what people might do in terms of breaching the barrier unknowingly. They are stretching what they know, and pushing onward, but they don't understand what this is all about.

A: Yes.

[Good night to Carla and Roger]

(L) Of the three pairs we were given, they each seem to be opposite to each other: Light and gravity, optics and atomic particles, matter and anti-matter...

(J) It's all about balance. What is the relation between gravity and light? What is the missing factor that allows third density and fourth density matter to achieve light speed without disintegration? What is the missing link between matter and consciousness?

(L) What is the missing link? Well, I think the relationship is right there. What is it that slows down light causing photons to manifest, collapsing the wave, so to speak, and creating matter?

(J) It may be that this same factor that allows third density to achieve light speed without disintegration. What is the missing link between matter and consciousness?

(L) Well, the relationship is there. We were told we were getting close when we said "consciousness" but that it was not our consciousness, but that of Level Seven.

(J) They said that "creation" was a recycling.

Q: (L) Are you still there?

A: As always, Laura, do you think we go out to lunch or something?

Q: [Laughter]

A: You keep asking if we are here?!?

Q: (T) Did you enjoy talking to Roger and would you like to talk to him again?

A: Yes. Will.

Q: (L) Am I getting warm when I say... we have light and gravity, optics and atomic particles, matter and anti-matter, all are ways of talking about a transition... are these three pairs of relationships?

A: Close.

Q: (L) What is the thing that collapses the wave? Is it consciousness?

A: Yes...

Q: (L) There is more. Can this consciousness be expressed...

(T) We are trying to get from a third density concept to a fourth density concept where there is no physicality, per se. At fourth density they don't have a problem with going at the speed of light and disintegrating, because it doesn't exist there...

A: Close.

Q: (T) So, for us to try and think of this in third density...

A: Variable physicality is the key.

Q: (L) What makes the physicality variable?

A: Awareness of link between consciousness and matter.

Q: (L) What is the link between consciousness and matter?

A: Illusion.

Q: (L) What is the nature of the illusion?

(T) That there isn't any connection between consciousness and matter. It is only an illusion that there is. It is part of the third density...

A: No. Illusion is that there is not.

Q: (L) The illusion is that there is no link between consciousness and matter.

A: Yes.

Q: (T) The illusion is that there is not a link. In third density...

(L) I got it!

(T) Don't disappear on me now! [Laughter] The relationship is that consciousness is matter.

A: Close. What about vice versa?

Q: (L) Just reverse everything. Light is gravity. Optics are atomic particles, matter is anti-matter... just reverse everything to understand the next level... it can't be that easy.

(J) Wait a second: gravity equals light, atomic particles equals optics, anti-matter equals matter? It is all about balance.

(L) And the answer must always be zero.

A: And zero is infinity.

Q: (L) So, you are saying that it is not that there is a link, the illusion is that there is separation. There is no difference, they are the same?

A: Yes.

Q: (T) If you warp space/time you travel by bringing your destination to you.

(L) Or, you can reverse that and understand that there is no distance between us and, say, Alpha Centauri, it is the alteration of perception that turns the axis and creates the illusion of distance.

A: Now, all you need is the "technology."

Q: (T) The technology is being developed right now.

(J) The technology has probably already been developed, it is just suppressed.

A: Yes.

Q: (L) I have a very strange sense that this interaction has ramifications?

A: Yes.

Q: (L) A hint?

A: We could but won't at this "time."

Q: (T) Are these major ramifications?

A: Yes.

Q: (L) Is there anything further for this evening?

A: No.

Q: (L) Then we will say thank you and good-night.

A: Good night.

One of the most significant things about this session was the revelation to me that it just *might* be possible to solve some of the great mysteries of our world with the help of the Cassiopaeans.

Yes, it is so that many, many sources of similar ilk have made claims to having done so – at least in philosophical terms – but here we had a real, live physicist who just possibly could figure out and ask the right questions, and then take the answers and translate them into usable, technological terms for the betterment of all humanity, not just "true believers."

I was enthralled by the fact that they had no problems talking with Prof. Santilli about physics though my stomach had knotted up at the beginning of the session from thinking that this was going to prove to me that the Cassiopaeans were just a chimera of my own subconscious – they would fail the test. But they didn't. Of course, they weren't giving anything away except clues, but the fact that they could do that was astonishing to me. It opened an endless vista of possibilities.

In addition to such considerations, the effect on me was also pronounced. It seemed that even when the session was over and I had gone to bed, I was still "channeling". My head was filled with ideas and images too deep for words and I was impatient to get on with the "project."

We waited for Prof. Santilli to return from Europe to see what the "ramifications" of the session would be. When he returned, he seemed to have a different "attitude" toward the Cassiopaeans, and it became clear that he did not wish to be associated with such a "bizarre" experiment. It was rather like the initial reaction of the MUFON group, which then changed so drastically that we were reduced from an hour of time to 15 minutes.

Something strange was going on. So much for our anticipation of help from such quarters. I put my hopes of delving into physics more deeply on the shelf, and over a year passed before we were to come back to the subject again.

But still, in terms of the "Wave" effect, it seemed that something about our position had changed, even if only in subtle ways. New doors had been opened in our minds and the Winds of Eternity were blowing our little ship toward some destination unknown.

CHAPTER 5
PERPENDICULAR REALITIES, TESSERACTS, AND OTHER ODD PHENOMENA...

In between the MUFON "Demo" session in March of 1995, and the visit of Dr. Santilli in May of the same year, there was another strange concept that the Cassiopaeans introduced to us that relates, it seems, to The Wave. I did not insert it in the chronological sequence because I felt it would have distracted from the series of events that resulted from our interactions with MUFON, but in certain way, it connects them – though the connection was only apparent in retrospect.

In this session again, in an unusual way, the Cassiopaeans brought up a matter, which led us step by step into the idea they wanted us to grasp; and this time T was the catalyst. I think it would be better for you, the reader, to read it exactly as it happened without any prior commentary, saving all that for afterward. I have put a couple of remarks in bold type just so you might keep them in mind.

04-29-95

Q: (L) Well, we were a little late getting started tonight...

A: T, was it October 1964?

Q: (L) To what does this question refer?

A: Ask T! Lake, yellow brick and brown brick buildings, cool day, fences, large cobalt colored cylinder, oscillating...

Q: (T) I would have been 14. I was a freshman... my father's cousin had a place at Keuka Lake and we used to go there and visit all the time... fences? I don't remember anything. I'm sorry. I'm drawing a blank.

A: Images we see... Now we see Victorian houses, green gabled roof... field... brown brick buildings...

Q: (T) October?

A: We asked you.

Q: (T) Dark blue? (J) Cobalt blue. (T) Dark blue, almost a black color? (J) Cobalt is a bright blue.

A: Cobalt is metallic navy blue.

Q: (T) Well, my brother wasn't home... I know what you are talking about! Yes, I did see something. I don't know if it was in October of 1964, but I remember seeing it!

A: Okay, now we are getting somewhere... what do you think happened to you that day?

Q: (T) I don't remember anything happening other than that I saw the object; it came floating over the house and then floated off in the other direction. I don't remember anything else happening. I stood outside, watched it come, watched it go; and I stood outside and watched it for quite some time.

A: Neighborhood, what appearance?

Q: (T) It looked just like the neighborhood. It didn't seem any different. I don't remember...

A: Describe...

Q: (T) There was a Fifties development out on the edge of the city limits of Rochester, surrounded by most of Kodak – out in that area – most of Rochester; across the street was a field with a schoolyard surrounded by a fence. A large, two-story brown school building, brown, or red brick... that I went to grammar school in. I don't know about yellow brick buildings, but our house was green at the time and the next door neighbor's house was yellow at the time with white fancy little trim stuff across the roof. It wasn't gabled, but it looked gabled. There were little gables over the front doors of most of the houses. The doors came out to the front and there was a little peak. There was a stadium on the other side of the schoolyard, a ways back for Aquinas football games and their stadium. Some fields and one of the last remaining wooded areas that was in the city limits that wasn't a park down the street... a set of railroad tracks about five blocks to the East. The lake, Lake Ontario, Rochester is right up against it, we were about seven miles, eight miles from there, maybe ten. I used to ride up there on my bike and back... the neighborhood itself didn't look any different because I watched the thing come in over the field. I remember my mother, I don't know if my brother was there, but I remember my mother and my neighbor. The neighbor woman was standing out on the front walk talking and they called me because I was in the house watching TV. I don't know if it was October though because it was still warm, sunny. It came in from high over the West, over a field, by the stadium, came down toward us, and came right toward us. I thought it was moving right at us. It didn't start moving right at us until we were looking at it...

A: Was.

Q: (T) Yes. Was moving toward us. It seemed to change direction when I came out and started looking at it. It went right over and...

A: Objective was you.

Q: (T) The objective was me? I don't think I was picked up at that time.

A: Oh yeah?

Q: (T) Well there were people standing there...

A: Time "freezes" during abduction.

Q: (T) The object had the distinctive falling leaf motion to it, which I thought was an extremely odd thing for it to do. It came right over the edge of the house on the side of the house, where, sometime in later years, I had something happen to me when I was in the basement. It was right over where I would have been sleeping...

A: Oscillating.

Q: (T) I thought it sure looked metallic and I wished I had a little pellet gun and could pop a pellet at it; it wasn't more than about 50 feet up in the air. It was maybe 10 to 15 feet long and maybe about 3 or 4 feet around. It looked like a wiener rounded on both ends but not as fat; it was longer and thinner. (F) It looked like a hotdog? (T) It looked metallic to me. It was smooth, perfectly smooth. (L) What are we getting to here? This was obviously brought up for a reason. If T was abducted...

A: Crossroads.

Q: (L) It was a crossroads in T's life?

A: And now... connection completed.

Q: (T) I'm not following this...

A: Access your recent dreams.

Q: (T) Recent dreams... I dreamed something about moving into a building and I had something that had a power cord or something that went outside... a connection of some kind... I don't remember them... they are just very vivid. Could something have happened to me just recently that started with that experience?

A: Yes.

Q: (T) It has to do with what we are doing here, but this isn't the completed connection we are talking about?

A: Not exactly.

Q: (T) The connection that was completed was all about something else?

A: Interrelated.

Q: (T) Does it have to do with my job?

A: In part.

Q: (T) Does it have to do with the fact that I am saying certain things to people at work, or wherever I can, when I talk about events that are happening these days and trying to raise their level of thinking on these things?

A: Yes, now, let's explore your friends and relationships and experiences in the years immediately following the event to see if we can "dig up" something of startling significance!!!

Q: (T) Are we sure this is 1964 and not 1974?

A: T, you know better!

Q: (T) I'm just asking because that event and the event that happened in winter with the voices outside the window and all the weirdness that happened that night seemed to be a lot closer together and that other event happened in the 70s, sometime. That was somewhere close to my trip out to Arizona and the weirdness out there with the car and all that.

A: Oh, there is sooooo much, isn't there T! It is time to divulge.

Q: (T) After high school. But, in those days I was mainly hanging out with some people I met over at Edison. Tom ___, a lot of people named Tom. I used to go to the lake and take drives around it at night. We just used up gas. I felt comfortable because I did a lot of things but most of the people I knew didn't get along with each other. I still do this today; I have learned from hard experience that I can't mix my friends. I learned at that time that every person in any group had a counterpart in any other group. Groups may be different, but they all have the same make-up, and I was always "my" person in each of a number of groups. There was nobody in any of the groups I hung out with that was like me; I was that individual for several groups. Does it have to do with when I got my driver's license and we all used to drive around a lot out in the country? We drove all through the lakes area...

A: Some.

Q: (T) We used to drive all through the hills out there at night... long drives. (L) Did something happen on one of these drives?

A: Maybe...

Q: (T) Does this have something to do with that bizarre town I came across one night and never was able to find again? Is that tied in here somehow?

A: Yes.

Q: (T) Strangest town I have ever seen. Talk about David Lynch! I was driving down through southwest New York one night. I was out of high school. I used to get stoned then too, so a lot of my experiences aren't dependable because I got stoned. I went through a town one night down there in the Southern Tier, in the Finger Lakes area, and it was the strangest thing. I have been through all these little towns, and there's usually people and stuff. Not a lot, but at least somebody around. It was about nine or ten o'clock, and I went through this town; it was two story buildings built right up to this two lane main street, with a little narrow sidewalk, and it was like driving into a canyon, and the buildings went straight up into the air. There was a streetlight every so far, but they were those little yellowish bulbs that don't cast much light on the street. There was absolutely nobody out there. There was nobody in any of the buildings, they were all boarded up and shut down. It looked like a town but it didn't look like a town. It went about four blocks. I came back out of it, turned around and drove through it again because I didn't believe it. I could never find it again, and I didn't know the name of it.

A: Discover.

Q: (S) It was the Twilight Zone... (T) Was this town..?

A: Yes.

Q: (L) You drove into another reality. (T) It wasn't really a town, was it?

A: Nope.

Q: (T) It gave me the willies. And, I turned around and drove through it a second time because I didn't believe it was there. (S) Were you by yourself? (T) Yes, I was all alone. There was nobody with me. One signal light that looked like it was out of the 1920s. Old street lamps... like a ghost town, literally. (L) What are you guys trying to tell us here about T or through T? Was the recent, connected event you mentioned private to T and happened in his life only?

A: Yes.

Q: (T) Each of my relationships then was with an individual who thought for themselves, they understood things; they had their own experiences that were different from most people, and knew that most people could not relate or understand. It doesn't have to be abduction experiences, but they have had life experiences...

A: Yes, but that is the sign of something more significant.

Q: (T) Is it the fact that I am able to form relationships with vastly different types of individuals?

A: All originate from same "plane."

Q: (L) In other words, he formed relationships with others like himself? And, did they all originate from the same plane, as in somewhere else?

A: Close.

Q: (L) Did the ship we started off with have a lot to do with interacting with all of these other people that T formed friendships and relationships with subsequent to this time?

A: Yes, but not central issue.

Q: (T) Do we all share a common experience?

A: Close.

Q: (L) Do they all share a common origin?

A: Yes.

Q: (L) And what is that origin?

A: Neormm.

Q: (L) Neormm?

A: Closest English equivalent.

Q: (L) Is that a place?

A: Yes.

Q: (L) Where is it?

A: Check star guides.

Q: (T) Is this a star? All of us are from another star that I've formed relationships like that with – the special ones that I would consider lasting?

A: In perpendicular reality.

Q: (L) All right! Where are we now? We have discovered that T has a thing called a "Perpendicular Reality" that has been running through his life and probably is an ongoing thing, is this correct?

A: Yes.

Q: (T) What is a perpendicular reality?

A: Intersection is at realm border.

Q: (L) So, in other words, you could follow along in your mind to the realm border because you have an intersecting reality with it. Is that correct?

A: No. They merge.

Q: (L) Okay, we have discovered the significance of the fact that T is part alien with a perpendicular alien reality that causes him to interact with other people who also have these perpendicular realities. What's the point? [Laughter] (S) Something to do! (J) It's a hobby.

A: "Point" is third density concept, and you need "refresher" course!

Q: (T) "Remedial Cassiopaean 101." (L) Well, I am just trying to understand what this whole thing is all about. What are we getting at here?

A: Then learn from what we communicate to you and what you already have "locked up" inside of you, i.e. *time to get the key!*

Q: (L) What I think is, maybe everybody does this, right now on the planet; there are always different groups that are forming connections with other people with whom they share an alternate reality. (J) In other words, we are all being attracted to each other? (F) Right. That makes sense. (L) In which case, what alternate reality do we share or do we share *no* alternate reality and is each person *a representative of an alternate reality different from each other and are a connection point?*

A: Latter concept is exactly correct!

Q: (T) We are what is common to each other in our group?

A: What did we say about increasing power?

Q: (L) Regarding "keys," I have heard the concept, written or talked about, that certain people, or perhaps everybody, have locked up inside themselves "pockets of energy," for lack of a better term, or knowledge as in electromagnetic patterning in their fields... and forming groups in this way would be...

A: Like putting together the pieces of the puzzle.

Q: (L) We are the pieces of the puzzle?

A: Draw on a piece of paper one perpendicular intersection.

Q: [We get paper and draw figure.] (L) Like that?

A: No, make it like an upside down "T"

Q: [T tries again] (L) Why don't you just draw it on the board for us? [Clamps pencil next to planchette on piece of paper] Okay guys, draw! [The planchette draws an inner circle surrounded by an outer circle, connected by seven spokes – rather like a wagon wheel.]

Q: (J) Is this like a crop circle?

A: Has been done, yes. Designates union of perpendicular realities.

Q: (L) Was the town that T went through one of the perpendicular reality towns?

A: Close. You need seven spokes.

Q: (L) There's that number seven again! Each person in the group is a spoke?

A: Yes.

Q: (L) Is there more to this concept that we are going to discover as we go along?

A: Of course!

Q: (L) Once the seven spokes are in place in terms of persons, is that going to increase our power/knowledge exponentially?

A: Explosively.

Q: (T) Okay, we have the image on the paper with seven spokes. What do we do with it next?

A: Open. Will fall into place, now you must ponder the significance and we must say goodnight!

When reading back over this session with hindsight, it seems to me that the "completed connection" the Cassiopaeans referred to might have been the fact that T brought our little group together with the MUFON group, which then led to the "Demo" session at the second MUFON group, and subsequently, to the "Santilli Session" which had significant repercussions later that were unforeseen by us at the time. But, actually, I think that the hints in this session really deserve deeper analysis, particularly regarding the strange stellar location designated as "Neormm" by the Cassiopaeans. This session is still a puzzle to me, and if anyone has any insights, I will appreciate hearing them.

We *did* come back to the issue of "Perpendicular Realities" a little later, and the subject was expanded in a very interesting way:

06-17-95

Q: (T) Several sessions back when we were discussing "Perpendicular Realities" you were talking about something that happened to me and that I had to look back over my life and analyze my relationships with other people from a certain point up until now and you said that this was a perpendicular reality. What is the definition of a perpendicular reality?

A: The perpendicular reality primarily, though not exclusively, refers to one's life path and how one's life path fits together in the cycle or in a wheel when connected with those of a similar life path. If you can picture an inlaid wheel formed by a circle within a circle, and adjoining partitions in a perfect balance, that would be the best representation of perpendicular reality for it does not completely involve one individual's experience, but rather a group of individual's experience for the progression of a greater purpose, if you understand what we mean. This is what we mean when we say: "perpendicular reality." Picture again, a circle within a circle adjoined by equally spaced partitions in a perfect cycle. That is perpendicular reality.

Q: (T) You had us draw this symbol and put seven spokes or partitions between the two circles.

A: Correct.

Q: (T) Is seven the optimal number?

A: Seven is always the optimal number. There are seven levels of density. This reflects through all phases of reality.

Q: (T) The people that I interacted with during this time, they also have gone on to do other things that they were supposed to be doing because of their interaction with me in this perpendicular reality that we all existed in?

A: That's correct.

Q: (T) You also said that each of us in this group came from a different perpendicular reality.

A: That is correct.

Q: (T) Is it at this point where we merge our different perpendicular realities in order to learn from each other's experiences?

A: That could be described as correct.

Q: (L) It was said at the time that the inner circle was the connection with this reality and that the outer circle and connecting segments were where the perpendicular reality is "joined with the wave." Is it implied in that statement that the forming of this conduit through these perpendicular realities is instrumental in bringing forth this wave, bringing forth this change, this dimensional shift, or density shift, and is that something that is being done in other places?

A: We wish to congratulate you for asking six questions in one. [(T) One more question and you would have a perfect perpendicular question!] Mirth!

Q: (L) Are we connected in some way with the wave, individually and as a group?

A: Well, of course. Everything is connected to the wave.

Q: (L) Are we, by connecting into this wheel, so to speak, activating the wave in some way?

A: We are not clear about your interesting interpretation there, but it is true that you have an interactive relationship with the wave... However, as stated before, you are in an interactive relationship with the wave in a sense, in that the wave is a part of your reality, always has been and always will be. And, of course, it does involve your progress through the Grand Cycle. And the perpendicular reality is again, of course, advancement from the core outward, which is yet another reflection of all reality and all that exists. Now, we wish to return to the visual representation as mentioned previously. If you notice the core circle connects with all seven sections to the outer circle. Now, picture that outer circle as being an ever expanding circle, and each one of the seven segments as being an ever-expanding line. Of course, now, this will expand outward in a circular or cyclical pattern. Please picture visually an expanding outer circle and a non-expanding inner circle. Contemplate that and then please give us your feelings as to what that represents.

Q: (L) Does it represent an expansion of our knowledge and consciousness?

A: That's part of it.

Q: (L) Does it represent also expanding influence of what and who we are on that which is around us?

A: That is correct. Contemplate if you will, *the ever-expanding outer circle and the non-expanding inner circle*, and of course the seven partitions also moving outwardly. What type of shape does that form in your mind's eye?

Q: (L) A wheel?

A: Is that all?

Q: (T) A pie?

A: Keep going.

Q: (L) An eye.

A: Now we are starting to turn it into a sphere! Why would it turn into a sphere?

Q: (L) How can it turn into a sphere?

A: How can it not!

Q: (SV) It is going in ALL directions, not just flat...

A: Is a straight line a straight line or a...

Q: (L) Oh, you're not talking about a circle?

A: We are talking about a circle. What becomes of a circle if you expand it outward forever?

Q: (J) It disappears.

A: It disappears? How can it disappear? Where does it disappear to? We ask you that, J? J?

Q: (J) Visually, as the outer circle expands, the inner circle becomes smaller and smaller until it disappears. As you continue to expand out with the outer circle, the inner circle disappears.

A: But where does it disappear to?

Q: (J) A black hole?

A: A black hole. Well, that's a possibility. But, we really didn't want you to concentrate so heavily on the smaller circle, now did we? It's the outer circle.

Q: (T) The outer circle is used to encompass more and more.

A: And what shape does it begin to take on? We want you to look at this outer circle expanding outward!

Q: (J) Are we to assume that the seven spokes remain the same size in relation to the circle?

A: Well, answer that question for yourself.

Q: (L) Okay, we are looking at it as a plane representation. As a flat surface.

A: Well, what happens to a flat surface if you extend it outward forever?

Q: (L) Well, we don't know. That, that... (SV) It keeps on going.

A: It keeps on going?

Q: (L) Yeah, bigger and flatter!

A: It does? What happens to a line if you extend it forever and ever?

Q: (L and S) It keeps on going.

A: It does? Where does it go to?

Q: (SV) Forever. (J) Back to itself. (L) We don't know that.

A: Oh, someone said "Back to itself." And why don't we know that?

Q: (L) Because we don't. It is conjectured that space is curved...

A: "Because we don't know. Now, why don't we know?

Q: (L) Because we haven't been there.

A: Had Columbus been outside of Italy and Spain?

Q: (L) Well, of course Columbus had an idea that there was something but he hadn't been there, no. But he went and checked it out.

A: Did he have just an idea?

Q: (L) Well, pretty much, I guess.

A: Hmmm. That's not the way we remember it. The way we remember it is that he had instinct and imagination and when he married his instinct with imagination, it became reality. And, when it became reality, he had created a reality which he was fully confident would be manifest in the physical third density reality. It wasn't that he was confident. He knew it to be so. He didn't stop himself by adding prejudice to the equation, which is what you are doing when you say: "Well, we don't know what happens because we have never been there!" Think logically, please. We have told you so many times that everything is a Grand Cycle. If it's a Grand Cycle, we have told you about circles within circles. We have told you about cycles. We have told you about short wave cycles and long wave cycles. Now, after all this information that you have asked of us, which we have more than happily given to you, would you expect that a straight line would just go out forever and ever and ever as a straight line? How could it possibly do that? What happens, if you take, on your third density earth, and you draw a straight line to the East or to the West or to the North or to the South...?

Q: (J) It comes all the way back to itself.

A: Right...

Q: (L) Okay, so we're living in a big globe!

A: Are we?

Q: (L) Well, that is what it sounds like, a big circle?

A: Oh, my, my, my. You need more study and learning, my dear. Need more study. Even your Albert Einstein had a theory about what happened.

Q: (L) Yes, but that was just a theory.

A: Oh, well we guess then it must be dropped. We'll never know. It's just a theory. Well, we'll just forget about it.

Q: (T) I'm still expanding the circle... (SV) Me too.

A: Very good, that was the idea. It keeps going and going and going.

Q: (L) Well, mine does too, but it hasn't come back and met anything. So, what's the point?

A: Does there need to be a point?

Q: (L) Of course!

A: Who says? We are trying to help you learn. When do you expect to shut down this process?

Q: (J) Never. (L) Gee, I hope never.

A: Then there never is a point!

Q: (J) Point taken! (L) There is no point. [Laughter.] Well, if you expand the circle outward and continue expanding it in all directions, it pulls the seven spokes with it, which encompasses more and more space in a cross section, and then turns that circle, you have a sphere.

A: Precisely. But Laura says that means we are living in a big globe. And, maybe we are.

Q: (T) Well, it wouldn't be a big globe; so to speak, it would only be a big globe within the circle. If the circle continues to expand, it would just continue to go outward and outward and the globe would become bigger and bigger and bigger... (L) You're making me nervous... (T) But it goes outward forever... cause there is no end to going out...

A: There isn't?

Q: (SV) Nope.

A: Well, then maybe there's no beginning.

Q: (T) Well, there wouldn't be a beginning, just a big, open void. An infinite void...

A: If there's no end and no beginning, then what do you have?

Q: (L) No point. (J) The here and now.

A: The here and now which are also the future and the past. Everything that was, is, and will be, all at once. This is why only a very few of your third density persons have been able to understand space travel, because even though traveling into space in your third density is every bit as third density as lying on your bed at night in your comfortable home, the time reference is taken away. Something that you hold very close to your bosom as if it were your mother. And, it is the biggest illusion that you have. We have repeatedly told you over and over that there is no time, and yet, of course, you have been so brainwashed into this concept that you cannot get rid of it no matter what you do, now can you? Imagine going out into space. You'd be lost when confronted with reality that everything is completely all at one? Would you not? Picture yourself floating around in space!

Q: (T) Does the sphere keep expanding... as the circle expands and you turn the circle 180 degrees, you get a sphere. As the sphere continues to expand it, you take a point on the outer edge of the sphere in order to take the sphere about itself; you get a donut, an ever-expanding inner tube. If you take that and twist it, you get an even larger inner tube. It just continues to expand and encompasses more space...

A: And now, when you merge densities, or traverse densities, what you have is the merging of physical reality and ethereal reality, which involves thought form versus physicality. When you can merge those perfectly, what you realize then, is that the reason there is no beginning and no end is merely because there is no need for you to contemplate a beginning or an end after you have completed your development. When you are at union with the One at Seventh density, that is when you have accomplished this and then there is no longer any need for difference between physical and ethereal forms.

Q: (SV) I want to ask one question: If there is no time, there is no past and no future; there are no past lives and no future lives, there is no such thing as reincarnation, then how can you be us...

A: Yes, there is reincarnation. You are getting ahead of yourself there. We never said there is no reincarnation.

Q: (SV) But, if there is no time? (J) It is our perception of it. (L) It is all happening simultaneously. We are having all of these lifetimes at once. (SV) Is there a way that we can connect ourselves with all our other selves?

A: Picture it this way: we will access some of your memory banks and give you another reference which, interestingly enough, fits very closely with the perpendicular reality wheel that we described earlier. You know what a slide projector looks like? To give you some feeling of what this expanded nature of reality really is, picture yourself watching a big slide presentation with a big slide wheel on the projector. At any given point along the way you are watching one particular slide. But, all the rest of the slides are present on the wheel, are they not? And, of course, this fits in with the perpendicular reality, which fits in with the circles within circles and cycles within cycles, which also fits in the Grand Cycle, which also fits in with what we have told you before: All there is is lessons. That's all there is. And we ask that you enjoy them as you are watching the slide presentation...

Q: (J) In that analogy, the light that shines through the slide, as it projects it upon the screen, is our perception.

A: And, if you look back at the center of the projector, you see the origin and essence of all creation itself, which, is Level Seven where you are in union with the One.

Now, let's go in another direction for a moment. Let's look at my presentation of Ouspensky's discussion of the fourth dimension of time, as drawn from his book, *Tertium Organum*:

We say that space is infinite – that it is illimitable in both scope and direction. (There may be some who postulate an outer limit to space, but what they propose as being outside that limit is an even greater difficulty than that of infinity.) Space, as we perceive it, has only three dimensions: length, width, and height. We define this condition as three independent directions – that is, each measurement lies at right angles to the others simultaneously.

But, this is a contradiction. For, if space is infinite, then it must possess an infinite number of lines perpendicular and not parallel to one another.

Is infinity then foolishness, and does space necessarily have a limit? If it does have a limit, in what space does our space exist? But, if space does possess an infinite number of lines perpendicular to one another, then we must ask why we can only perceive three. If we exist in a condition of mind that perceives only three dimensions, this must mean that the properties of space are created – or differentiated – by certain attributes within us. For some reason or another, the Whole is inaccessible to us.

Ouspensky wrote in an essay in 1908, entitled *The Fourth Dimension:*

> We may have very good reason for saying that we are ourselves beings of four dimensions and we are turned towards the third dimension with only one of our sides, i.e., with only a small part of our being. Only this part of us lives in three dimensions, and we are conscious only of this part as our body. The greater part of our being lives in the fourth dimension, but we are unconscious of this greater part of ourselves. Or it would be still more true to say that we live in a four-dimensional world, but are conscious of ourselves only in a three dimensional world.

The fact is, Ouspensky was greatly influenced in his thinking by Charles Howard Hinton, an English mathematician. But, long before Hinton had a clue about the ideas of the "fourth dimension," there was Georg Bernhard Riemann.

Michio Kaku tells the story in his book *Hyperspace: A Scientific Odyssey Through Parallel Universes, Time Warps, and the 10th Dimension* (Oxford University Press, 1994) and I have pretty much followed his outline, though reducing the length and complexity of the story.

On June 10, 1854, at the University of Göttingen, Germany, Riemann gave a lecture entitled *On the Hypotheses Which Lie at the Foundation of Geometry*, sounding the death knell of the classical, linear view of the universe and introduced the theory of higher dimensions. As I have written elsewhere, the prevailing view of physics eventually filters down to affect all our cultural and social interactions, and it was only 30 or so years after Riemann's talk that the "mysterious fourth dimension" would begin to profoundly affect art, philosophy and literature.

Sixty years after, Einstein used four-dimensional Riemannian geometry to explain the creation of the Universe and its evolution, and 130 years later, physicists would use ten-dimensional geometry to attempt to unite all the laws of the physical universe.

Euclidean geometry holds that space is three dimensional and "flat." In flat space, angles in a triangle always add to 180 degrees which omits the possibility that space can be curved, as on a sphere. For two thousand years, Euclid was "king" and all of Christendom marveled at his insights. Cathedrals were built and civilizations were born according to the principles of Euclid. Euclid and the Church – strange, but devoted bedfellows.

Most people can remember struggling with the theorems of Euclid: that the circumference of a circle is *pi* times the diameter, and that parallel lines never intersect. It was always pretty standard stuff except for one little problem that most people aren't aware of: try as they would for centuries, the greatest mathematicians simply could not *prove* these deceptively simple propositions. As long as you stayed in "flatland," you were safe with Euclid. The instant you wandered into curved space, Euclid was your nemesis.

Riemann rebelled against the so-called "mathematical precision" of Euclid, because it was apparent to him that the natural world is *not* made up of Euclid's flat, idealized, geometric figures. It was clear that the *real* world was made up of curves that bend and twist in infinite variety.

Euclid said, "It is obvious" that a point has no dimension at all. A line has one dimension: length. A plane has two dimensions: length and breadth. A solid has three dimensions: length, breadth, and height. And that's it! There is no more! Nothing has four dimensions, according to Euclid.

Another Greek who has dominated our culture for a very long time, Aristotle, stated categorically that the fourth spatial dimension was impossible. Ptolemy, the Egyptianized Greek went even further and constructed a "proof" that the fourth dimension was impossible. If you draw three mutually perpendicular lines, and then try to draw a fourth line that is perpendicular to the other three lines, you will discover that it is impossible. More than three mutually perpendicular lines are not only impossible to draw, they are impossible to comprehend.

But, what Ptolemy *really* did was to demonstrate that it is impossible to visualize the fourth dimension with our three-dimensional brains! Today, mathematicians and physicists *know* that there are many objects that can be shown to exist mathematically, which cannot be visualized.

As Michio Kaku writes, "Ptolemy may go down in history as the man who opposed two great ideas in science: the sun-centered solar system and the fourth dimension."

It is a curious thing that many mathematicians, obviously deeply influenced by Christianity, and their faith in the Bible as the "True and only word of God," regularly denounced the idea of the fourth dimension calling it a "monster in nature." And so, Euclid and the Church dominated our minds, brainwashing humanity into thinking that things cannot exist that we cannot picture in our minds. It was, oddly enough when you consider the purported "spiritual goals" of religion, a curious descent into gross materialism.

As mentioned, the story of Riemann and how and why he prepared his famous lecture is nicely told in Michio Kaku's *Hyperspace*, well worth reading. But, what concerns us here is that Riemann developed the idea of the *metric tensor* and also was one of the first to discuss *multiple connected spaces, or wormholes*. To visualize this, take two sheets of paper and place one on top of the other. Make a little cut on each with knife or scissors, and glue the sheets together along the two cuts only. If a bug lives on the top sheet, he may one day accidentally walk into the cut and find himself on the bottom sheet. He will be puzzled because everything is in the wrong place. After much experimentation, the bug may discover that he can re-emerge into his original world by passing again through the cut. As long as he walks around the cut, everything is fine and looks normal, but when he tries to take the "short-cut" he has a problem.

Lewis Carroll used "Riemann's cuts" with great effect in his book *Through the Looking-Glass*. Riemann's cut *is* the looking glass.

Soon after Riemann, researchers all over Europe began to popularize the idea of the fourth dimension for the layperson. As it happened, Riemann's mathematics was so far in advance of the thinking of the day that there was no *physical* principle to guide further research. It was only after another hundred years had passed that physicists even caught up with him! But, one thing that *did* happen was the realization that a being from the fourth dimension would have what would seem to us, God-like powers. Kaku writes:

> Imagine being able to walk through walls.
>
> You wouldn't have to bother with opening doors; you could pass right through them. You wouldn't have to go around buildings; you could enter them through their walls and pillars and out through the back wall. You wouldn't have to detour around mountains; you could step right into them. When hungry, you could simply reach through the refrigerator door without opening it. You could never be accidentally locked outside your car; you could simply step through the car door.
>
> Imagine being able to disappear or reappear at will.
>
> Instead of driving to school or work, you would just vanish and rematerialize in your classroom or office. You wouldn't need an airplane to visit far-away places, you could just vanish and rematerialize where you wanted. You would never be stuck in city traffic during rush hours; you and your car would simply disappear and rematerialize at your destination.
>
> Imagine having x-ray eyes.
>
> You would be able to see accidents happening from a distance. After vanishing and rematerializing at the site of any accident, you

could see exactly where the victims were, even if they were buried under debris.

Imagine being able to reach into an object without opening it.

You could extract the sections from an orange without peeling or cutting it. You would be hailed as a master surgeon, with the ability to repair the internal organs of patients without ever cutting the skin, thereby greatly reducing pain and the risk of infection. You would simply reach into the person's body, passing directly through the skin, and perform the delicate operation.

Imagine what a criminal could do with these powers. He could enter the most heavily guarded bank. He could see through the massive doors of the vault for the valuables and case and reach inside and pull them out. He could then stroll outside as the bullets from the guards passed right through him.

With these powers, no prison could hold a criminal. No secrets could be kept from us. No treasures could be hidden from us. No obstructions could stop us. We would truly be miracle workers, performing feats beyond the comprehension of mortals. We would also be omnipotent.

What being could possess such God-like power? The answer: a being from a higher-dimensional world.

In 1877, a scandal in London brought the idea of the fourth dimension to public awareness in a big way. A psychic named Henry Slade was holding séances in the homes of prominent people, and was arrested for fraud "using subtle crafts and devices, by palmistry and otherwise" (Kaku).

Slade was convicted of fraud by the court, but he insisted that he could prove his innocence by duplicating his feats before a scientific commission and Johann Zöllner, professor of physics and astronomy at the University of Leipzig, gathered together a group of scientists who were willing to take a scientific look. Their reason for doing so was made public and consisted in declaring that the feats Slade claimed to be doing were, indeed, possible by manipulating objects in the fourth dimension! In so doing, the media coverage gave the public a real idea of just exactly what was possible in this strange world of ours.

Among Slade's defenders were William Crookes, inventor of the cathode ray tube; Wilhelm Weber, Gauss's collaborator and the mentor of Riemann; J.J. Thompson, who won the Nobel Prize in 1906 for the discovery of the electron; Lord Rayleigh, one of the greatest classical physicists of the late nineteenth century and winner of the Nobel Prize in 1904. Kaku writes:

> First, Slade was given two separate, unbroken wooden rings. Could he push one wooden ring past the other, so that they were intertwined without breaking it? If Slade succeeded, Zöllner wrote, it would "represent a miracle, that is, a phenomenon which our conceptions heretofore of physical and organic processes would be absolutely incompetent to explain."
>
> Second, he was given the shell of a sea snail, which twisted either to the right or to the left. Could Slade transform a right-handed shell into a left-handed shell and vice versa?
>
> Third, he was given a closed loop of rope made of dried animal gut. Could he make a knot in the circular rope without cutting it?
>
> Slade was also given variations of these tests. For example, a rope was tied into a right-handed knot and its ends were sealed with wax and impressed with Zöllner's personal seal. Slade was asked to untie the knot, without breaking the wax seal, and retie the rope in a left-handed knot. Since knots can always be untied in the fourth dimension, this feat should be easy for a fourth-dimensional person. Slade was also asked to remove the contents of a sealed bottle without breaking the bottle.
>
> Could Slade demonstrate this astounding ability?
>
> Today we realize that the manipulation of higher-dimensional space, as claimed by Slade, would require a technology far in advance of anything possible on this planet for the conceivable future. However, what is interesting about this notorious case is that Zöllner correctly concluded that Slade's feats of wizardry could be explained if one could somehow move objects through the fourth dimension.
>
> For example, in three dimensions, separate rings cannot be pushed through each other until they intertwine without breaking them. Similarly, closed, circular pieces of rope cannot be twisted into knots without cutting them. However, in higher dimensions, knots are easily unraveled and rings can be intertwined. This is because there is "more room" in which to move ropes past each other and rings into each other. If the fourth dimension existed, ropes and rings could be lifted off our universe, intertwined, and then returned to our world. In fact, in the fourth dimensions, knots can never remain tied. They can always be unraveled without cutting the rope. This feat is impossible in three dimensions, but trivial in the fourth. The third dimension, as it turns out, is the only dimensions in which knots stay knotted!

Similarly, in three dimensions it is impossible to convert a rigid left-handed object into a right-handed one. Humans are born with hearts on their left side, and no surgeon, no matter how skilled, can reverse human internal organs. This is possible (as first pointed out by mathematician August Mobius in 1827) only if we lift the body out of our universe, rotate it in the fourth dimension, and then reinsert it back into our universe.

Zöllner sparked a storm of controversy when, publishing in both the *Quarterly Journal of Science and Transcendental Physics*, he claimed that Slade amazed his audiences with these "miraculous" feats during séances in the presence of distinguished scientists.

Zöllner's spirited defense of Slade's feats was sensationalized throughout London society. Supporting Zöllner's claims was his circle of reputable scientists, including Weber and Crookes. These were not average scientists, but masters of the art of science and seasoned observers of experiment. They had spent a lifetime working with natural phenomena, and now before their eyes, Slade was performing feats that were possible only if spirits lived in the fourth dimension.

There were, of course, savage critics and detractors but, in my opinion, none of their arguments hold water. In fact, such evidence has been demonstrated time and again over the centuries, far into the distant past, and there have always been detractors and "savages" criticizing on behalf of their materialist masters or gods.

The interesting thing about Kaku's descriptions of the abilities of a "fourth dimensional being" is that they happen to be precisely the type of things that characterize the "Alien Phenomenon" that interacts with our reality to a greater and greater extent with each passing year. What's more, there is a great body of evidence that beings with such powers have interacted with humanity for a very long time, though in ages past they were called fairies, demons, vampires, and so forth. Further, these abilities that are being described as "fourth dimensional," are exactly what the Cassiopaeans term "fourth density," rather than dimension.

In 1884, after a decade of controversy, Edwin Abbot, headmaster of the City of London School, wrote the novel *Flatland: A Romance of Many Dimensions by a Square*. Abbot was a clergyman, which wasn't too surprising because they now had a "place" to put heaven and hell and angels and demons – in the fourth dimension (which probably wasn't too far off in terms of accuracy!). The unique thing about *Flatland* was that is was also a biting satire of social criticism. Abbot poked fun at the pious people who denied the possibility of the fourth dimension. It is a book well worth reading for the many examples it makes of bigotry and narrow mindedness that prevail, even today, in scientific and religious communities.

Flatland paved the way for more artistic fourth dimensional expressions, including works by Oscar Wilde, H.G. Wells, Lewis Carroll, Joseph Conrad and others. The development of many of the "occult societies" including Theosophy was influenced by the ideas of the fourth dimension. It was, as we could say today, the "latest fad" of that time.

This had a good side and a bad side. On the bad side, serious scientists sort of "distanced" themselves from the "tabloid like" nature of the subject just as they distance themselves from anything having to do with "aliens" today. On the good side, it became a cultural metaphor. Cubism and Expressionism were influenced by the fourth dimensional non-Euclidean geometries.

Charles Howard Hinton brought the fourth dimension to America. At Oxford, Hinton had been trying to figure out ways to visualize the fourth dimension. As a mathematician, he knew that one cannot visualize a four-dimensional object in its entirety, but you can visualize a cross section of one.

After some personal problems, Hinton came to America, worked for a time at Princeton, and later at the Patent Office in Washington. He spent years developing clever ways for the average person to "see" four-dimensional objects. Eventually, he perfected special cubes that, if one tried hard enough, could allow one to visualize hypercubes, or cubes in four dimensions. These would eventually be called Hinton's cubes. He coined the name for an "unraveled" hypercube: *Tesseract*.

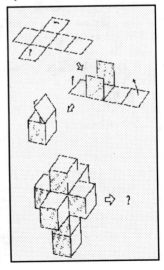

Flatlanders cannot visualize a cube, but they can conceptualize a three-dimensional cube by unraveling it. To a Flatlander, a cube, when unfolded, resembles a cross, consisting of six squares as the figure below shows. In the same way, we cannot visualize a four-dimensional hypercube but, if we "unfold" it, we have *a series of cubes arranged in a cross like Tesseract*. Although this looks like a "solid, stable" object of three dimensions, the idea is to understand that it is really just our representation of the hypercube which is "wrapped up" in 4 dimensional space the same way the "cross" figure "wraps up" into a cube when going from 2 dimensional space to 3 dimensional space.

As the reader might guess, Hinton's cubes soon became objects of "mystical importance." It was claimed that a person could catch glimpses of the fourth dimension by meditating on one of them. His disciples spent hours contemplating these cubes until they attained the ability to mentally rearrange and reassemble them via the fourth dimension into a hypercube. Those who could perform this mental feat, it was said, would attain the highest state of nirvana!

Hinton's greatest contribution to the matter of the fourth dimension was his popularization of higher dimensional figures. These are useful in many ways because even *professional mathematicians conceptualize higher-dimensional objects via their cross sections, their unraveling, and their shadows.*

The reader might want to have a look at *The Monster from Nowhere* by Nelson Bond, which describes how a monster from the fourth dimension might manifest in our own. There are some bizarre descriptions that actually reflect some cases of "alien manifestation" in our own times.

Now, where are we with all of this?

I think we can understand that everyone has a "connection" to The Wave, or Realm Border, via a fourth dimension-like "cut" or wormhole called a "Perpendicular Reality." Whether they can access it or not is another question. And, whether it needs more than one person to "produce" or "manifest" the "cut" is still another. If the latter idea is correct, we might conjecture that groups of seven individuals, if they are the *right* seven individuals (determined by each group dynamic) can interact in such a way as to bring exponential knowledge and awareness to each and every member of the group, thereby "opening" the cut, or wormhole, is a further consideration.

Such groups would be called "conduits" as the Cassiopaeans have denoted them, and, as we learned earlier, a conduit is a sort of "escape hatch" that can be activated upon the arrival of The Wave.

But, exactly how might such a thing work? Well, as we went along, more bits and pieces of the puzzle came our way though, at this point, the Santilli session was the last time The Wave was discussed for almost a year. We wouldn't come back to it until June 1996 when much water had gone over the dam and under the bridge. Changes, changes, changes.[33]

When it finally was discussed again, it was because I started off with a question about something that was seemingly unrelated. And, in this case, the "wave" that was brought up did not seem, at that moment, to be related to The Wave, as we are discussing it. It was only later that we began to suspect a connection.

Just to give a little background about what prompted the questions that led to the next series of clues, I had purchased a book entitled *The Sufi Path of Knowledge* by William Chittick at some point simply because I wanted to be better informed about the Sufis as a result of my interest in the writings of Ouspensky and Gurdjieff. I had even asked a bit about Ouspensky's presentation of 2nd dimensional awareness relating to what the Cassiopaeans called "2nd density."

02-11-95

Q: (L) Earlier we were reading from Ouspensky's Tertium Organum about perceptions. Was this a fairly accurate description of the state of our perceptions and the state of 2nd density perceptions?

A: Yes.

Let me note again that it seems that the mathematical explication of dimensions is more in line with what the Cassiopaeans are describing as *densities*, while "alternate realities" is more along the line of the "popular" understanding of dimensions. There is certainly a lot of misunderstanding and misconception out there amongst many New Age gurus regarding these subjects. And, the sad thing is that they use the words without any comprehension of the mathematical precision and deeper meanings, and many people are being fed a load of hooey with these "word salads." At the same time, there are many who have the understanding, but haven't got the proper vocabulary to express it, and thus the conflict between inspired perception and science is endlessly perpetuated. But, that's a story for another time.

During and after the period of deep level change in my own life, I have to admit that I was really pretty angry with the Cassiopaeans. I mean, here they were, supposedly 6th density light beings who had been chatting with us for some time, who, one would think, could

---

[33] It was during this period that I asked my ex for a divorce and Tom French has described my condition quite well in his article. The interested reader can find the piece on the Times website at www.sptimes.com.

advise me in ways that would prevent pain and suffering, or dire and dreadful events, and all I had experienced from the moment I began to put their suggestions into effect was constant, unmitigated attack on my psyche, my person, and even my family. I complained to them one night:

02-11-96

Q: (L) I have written to a *lot* of people... when am I going to find what I am looking for?

A: Did we not tell you, did we not advise you about the network??!??

Q: (L) Of course...

A: And what did you do?

Q: (L) Well, I got online as soon as I could...

A: And what happened?

Q: (L) The Lizzies tried to kill me! [laughter]

A: The Lizard Force, i.e. STS, has been attacking you since day one. We have been advising you only for 1.5 years, as you measure it.

Q: (L) The situation is such that I am running out of force from working against this constant oppression and opposition. Can you tell me if I will ever have some peace of mind so that I can continue to function?

A: Have we?

And, they had... in many subtle ways. The only problem was, it was never specific. It was like being told there was a treasure in a labyrinth that I was supposed to find, and being put into it blindfolded. Sure, the Cassiopaeans were there on the side sort of whispering, "You're getting warm now! Oops! You're cold... colder... ICE cold...! Okay, yes... getting warm... warmer... hot, hot!"

But, that was something of a crazy way to live. I didn't realize at the time that they were teaching me to discern things in a way and at a level that is rarely accessed by even those who spend their lives in the realms of metaphysics and the paranormal. I was just frustrated and angry like a child who was having a hard time doing math, not realizing how valuable the practice lessons would become.

But, it was a process that seemed to be taking forever. Several months went by with no sessions because I was ill or depressed or just too tired to make the effort. When we finally did have another session at one point, I complained again:

06-01-96

Q: (L) Several people have pointed out to me, only since we have begun this channeling project that all these dreadful things have happened in my life. My life is a shambles!

A: "Dreadful is subjective."

Q: (L) I would say that the physical things that have happened to me, the collapse of my marriage, the things that have happened to my children, are pretty damn dreadful, subjectively or otherwise!

A: Before these changes began to manifest, you were deeper into the "deadly illusion" than you are now. Emergence is, by its very nature, uncomfortable. But, it has and will, empower you, we promise!!!!!!!!

Q: (L) It is a very trying time now. I am having a difficult time just coping.

A: And there have been others, and will be others, but that does not mean that the rewards will be slight. You are on a path of destiny, and there is no turning back now.

In the frame of mind I was, that sounded foreboding! I had no enthusiasm for anything, and I was in a constant state of physical crisis from one illness after another. But, during the periods of sickness or tiredness and/or depression, I began to idly flip through this book on the teachings of Muhyi al-Din Muhammad ibn 'Ali ibn al-'Arabi which had sat unopened on the shelf for a couple of years.

As I began to read bits and pieces, I was stunned at the similarity of the teachings to what the Cassiopaeans had been saying. I was also pretty excited to find that the very things I was suffering were not unusual for someone who was receiving what was called an "unveiling." This gave me the heart to decide on another session at which the following exchange took place:

06-15-96

Q: (L) As you know, I have been studying the Sufi teachings, and I am discovering so many similarities in these Sufi "unveilings" to what we have been receiving through this source, that I am really quite amazed, to say the least. So, my question is: could what we are doing here be considered an ongoing, incremental, "unveiling," as they call it?

A: Yes.

Q: (L) Now, from what I am reading, in the process of unveiling, at certain points, when the knowledge base has been sufficiently expanded, inner unveilings then begin to occur. Is this part of the present process?

A: Maybe.

Q: (L) My experience has been, over the past couple of years, that whenever there is a significant increase in knowledge, that it is sort of cyclical – I go through a depression before I can assimilate – and it is like an inner transformation from one level to another. Is there something we can do, and if so, is it desirable, to increase or facilitate this process in some way?

A: It is a natural process, let it be.

Q: (L) One of the things that Al-'Arabi writes about is the ontological levels of being. Concentric circles, so to speak, of states of being. And each state defines relationships in terms of knowledge and awareness. At each higher level you are closer to a direct relationship with the core of existence, and on the outer edges, you are in closer relationship with matter. This pretty well explicates the 7 densities you have described for us and he says there are 7 also. He also talks about the "outraying" and the "inward moving" toward knowledge. My thought was that certain beings, such as fourth density STS, and other STS beings of third density, who think that they are creating a situation where they will accrue power to themselves, may, in fact, be part of the "outraying" or dispersion into matter. Is this a correct perception?

A: Close.

Q: (L) Al-'Arabi says, and this echoes what you have said, that you can stay in the illusion where you are, you can move downward or upward. Is this, in part, whichever direction you choose, a function of your position on the cycle?

A: It is more complex than that.

Q: (L) Well, I am sure of that. Al-'Arabi presents a very complex analysis and he probably didn't know it all either... Nevertheless, it almost word-for-word reflects things that have been given directly to us through this source.

A: Now, learn, read, research all you can about *unstable gravity waves*.

Q: (L) Okay. Unstable gravity waves. I'll see what I can find. Is there something more about this?

A: Meditate too!

Q: (L) Yes. Well, they have been telling us to meditate. Have you been meditating, Frank? (F) Not lately.

A: We mean for you, Laura, to meditate about unstable gravity waves as part of research. Unstable gravity waves unlock as yet unknown secrets of quantum physics to make the picture crystal clear.

Q: (L) Gravity seems to be a property of matter. Is that correct?

A: And... antimatter!

Q: (L) Is the gravity that is a property of antimatter "antigravity?" Or, is it just gravity on the other side, so to speak?

A: Binder. Gravity binds all that is physical with all that is ethereal through unstable gravity waves!!!

Q: (L) Is antimatter what we refer to as "ethereal" existence?

A: Pathway to. Doorway to.

Q: (L) Do unstable gravity waves emanate from 7th density?

A: Throughout. There is no emanation point.

Q: (L) So, they are a property or attribute of the existence of matter, and the binder of matter to ethereal ideation?

A: Sort of, but they are a property of anti-matter, too!

Q: (L) So, through unstable gravity waves, you can access other densities?

A: Everything.

Q: (L) Can you generate them mechanically?

A: Generation is really collecting and dispersing.

Q: (L) Okay, what kind of a device would collect and disperse gravity waves? Is this what spirals do?

A: On the way to. When you wrote Noah (The Noah Syndrome) where did you place gravity?

Q: (L) I thought that gravity was an indicator of the consumption of electricity; that gravity was a byproduct of a continuous flow of electrical energy...

A: Gravity is no byproduct! It is the central ingredient of all existence!

Q: (L) I was evaluating by electric flow and consumption... and I was thinking that electricity was evidence of some sort of consciousness, and that gravity was evidence that a planet that had it, had life...

A: We have told you before that planets and stars are windows. And where does the gravity go?

Q: (L) Well, where does gravity go? The sun is a window. Even our planet must be a window!

A: You have it too!! Gravity is all there is.

Q: (L) Is light the emanation of gravity?

A: No.

Q: (L) What is light?

A: Gravity. Gravity is "God."

Q: (L) But, I thought God was light?

A: If gravity is everything, what isn't it? Light is energy expression generated by gravity. Please name something that is not gravity.

Q: (L) Well, if gravity is everything, there is nothing that is not gravity, well, fine! What is absolute nothingness?

A: A mere thought.

Q: (L) So, there is no such thing as non-existence?

A: Yes, there is.

Q: (L) Do thoughts produce gravity?

A: Yes.

Q: (L) Does sound produce gravity?

A: Yes.

Q: (L) Can sound manipulate gravity?

A: Yes.

Q: (L) Can it be done with the human voice?

A: Yes.

Q: (L) Can it be done tonally or by power through thought?

A: Both. Gravity is manipulated by sound when thought manipulated by gravity chooses to produce sound, which manipulates gravity.

Q: (L) Now, did the fellow who built the Coral Castle[34] spin in his airplane seat while thinking his manipulations into place?

---

[34] Coral Castle was built in the early 20th century by an eccentric Latvian recluse named Edward Leedskalnin. Edward Leedskalnin was a 100 pound – 5 foot tall man – who wound up in Homestead, Florida – on a ten-acre tract of land just south of Miami, Florida. Somehow he managed to single-handedly lift and maneuver blocks of coral weighing up to 30 tons each and create not only a castle but other things. How Edward did his work has never been discovered, though he labored for 30 years. He worked alone – at night – and seemed to know when he was being watched. On those occasions – he never lifted any of the stones. Many articles claim that he found the same secrets of levitation as those used by the supposed builders of the Pyramids of Egypt – among other megalithic sites around the world whose creation remain unexplained.

Edward Leedskalnin was quoted as saying, "I have discovered the secrets of the pyramids, and have found out how the Egyptians and the ancient builders in Peru,

A: No. He spun when gravity chose to manipulate him to spin in order to manipulate gravity.

Q: (L) Does gravity have consciousness?

A: Yes.

Q: (L) Is it ever possible for the individual to do the choosing, or is it gravity that *is* him that chose?

A: The gravity that was inside him was all the gravity in existence.

Q: (L) Well, I thought the Sufis were tough! (F) Well, it's probably because of your studies that this door opened. (L) Good grief! What have I done! All right. I am confused.

A: No you are not.

Q: (L) Then, just put it this way: I am befuddled and overloaded.

A: Befuddling is fun!

Q: (L) Well, I guess that if any of this is going to be of particular significance to us, then we will certainly find out the details as we go along.

A: How many times do we have to tell you?!?! The entire sum total of all existence exists within each of you, and vice versa.

Q: (L) Then what is the explanation for the "manyness" that we perceive?

A: Perception of 3rd density.

Q: (L) So, the entire universe is inside me... okay, that's... I understand. Oddly enough, I do. The problem is accessing it, stripping away the veils.

A: That is the fun part.

Q: (L) So, the fellow who built the Coral Castle was able to access this. Consistently or only intermittently?

A: Partially.

Q: (L) According to what I understand, at the speed of light, there is no mass, no time, and no gravity. How can this be?

A: No mass, no time, but yes, gravity.

Q: (L) A photon has gravity?

A: Gravity supercedes light speed.

Yucatan, and Asia, with only primitive tools, raised and set in place blocks of stone weighing many tons!"

In total, Edward quarried over eleven hundred tons of coral rock for his castle, using tools fashioned from wrecking-yard junk, never revealing how he managed to rise, and position, the massive coral blocks that make up the compound.

Q: (L) Gravity waves are faster than light?

A: Yes.

Q: (L) What would make a gravity wave unstable?

A: Utilization.

Q: (L) I feel like I am missing a really big point here...

A: You are, but you can only find it at your own pace. And on that note, good night.

By this time, all of those who have thought, from time to time, that I am a little slow on the uptake, are convinced of it! It is true that I had read and studied for many years to discover the secrets of our existence in this world, and I had thought, at one time, I had a pretty good handle on all of it for a layperson. Now, all of that was just being tossed out the window and I was back in first grade, or so it seemed. And, in this school, I was apparently *not* the brightest student!

There are a number of points in this last session that strike me (in retrospect, of course!) as being worthy of keeping in mind as we go along in solving this puzzle of how to get out of Oz and back to Kansas, and they are:

> Unstable gravity waves unlock as yet unknown secrets of quantum physics to make the picture crystal clear.
>
> Gravity seems to be a property of matter and antimatter! Antimatter is the pathway or doorway to "ethereal" existence. Gravity binds all that is physical with all that is ethereal through unstable gravity waves!!!
>
> Thus, through unstable gravity waves, you can access not only other densities, but also everything else.
>
> Mechanical "generation" of gravity waves is really collecting and dispersing.
>
> Spirals are "On the way to" a mechanical means of collecting and dispersing gravity waves.
>
> Gravity is the central ingredient of all existence! You have it too!!
>
> Thoughts produce gravity. And, by relation, so does knowledge and awareness. Remembering, of course, that knowledge and awareness are the "keys" to forming a conduit, and we think that a "conduit" is a Perpendicular Reality, or something similar to Riemann's Cut, or a Wormhole.

I don't know if you, the reader, are thinking what I am thinking about all of this, but keep the above in mind as we continue to try to discover the nature of The Wave and how best to be prepared to interact with it to our benefit.

CHAPTER 6
ANIMAL PSYCHOLOGY
OR
THAT WHICH WAS A, WILL BE A. THAT WHICH WAS NOT-A, WILL BE NOT-A. EVERYTHING WAS AND WILL BE EITHER A OR NOT-A.

02-11-95

Q: (L) Earlier we were reading from Ouspensky's Tertium Organum about perceptions, was this a fairly accurate description of the state of our perceptions and the state of 2nd density perceptions?

A: Yes.

Q: (L) Okay, now making a jump with that, as to fourth density perception, is the fourth density perception...

A: Wait and see.

I know that a number of you are wondering about that remark about Ouspensky's description of the perceptions of 2nd density which was mentioned in Chapter 5 because you have written to ask me what, exactly, it was. Before I get into the Cassiopaean discussion here, I want to quote that passage we discussed because the issue will come up again in this chapter, and the reader might like to be familiar with what it says because everyone seems to want to know exactly *why* it is, and *how* it is, that we can be living in a world of such vastly different perceptions, and that these can have so profound an impact on us that it is possible that *we live and move among beings that we cannot perceive.*

There is also the issue of what our own perceptions might be like after "graduation" to fourth density, and that is a question we would all like to have answered. So, perhaps, in his speculations on the matter, Ouspensky gave us some clues, though it is pretty certain that it was not all correct.

In fact, Ark and I have debated rather long over whether to share this extract or not because of what he perceives to be serious flaws in Ouspensky's "scientific arguments." Ark says they are not scientific at all and that Ouspensky makes leaps of assumption and statements without proof.

That may be true, but the point of the passage was to get something of an inkling of what might be the differences between human and animal experience of the world around us so that we might have a framework from which to speculate further.

The extract is going to be a little long, but I just didn't see how I could shorten it without really losing something important. Even though the language is a little "dated," since it was written in the 20's or earlier, Ouspensky is pretty concise and economical with his words and there are very few that are "extra." But, the end result will be that, even for those who cannot just go out and buy the book, there will be a good understanding of what we are talking about from here on out when we talk about density "perceptions." And it is this idea of the differences that I want to convey, not necessarily the specifics as outlined by Ouspensky. So, please read it through even if you don't at first see the relevance, and you may be surprised at some of the ideas that will start popping up!

From Tertium Organum:

> The basic unit of our perception is a sensation. A sensation is an elementary change in the state of our inner life, produced, or so it appears to us, either by some change in the state of the outer world in relation to our inner life, or by a change in our inner life in relation to the outer world. ...It is sufficient to define a sensation as an elementary change in the state of the inner life. Experiencing a sensation, we assume it to be, so to speak, a reflection of some kind of change in the external world.
>
> The sensations experienced by us leave a certain trace in our memory. In accumulating, memories of sensations begin to blend in our consciousness into groups according to their similarity, to become associated, to be put together, or to be contrasted. Sensations, usually experienced in close connection with one another, will arise in our memory preserving the same connection. And gradually, out of memories of sensations there are formed representations.
>
> Representations are, so to speak, group memories of sensations. In the formation of representations, the grouping of sensations follows

two clearly defined directions. The first direction is according to the character of the sensations: thus sensation of yellow colour will be linked with other sensations of yellow colour, and sensation of acid taste, with other sensations of acid taste. The second direction is according to the time of receiving the sensation.

When one group, forming one representation, contains different sensations experienced simultaneously, the memory of this definite group of sensations is attributed to a common cause. The "common cause" is projected into the external world, as the object; and it is assumed that the given representation reflects the real properties of this object.

Such a group memory constitutes a representation, as for instance, the representation of a tree – this tree. Into this group enters the green colour of the leaves, their smell, their shade, the sound of the wind in the branches, and so on. All these things, taken together, form as it were, the focus of rays emitted by our mind and gradually focused on the external object, which may coincide with it either badly or well.

In the further complexities of mental life, memories of representations undergo the same process as memories of sensations. In accumulating, memories of representations or "images of representation" become associated along the most varied lines, are put together, contrasted, form groups and, in the end, give rise to concepts.

Thus, out of the various sensations experienced at different times (in groups), there arises in a child the representation of a tree (this tree), and later, out of the images of representations of different trees is formed the concept of a tree, i.e. not of this particular tree but of a tree in general. The formation of concepts leads to the formation of words and the appearance of speech.

Speech consists of words; every word expresses a concept. A concept and a word are really the same thing, only the one (the concept) stands, as it were, for the inner aspect, while the other (the word) stands for the outer aspect. The word is the algebraic sign of a thing.

In our speech words express concepts or ideas. Ideas are broader concepts; they are not a group sign for similar representations, but embrace groups of dissimilar representations, or even groups of concepts. Thus an idea is a complex or an abstract concept.

At the present moment an average man, taken as a standard, has three units of mental life – sensation, representation and concept.

Observation further shows us that in some people at certain moments there appears, as it were, a fourth unit of mental life, which different authors and schools call by different names, but in which the element of perception of the element of ideas is always connected with the emotional element. If Kant's idea is true, if space with its characteristics is a property of our consciousness and not a property of the external world, then the three-dimensionality of the world must in some way be dependent on the constitution of our mental apparatus.

Concretely, the question may be put in this way: What is the relation of the three-dimensional extension of the world to the fact that our mental apparatus contains sensations, representations and concepts, and that they stand exactly in this order?

We have a mental apparatus of this kind and the world is three-dimensional. How to prove that the three-dimensionality of the world depends on this particular constitution of our mental apparatus?

If we were able to alter our mental apparatus and observe that the world around us changed with these alterations, this would prove to us the dependence of the properties of space on the properties of our mind. If the above mentioned higher form of inner life, which now appears only accidentally depending on some little-known conditions, could be rendered as definite, as precise, as obedient to our will as a concept, and if, through this, the number of characteristics of space increased, i.e. if space, instead of being three-dimensional, became four dimensional, this would confirm our supposition and prove Kant's idea that space with its properties is the form of our sense perception.

If we could reduce the number of units of our mental life and deliberately deprive ourselves or some other man of concepts, leaving his or our mind to operate by representations and sensations alone; and if, through this, the number of characteristics of the space surrounding us diminished, i.e. if for that man the world were to become two-dimensional instead of three-dimensional and, with a further limitation of his mental apparatus, i.e. with depriving him of representations, it were to become one-dimensional, this would confirm our surmise and Kant's thought could be regarded as proved.

Thus, Kant's idea could be proved experimentally if we were able to ascertain that for a being possessing nothing but sensations the world is one-dimensional; for a being possessing sensations and representations it is two-dimensional; and for a being possessing, in addition to concepts and ideas, also higher forms of perception, the world is four-dimensional.

Kant's proposition regarding the subjective character of the idea of space could be taken as proved if:

a) For a being possessing nothing but sensations, our entire world with all its variety of forms appears as one line; if the universe of this being had one dimension, i.e. if this being were one-dimensional by virtue of the properties of his perception; and

b) For a being possessing the capacity of forming representations in addition to his ability of experiencing sensations, the world had a two-dimensional extension, i.e. if our entire world with its blue skies, clouds, green trees, mountains and precipices, appeared to him merely as a plane; if the universe of this being had only two dimensions, that is, if this being were two-dimensional by virtue of the properties of his perception.

More briefly, Kant's proposition would be proved if we saw that for a given subject the number of characteristics of the world changed according to the change of his mental apparatus.

It does not seem possible to carry out such an experiment of reducing mental characteristics, for we do not know how to restrict our own or someone else's mental apparatus with the ordinary means at our disposal. Experiments of augmenting mental characteristics exist but, for many different reasons, they are not sufficiently convincing. The main reason is that an increase of mental faculties produces in our inner world so much that is new, that this new masks any changes which take place simultaneously in our usual perceptions of the world. We feel the new but cannot exactly define the difference.

A whole series of teachings and religious and philosophical doctrines have as their professed or hidden aim precisely this expansion of consciousness. This is the aim of mysticism of all times and all religions, the aim of occultism, the aim of the Eastern Yoga. But the question of the expansion of consciousness requires special study.

In the meantime, in order to prove the contention stated above about the change of the world as a result of a change in the mental apparatus, it is sufficient to examine the hypothesis about the possibility of a lesser number of mental characteristics.

If we do not know how to carry out experiments in this direction, perhaps observation is possible. We must ask ourselves the question: Are there in the world beings whose mental life is below ours in the required sense?

Such beings, whose mental life is below ours, undoubtedly exist. They are animals. We know very little about what constitutes the difference between the mental processes of an animal and the mental processes of a man; our ordinary 'conversational psychology' is altogether ignorant of it. As a rule we entirely deny the existence of reason in animals, or, on the contrary, we ascribe to them our own psychology, but 'limited' – though how and in what respect it is limited, we do not know. And then we say that an animal has no reason but has instinct. But we have a very hazy idea of what instinct may mean. I am speaking now not only of popular, but also of 'scientific', psychology.

Let us, however, try to examine what instinct is and what animal mentality is like. In the first place, let us examine the actions of an animal and determine in what way they differ from ours. If they are instinctive actions, what does it mean?

We distinguish in living beings reflex actions, instinctive actions, rational actions, and automatic actions. Reflex actions are simply *responses by motion*, reactions to external irritations, always occurring in the same manner, irrespective of their usefulness or uselessness, expediency or inexpediency in a given instance. Their origin and laws are the outcome of the simple *irritability* of the cell.

What is meant by *irritability* of the cell and what are these laws?

By irritability of the cell is meant its capacity to respond by motion to external irritations. Experiments with the simplest living one-cell organisms proved that irritability is governed by strictly definite laws. The cell responds by motion to an external irritation. The force of the responsive motion is increased with the increase of the force of irritation, but it has not been possible to establish the exact ratio. In order to provoke a responsive motion, the irritation must be sufficiently strong. Every irritation experienced leaves a *certain trace* in the cell, rendering it more susceptible to further irritations. This is proved by the fact that to a *repeated* irritation of an *equal force* the cell responds with a stronger movement than to the first irritation. And, if irritations are further repeated, the cell would respond to them with an increasingly stronger motion, up to a certain limit. Having reached this limit, the cell becomes *tired*, as it were, and begins to respond to the same irritation by increasingly weaker reactions. The cell appears to become used to the irritation. It becomes for the cell part of its *permanent surroundings* and the cell ceases to react to it, for it reacts only to *changes* in the permanent conditions. If from the very beginning the irritation is too weak to produce a responsive motion, it still leaves a certain *invisible* trace in the cell. This is shown by the fact that, by repeating weak irritations, it is possible to make the cell react to them. Thus in the *laws of irritability* we see what seem to be the rudiments of the capacities of memory, fatigue and habit. The cell produces the illusion of a *being,* which, if not conscious and reasoning, is at least capable of remembering, capable of forming habits and of getting tired.

If we are almost deceived by a cell, how much easier it is for us to be deceived by an animal with its complex life. But let us return to our analysis of *actions*.

By reflex actions of an organism are meant actions where the whole organism or its separate parts act *as the cell does*, i.e. within the limits of the law of irritability. We observe such actions both in man and in animals. A shudder runs through a man from sudden cold or from an unexpected touch. He blinks if some object quickly approaches or touches him. If a man sits with his leg hanging loosely, his foot jerks forward if the tendon immediately below the knee is hit. These movements happen independently of consciousness and may happen even contrary to consciousness. As a rule consciousness perceives them as an already accomplished fact. And these movements need not necessarily be expedient. The foot will jerk forward if the tendon is hit even if there is a knife or fire in front of it.

By instinctive actions are meant actions, which are expedient but performed without any consciousness of *choice* or consciousness of *purpose*.

They arise with the appearance of an emotional quality in a sensation, i.e. from the moment when the feeling of pleasure or pain becomes connected with the sensation.

And indeed, before the appearance of human intellect, 'actions' in all the animal kingdom are governed by the tendency to obtain or keep pleasure, or to avoid pain. We may say with the utmost certainty that instinct is pleasure-pain which, like the positive and negative poles of an electromagnet, repels and attracts an animal in one or another direction, thus forcing it to perform a whole series of complicated actions, at times so expedient as to appear conscious; and not only conscious, but based on a foresight of the future almost bordering on clairvoyance, such as the migration of birds, the building of nests for the young still unborn, the finding of the way south in the autumn and north in the spring, and so on. But in actual fact all these actions are explained solely by instinct, i.e. by subordination to *pleasure-pain*.

In the course of periods in which thousands of years may be counted as days, there was evolved in all animals, through selection, a type that lives according to this subordination. This subordination is expedient, i.e. its results lead to the *required* aim. It is quite clear why this is so. *If the feeling of pleasure proceeded from something harmful,* a given species could not live and would soon die out. Instinct is the guiding factor of its life, but only so long as instinct is expedient. As soon as it ceases to be expedient, it becomes the guiding factor of death, and the species very soon dies out.

Normally, 'pleasure-pain' is pleasant and unpleasant not *for* the usefulness or the harm it brings, but *as a consequence* of it. Influences, which had proved *useful* to a given species during its vegetable life, begin to be experienced as *pleasant* with the transition to animal life; harmful influences are experienced as unpleasant. One and the same influence – say a certain temperature – may be useful and pleasant for one species and harmful and unpleasant for another. It is clear, therefore, that subordination to 'pleasure-pain' should be expedient. The pleasant is *pleasant* because it is *useful;* the unpleasant is *unpleasant* because it is *harmful.*

The next stage after instinctive actions consists of rational and automatic actions. By rational action is meant an action known to the acting subject *before it is performed* – an action that the acting subject can name, define, explain and whose cause and purpose he can point out – *before it has taken place.*

By automatic actions are meant actions, which have been rational for a given subject but have since become customary and unconscious through frequent repetition. The automatic actions learned by trained animals were previously rational not in the animal but in the trainer. Such actions often seem quite rational, but this is pure illusion. The animal remembers the order of actions and so its actions appear to be thought out and expedient. And it is true they were thought out, *but not by it.* Automatic actions are often confused with instinctive actions; and indeed they do resemble the instinctive, but at the same time there is an enormous difference between them. Automatic actions are created by the subject in the course of his own life. And, before becoming automatic, they must for a long time remain rational for him or for another person.

Instinctive actions are created during the lifetime of a *species* and the capacity to perform them is handed down, in a ready-made form, through heredity. Automatic actions *may* be called the instinctive actions, which a given subject has evolved for himself. Instinctive actions *cannot* be called automatic actions evolved by a given species, because they *never were* rational for separate individuals of that species, but are the result of a complex series of reflexes.

Reflexes, instinctive actions and 'rational' actions may be regarded as reflected, i.e. as not independent.

The first, the second, and the third come not from man himself but from the external world. A man is merely a transmitting or transforming station of forces; all his actions *belonging to these three categories* are produced by impressions coming from the external world. In these three kinds of actions man is actually an automaton, either unaware or aware of his actions. Nothing comes from himself.

Only the highest category of actions, i.e. conscious actions (which, generally speaking, we do not observe, since we confuse them with rational actions, mainly because we call 'rational' actions conscious) – depend not only on the impressions coming from the external world, but on something else besides. But the capacity for such actions is very rarely met with and only very few people have it. These people may be defined as the *higher type of man*.

Having established the difference between actions, we must now return to the question: *How does the mental apparatus of an animal differ from that of a man?*

Of the four categories of actions only the two lower ones are accessible to animals. The category of 'rational' actions is not accessible to them. This is proved, first of all, by the fact that animals do not speak as we do.

It was shown earlier that the possession of speech is indissolubly connected with the possession of concepts. Consequently, we may say that animals do not possess concepts.

Is this true – and is the possession of instinctive reason possible without possessing concepts?

All that we know about instinctive reason tells us that it operates while possessing only representations and sensations, and on the lower levels possessing only sensations. The mental apparatus which thinks by means of representations must be identical with instinctive reason which enables it to make that *selection* from among the available representations which, from outside, produces the impression of reasoning and drawing conclusions. In reality, an animal does not think out its actions, but lives by emotions, obeying the emotion that is strongest at a given moment. Although it is true that in the life of an animal there may be very acute moments, when it is faced with the necessity of making a *selection* from a certain series of representations. In that case, at a given moment, its actions may appear to be reasoned out. For instance, an animal, faced with danger, often acts with surprising caution and intelligence.

But in reality the actions of an animal are governed not by thoughts but mostly by emotional memory and motor representations. It has been shown earlier that emotions are expedient and, in a normal being, obedience to them should also be expedient. In an animal, every representation, every remembered image is connected with some emotional sensation and emotional recollection; there are no *unemotional* cold thoughts or images in the nature of an animal. Or, if there are some, they are inactive, incapable of moving it to any action.

Thus, all the actions of animals, at times very complex, expedient and seemingly rational, can be explained without assuming the existence in them of concepts, reasoning and mental conclusions.

On the contrary, we must admit that animals *have no concepts*. The proof of this is that they have no speech. If we take two *men* of different nationalities, different races, each ignorant of the language of the other, and settle them to live together, they will immediately find means of communicating with each other. One would draw with his finger a circle; the other would draw another circle alongside the first. This is enough to establish that they can understand one another. If a thick stone wall were to separate people, again it would not deter them. One would knock three times; the other would also knock three times in reply – communication is established. The idea of communication with the inhabitants of another planet is based precisely on the system of light signals. On the earth it is proposed to make an enormous luminous circle or square. It should be noticed on Mars or somewhere over there and should be answered by a similar signal.

With animals we live side by side, yet we are unable to establish such communication with them. Evidently, the distance between us is greater, the difference deeper than between people separated by ignorance of language, stone walls and enormous distances.

Another proof of the absence of concepts in an animal is its incapacity of using a lever, i.e. its incapacity of arriving independently at an understanding of the significance and the action of a lever. The usual argument that an animal does not know how to use a lever simply because its organs – paws, etc. – are not adapted for such actions, does not bear criticism, because any animal can be *taught* to use a lever. This means that organs have nothing to do with it. The thing is simply that *by itself* an animal cannot arrive at the idea of a lever. The invention of a lever at once separated primitive man from the animals and it was inseparably connected with the appearance of concepts. The mental side of *understanding the action of a lever* lies in the construction of a correct syllogism. Without mentally constructing a syllogism it is impossible to understand the action of a lever. Without concepts it is impossible to construct a syllogism. In the mental sphere a syllogism is literally the same thing as a lever in the physical sphere.

The application of a lever distinguishes man from the animal as drastically as does speech. If some Martian scientists were to look at the Earth and study it objectively through a telescope, not hearing speech from afar nor entering into the subjective world of the inhabitants of the Earth and without any contact with it, they would divide the beings living on the Earth into two categories: those familiar with the action of a lever and those unfamiliar with it.

On the whole the psychology of animals is very obscure to us. The infinite number of observations made of all animals, from elephants to spiders, and the infinite number of anecdotes about the intelligence, perspicacity and moral qualities of animals change nothing in this respect. We represent animals either as living automatons or as stupid human beings. We are too shut up in the circle of our own mentality. We have no idea of any other mentality and involuntarily we think that the only kind of mentality possible is the one we possess. But this is an illusion, which prevents us from understanding life. If we were able to enter into the inner world of an animal and understand how it perceives, understands and acts, we would see many extremely interesting things.

For example, if we could represent to ourselves and re-create mentally the *logic* of the animal, it would greatly help us to understand our own logic and the laws of our thinking. Above all we would understand the conditional and relative character of our whole idea of the world.

An animal must have a very peculiar logic. Of course, it would not be logic in the true sense of the word, for logic presupposes the existence of *logos*, i.e. word or concept. Our usual logic, the one we live by, without which 'the cobbler will not be able to make shoes' can be brought down to the simple scheme formulated by Aristotle in those writings, which were published by his pupils under the general title of *Organon*, i.e. the 'Instrument' (of thought). This scheme consists in the following:

A is A.

A is not not-A.

Everything is either A or not-A.

The logic contained in this scheme – Aristotle's logic – is quite sufficient *for observation*. But for experiment it is insufficient, *for experiment*, takes place *in time*, whereas Aristotle's formulae do not take time into account. This was observed at the very dawn of the establishment of our experimental knowledge; it was noted by Roger Bacon and, some centuries later, was formulated by his famous namesake, Francis Bacon, in the treatise *Novum Organum* – 'New Instrument' (of thought). Briefly Bacon's formulation may be reduced to the following:

That which was A, will be A.

That which was not-A, will be not-A.

Everything was and will be either A or not-A.

All our scientific experience is built on these formulae, whether they are taken or not taken into account by our mind. And these same formulae actually serve as a basis for making shoes, for if a cobbler could not be sure that the leather bought yesterday would be leather tomorrow, he would probably not venture to make shoes but would look for some other more secure profession.

Logical formulae, both those of Aristotle and Bacon, are simply deduced from observation of facts and embrace nothing but the contents of these facts – and can embrace nothing more. They are not laws of *thinking* but merely laws of the external world, as we, or laws of our relationship to the external world perceive it.

If we were able to represent to ourselves the 'logic' of an animal, we would understand its relationship to the external world. Our chief mistake as regards the inner world of an animal lies in our ascribing to it our own logic. We think that *there is only one logic*, and that our logic is something absolute, something existing outside us and apart from us. Yet, in actual fact, it is merely the laws of the relation of our inner life to the outside world or the laws that our mind finds in the outside world. A different mind will find different laws.

The first difference between our logic and that of an animal is that the latter is not *general*. It is a particular logic in every case, for every separate representation. For animals there exists no classification according to common properties, i.e. classes, varieties and species. Every single object exists by itself; all its properties are specific properties.

This house and *that* house are, for an animal, totally different objects, because the one is *his* house and the other an *alien* house. Generally speaking, we recognize objects by their similarity; an animal must recognize them by their differences. It remembers every object by the signs, which have had for it the greatest emotional significance. In this form, i.e. with emotional qualities, representations are preserved in the memory of an animal. It is easy to see that it is much more difficult to preserve such representations in memory; consequently the memory of an animal is much more burdened than ours, although in the amount of knowledge and the number of things preserved in the memory an animal is far below us.

Having once seen an object, we refer it to a certain class, variety and species, attach it to one or another concept and connect it in our mind with one or another 'word', i.e. with an algebraic sign, then with another, defining it, and so on.

An animal has no concepts; it has no mental algebra with the help of which we think. It must know *a given object* and remember it with all its characteristics and peculiarities. Not a single forgotten characteristic will come back. But for us the main characteristics are implied in the concept with which we have connected the given object, and we can find it in our memory by any of its characteristic signs.

It is clear from this that an animal's memory is more burdened than ours, and that this is precisely the main cause that hinders the mental evolution of an animal. Its mind is too occupied. It has *no time* to move forward. It is possible to arrest the mental development of a child by making it learn by heart series of words and series of figures. An animal is exactly in the same position. And this explains the strange fact that an animal is *more intelligent when young.*

In a man the peak of his intellectual power is reached at a mature age, very often even in old age; in the case of an animal it is just the reverse. It is *receptive* only while it is young. With maturity its development becomes arrested and in old age it undoubtedly becomes retrogressive.

The logic of an animal, if we attempt to express it in formulae similar to those of Aristotle and Bacon, would be as follows:

The animal will understand the formula *A is A*.

It *will* say: I am I, and so on.

But it will not understand the formula *A is not not-A,* for *not-A* is a *concept.*

The animal will say: This is this. That is that. This is not that.

Or this man is this man. That man is that man. This man is not that man.

Later on I shall have to return to the logic of animals. For the moment it was only necessary to establish the fact that the psychology of animals is very distinctive and fundamentally different from ours. And it is not only distinctive but also very varied.

Among the animals known to us, even among domestic animals, psychological differences are so great as to put them on totally different levels. We do not notice this and put them all under one head – *'animals'.*

A goose has put its foot on a piece of watermelon rind, pulls at it with its beak but cannot pull it out, and it never occurs to it to lift its foot off the rind. This means that its mental processes are so vague that it has a very imperfect knowledge of its own body and does not properly distinguish it from other objects. This could not happen either with a dog or a cat. They know their bodies perfectly well. But in their relations to outside objects a dog and a cat are very different.

I have observed a dog, a 'very intelligent' setter. When the little rug on which he slept got mucked up and became uncomfortable to lie on, he understood that the discomfort was *outside him,* that it was in the rug and, more precisely, in the position of the rug. So he kept on worrying the rug with his teeth, twisting it and dragging it here and there, all the while growling, sighing and groaning until someone came to his assistance. But he could never manage to straighten out the rug by himself.

With a cat such a question could never even arise. A cat knows its body perfectly well, but everything *outside itself* it takes for granted, as something given. To *correct* the outside world, to accommodate it to its own comfort, would never occur to a cat. Maybe this is so because a cat lives more in another world, the world of dreams and fantasies, than in this one. Therefore, if there were something wrong with its bed, a cat would itself turn and twist a hundred times until it could settle down comfortably; or it would go and settle down in another place.

A monkey would of course spread out the rug quite easily.

Here are four beings, all quite different. And this is only one example of which one could easily find hundreds. And yet for us all this is *an animal.* We mix together many things that are totally different; our divisions are very often wrong and this hinders us in our examination of ourselves.

Moreover it would be quite incorrect to assert that the differences mentioned determine 'evolutionary stages', that animals of one type are *higher* or *lower* than others. The dog and the monkey by their *reason,* their ability to imitate and (the dog) by his fidelity to man seem to be higher than the cat, but the cat is infinitely superior to them in its intuition, its aesthetic sense, its independence and willpower. The dog and the monkey manifest themselves in their entirety. All that there is in them can be seen. But it is not without cause that the cat is regarded as a magical and occult animal. There is much in it that is hidden, much that it does not itself know. If one is to speak in terms of evolution it would be much more correct to say that these are animals of different evolutions, just as, in all probability, not one but several evolutions go on in mankind.

The recognition of several independent and, from a certain point of view, equivalent evolutions, developing entirely different properties, would lead us out of the labyrinth of endless contradictions in our understanding of *man* and would show the way to the understanding of the only real and important evolution for us, the evolution towards superman.

We have established the tremendous difference, which exists between the mentality of man and that of animals. This difference is bound to have a deep effect on the animal perception of the external world. But *how* and *in what?* This is precisely what we do not know and what we must endeavour to establish.

To do this we must return once more to *our* perception of the world and examine *in detail* how we perceive it; and then we must see how the world must be perceived by the animal with its limited mental equipment.

First of all we must take note of the fact that, as regards the external aspect and form of the world, our perception is extremely incorrect. We know that the world consists of solids, but we always see and touch *only surfaces*. We never see or touch *a solid*. A solid is already *a concept*, made up of a number of representations put together by means of reasoning and experience. For direct sensation only surfaces exist. Sensations of weight, mass, volume, which we *mentally* associate with a 'solid', are in reality connected for us with sensations of surfaces. We only know that this sensation of surfaces comes from a solid, but we never sense the solid itself. Maybe it is possible to call the composite sensation of surfaces, weight, mass, density, resistance and so on – 'sensation of a solid'. But we are obliged mentally to bind all these sensations into one and to call this general sensation – a solid. We sense directly only surfaces, and then, separately, weight; we never sense the resistance of a solid, as such.

But we *know* that the world does not consist of surfaces, we know that we see the world incorrectly. We know that we *never* see the world *as it really is*, not only in the philosophical sense of this expression, but even in the most ordinary *geometrical* sense. We have never seen a cube, a sphere, etc.; we have always seen only surfaces. Realizing this, we mentally correct what we see. Behind the surfaces we *think* the solid. But we can never *represent* a solid to ourselves; we cannot represent a cube or a sphere not in perspective, but from all sides at once.

It is clear that the world does not exist in perspective; yet we are unable to see it in any other way. We see everything only in perspective, i.e. in perceiving it; we distort the world with our eye. And we know that we distort it. We know that it is not as we see it. And mentally we continually *correct* what the eye sees, substituting the real content for those symbols of things, which our sight shows us.

Our sight is a complex faculty. It consists of visual sensations, *plus* the memory of sensations of touch. A child tries to touch everything he sees – the nose of his nurse, the moon, the dancing spot of reflected sunlight on the wall. He learns only gradually to distinguish between the near and the far *by sight alone*. But we know that even in mature years we are easily subject to optical illusions. We see distant objects as flat, i.e. even more incorrectly, for relief is, after all, a symbol indicating a certain property of objects. At a great distance a man is outlined for us in silhouette. This happens because at long range we can never touch anything, and our eye has not been trained to notice the differences in surfaces, which, at close range, are felt by the fingertips.

In this connection, observations made on the blind beginning to see are very interesting. The periodical *Slepetz* ('The Blind Man') 1912, contains a description, based on direct observation, of how men, blind from birth, learn to see after an operation, which has restored their sight. This is how a youth of seventeen describes his experiences after the restoration of his sight by the removal of a cataract. On the third day after the operation he was asked what he saw; he replied that he saw a vast expanse of light with dim objects moving in it. He did not distinguish these objects. Only after four days did he begin to distinguish them, and only after two weeks, when his eyes became used to the light, did he begin to make a practical use of his sight for the discernment of objects. He was shown all the colours of the spectrum and very quickly mastered them, except the yellow and the green, which he kept on confusing for a long time. A cube, a sphere and a pyramid, placed before him, seemed to him a square, a flat disc and a triangle. When a flat disc was placed next to the sphere, he could not see any difference between them. When asked to describe his first impression of the two figures, he answered that he noticed at once the difference between the cube and the sphere and realized that they were not drawings, but could not derive from them the representation of a square and a circle, until he felt in his fingertips the same sensation as though he had touched a square and a circle. When he was allowed to handle the cube, the sphere and the pyramid, he immediately identified these solids by touch and was very surprised at not having recognized them at once by sight. He had as yet no representation of space, of perspective. All objects appeared flat to him. Although he knew that the nose projected and the eyes were sunk in cavities, the human face also looked flat to his eyes. He was overjoyed at having his sight restored, but in the beginning looking at things tired him; impressions overwhelmed and exhausted him. This is why, while enjoying perfect sight, he at times reverted to touch, as a form of relaxation.

We are never able to see even a small bit of the external world as it is, i.e. *such as we know it to be*. We can never see a writing desk or a cupboard *simultaneously from all sides, as well as inside*. Our eye distorts the external world in a certain way to enable us, in looking about, to determine the position of objects relative to ourselves. But to look at the world *not from our own point of view* is impossible for us. And we are never able to have a correct view of it, a view not distorted by our eyesight.

Relief and perspective – these are the distortions of the objects by our eye. They are an optical illusion, a visual deception. A cube in perspective is only a conventional symbol of a three-dimensional cube. And everything we see is only a conventional image of that conventionally real three-dimensional world which our geometry studies – and not the real world itself. On the basis of what we see, we must guess what it really is. We know that what we see is incorrect, and we think of the world as being different from the way we see it. If we had no doubts about the correctness of our sight, if we knew that the world was such as we saw it, it stands to reason that we would think of it as we see it. In practice, however, we are constantly introducing corrections into what we see.

This capacity of introducing corrections in that which the eye sees necessarily implies the possession of concepts, for corrections are made by means of reasoning, which is impossible without concepts. Without this capacity of correcting what is seen by the eye we would see the world quite differently, i.e. much of what *actually exists* we would see wrongly, much of what *actually exists* we would not see at all, and we would see a great deal of what, in reality, *does not exist at all*.

In the first place, we would see an enormous number of *nonexistent movements*. For direct sensation, every movement of our own is connected with the movement of everything around us. We *know* that this movement is illusory, but we *see* it as real. Objects turn round before us, run past us, and outstrip one another. Houses, which we drive past slowly, turn about leisurely; if we drive fast, they turn quickly; trees suddenly spring up before us, run away and vanish.

This *apparent* animation of objects, together with dreams, provided, and still provides, the main food for the fantasy of fairy-tales.

In those cases the 'movements' of objects may be very complex. Look at the strange behaviour of a cornfield seen through the window of your railway carriage. It runs up to your very window, stops, turns about slowly and runs to one side. The trees in the wood clearly run at different speeds, outstripping one another. A whole landscape of illusory motion! And what of the sun which still continues, in all languages, to rise and set, and the movement of which was at one time so passionately defended!

This is how it all appears to us. And although we already know that all these movements are illusory, we still *see* them and are, at times, deceived.

How many more illusions we would see if we were unable mentally to unravel the causes that produce them, and were to regard everything as existing exactly as we see it?

I see it, therefore it is.

This assertion is the main source of all illusions.

The right way to put it would be:

I see it, therefore it is not. Or at any rate: I see it, therefore it is not so.

We can say the latter, but animals cannot. For them whatever they see — is. They have to believe what they see.

How does the world appear to animals?

For animals the world is a series of complex moving surfaces. Animals live in a *two-dimensional* world; their universe has the appearance and properties of a *surface*. And on this surface there take place a vast number of movements of the most varied and fantastic character.

Why should the world appear as a surface to animals?

First of all, it is because it appears as a surface *to us*.

But we *know* that the world is not a surface, whereas animals cannot know it. They accept everything as it appears. They cannot correct what the eye sees, or cannot do so to the same degree as we can.

We can measure in three directions; the quality of our mind enables us to do so. Animals can measure simultaneously only in two directions; they can never measure in three directions at once. This is due to the fact that, having no concepts, they are incapable of keeping in mind the measurements of the first direction while measuring the second and third.

I will explain this more clearly.

Let us imagine ourselves measuring a *cube*. In measuring a cube in three directions, we must, while measuring in one direction, keep in mind, *remember*, the two others. But things can only be kept in mind as concepts, i.e. we can remember them only by connecting them with various concepts, by labeling them in one or another way.

Thus, having labeled the first two directions — *length* and *breadth*, it is possible to measure the *height*. Otherwise it could not be done. As *representations* the first two measurements of a cube are absolutely identical and are bound to merge in our mind into one. An animal has no concepts, so it cannot label the first two measurements of the cube as length and breadth. Therefore, at the moment when it begins to measure the height of the cube, the first two measurements will merge into one. An animal measuring a cube, and possessing no concepts but only representations, will resemble a cat I once observed. She dragged her kittens – there were five or six of them – into different rooms and could not collect them together again. She would get hold of one, carry it over to another and put them side by side. Then she would start looking for the third, bring it along and place it with the other two. Then immediately she would seize the first, carry it to another room and put it there beside the fourth; then she would again run to the first room, catch hold of the second and drag it somewhere else to the fifth, and so on. For a whole hour the cat struggled with her kittens, genuinely harassed, but could do nothing. Clearly she had no concepts to help her remember how many kittens there were in all.

It is extremely important to explain to oneself an animal's relationship to the measurement of solids.

The whole point is that animals see nothing but surfaces. (This we can say with the utmost conviction, since we ourselves see nothing but surfaces.) Seeing only surfaces, animals can represent to themselves only two dimensions. The third dimension, side by side with the first two, can only be *thought*, i.e. this dimension must be a concept. But animals have no concepts; the third dimension appears also as a representation. Consequently, at the moment of its appearance, the first two representations invariably merge into one. Animals see the difference between two dimensions, but cannot see the difference between three. This difference can only be *known*. And in order to know that, concepts are necessary.

For animals identical representations are bound to merge into one, just as for us two simultaneous, identical phenomena taking place at one point must merge into one. For animals it would be one phenomenon, just as for us all identical, simultaneous phenomena taking place at one point are one phenomenon.

Thus animals will see the world as a surface, and will measure this surface only in two directions.

How then to explain the fact that, living in a two-dimensional world, or seeing themselves in a two-dimensional world, animals orientate perfectly well in our three-dimensional world? How to explain that a bird flies up and down, straight ahead and sideways, in all three directions; that a horse jumps fences and ditches; that a dog and a cat seem to understand the properties of depth and height together with length and breadth?

In order to explain this we must return once more to the fundamental principles of animal psychology. It has been pointed out earlier that many properties of objects, which we remember as the *general* properties of species and varieties, have to be remembered by animals as the *individual* properties of objects. In sorting out this enormous store of individual properties preserved in memory animals are helped by the emotional quality connected for them with each representation and each memory of a sensation.

An animal knows, say, two roads as two entirely separate phenomena *having nothing in common*; one phenomenon, i.e. one road consists of a series of definite representations coloured by definite emotional qualities; the other phenomenon, i.e. the other road, consists of a series of other definite representations, coloured by other qualities. We say that both the one and the other are roads, one leading to one place, the other to another. For the animal the two roads have nothing in common. But it remembers all the sequence of emotional qualities connected with the first road and the second road and so remembers both roads with their turnings, ditches, fences and so on.

Thus the memory of the definite properties of objects, which they have seen, helps animals to orientate in the world of phenomena. But, as a rule, when faced with new phenomena, animals are much more helpless than man.

Animals see two dimensions. They constantly sense the third dimension but do not see it. They sense it as something *transient,* as we sense *time.*

The surfaces which animals see possess for them many strange properties; these are, first of all *numerous and varied movements.*

It has been said already that all illusory movements must be perfectly real for them. These movements *seem* real to us also, but we *know* them to be illusory, as for instance the turning round of a house as we drive past, the springing up of a tree from round the corner, the movement of the moon among the clouds and so on.

In addition, many other movements will exist for animals, which we do not suspect. Actually a great many objects, completely motionless for us – indeed *all objects* – must appear to animals as *moving. And it is precisely in these movements that the third dimension of solids will be manifested for them, i.e. The third dimension of solids will appear to them as motion.*

Let us try to imagine how an animal perceives objects of the external world.

Let us suppose that a *large disc* is placed before an animal and, beside it, a *large sphere* of the same diameter.

Facing them directly at a certain distance, the animal will see two circles. If it starts walking round them, the animal will notice that the sphere remains a circle but the disc gradually narrows and becomes a narrow strip. As the animal continues to move round it, the strip begins to widen and gradually becomes again a circle. The sphere will not change its form as the animal moves round it, but strange phenomena will begin to occur in it as the animal draws near.

Let us try to understand how the animal will perceive the surface of the sphere as distinct from the surface of the disc.

One thing is certain – it will perceive a spherical surface *differently from us*. We perceive convexity or sphericity as *a property common to* many surfaces. Owing to the nature of its mental apparatus, the animal should perceive sphericity as an *individual property* of the given sphere. What should sphericity look like, taken as an individual property of a given sphere?

We can say with the utmost conviction that sphericity will appear to the animal as a movement of the surface it sees.

When the animal comes near to the sphere, in all probability what happens is something like this: the surface the animal sees springs into rapid motion; its centre projects forward, and all the other points begin to recede from the centre with a velocity proportionate to their distance from the centre (or the square of their distance from the centre).

This is the way in which the animal must sense a spherical surface. *It is reminiscent of the way we sense sound.* At a certain distance from the sphere the animal sees it as a plane. Approaching it and touching some point of the sphere, it sees that the relation of all the other points to that point *has changed* as compared with what it should be on a plane, as if all the other points have moved, have drawn aside. Touching another point it again sees all the other points withdrawing from it.

This property of the sphere will appear as its *motion,* as 'vibration'. And indeed the sphere will resemble a vibrating, undulating surface. In the same way *any angle* of a motionless object must appear as *motion* to the animal.

The animal can see an *angle* of a three-dimensional object only if it moves past it, and in that case the object will seem to have turned – a new side has appeared, and the old side has receded or moved aside. An angle will be perceived as a turning, a movement of the object, i.e. as something transient, *temporal,* i.e. as a change in the state of the object. Remembering the angles met with before – which the animal has *seen* as the motion of bodies – it will regard them as gone, finished, vanished, belonging to the *past*.

Of course, the animal cannot *reason* thus, but it will act as though this was its reasoning.

If the animal could think of phenomena (i.e. angles and curved surfaces), which have not yet entered its life, it would no doubt represent them to itself *only in time*. In other words, the animal could not allow them any real existence at the present moment when *they have not yet appeared*. If it could express an opinion about them, it would say that these angles *exist as a potentiality,* that they *will be,* but that *at present they are not*.

For a horse, the corner of a house past which it runs every day, is a *phenomenon, which recurs in certain circumstances,* but which still *takes place only in time;* it is not a spatial and constant property of the house.

For the animal an angle must be a time-phenomenon, instead of being a space-phenomenon as it is for us.

Thus we see that the animal will perceive the properties of our third dimension as movements and will refer these properties *to time*, to the past or future, or to the present, i.e. to the moment of transition of the future into the past.

This is an extremely important point and contains the key to the understanding of our own perception of the world; consequently we must examine it in greater detail.

So far we have considered higher animals: a dog, a cat, a horse. Let us now take a lower animal – a snail for example. We know nothing about its inner life, but we may be sure that its perception is very different from ours. In all probability a snail's sensations of its surroundings are very vague. It probably feels warmth, cold, light, darkness, hunger, and *instinctively* (i.e. incited by the pleasure-pain guidance) it crawls towards the uneaten edge of the leaf it sits on and draws away from a dead leaf. Its movements are governed by *pleasure-pain;* it always advances towards the one and retreats from the other. *It always moves on one line* – from the unpleasant towards the pleasant. And, in all probability, it knows and senses nothing except this line. This line constitutes the whole of its world. All the sensations *entering* from outside are sensed by the snail on its line of motion. And these come to it *out of time* – from potentiality they become actuality. For a snail the whole of our universe exists in the future and the past, i.e. *in time*. Only one line exists in the present; all the rest lies in time. It is more than probable that a snail is not aware of its own movements; making efforts with its whole body it moves forward towards the fresh edge of the leaf, but it seems to it that the leaf moves towards it, coming into being at that moment, appearing out of time, as the morning appears to us.

A snail is a one-dimensional being.

Higher animals – a dog, a cat, and a horse – are two-dimensional beings. To them space appears as a surface, *a plane*. Everything outside this plane lies for them in time.

Thus we see that a higher animal – a two-dimensional being as compared to a one-dimensional – *extracts one more dimension out of time.*

The world of a snail has one dimension – our second and third dimensions lie for it in time.

The world of a dog has two dimensions – our third dimension lies for it in time.

An animal may remember all the 'phenomena' it has observed, i.e. all the properties of three-dimensional bodies it has come into contact with, but it cannot know that that which for it is a recurring phenomenon is in reality a permanent property of a three-dimensional body – an angle, or curvature, or convexity.

This is the psychology of the perception of the world by a two-dimensional being.

For it a *new sun* will rise every day. Yesterday's sun has gone and will never recur again. Tomorrow's sun does not yet exist.

Rostand failed to understand the psychology of *Chantecler*. The cock could not think that he *awakened* the sun by his crowing. For him the sun does not go to sleep – it recedes into the past, vanishes, is annihilated, and *ceases to be*. Tomorrow, if it comes, there will be a new sun; just as for us there is a *new spring* each year. In order *to be* the sun cannot wake up; it must *come into being*, be born. An animal (if it could think without losing its characteristic psychology) could not believe in the appearance *today* of the same sun that was there *yesterday*. This is human reasoning.

For an animal a *new sun* rises every morning, just as for us a *new morning* comes every day, a *new spring* every year.

An animal is incapable of understanding that the sun is one and the same, whether today or yesterday – *exactly as we probably cannot understand that the morning is one, and the spring is one.*

The motion of objects which, for us, is not illusory but real, such as the motion of a rotating wheel or a moving carriage and so on, must, for an animal, differ greatly from the motion it sees in all objects which are motionless for us – that motion in the guise of which it sees the third dimension of bodies. This first motion (i.e. motion which is also real for us) must appear to it spontaneous, *alive*.

And these two kinds of motion will be incommensurable for it. An animal will be able to measure an angle or a convex surface, although it will not understand its true meaning and will regard it as motion. But it will never be able to measure real motion, i.e. motion that is real for us. To do this it is necessary to have *our conception of time* and measure all movements in relation to some more constant motion, i.e. compare all movements with one. As an animal has no concepts, it will not be able to do this. Therefore, movements of objects which are *real for us* will be incapable of measurement, and thus *incommensurable with* other movements which, for it, are real and capable of measurement, but for us are illusory, constituting in reality the third dimension of bodies.

The latter is inevitable. If an animal senses and measures *as motion* that which is not motion, it is clear that it cannot apply the same measure to that which is and that which is not motion.

But this does not mean that an animal cannot know the character of movements proceeding in our world and conform to them. On the contrary, we see that an animal orientates perfectly among the movements of objects of our three-dimensional world. In this it is helped by instinct, i.e. capacity, evolved through hundreds of centuries of selection, of performing expedient actions without consciousness of purpose. And an animal discriminates perfectly well between movements happening round it.

But, distinguishing between two kinds of phenomena – *two kinds of motion* – an animal is bound to explain one of them by some inner inexplicable property of objects, i.e. it will probably regard that kind of motion as the result of the *animation* of objects, and will regard moving objects *as alive*.

A kitten plays with a ball or with its own tail because the ball or the tail *runs away from it*.

A bear will fight with a beam until the beam throws him off the tree, because in the swinging beam he feels something alive and hostile.

A horse shies from a bush because the bush has suddenly turned round and waved a branch.

In the latter case the bush may not have moved at all – it was the horse that was running. But it *appeared* to move; therefore, it was alive. Probably everything that moves is alive for an animal. Why does a dog bark so furiously at a passing carriage? We do not quite understand it. We do not see how a passing carriage turns, twists and grimaces in the eyes of a dog. It is full of life – the wheels, the roof, the mudguards, the seats, and the passengers – all this is moving, turning…

Now let us summarize our deductions.

We have established that a man possesses sensations, representations and concepts; that higher animals possess sensations and representations, and lower animals only sensations. We deduced that an animal has no concepts mainly from the fact that it has no words, no speech. We have further established that, having no concepts, animals cannot comprehend the third dimension and only see the world as a surface. In other words they have no means, no instrument, for correcting their wrong sensations of the world. Then we found that, seeing the world as a surface, animals see on this surface a great many *movements* non-existent for us. That is, all those properties of bodies which we regard as the properties of their three-dimensionality, must appear as movements to them. Thus an angle and a spherical surface must appear to them as motion of the plane. Further, we came to the conclusion that everything that, for us, belongs to the domain of the third dimension as something *constant,* animals must regard as transient occurrences happening to objects – as time-phenomena.

Thus, in all its relations to the world an animal proves to be completely analogous to the unreal two-dimensional being, which we have supposed, lived on a plane. The whole of our world appears to an animal as a plane through which phenomena are passing, moving according to time or in time.

So we can say that we have established the following: that with a certain limitation of the mental apparatus which perceives the external world, for a subject possessing such an apparatus the whole aspect and all the properties of the world must change. And two subjects, living side by side but possessing different mental apparatuses, must live in different worlds – the properties of the extension of the world must be quite different for them. Moreover, we have seen conditions – not artificial and invented but actually existing in nature, i.e. the mental conditions of the life of animals – in which the world appears as a plane or even as a line.

In other words we have established that the three-dimensional extension of the world depends for us on the properties of our mental apparatus; or, that the world's three-dimensionality is not its own property, but merely the property of *our perception* of the world.

To put it differently, the three-dimensionality of the world is the property of its reflection in our consciousness.

If all this is so, it is clear that we have really proved the dependence of space on *space-sense*. And, since we have proved the *existence* of a space-sense *lower than ours*, by this very fact we have proved the possibility of a space-sense *higher than ours*.

And we must admit that if a *fourth unit* of thinking becomes formed in us, as different from the concept as the concept is different from the representation, then, simultaneously with this, there will appear for us in the surrounding world a fourth characteristic which we may call geometrically a fourth direction or a fourth perpendicular, because this characteristic will contain properties of objects perpendicular to all properties known to us and not parallel to any of them. In other words, we shall see or feel ourselves not in a space of three, but of four dimensions, and the surrounding objects as well as our own bodies will reveal the *general properties* of the fourth dimension which we had not noticed before or which we had regarded as individual properties of objects (or their motion), just as animals regard the extension of objects in the third dimension as their motion.

Having seen or felt ourselves in the world of four dimensions, we shall find that the world of three dimensions has not and never had any real existence that it was a creation of our fantasy, a phantom, a spectre, a delusion, an optical illusion, anything you like, but not reality.

All this is far from being a 'hypothesis', a supposition; it is an exact *fact,* as much of a fact as the existence of infinity. For the sake of its own existence, positivism had somehow to do away with infinity or at least to call it a 'hypothesis', which may or may not be true. But infinity is not a hypothesis; it is a fact. And just such a fact is also the multi-dimensionality of space and all that it implies, i.e. the unreality of everything three-dimensional.

I don't know about anybody else, but when I had read the above passage *after* the Cassiopaeans talked to us about fourth density perception, I became acutely aware of the gulf between our perception of our world and what it must actually BE. We will come back to Ouspensky and his speculations about higher density perceptions rather soon, but for now we must return to our narrative regarding The Wave and the incremental revelations, where they led and what we understand at the present.

About a week after my "Sufi" question led to the subject of "Unstable Gravity Waves," I decided to ask some questions about the densities. I was really just trying to get a handle on *why* it is that we can only perceive things in the narrow frame of our reality. I wanted to know how things that are supposed to exist in other "realms" are veiled from us. I couldn't quite grasp the difference between fourth density and 5th density because so many famous or well-known teachings seem to talk about physical realms and then – poof! – you go to the ethereal or "astral" realms.

The Cassiopaeans seemed to be saying that there was something "paraphysical" that was a sort of intermediate level – it was physical but in a peculiar way – and you could "die" there and then go to the "astral" or ethereal realms. This was a completely new idea; it seemed to me, and worth having a closer look. So, I launched into the subject:

06-22-96

Q: (L) Tonight, I would like to ask about 5th density. How does the "dividing line" between the 4 physical densities and 5th function?

A: Recycling zone, one must have direct contact in perfect balance with those on 6th density in order to fulfill the need for contemplation/learning phase while in between incarnations of 1st through 4th densities.

Q: (L) When a person finishes all their experiences on 1st through fourth density, do they then remain at 5th for a period before to moving to 6th?

A: Yes.

Q: (L) When you die in third and go to 5th, do you pass through or see 4th?

A: No.

Q: (L) When you are in 5th density, is part of your service to be a guide? Are there two kinds of beings on 5th: those who are there for the recycling, and those whose level it simply IS? (I had heard a lot of different teachings to this effect – that "dead dudes" could choose to be "guides" or whatever. I was a little confused about how this whole thing worked.)

A: No. All are as one in timeless understanding of all there is.

Q: (L) If, at 5th density a person has timeless understanding, what is it about them that determines that they will "recycle" as opposed to moving to 6th from 5th?

A: Contemplation reveals needed destiny.

Q: (L) So, being united with other beings on 5th, you come to some sort of understanding about your lessons...

A: Balanced. And this, my dear, is another example of gravity as the binder of all creation... "The Great Equalizer!"

Q: (L) In this picture in my mind, the cycle moves out in dispersion, begins to accrete and return to the source. Is this correct?

A: Close.

Q: (L) Is this, in fact, that exactly half of all that exists is moving into imbalance, while the other half is moving into balance?

A: Close.

Q: (L) All the cosmos? All that exists?

A: Yes.

Q: (L) Is it possible that one area of the cosmos has more of the balance-seeking energy while another has more of that which is seeking imbalance?

A: Oh yes!

Q: (L) Is the Earth one of those areas that are more imbalanced than balanced at the present time?

A: Yes, but rapidly moving back toward balance.

Q: (L) Is the Realm Border part of this balancing?

A: Yes.

Q: (V) A few weeks ago several of us began to suffer from internal heat, insomnia, and other things. What was this?

A: Image. Deep conjunction of fibrous linkage in DNA structure.

Q: (V) Well, I want to know if it is in my mind that I get so hot, or does my body temperature actually elevate?

A: Only on 4th. Bleed through, get used to those!

Q: (L) Does this mean we are actually experiencing a bleed through of fourth density?

A: Image.

Q: (V) Are the little flashes of light I see also a manifestation of this?

A: Maybe so, but try to concentrate on the ethereal significance, rather than the physical.

Q: (L) When you say "deep conjunction of fibrous linkage," does this mean that we are conjoining with a linkage to a fourth density body that is growing, developing?

A: Slowly, but surely. We have told you before that the upcoming "changes" relate to the spiritual and awareness factors rather than the much publicized physical. Symbolism is always a necessary tool in teaching. But, the trick is to read the hidden lessons represented by the symbology, not to get hung up on the literal meanings of the symbols!

Q: (L) You say that the symbology has to do with hidden meanings. The symbology that you used was "image" and "deep fibrous linkage" of DNA. Now, is that a physical, symbolic image?

A: Yes.

Q: (L) What is your definition of "image?" We have many.

A: Learning is fun, Laura, as you have repeatedly found!

Q: (L) Well, I am so hot now that I really need to know about this! And, how come I am always the one who gets assigned the job of figuring everything out?

A: Because you have asked for the "power" to figure out the most important issues in all of reality. And, we have been assisting you in your empowerment.

Q: (L) Image. DNA linkage. (V) "Power" was in quotes.

A: Leave that alone for now, you will know soon enough.

Q: (V) Is this fourth density body something that already exists so that we could communicate with it?

A: Habeas Corpus?

Q: (V) Well, they just said... (L) Well, what they must mean is that you ARE it – you are transforming little by little and all of the unpleasant little side-effects are just part of it.

A: Yes.

Q: (V) Righteous! (L) T__A__ showed me a couple of acupuncture points that seem to induce an altered state. Is this, as he says, a way to open the door to the subconscious?

A: Stimulates endorphins.

Q: (L) Is there any point on the body that *can* be used to assist in opening the gate to the subconscious?

A: No such assistance is needed. First, we would like to suggest that you seek a "spin" doctor for your quest!!

Q: (L) Would a "spin" doctor be a Sufi master?

A: One example.

Q: (L) Yes. They keep bringing up things involving spinning.

A: Hilliard. Leedskallen. Coral Castle.

Q: (L) Well, they are really pushing on this gravity thing. Can I ask a question on another subject?

A: You can ask about the Easter Bunny, if you wish.

Q: (L) Is third density awareness the only density with perception of time?

A: No.

Q: (L) Well, what others?

A: 4,5,6,7.

Q: (L) But I thought that time perception was an illusion?

A: YOUR perception of it is an illusion. Remember the example of the dogs and cats riding in a car?

Q: (L) Yes. Ouspensky and the horse. So, time, as an essential thing, *does* exist?

A: But not as you know it. When we refer to "timelessness," we are speaking from the standpoint of your familiarity only.

Q: (L) Does time then exist, and does space have a limit?

A: You are getting confused because your inborn linear perception is clouding the image your efforts are trying to produce.

Q: (L) Okay, let's go back to the "balancing" of Earth. How can this be done?

A: Vague question.

Q: (L) Let me try this: the "buckets of love and light" group say that it is going to be balanced because everyone is going to think nice thoughts, and all of their buckets of love and light are going to eventually reach a critical mass and spill over onto all the rest of humanity and all of the bad guys are going to be transformed into good guys. This is the standard version. Is this what you mean?

A: No.

Q: (L) Swell! Is the energy that is being manifested in the positive, on and around the planet, is it going to reduce the level of negativity in the beings existing on the planet?

A: This is not the point. When "Earth" becomes a fourth density realm, all the forces, both STS and STO shall be in direct contact with one another... It will be a "level playing field," thus, balanced.

Q: (L) Speaking of balance, one of the crop circles you interpreted was an "astronomical twin phenomenon." What is an astronomical twin phenomenon?

A: Many perfectly synchronous meanings. Duplicity of, as in "Alice through the looking glass."

Q: (L) Double images. Hmmm... Does this relate to matter and antimatter?

A: Yes, and...

Q: (L) Gravity and manifesting on one side and manifesting a mirror image on the other...

A: Yes, and... Astronomical.

Q: (L) Okay, that relates to stars and planets... astronomical in terms of another universe, an alternate universe composed of antimatter?

A: Yes, and...

Q: (L) Is this alternate universe of antimatter the point from which phenomena occur or are manifested in our universe?

A: More like doorway or "conduit."

Q: (L) Is this alternate universe the means by which we must travel to fourth density? Is it like a veil, or an abyss of some sort?

A: Think of it as the highway. Realm Border is traveling wave.

Q: (L) Okay, you say "traveling wave," and then you say that antimatter is the highway. Does this mean moving through antimatter or interacting in some way with antimatter via the impetus of the traveling wave, or realm border?

A: Bends space/time, this is where your unstable gravity waves can be utilized.

Q: (L) Utilizing antimatter by creating an EM field, which collapses the gravity wave, allows antimatter to unite with matter, creating a portal through which space/time can be bent, or traveled through via this "bending." In other words, producing an EM field, which results in a sort of bringing in the antimatter, *is* the bending of space/time? Is that it?

A: Yes.

Q: (V) Is there a portal for each person, or one large portal?

A: No.

Q: (V) So we move through a portal in masses?

A: No.

Q: (V) If there are not personal portals for one person, or portals for groups of people...

A: *Portal is where you desire it to be.* With proper technology you can create a portal where desired. There are unlimited options.

Q: (L) Proper technology. Unstable gravity waves. And once you told us to study Tesla coils... antimatter... destabilizing the gravity waves *through* EM generation allows the antimatter to interact with matter which then creates a portal... is it in the antimatter universe that all this traveling back and forth is done by aliens when they abduct people?

A: Close. They transport through it, but most abductions take place in either 3rd or fourth density.

Q: (L) Is this movement through the antimatter universe, is this what people perceive in their abductions as the "wall of fire?" The coming apart. The demolecularizing?

A: No. That is TransDimensional Atomic Remolecularization.

Q: (L) Okay, if a person were passing into the antimatter universe, how would they perceive it?

A: They wouldn't.

Q: (L) Why?

A: No space; no time.

Q: (L) Antimatter universe has no space and no time... so, the antimatter universe is possibly where the poor guys of Flight 19 are?

A: Yes.

Q: (L) And you can get stuck in this place?

A: Yes. And if you are in a time warp cocoon, you are hyperconscious, i.e. you perceive "zero time" as if it were literally millions of years that is if the cycle is connected or closed, as in "Philadelphia Experiment." And, on that note, good night.

Now, I want to put two remarks from the above transcript together:

When "Earth" becomes a fourth density realm, all the forces, both STS and STO shall be in direct contact with one another... It will be a "level playing field," thus, balanced.

Q: (L) So, being united with other beings on 5th, you come to some sort of understanding about your lessons...

A: Balanced. And this, my dear, is another example of gravity as the binder of all creation... "The Great Equalizer!"

Remembering what was said about the "essence beings" in Chapter 2:

Q: (L) Are there other parts of us in all realms doing other things at this moment?

A: Yes.

Q: (L) And how is this going to be affected by the realm border crossing?

A: Will merge.

Q: (L) Do we need to do extensive hypnosis to bring these aspects of ourselves up and deal with these things a little at a time?

A: Will happen involuntarily. Will be like a thermonuclear blast.

And what was said in our "Oz" discussion:

Q: (T) Now, when those who move into fourth density make the move, will they experience completeness or merge with all other densities of their being, at that point, even if it is for a short time?

A: For one immeasurably small instant, this is what is meant by "illumination"!

Q: (T) But, for that small instant, because there really is no time, maybe an instant or an aeon, depending on how any individual might measure it; we might experience oneness with ourselves?

A: It may seem to last "forever."

Q: (L) Is this what is known as the "rapture?"

A: Some have attempted to explain instinctive thought patterns this way.

It seems we have identified our Wave – it is a Gravity Wave.

So far, so good, right? Is everybody with me here? Do we all know what it is I am trying to find out with these questions?

I thought so. And what's more, I thought I was getting a handle on the thing. I thought I had a clue. I had become so intensely driven by the references to gravity waves unlocking the secrets of physics that I couldn't even sleep at night for all the visions of Nobel Prizes dancing in my head!

There I was, Mrs. Average America with five kids and a spirit board in the room next to my kitchen that was going to give me the secrets to unlock all the mysteries of space, time, and being!

I was going to do it for all the women in the world who had been treated like second class citizens since that wily old Lizard Jehovah/Yahweh sent the apple to Eve. I was going to do it for all the unsung heroes and home grown geniuses who eke out their lives in quiet desperation, asking the heavens at night, "Why am I here? What must I do?" My handy dandy little spirit board was going to give me the *new* Theory of Everything! I was going to wrap it all up in a nice, neat little package and mail it to the nearest university, and they were going to just go gaga over it and send me to Stockholm to pick up my medal!

What a heady feeling! I should have seen it coming, but I didn't. The pit, that is. You know, the one that pride digs? I fell into it at the next session.

CHAPTER 7
BALLOONS, ANTI-BALLOONS AND FIREWORKS
OR
LAURA FALLS INTO THE PIT AND ARK COMES TO THE RESCUE

As I said, I was starting to feel pretty confident with this channeling thing we had going on here. For somebody who, as a rule, finds most channeled material to be mindless psychobabble at best, or insidious disinformation leading to destruction at worst, I was becoming rather fascinated by the material the Cassiopaeans were delivering.

After a couple of years of holding everything they said in deepest suspicion, looking for the flaws, being a super skeptic, I was now beginning to think that I had invented the wheel! After all, it seemed they could hold their own in a discussion with a "real" scientist; they produced information that was initially thought to be incredible or nonsense, which then checked out in amazing ways; and most of all, they very carefully avoided any kind of "interference" in our personal lives in a direct way, while the information they were imparting to us, if considered and added to our criteria for evaluating our reality, seemed to help enormously in sorting through problems and understanding what was going on "under the surface."

They were, in effect, not giving us fish, but teaching us to fish.

And, of course, with this growing confidence, I decided to run a "tighter ship," so to speak. No more fun and games. Let's get right down to business here and solve this puzzle and go home!

06-29-96

Q: (L) Well, I would like to get directly to my questions as they have developed during the past few days. The first thing is in regard to the Santilli session: is awareness equal to gravity?

A: It is a part therein.

Q: (L) Does accumulation of knowledge and awareness correspond to an increase in gravity?

A: No.

Q: (L) You said that energy can change the value of the density. The value of the density, as I understand it, is either plus or minus. Does this mean that pumping energy into third density from another realm of space/time can intensify the gravity to such a state that it changes its unit and becomes antimatter?

A: No.

Q: (L) You said that EM was the same as gravity. Does an increase in EM, the collection of EM or the production of an EM wave, does this increase gravity on those things or objects or persons subjected to it?

A: Gravity does not ever get increased or decreased; it is merely collected and dispersed.

Q: (L) If gravity is collected and dispersed, and planets and stars are windows, and you say that human beings "have" gravity, does that mean that the human beings, or the life forms on a given planet or in a given solar system, are the collectors of this gravity?

A: No. Gravity is the Collector of human beings and all else! Make "collector" singular.

Q: (L) Is STO the equivalent of dispersing gravity?

A: No, STO is a REFLECTION of the existence of gravity dispersal.

Q: (L) Is STS also dispersal of gravity?

A: No. Collection is reflected. STS is reflection or reflected by collection of gravity.

Q: (L) You said that changing the unit involves movement to another density. You also said that antimatter realm is the door to, or the pathway to, ethereal existence. Is fourth density, therefore, an antimatter universe?

A: No.

Q: (L) Do the beings in fourth density manifest in an antimatter state?

A: Both.

Q: (L) Is fourth density a density where both matter and antimatter are in balance?

A: Not in balance, in evidence.

Q: (L) So matter and antimatter are both available for utilization by individuals according to will and awareness?

A: Close. Antimatter and matter are balanced everywhere.

Q: (L) You say that *increasing awareness* was "a part therein," of gravity. So, if a person is increasing awareness, do they also increase in gravity?

A: No.

Q: (L) What is the relationship between the increasing awareness and gravity?

A: Nothing direct.

Q: (L) I am trying to find out what effect increasing awareness has on human beings in relation to this unstable gravity wave you have mentioned, as well as the *oncoming "wave."*

A: You are trying to "marry" two *parallels*. [Note that the intent here is that "increasing awareness" is parallel to the "oncoming wave."]

Q: (L) We have two parallels... okay... so if one is exponential increasing in awareness, the sign of the units of bodily energy does not change?

A: You are still attempting to generate.

Q: (L) Well, I am just trying to get a grip on some ideas here...

A: Then change the thought pattern. Gravity is the "stuff" of all existence; therefore it has an unchanging property of quantity.

Q: (L) So, gravity is not being "used," per se?

A: Close. You can utilize gravity, but you cannot "use" it. You cannot increase or decrease that which is in perfectly balanced static state.

Q: (L) So, gravity is in a perfectly "static" state. Yet, it can be "utilized." Can you make clear for me the transition from the static state to utilization? What occurs?

A: There is no transition, just application.

Q: (L) What occurs from the perfectly static state to the application mode? Is anybody following me?

A: No, including us!

Q: (L) Wonderful! What I am trying to get at is, 1) gravity exists in a static state; 2) light is an energy expression of gravity, therefore it is utilization? Correct?

A: No. Light is an expression of gravitational energy.

Q: (L) Well, when one has an expression, it expresses onto, into, or to something somewhere...

A: It does? If a tree falls in the forest, and nothing is there to hear it, does it make a sound?

Q: (L) You are saying that gravity is everywhere in balance and static, and then you say that utilization causes unstable gravity waves. And then you say that gravity is God, and that God is all creation, and we are a part of all creation, and, therefore, we are of God, and gravity. So, what I am trying to get at here is: what is the thing, the event, the manifestation, the mode of utilization that takes gravity from a perfectly static state to an unstable state, if you are saying it is always perfectly balanced. That does not make sense to me.

A: Instability does not automatically mean non-static. *Unstable waves can be static in their instability.*

Q: (L) None of this makes a whole lot of sense. I thought I was beginning to understand it, and obviously I don't have a clue. Let's try a different direction. You said that the universe consists of equal amounts of matter and antimatter. Are the first three densities, densities of matter?

A: And antimatter.

Q: (L) Are there equal amounts of matter and antimatter at all densities?

A: Yes. Remember, density refers to one's conscious awareness only. *Once one is aware, ALL* [many spirals of the planchette] *conforms to that awareness.*

Q: (L) What is it about the oncoming wave that is going to make any given person aware?

A: Not yet... First: your prophets have always used 3rd density symbology to try to convey fourth density realities. You are attempting to gather 3rd density answers to explain 4th through 7th density principles. This is why you are getting frustrated, because it doesn't "mesh."

Q: (L) Are manifestations in third density simply loci of collection of gravity?

A: In part. But, so are manifestations on all densities. What do you suppose the opposite of gravity is?

Q: (L) Antigravity?

A: Yes.

Q: (L) So, if all that exists were like a blown up balloon, and the surface of the balloon represents the static state of gravity, 7th density maybe... and it begins to bump out in different places... and all these little bumps are loci of manifestation of various densities – and this is very simplified, I am just trying to get an image – is this getting, even very simplistically, to an idea that I can work with?

A: As long as you have an "antiballoon" too.

Q: (L) So, can we make the outer surface of the balloon a balloon, and the inner surface or the air the "antiballoon?"

A: No.

Q: (L) Two balloons next to one another?

A: No. A nonballoon.

Q: (L) A nonballoon?!! You are making me CRAZY! You are saying that NOTHING exists! We are just not even HERE! I mean! Let's just turn out the lights and say "sayonara!"

A: No.

Q: (L) Well, for God's SAKE! Help me out with a visual on this! [Pause and deep breath – everyone in the room looking at me expectantly] Okay, a balloon in front of a mirror, the reflection of the balloon is the "nonballoon?"

A: No.

Q: (L) The nonballoon is when the balloon switches off – but it does it so fast you are not aware of it – like a pulsation...? I mean... I am desperate here!

A: You see, my dear, when you arrive at fourth density, then you will see.

Q: (L) Well, how in the heck am I supposed to get there if I can't "get it?"

A: Who says you have to "get it" before you get there?

Q: (L) Well, that leads us right back to: what is the wave going to do to expand this awareness? Because, if the wave is what "gets you there," what makes this so?

A: No. It is like this: After you have completed all your lessons in "third grade," where do you go?

Q: (L) So, it is a question of...

A: Answer, please.

Q: (L) You go to fourth grade.

A: Okay, now, do you have to already be in 4th grade in order to be allowed to go there? Answer.

Q: (L) No. But you have to know all the third density things...

A: Yes. More apropos: you have to have learned all of the lessons.

Q: (L) What kind of lessons are we talking about here?

A: Karmic and simple understandings.

Q: (L) What are the key elements of these understandings, and are they fairly universal?

A: They are universal.

Q: (L) What are they?

A: We cannot tell you that.

Q: (L) Swell! My night would not have been complete without that! Do the lessons have to do with discovering the MEANINGS of the symbology of third density existence, seeing behind the veil... and reacting to things according to a true free choice? Giving each thing or person or event its due as the Sufis teach?

A: Okay. But you cannot force the issue. When you have learned, you have learned!

Q: (L) I just want to make sure that I am doing the most I can do. I don't want to have to come back to third density.

A: You cannot, so just enjoy the ride. Learning is fun!

Q: (L) Now, you told me research and meditate upon unstable gravity waves. And, that once I understood this, quantum physics would be perfectly clear to me, and basically everything would be perfectly clear. Now, I have been struggling with this...

A: That is just the point, Laura! When it is a struggle, you are not learning. So stop struggling and meditate i.e. enjoy the ride.

So, I fell into the pit of ego – I thought I had a clue. But how the dickens can you stop struggling and "enjoy the ride" when the whole world seems to be an out-of-control train heading straight for a bridge that has been washed out by a dam that has collapsed in a torrential downpour? At least that is what it seemed like at the time. I needed to understand. I needed to know what was going on here on the Big Blue Marble. I *really* needed those answers!

So, since the Cassiopaeans had suggested that I do research on gravity waves, that is exactly what I decided to do. I went to the library and struck out. Nothing there. I did a rather primitive internet search (I wasn't very computer smart at the time) and found a couple of odd references that made no sense, and finally decided to do something rather more daring.

I figured that Dr. Santilli *must* be the answer! If he had lost interest in the Cassiopaeans, maybe I could rekindle it. I put together the material from the Santilli session with the subsequent gravity wave material delivered over a year later, and typed it all up very nicely and faxed it to him along with a request that he have a look at what had come up since he had visited. I was sure he would be interested and things would just take off from there.

Nope. Barely a flicker of a response.

Okay, Plan A flopped; Plan B: obtain permission from Dr. Santilli to use his name and then post the material on the internet in the hopes that someone would read it who knew something about gravity waves and would reciprocate with more information I could work with. Fortunately, he was gracious enough to consent, and I dutifully sent the whole sequence of remarks to Col. Steve Wilson for his opinion, and to ask if he would post it to his Skywatch mail group. Col. Wilson was very interested in the material, and the Cassiopaeans as well, since we had exchanged a number of previous e-mails on many subjects. It was his opinion that the Cassiopaeans were certainly revealing information that was accurate and that he could verify. But some of the information he could neither verify nor comment on.

Col. Wilson posted the Santilli session to the mail group on the 27th of June 1996, and I settled down to wait and see if anyone who could point me in the right direction for my research would read it. The subject field of the message read: "Dr. Roger Santilli and the Cassiopaeans…" I thought it was catchy enough that people wouldn't just delete it out of hand.

I admit to having been more than a little paranoid about sending this material out this way. After all, I had already experienced some pretty vicious attacks from various sources that I will detail another time, and it was clear to me that there was possibly some danger to myself in making public the Cassiopaean information in some of the more "sensitive" areas. But, I was desperate, and understood that being desperate called for desperate measures.

Nothing happened. Nobody commented on the post. Nothing was said by a single soul on that supposedly humongous mail group. I had played my cards and lost. There would be no more information about gravity waves.

The Fourth of July was coming up and my aunt invited me to come to her house to celebrate since there were also a couple of family birthdays – one on the 3rd and one on the 5th – so we were going to do the whole family celebration thing and go to a fireworks exhibition and barbeque. I was pretty depressed but the kids wanted to go, and since I was finally recovering somewhat from my months of disability, I thought I would chance it and make the trip. Besides, my cousin is an aerospace engineer and I had decided that I would sort of "come out of the closet" about my channeling activities and enlist his help in looking at the material and seeing if he could come up with any "real" physics or math that would further the project. Heck, who knows? Maybe he would know something about gravity waves!

So, we went. It's about 150 miles there and usually takes over three hours with the traffic, but it seemed like a lot less with the kids so excited and happy to be "on the road." We barreled along through the North Florida woods with the tape player blasting us with U2 and Pink Floyd all the way. I must have heard "Are we THERE yet?" at least a hundred times.

The barbeque was nice and I won a fishing rod in a raffle for the local volunteer fire department. The kids had a great time with the cousins, but I was tiring rapidly and couldn't keep up with all the activity. My aerospace engineer cousin either knew nothing about gravity waves or thought it wasn't a suitable subject to discuss with a woman. His attitude seemed to be humorously condescending, so the conversation went nowhere. So there I was, wandering around in the heat, humidity, and bugs, wondering just what the heck was I going to do next. We stayed overnight and I had a strange experience there sleeping in a strange bed. I was feeling so completely alone – more than I ever had in my life – and I wanted so badly to solve these problems about our reality, our existence, our place in the universe, but I just couldn't seem to connect with a single, solitary person who was as driven as I was to understand *why? How?* And all that. I actually began to cry from the frustration and I was shouting the question at the universe in my mind. It seemed to echo and re-echo endlessly into the vastness of space, which frightened me, but then an odd sensation of comfort, of destiny seemed to settle over me like a blanket. I just knew that an answer would come if I persisted.

The strangest feeling of disconnectedness from that environment of mindless celebration grew in me all through the next day, and I got more and more restless with each passing moment. I felt like I was going to jump out of my skin.

Finally, I could stand it no longer and I told the children that as soon as the fireworks were over we were going home. Thankfully, they were tired enough from all their activities that the thought of sleeping in their own beds made them agreeable, and we made our apologies for not staying the full three days and headed out with the last "rocket's red glare" showering down over the softball field in that little backwoods, North Florida town which boasted a single traffic light but one of the best fireworks shows I have ever seen!

On the road again. Night driving in the Florida backwoods – one of life's great pleasures. Minimal traffic, soft scented air blowing in the windows, smooth, two-lane blacktop between towering pine trees for miles and miles. The children were soon asleep and I drove straight home, arriving not long after midnight. I put everyone to bed and had a long, relaxing soak in the tub before putting myself to bed. But, just before turning in, I decided to check my e-mail to see if anybody had sent me anything at all.

"You have mail!" the computer informed me.

And I did.

Subject: Dr. Roger Santilli and the Cassiopaeans...

Send reply to: ajad@physik.uni-bielefeld.de

Date sent: Fri, 5 Jul 1996 19:07:43 +1

Hi, Which is the address (e-mail?) of Dr. Roger Santilli? I would like to take a look at his papers.

Thanks.

ark

What a funny name! And what a funny feeling it gave me. Subtle, indistinct, like a small draft of warm air across my cheek.

"Nothing," my conscious mind scolded! After all, this person with the funny name only wanted Santilli's e-mail, and had nothing at all to say about the Cassiopaeans. What a disappointment! But, it was the first "nibble" in the 8 days since I had sent out the material.

I swallowed my disappointment and decided to be as helpful as possible.

The end result was this: indeed, the Cassiopaeans were correct when they said that our little demo at the MUFON meeting was "predestiined." Because it created a situation that caught the attention of Santilli, and because, a year later, I posted the Santilli session on a mail list on the internet, it was forwarded to a physicist who *was* interested in the Cassiopaean material. And not just *any* physicist – a physicist with a good reputation, a *Humboldt Prize-Winning physicist* with a list of publications as long as my arm, and a specialist in the areas necessary to work on the very problems that had haunted my mind all my life. Moreover, he was as driven to understand and solve them as I was.

Above: The ancient megalith on which Ark was sitting while writing in his research journal about gravity waves.

Below: The view from Ark's office window in Firenze. The buildings of the University there are very old – formerly a monastery.

And, the curious fact is that he was actually writing about gravity waves in his research journal during the same time period that the Cassiopaeans were urging *me* to research them. He was sitting on a broken, ancient megalith along the side of one of his favorite walks in Firenze and he decided, on the day after I first wrote back to him, to go and photograph that stone as a sort of "document" of the event.

Another interesting thing is that one might even think that a physicist *is* a "spin doctor".

06-22-96

Q: (L) Is there any point on the body that *can* be used to assist in opening the gate to the subconscious?

A: No such assistance is needed. First, we would like to suggest that you seek a "spin" doctor for your quest!!

Certainly, the strange events I recounted in the previous chapter that occurred only after meeting Ark suggest that this relationship was destined to "open the gates to the subconscious" in me.

At a very early point in our relationship we agreed that our "quest" was the very thing that had brought us together, so we were certainly going to begin working together on it right away. Ark would read sections of the transcripts, and compose questions that he sent to me via e-mail. He would also ask questions about the many subjects that he had become familiar with in his own research.

Nine days after that first e-mail, Ark "participated" in a session. In a curious way it brought us back around to the subject of The Wave.

07-14-96

Q: (L) First of all, I have had some contact with a physicist who is interested in the material. And, because of this, I was motivated to pick up a book I had read many years ago about the German occupation of Poland, and there were some very strange things said in this book, and some funny synchronous numbers... It just seemed to be a prototype of the present reality in global terms. My question is: is there some synchronous implication between this contact, the reading of this book when I was 11 years old, and the material we have received through this source?

A: Open.

Q: (L) You have said that the Holocaust was basically a 'practice run' for the ultimate space invasion. Was Hitler's agenda a practice run for a future scenario?

A: Close. Was a "testing" of the will.

Q: (L) Whose will was being tested?

A: Yours.

Q: (L) Me specifically, or the planet?

A: Latter.

Q: (L) In terms of this scenario, is there some lesson that we can learn about what may or may not occur through this book I have mentioned?

A: Maybe, but suggest you learn to blend mosaic consciousness.

Q: (L) What is mosaic consciousness?

A: Thinking in internally spherical terms, rather than using linear "point blank" approach. The whole picture is seen by seeing the whole scene. Picture yourself as being at the center of a mosaic.

Q: (L) Okay, I know what you are saying, but I just don't think that there is any way I can DO this!

A: Yes you can!

Q: (L) Okay. Okay. This whole situation, this Polish connection, this German connection,[35] the American and alien things, the soldier/Nephilim thing, these are all manifestations of a Realm Border Crossing, am I correct?

A: Close.

Q: (L) And some of the manifestations of a Realm Border Crossing are that some people graduate or transition to fourth density, that their awareness changes, everything changes, the playing field is leveled. So, what happened in Germany was a 'practice run' but what is going to happen is that the 'playing field' is going to be leveled, so it will not be exactly the same scenario, is this a correct assessment?

A: Maybe. All right, my dear, you want the facts, so we will give them to you, and hopefully you will comprehend. If not now, then when necessary maybe…

Fact number one: All there is is lessons.

Fact two: This is one big school.

Fact three: Timing as you perceive it, is never, *never* definite.

Fact four: What is to happen, as you state it, is a ways off, and will not occur until you have reached that point on the learning cycle, and you are not close yet.

Fact five: The learning cycle is variable, and progress along it is determined by events and circumstances as they unfold.

Q: (L) So, the events and circumstances of our lives, individually and collectively, can indicate where we are on this learning cycle? And we are asking to have things told to us, or revealed to us about things that are, in themselves, the necessary lessons? And it would

---

[35] The past life situation described in *Amazing Grace* is what is referred to here. All my life I was haunted by dreams and images of a past life in Nazi Germany where I was married to a Jew who was arrested. Our four children were also taken away to camps. I committed suicide as a result of my grief for my family. I spent my whole life wondering where my husband of that time was. Upon meeting Ark, both of us experienced phenomena that suggested strongly that he was, indeed, that "Lost Love" from another life, perhaps even many other lives. As the Cassiopaeans remarked at a later point, we were "complementary souls."

be virtually useless to be told about them since they must be experienced?

A: Partly correct. If you want hints, then hints shall we give. But, if you are looking for a "road map?" Forgetitski!

Q: (L) Okay, we want some hints. And Ark wants some hints, too! He wants to know if we can invent a tool that enhances free will?

A: No tool is needed because of facts 3, 4, and 5.

Q: (L) Ummm... So, when a person is being hypnotized and controlled from outside, because that is the matter of concern we were discussing earlier, they are hypnotized and controlled until they learn to stop it?

A: Yes.

Q: (L) So, using the analogy of the Prodigal Son in the pigsty, they just have to wallow in it and suffer until they have had enough?

A: Using your analogy of the bicycle: Is there a tool that makes it unnecessary for the child to learn how to ride the bicycle in order to know how to ride it?

Q: (MM) Don't you get more free will by assimilating knowledge?

A: Yes!! Yes!!

Q: (L) So, in other words, knowledge and awareness makes you aware that you have free will, and also makes you aware of what actions actually *are* acts of free will, and therefore, when you know or suspect the difference between the lies and deception and truth, then you are in a position to be in control of your life?

A: *Yes.*

Q: (L) Ark also wants to ask... well, his problem is faith, as he said it to me.

A: Faith comes also from knowledge, and as we have stated before... False knowledge is worse than no knowledge at all!!!!!

Q: (L) So, it is important to take each and every thing that is being learned or analyzed, and take it completely apart and dig in every direction around it, and even in related directions, to *fully* ascertain that it is true? As C.S. Lewis said, knowledge is like a rope... as long as you are using it to tie up a box, it doesn't matter whether it is perfect or not, but if you have to use it to hang over a precipice, then it behooves you to make absolutely certain that it is strong enough to support your weight.

A: Yes.

Q: (L) Okay, Ark asks about this: "In 1979, Project Phoenix, with the assistance of the Grays, was successful in producing a mind amplifier." Is this true?

A: Nope!

Q: (L) Okay! That was pretty precise! Next: "Is it possible that, under drug influence, psychics, or those with mental capabilities above the norm, can be hooked up to some type of machine and are enabled thereby to create some type of physical form?"

A: Possible. Now review: The "Grays" are cybergenetic probes of the "Lizard" beings, so just exactly who is doing the assisting? And who is *behind* the Lizard types?? Could it be your ancestors, perhaps!?!

Q: (L) It says here: "The fire within man that is characterized as passion is the secret that can be utilized. The secret to all things is passion. With passion all things are possible. The amplification experiments of the Phoenix Project have been explained as having amplified brain waves. In fact, it amplified the passion of the subject. It was that 'inner will' of the subject that was amplified, that inner spirit within all of us is that driving force is manifested as electrical energy. Master that force and you cannot be controlled, the universe is yours. Master the inner spirit and you shall master the physical." Comments please.

A: First things first: Who is doing the assisting? And how is the assisting being done?!!!!!!???

Q: (L) Well, they say that the Grays are assisting the Consortium; this is the Hopi material... Who is doing the assisting? Hmmmm... Give me a clue... I think that the Nordic aliens are controlling the Lizards, who created the Grays, which are probes of the Lizards, and are purportedly assisting the Consortium...

A: Assisting? Or maybe influencing?!? And if so, how so?!? And, is not this the whole point? Are you not ultimately influenced always?!? In EVERYTHING you do? We have stated thus numerous times... So, please let us not get off the track, okay?

Q: (L) In other words, as long as we are in the pigsty, we are in the pigsty, and until we get *out* of it, we are *in* it?

A: Until you reach that point on the learning cycle.

Q: (MM) What is this chemical they use with these psychics, per se, is it the 'akashic chemical?'

A: That information you refer to is false in its entirety! "Passion" does not set one "free," quite the opposite!

Q: (L) But what if your passion is for knowledge?

A: That is not passion. It is soul questing.

Q: (L) What is it that gives some people this drive, this steamroller effect, that they are determined to get to the absolute bottom of everything and strip away every lie until there is nothing left but the naked truth? What is the source of this desire?

A: Wrong concept. It is simply that one is at that point on the learning cycle. At that point, no drive is needed.

Q: (L) So, you more or less are there because some critical mass has been reached that 'jumps' you to the point where seeking truth is simply who you are? It defines the parameters of your being. Is it like a 360 degree circle, and each person is a different point on the circle, and the whole thing cycles, and you never change relative to the people behind and in front of you, and the only real thing you can do to help anyone is to move the circle by moving yourself, thereby pushing the one ahead of you up, and pulling the one behind you into your previous place? And where you are on the cycle determines what you do?

A: It is a single cycle, yes. There is only one learning cycle, and where you are upon it, determines your EXPERIENCES, and vice versa.

Q: (L) Is there ever any point where lines connect from one point on the cycle so that you can 'jump' from one point to another? Like a wormhole in space or something?

A: Refer to facts 1 and 2 and 3.

Q: (L) So, no short cuts?

A: Now, refer to 3, 4 and 5.

Q: (L) So, certain events and circumstances could help a person to make 'leaps?'

A: No "leap", acceleration.

Q: (L) One thing, previously when we were talking about unstable gravity waves, and I asked what caused them to become unstable, you said 'utilization,' and that STO was dispersion, and STS was 'collection' of gravity. I have made a few conjectures about this and would like to ask, does this mean that in giving to others, even if what you are giving is a withholding of assistance because you know that assistance would only *prolong* the lesson, is dispersing gravity, and exerting mental or other control over others, even if one is *unaware* that they are attaching energy drains to another, also a form of collecting gravity?

A: Close.

Q: (L) So, when you collect gravity, you become like a black hole, you cave in on yourself?

A: Ultimately.

Q: (L) And it seems to me that one of the objectives of what we are doing is releasing the gravity collected in ourselves?

A: If that is your choice, or if that is your path.

Q: (L) Is choice as intimately connected with the path, as I understand it? Is it just simply part of how you are configured in your soul essence?

A: Close.

Q: (L) And there are people for whom STS is simply their choice. It is their path.

A: Close.

Q: (L) So, it is a judgment and a disservice to try to convert someone to your path, even if you perceive the end result of the path they are on, that it leads to dissolution? It is still *their chosen path?*

A: Yes.

Q: (L) And, if you send 'buckets of love and light' to such a one, and that is their path, you are violating their free will?

A: You might as well send "buckets" of vomit, as that is how they will react. Judgment is STS.

Q: (L) You told us before that stars and planets are portals, or openings into other densities. Is it possible that this oncoming wave, this Realm Border Crossing will be accessed through these types of portals, that it is not something that is actually in our 'space,' but that it would emanate through stars and planets? Am I onto something here?

A: You may be starting down a long path. Just remember: All prophecies attached to calendar dates are useless unless you wish to be sucked up by the fourth density STS forces!

Q: (L) Speaking of being sucked up by fourth density STS forces, MM was told by her local Hindu gathering that she was "vacuuming" up their energies and they invited her to either get with the program or find another group to hang out with. What kind of an interaction was this? Why were they so uncomfortable in her presence?

A: Because they wished to be worshipped.

Q: (L) Does that mean that being worshipped is the equivalent of sucking energy?

A: Close.

Q: (L) Now, I am curious about the doggie image that was on the photo that MM took and showed to me?

A: In these times, 2nd density creatures will collect more and more attachments.

Q: (L) Are these attachments like other entities?

A: Yes, and others.

Q: (L) When they are collecting these attachments, are they collecting them from us, as in protecting?

A: No.

Q: (L) Are they being used to collect attachments to be detrimental to us?

A: Yes.

Q: (L) Why are our animals picking up attachments?

A: Because of vibrational frequency intensifications, i.e. The Wave.

Q: (L) Is there something we could do? I mean, are we supposed to get rid of pets?

A: We would never suggest something as harsh as this. However, beware: third density STS orientation includes the thought of "dominion" over 2nd density, and this is merely a continuation of the energy buildups of the approach of The Wave... Some of the lessons are interesting indeed. *When you assume that capture and imprisonment of those of lesser capacity than you is for "their good," why should not you expect those of greater capacity than you to assume the same regarding you?!?* We would like you to ponder this further. We suspect there is much to be gained from insights lurking there.

The Wave subject was put on hold at this point because so many "real life" activities took priority – such as working in the direction of Ark's first visit and details about how to arrange our future so that we could work together in real space/time rather than in an amorphous virtual reality.

But, when all of the matters finally began to sort themselves out, we eventually came back to the subject. But, by this time, we were learning that we had to do our homework, there was no free lunch, and the goal of solving the greatest mysteries of reality was going to be a pretty big project.

AFTERWORD

As some readers may know, *The Wave* was originally published online, amounting to almost a thousand pages of printed text. Thus, we have decided to publish the series in multiple volumes. The originally published material is included in volumes one, two, three, four, and eight. Books five, six, and seven include material originally published as *The Adventures Series*, which deals with events surrounding the writing of the original Wave material.

Here's a rundown of the Wave volumes and the subjects dealt with in each:

Book One: *Riding the Wave* – The hyperdimensional nature of reality, including the UFO/Alien phenomenon, hypnosis, channeling, hyperdimensions, and the concept of the Wave.

Book Two: *Soul Hackers* – The subjective nature of life on our planet, including an in depth critique of New Age "you create your own reality" philosophy and its purveyors, hyperdimensional "window-fallers", mind-control, and the process of learning to see reality objectively.

Book Three: *Stripped to the Bone* – Roswell, "Nexus Seven," the holy grail, the ancient science of alchemy, and esoteric initiation.

Book Four: *The Terror of History* – "Organic portals," the Oak Island mystery, the Priory of Sion, and the history of the Jews.

Books Five: *Petty Tyrants,* and Six: *Facing the Unknown* – The Matrix-like theological 'drama of souls', including a behind the scenes look at the events surrounding the writing of *The Wave*, the symbolic nature of reality, semiotics, petty tyrants, and the strange death of Morris Jessup.

Book Seven: *Almost Human* – Cyclic catastrophe, conspiracy, psychopathy, and the true motivations of the power elite and their control of information.

(*Note:* With the exception of books five and six, the Wave books can be read in any order.)

The introduction to the series on the website says:

> The Wave is a term used to describe a Macro-Cosmic Quantum Wave Collapse producing both a physical and a "metaphysical" change to the Earth's cosmic environment theorized to be

statistically probable sometime in the early 21st century. This event is variously described by other sources as the planetary shift to 4th density, shift of the ages, harvest, etc., and is most often placed around the end of 2012. The subject of The Wave begins with a UFO abduction account, a transcript of an actual hypnotic regression session, that refers to a global cataclysmic change.

The fact is, in the past three years, we have made much progress in our understanding of The Wave and our relationship to it. I will be adding material to the end of this book version of the series, that will not appear on the website, that will include this information, and, finally, we will have a conclusion to *The Wave*. Whether or not that conclusion is correct remains to be seen.

I don't think we have very long to wait to find out.

BIBLIOGRAPHY

Allen, Gary. *None Dare Call It Conspiracy*. Seal Beach, California: Concord, 1972.
Baldwin, William J., D.D.S., Ph.D. *Spirit Releasement Therapy: A Technique Manual*. Falls Church, VA: Human Potential Foundation, 1993.
Bastide, Jean. *La memoire des OVNI: Des argonauts aux extraterrestres*. Mercure de France, 1978.
Boëdec, Jean-Francois. *Fantastiques recontres au bout du monde: les apparitions de phenomenes aerospatiaux non identifies dans le finistere*. Plomeur: Editions Le Signor, 1982.
Briggs, Katharine. *The Encylopedia of Fairies*. New York: Pantheon Books, 1976.
Campbell, Joseph. *The Hero with a Thousand Faces*. Princeton: Princeton University Press, 1973.
Chittick, William. *The Sufi Path of Knowledge*. Albany: State University of New York, 1989.
Cohen, Stanley. *States of Denial: Knowing about Atrocities and Suffering*. Cambridge: Polity Press; Malden, MA: Blackwell Publishers, 2001.
Corso, Col. Philip J., with William J. Birnes. *The Day After Roswell*. New York: Pocket Books, 1998.
Curran, Robert. *The Haunted: One Family's Nightmare*. New York: St. Martins Press, 1988.
Dolan, Richard. *UFOs and the National Security State*. Hampton Roads, second edition, 2002.
Ecker, Don. "The Human Mutilation Factor": http://www.paranetinfo.com/UFO_Files/ufo/hummute.txt
Eco, Umberto. *The Search for the Perfect Language*. Oxford: Blackwell, 1995.
Fawcett, Lawrence, and Barry J. Greenwood. *Clear intent: The government coverup of the UFO experience*. Englewood Cliffs: Prentice-Hall, 1984.
Fort, Charles. *The Complete Books of Charles Fort*. New York: Dover Publications, Inc., 1974.
Fowler, Raymond E. *The Andreasson Affair*. New York: Bantam Books, 1979.
Fuller, John G. *The Interrupted Journey*. New York: Dell, 1967.
Godwin, Joscelyn. *Arktos: The Polar Myth*. Kempton: Adventures Unlimited Press, 1996.
Hopkins, Budd. *Missing Time*. New York: Ballantine Books, 1981.
Hurley, Matthew. *The Alien Chronicles: Compelling evidence for extraterrestrial encounters in art & texts since ancient times*. Quester Publications, 2003.
Hynek, J. Allen. *The UFO Experience: A Scientific Enquiry*. New York: Ballantine Books, 1977.
____. Speech at the United Nations, Nov. 27th 1978. *UFOEVIDENCE.com*: http://www.ufoevidence.org/documents/doc757.htm
____. Speech at AIAA 13th Aerospace Sciences Meeting Pasadena, Calif., January 20-22, 1975. *nicap.org*: http://www.nicap.org/emerge.htm

Kaku, Michio. *Hyperspace: A Scientific Odyssey Through Parallel Universes, Time Warps, and the 10th Dimension.* Oxford University Press, 1994.

Mack, John E., M.D. *Abduction: Human Encounters with Aliens.* New York: Ballantine Books, 1994.

Marchetti, Victor, and John D. Marks. *The CIA and the Cult of Intelligence.* New York: Laurel, 1980.

Marrs, Jim. *The Alien Agenda.* New York: Harper Collins, 1997.

Osborn, Nancy. *The Demon Syndrome.* New York: Bantam Books, 1983.

Ouspensky, P. D. *Tertium Organum: A Key to the Enigmas of the World.* New York: Vintage Books, 1981.

____. *In Search of the Miraculous: Fragments of an Unknown Teaching.* San Diego: Harvest/HBJ, 1977.

Picknett, Lynn, and Clive Prince. *The Stargate Conspiracy: The Truth About Extraterrestrial Life and the Mysteries of Ancient Egypt.* New York, Berkley, 1999.

Sitchin, Zecharia. *The 12th Planet: Book 1 of the Earth Chronicles.* New York: Avon Books, 1978.

Tacitus, trans. Kenneth Wellesley. *The Histories.* London: Penguin Books, 1964.

Topper, Michael. "Channeling, UFOs and the Positive/Negative Realms Beyond This World". http://zelator.topcities.com/text1.htm

Turner, Karla, Ph.D. *Into the Fringe: A True Story of Alien Abduction.* New York: Berkley, 1992.

____. *Taken: Inside the Alien-Human Agenda.* Tallahassee: Rose Printing Company, Inc., 1994.

Turner, Karla, Ph.D., with Ted Rice. *Masquerade of Angels.* Kelt Works, 1994.

Turner, Elton. "Alien Behavior: Concept or Precept?" *Contact Forum,* September/October, 1994: http://www.karlaturner.org/articles/alien_behavior.html

Vallee, Jacques. *Passport to Magonia.* Chicago: H. Regnery Co., 1969.

____. *The Invisible College: What a group of scientists has discovered about UFOs.* New York: Dutton, 1975.

____. *Messengers of Deception: UFO Contacts and Cults.* Berkeley: And/Or Press, 1979.

____. *Dimensions.* New York: Contemporary Books, 1988.

____. *Forbidden Science: Journals 1957-1969.* New York. Marlowe and Co., 1996.

Vallee, Jacques F. and Eric W. Davis. "Incommensurability, Orthodoxy and the Physics of High Strangeness: A 6-layer Model for Anomalous Phenomena", *National Institute for Discovery Science*: http://www.nidsci.org/pdf/vallee_davis.pdf

Velikovsky, Immanuel. *Worlds in Collision.* New York: Dell, 1965.

Von Daniken, Erich. *Chariots of the Gods?* Putnam Books, 1970.